The Fall

INTERNATIONAL STUDIES IN GLOBAL CHANGE

Edited by **Toms R. Burns**, Uppsala University, Sweden
Thomas Dietz, George Mason University, Fairfax, Virginia, USA

This book series is devoted to investigations of human ecology, technology and management and their interrelations. It will include theoretical and methodological contributions to the analysis of social systems and their transformation, technology, risk, environmental problems, energy and natural resources, population growth, public health, and global economic and societal developments.

Volume 10
THE MANAGEMENT OF UNCERTAINTY
Learning from Chernobyl
Angela Liberatore

Volume 11
THE FALL
A Comparative Study of the End of Communism in Czechoslovakia, East Germany, Hungary and Poland
Steven Saxonberg

The Fall

A COMPARATIVE STUDY OF THE END OF COMMUNISM IN
CZECHOSLOVAKIA, EAST GERMANY, HUNGARY AND POLAND

Steven Saxonberg

Uppsala University, Sweden

harwood academic publishers
Australia • Canada • France • Germany • India • Japan
Luxembourg • Malaysia • The Netherlands • Russia
Singapore • Switzerland

Amsteldijk 166
1st Floor
1079 LH Amsterdam
The Netherlands

British Library Cataloguing in Publication Data

A catalogue record for this book is available from the British Library.

ISBN: 90-5823-097-X
ISSN: 1055-7180

TABLE OF CONTENTS

FOREWORD

Seymore Martin Lipset
George Mason University and The Hoover Institution,
Stanford University, USA

Dr Saxonberg's book attempts to explain one of the most important events of this century: the collapse of communism in Eastern Europe. The book follows the pluralist tradition in emphasizing the conflicts of interests between the various groups within the party-state and in bringing civil society into the analysis. At the same time, Saxonberg avoids the mistakes of some pluralist theorists who have tended to downplay the differences between the communist regimes in Eastern Europe and their capitalist democratic neighbors in the West.

Saxonberg works mainly on what Robert Merton has called the middle-range, rather than the grand theory level. He seeks to explain the type of change that occurred in a certain geographic area in a certain period of time. Furthermore, he concentrates on explaining the differences between the types of change in various countries, rather than the similarities. He combines institutional and cognitive analyses, an approach which may be applied to understanding events and developments in the non-communist part of the world as well. He even applies some Marxist ideas to help account for the policy failures of 'Marxists.'

Many explanations have arisen post-mortem about the collapse of the communist regimes, which do not necessarily fall into the conventional totalitarian/pluralist theoretical divide. Saxonberg shows that many of these approaches are inadequate. Thus, he disposes of the frequent claim that the USA's arms build-up caused the economic crisis, by showing that even those East European countries—such as Hungary—with relatively low levels of military spending also suffered economically. Indeed, it is not even certain that military spending increased for the Eastern European countries. For example, the post-communist official statistical yearbook for East Germany indicates that its defense spending actually decreased during the 1980s. Since the yearbook came out after the communist regime had collapsed, the statistics should be relatively reliable.

Saxonberg also criticizes the argument that the emergence of the institutions of civil society brought about the downfall. In none of the countries—with the partial exception of Poland—was there a highly developed civil society, hence it is simply wrong to suggest that the mobilization of an active civil society brought these regimes down. Moreover, the dichotomy of the civil society versus the state does not hold up well in these societies. For instance, in the Hungarian case, reformers within the party-state actually took the initiative to start some of the independent organizations, and even encouraged dissidents to form their own political parties, so that the reformers would have groups with which they could negotiate. There was, of course, a complicated interplay between the party-state and the citizenry. In Hungary, scholars at state-run research institutes and state-run universities wrote critical reports about economy and society, which convinced some of the communist leaders that change was necessary.

Saxonberg points to the need to differentiate the liberalizations among the communist countries. Those such as Poland and Hungary with the most open social climate in the communist world allowed for a dynamic interplay between the party-political elite and dissident intellectuals. Scholars and dissidents could take advantage of the relatively open climate to publish articles at home or abroad, which in turn influenced the thinking of the political elite. Since reformers among the latter were becoming increasingly concerned that their economies were failing, they did not need the direct pressure of a strong civil society to convince themselves that change was necessary.

Saxonberg develops a three-level scheme of interests. At the meta-level are 'postulated interests,' which come close to the idea of 'objective' or 'systemic' interests. He postulates that the exploited everywhere have an interest in improving their position. Weber's influence on this work is found in the discussion of institutions. Saxonberg discusses the legitimacy crisis of the communist regimes and their attempts to get the populace to accept their rule. He argues that national differences in the degree of 'pragmatic acceptance' of the regimes had enormous influence on their behaviors in 1989.

Finally, he discusses the actors' perceptions of their interests. Here 'perception' is the key word, because it suggests the need to analyze psychological mechanisms which may influence the perception of interests in ways that are not necessarily 'rational.' Criticizing the rational choice model of actors who calculate costs and benefits, Saxonberg argues that emotive factors, such as frustrated rising expectations and outrage at regime repression, were particularly important in inducing citizens to engage in collective action against the communist regimes.

Soviet-type societies are viewed from a class perspective, in which the members of the party-state apparatus constitute the ruling class. The exploited classes include the workers, the professionals, white collar workers, and peasants. Since peasants did not play an important role in the collapse of the Soviet-type systems, they are left out of the analysis. Saxonberg explores the behavior of the strata of intellectuals (such as authors, priests, philosophers, etc.). Although many social scientists have traditionally grouped professionals and intellectuals together, this study concludes that the members of the two groups had varying interests, and that they behaved differently under the Soviet-type systems.

The Fall is highly original, synthesizing neo-institutionalism, Marxism, and political psychology. Saxonberg presents a highly ambitious and complex analysis of the downfall of communism in Eastern Europe that is well worth our reading.

ACKNOWLEDGEMENTS

I have been very fortunate in writing this book, which began as a doctoral dissertation, and which I defended successfully in June 1997. As a graduate student in the Department of Government at Uppsala University, I benefited greatly from the supervision of my two advisors, Olle Törnquist and Stefan Björklund. After I completed the manuscript, the Department of Government selected a review committee to read through the book. One of its members, Lars Nord, shared his critical comments with me and gave me constructive suggestions for improvement. At the next stage—when I defended my dissertation—I was again fortunate to have an excellent opponent, Ole Nørgaard, from Aarhus University in Denmark. He kept in touch with me after my defense and continued to discuss several points with me.

Perhaps my best bit of good fortune came directly after I defended my dissertation. One of the members of the examination committee, Tom R. Burns (Department of Sociology, Uppsala University), decided to publish my book in a series he is editing on global change. He also gave me enormous help in revising the book. In addition, he put me in contact with Helena Flam (Department of Sociology, Leipzig University), who gave me particularly helpful suggestions concerning the theoretical portion of the book.

This book would not have been possible without many months of field work. The Department of Government was very generous in this regard too, twice granting me extra funding to spend time in Prague in 1992 and 1993, where I was a guest researcher at the Charles University and University of Economics. Uppsala University supported me as well, by allowing me to go to the Jagiellonian University in 1995 in Cracow as part of a faculty-exchange program between the two universities. The Swedish Institute deserves special thanks for funding my stay at the Central European University in 1995 and my one-year stay in Prague during the 1997–98 academic year, where again I was a guest of the Charles University. I did most of my revisions on the book during this one-year stay in Prague.

I have also benefited from comments from Mattias Burrell, Jouni Reinikainen and Lenka Rovná.

Finally, I want to thank Peter Mayers for his careful copyediting of my final manuscript.

ABBREVIATIONS

ČSSR *Československá socialistická republika* (Czechoslovak Socialist Republic)

DA *Demokratischer Aufbruch* ('Democratic Uprising,' group in East Germany which first aimed at dialogue and wanted to maintain a 'socialist system,' later allied itself with the conservative West German Christian Democrats)

DAMU *Divadelní fakulta Akademie múzických uměni* ('Dramatical Academy of Musical Arts' in Prague)

FDJ *Freie Deutsche Jugend* ('Free German Youth' in the GDR)

FIDESZ 'Young Democrats' (independent youth movement in Hungary, which participated in the Round Table talks and later became a political party)

FRG Federal Republic of Germany (West Germany)

GDR German Democratic Republic (East Germany)

MDF 'Hungarian Democratic Forum' (a conservative Hungarian party which participated in the Round Table talks and won the first free elections)

MOST 'Bridge' (A Czech organization that aimed at starting negotiations between the government and opposition)

NF *Neues Forum* ('New Forum,' the main East German opposition group)

OF *Občanské Forum* ('Civic Forum,' the main Czech opposition group)

SED *Sozialistiche Einheitspartei Deutschlands* ('The Socialist Unity Party of Germany,' the East German Communist Party, which incorporated the old Social Democratic Party)

SSM *Socialistický svaz mládeže* ('The Socialist Youth Union,' it was the official youth organization in Czechoslovakia)

Stasi *Staatssicherheit* ('State Security,' the East German secret police)

StB *Statní bezpečnost* ('State Security', the Czechoslovak secret police)

STUHA 'Ribbon' (name of the Independent Student Organization formed in Prague)

SZDSZ 'Alliance of Free Democrats' (a liberal party in Hungary which participated in the Round Table talks)

VPN *Verejnosf proti násiliu* ('Public Against Violence,' the main Slovak opposition group)

Part I:

THEORY

Chapter 1

THE COLLAPSE

"The system is terrible and does not work; yet it will last forever—if not longer." This first sentence sums up the basic Western attitude toward the Communist-led regimes in Eastern Europe before 1989. "The system *had to* collapse, although nobody expected it." This next sentence sums up much of the subsequent writing about the monumental events of 1989. It would be inappropriate, however, to blame experts for failing to predict these events. As Alexander George (1991: 469) asserts, "theory inevitably struggles to catch up with reality and often has great difficulty trying to cope with real-world complexity." "Theory does better," he adds, "in explaining what has happened than in predicting it."

Fortunately, I began my study several years after the collapse of the Soviet-type regimes[1] in Eastern Europe, so I have been spared the difficult task of making predictions. Yet, the rich body of literature produced by Alexander George shows it can still be extremely interesting to interpret historical events from a variety of theoretical perspectives. Even if we will never be able to predict social developments, such studies can help us understand the world.

In this book, I concentrate on a question which most theorists have neglected: the variation in the processes by which the different regimes collapsed in 1989, and the reasons for this. In particular, I want to know why Poland and Hungary accomplished a negotiated

---

1. I prefer the neutral term "Soviet-type system." Calling these countries Communist implies they had reached the Communist stage of development. Yet not even the regimes themselves claimed to have reached that stage. I use the term "Communist," therefore, solely to denote a member of one of the Communist parties (none of which, incidentally, featured the term "Communist" in their official name, except for the Czechoslovak Communist Party). One popular alternative has been to term these countries "state-socialist." This usage implies that these states were indeed socialist, and that theirs was a negative, state-oriented socialism. I am opposed, however, to using the term "socialist" (even when combined with some kind of adjective) to refer to a system in which "not a single constituent of the original Marxian project has been 'realized'..." (Fehér 1992: 17). Some theorists have considered these countries to be transitional societies situated between capitalism and socialism (see Trotsky 1937 & 1942, ch. 2; cf. Eklund & Reichard 1976, Mandel 1991, Therborn 1971 & 1980 and Ticktin 1987 & 1992). In my view, the Soviet-type system was a socioeconomic system sui generis, with its own mode of production.

"institutional compromise" with the opposition, while neighboring East Germany (the GDR or "German Democratic Republic") and Czechoslovakia (the ČSSR or *Československá socialistická republika*) experienced a non-violent revolution.

Poland and Hungary saw an institutional compromise, because the impetus for change came from the elite, which undertook negotiations with the opposition over the shape of the new institutions.[2] The GDR and ČSSR experienced a revolution, because the impetus for change came directly from the mobilization of a broad-based opposition engaged in non-accepted means[3] of mass collective action;[4] the result was systemic change in both the political and the socioeconomic systems.[5]

My inquiry into the differences in the process of change leads to three basic questions.

1) *Why did the Polish and Hungarian rulers take the initiative for negotiations, while their East German and Czechoslovak comrades tried to avoid negotiating?* The leaders of the latter two

---

2. The term "institutional compromise" comes from Przeworski (1988). He has also used the terms "institutional agreements" (1986) and "democracy with guarantees" (1991). I favor the term "institutional compromise" because it emphasizes the fact that both the regime and the opposition try, through negotiations, to shape the future democratic institutions to their own advantage—while exhibiting, at the same time, some willingness to compromise. Przeworski concludes, in all three works, that the ruling elites will not agree to a democratic transition unless they can obtain some guarantees that their basic interests will not be harmed. I prefer a broader interpretation of the term, in which a compromise merely requires a compromise, without any special guarantees. The question of whether or not elites always require guarantees before agreeing to compromise can then be settled by empirical research.

3. Note that "non-accepted means" does not necessarily include violence. Traditionally, most authors attempting to define revolutions have included the use of violence as a necessary condition—see, for example, Freeman (1972: 345 & 349), Gurr (1970: 4), Johnson (1983: 1), Stone (1966: 159) and Zagorin (1973: 28). None of these authors, even try, however, to explain *why* this must be the case. Why should an armed uprising by a few dozen army officers be considered more revolutionary than the successful mobilization of millions of citizens using such non-violent methods as strikes and demonstrations? The essence of a revolution does not lie in the use of violence, but rather in the successful mobilization of masses of people against a regime.

4. Some authors are only interested in the type of change, rather than in the process. See, for example, Clapham (1985: 160) and Allardt (1971: 29). However, the dynamic processes involved in e.g. an elitist, military *coup* which issues in a radical regime are very different than those involved in a mass social movement. It would be virtually impossible, accordingly, to devise a theory capable of explaining both types of political change.

5. Since I have included the criterion that the change in question be systemic—in the sense that it affect not only the political but also the socioeconomic system—I limit myself to what have traditionally been called "social revolutions." Yet my usage here differs from the classical definitions. In contrast to Skocpol (1979: 4), for example, I do not include "rapid change" in my definition, since it is hard to determine how fast a change must be to be qualify as "rapid."

countries waited until they were confronted by a mass movement. Then, instead of trying to keep their power, they simply gave up.

2) *How were mass movements able to emerge during such a short time span?* This is especially intriguing because, in contrast to the people of Poland, the populations of the GDR and ČSSR had been rather passive until 1989.

3) *What were the underlying causes of the crisis from which the entire Soviet bloc suffered?* Since the collapse did not occur in a vacuum, we can reasonably assume the existence of certain similar background variables which caused the general crisis. The leaders of these countries made different choices, but the similar background variables likely set the process of collapse into motion.

I start this chapter with a brief review of the major events, in order to provide the reader with a basic picture of what happened. Once the reader has this picture in mind, I proceed to review the theoretical discourse. In particular, I discuss the extent to which several major scholars answer the questions above concerning the differences in the process of collapse, and the underlying causes for them.

THE EVENTS

Institutional Compromise in Poland

During the Brezhnev years, Western observers generally believed the Soviet-bloc countries were extremely stable. The Polish leader Gierek shared this view of immense stability. To his surprise, a strike broke out at the Lenin Shipyard when he announced price hikes on July 1, 1980 (Touraine et al. 1982: 197). The leader of the strike, Lech Wałęsa, announced the strike had ended after management had agreed to increase wages by 200 zlotys. But his colleagues wanted to keep striking *in solidarity* with the workers at other plants who had not received similar wage increases. Thus was *Solidarność* ("Solidarity") born (Touraine et al. 1982: 37). By the end of August, the union had signed the historic Gdańsk accords with the Communist regime. Now, for the first time in the history of the Soviet bloc, workers received the right to strike and to form free trade unions. *Solidarność* membership quickly reached 10 million.[6] One and a half years and two Communist

---

6. For membership estimates, see Wesołowski (1990: 452), Ost (1990: 220) and Barker & Weber (1982: 26).

general secretaries later, martial law was declared: *Solidarność* was banned and its leaders were arrested.

Following these initial oppressive measures, the regime tried throughout the decade to coopt society into supporting the regime. This included replacing the old Communist union with a new one (OPZZ), establishing a constitutional tribunal, installing an ombudsman, setting up the Patriotic Movement for National Rebirth (PRON), and creating a consultative council. In 1987, finally, Jaruzelski held a referendum on economic reform. Although it obtained nearly two-thirds of the votes, the referendum failed. The Communists were so certain of victory that they required the support of the majority of *eligible* voters, rather than just a majority of those voting.

After several years of tranquillity, waves of wild-cat strikes broke out in May and August 1988 among younger workers unconnected to *Solidarność*. Local and national *Solidarność* leaders joined in later. They considered these actions premature, however, and the strikes did not develop into the mass mobilization of 1980–1981 (Tymowski 1993: 194; cf. Zubek 1991: 359).

On August 26, faced with several strikes and a rapidly deteriorating economy, the interior minister, General Kiszczak, proposed a "round table" discussion with "various social and working circles" (Janowski 1992: 163).[7] In response, Wałęsa used his authority to end the strikes. Almost half a year later—on February 6, 1989—the round table talks officially began, and in a tranquil atmosphere.

The negotiations eventually resulted in semi-free elections. Seats to the senate were openly contested, while two-thirds of the seats in the lower house of parliament were reserved for the ruling Communists and their allies (for the dates, see East 1992: 128–131). The Communists did not win a single senate seat in these elections. In the lower house, the *Sejm*, they took only their allotted seats. After this debacle, the "allied" parties started acting like autonomous organizations, and undertook to build a government with *Solidarność*.

Since the regime had announced its willingness to talk to the opposition at a time when some strikes were taking place, one might claim that Poland actually experienced revolutionary change. It is possible that *if* the regime had not taken action, the strikes would eventually have developed into a mass movement that could have brought down

---

7. Ziemer (1989a: 805) places the date one day later.

the regime. However, the Polish rulers took action to neutralize the opposition before such a mass movement could emerge. As some observers note, the regime called for the talks in order to keep the opposition demobilized, and to allow for a compromise among the moderate forces on both sides (see Staniszkis 1991). And they succeeded, inasmuch as not a single major strike place took place after August 1988.

Far from leading a revolutionary upheaval, the *Solidarność* leadership which faced the regime in 1989 was much weaker than it had been during the more revolutionary period of 1980–1981. Even when the union was re-legalized in 1989, it was unable to recruit more than 1.5 million members—just 15% of its previous total.[8]

As I shall argue later on, the leaders of the regime did not decide to meet with the opposition because a revolutionary, mass-based social movement forced them to. They did so, rather, because they actually *wanted* a negotiating partner. They feared, namely, that they would otherwise lose control over the economy, inasmuch as they believed themselves lacking in the legitimacy necessary for carrying out economic reforms which would lower living standards over the next few years. Thus they needed an opposition leadership which they could coopt into sharing responsibility for the reforms. They did not wish, therefore, to destroy the main opposition group; rather, they sought the preservation of this potentially viable negotiating partner. In other words, the impetus for change came from the regime, which took the initiative for negotiating an institutional compromise.

Institutional Compromise in Hungary

In the same month that semi-free elections took place in Poland, trilateral talks began in Hungary between the Communists, the opposition parties, and other interest groups. Only a few years earlier, Hungary had seemed remarkably stable, having had the same leader for over 30 years. During the 1970s, moreover, Janos Kádár's brand of "goulash socialism" was relatively successful. Market-oriented reforms gave enterprises more autonomy from state planners. As a result, the quality and supply of consumer goods increased. Hungary had the highest-quality consumer goods within the Soviet bloc.

---

8. Wesołowski (1990: 452). Szelenyi (1991: xii) claims that membership went down from 80% in 1980 to 10–30% in 1989?. Ost (1990: 220) also claims that, by October 1989, the union had just over 20% of the members it had had at its height in 1981.

At the start of the next decade, however, the country faced a mounting debt crisis, declining investment, and lowered real wages. To deal with the worsening economic situation, the regime devised a series of economic reforms. These aimed at increasing enterprise autonomy further. They also included price reform (to bring domestic prices into line with world prices), a gradual relaxation of wage regulation, and greater tolerance for private entrepreneurship within the "second economy" (cf. Swain 1992: 134–146 and Marer 1989: 58–61). The reforms failed to alleviate the problems, however, as hard-currency debts continued to rise and hyperinflation loomed.

Under these economic strains, the population began to lose confidence in the regime.[9] Yet, no significant strike movements emerged, although the discontent of the people was increasing. Nor were there any nationwide, mass demonstrations against the government (Bruszt 1990: 366–7). Nevertheless, small opposition organizations formed during the late 1980s.

Taking advantage of the new climate brought about by Gorbachev's policies, the reform Communists became increasingly vocal in Hungary. Their first major triumph was the replacement of Kádár by Grósz on May 27, 1988 (see Schöpflin, Tökés, & Völgyes 1988 for details). Upon becoming general secretary, however, Grósz became more conservative. Then, in February 1989, the Central Committee went against the general secretary and passed a resolution calling for the creation of a multi-party system (Bruszt 1990: 374). Contrary to popular belief, then, it was the Hungarian rather than the Polish Communist leaders who were the first to advocate competitive elections openly. In June, official trilateral negotiations were opened between the Communists, the opposition parties, and other social organizations (Bruszt 1990: 367).

Like their Polish counterparts, the Hungarian rulers took the initiative for negotiations over an institutional compromise. In contrast to the Polish accord, however, the agreement in Hungary provided for completely free elections. The Communists did not demand any special status or reserved seats. While the rulers favored majority elections, the opposition preferred proportional representation. They

---

9. Swain (1992: 13–14) and Hankiss (1989b: 50) cite public opinion polls showing a declining popularity for the regime. In coming chapters, I discuss the problem of doing reliable surveys under a dictatorship. It suffices to note here, however, that these findings have not been contested in Hungary. In later chapters I cite former Communist functionaries who agree that the Party was losing support.

reached a compromise. 176 MPs were to be elected in single-member districts, 152 from regional party lists, and 58 from national party lists (Körösényi 1992b: 74). The biggest battle was over the question of the presidency. The regime wanted direct elections, since they assumed that their candidate, Pozsgay, would probably win. For the same reason, two of the opposition groups—FIDESZ (Federation of Young Democrats) and SZDSZ (Alliance of Free Democrats)—advocated parliamentary election of the president. They calculated that the combined opposition parties would have a majority in the new parliament. The two parties refused to sign the final agreement and instead started a petition drive for a referendum on the issue. The leaders of the more moderate opposition party, the MDF (the Hungarian Democratic Forum)—which had close contacts with Pozsgay—encouraged its supporters to boycott the referendum. In the end, the proposal for parliamentary election of the president passed with a mere 50.1% of the votes (for the statistics, see Körösényi 1992a: 9, footnote 19). At this point, it became clear that the president would be a non-Communist. In the ensuing election campaign, the major parties, including the MDF, took an increasingly anti-Communist stance. A change of leadership within the MDF made cooperation with the reform Communists impossible. Following the elections, the MDF formed a government with several small conservative parties, sending the FIDESZ and SZDSZ as well as the reform Communists into the opposition.

Revolutionary GDR

The German Democratic Republic (GDR), under the diehard conservative regime of Erich Honecker, was the most orthodox of the four countries. Although the economic situation worsened in the 1980s, General Secretary Honecker insisted on continuing along the neo-Stalinist path. Thus, he maintained tight control over the ideological, political, social and economic spheres of society. Nevertheless, peace, environmental, civil rights and women's groups began to emerge in the early 1980s. Often they operated under the aegis of the Evangelical Church. Although the leadership of the Church was rather cautious and sought accommodation with the state, several radical ministers allowed these alternative groups access to their parish buildings. By the latter half of the 1980s, furthermore, civil rights groups had emerged as well.[10]

---

10. For information about these groups, see Kühnel & Sallmon-Metzner (1991), Meuschel (1989–90), Reiβig (1993), Rüddensklau (1992) and Wielgohs & Schultz (1990 and 1993).

The Honecker regime frustrated any hopes that Gorbachev's *glasnost* might spread to the land of stability and orthodoxy. Instead, the neo-Stalinists embarked on a "re-ideologization" campaign (Walter 1990: 105). As it became clearer that Honecker would not reconsider his policies, citizens started looking for ways to escape from the temple of orthodoxy. During the summer of 1989, increasing numbers of young East Germans began travelling to Hungary, where the reformist Communists had been negotiating with the opposition over the first completely free elections in a Soviet-bloc country. Sensing a possible crack in the "Iron Curtain," the East German refugees hoped the Hungarian regime would prove the sincerity of its new democratic face by allowing them to flee via Austria to the Federal Republic of Germany (FRG). On September 11, the Hungarian government announced it was allowing all East German refugees to emigrate to the West (Spittmann & Helwig 1990: 4). That same night, over 25,000 East Germans eagerly took advantage of this opportunity. Now that the dam was breached, the flood of emigration continued for the rest of the year.

The turning point came on October 7, 1989. When Gorbachev arrived to participate in the 40th anniversary of the GDR, thousands of cheering protesters greeted him. They demanded his *glasnost* for their own country. The security forces violently repressed the ensuing demonstrations in East Berlin, Leipzig, Dresden and other cities. Yet that did not stop thousands of demonstrators from taking to the streets on the following day. On Monday, October 9, about 70,000 people joined the weekly Leipzig prayer for peace. As the demonstrations continued expanding, the Politburo announced the resignation of General Secretary Honecker (based partially on Spittmann & Helwig 1990: 8–11). However, the new general secretary, Egon Krenz, was unable to stop the exodus from the country.

During October and November, the mass exodus continued. The demonstrations, meanwhile, grew larger. About 300,000 attended a protest rally in Leipzig on October 30, and over a half million took part in Berlin on November 4. On November 7, the entire cabinet resigned. The Politburo followed the next day. One day later, Günter Schabowski announced that citizens would be able to travel freely (Reich 1990: 81). That night large groups of East Germans headed across the Berlin border. Once the wall came tumbling down, the Communists were never able to retake the initiative. Over the course of the following weeks the situation changed swiftly. Krenz resigned and Prime Minister Modrow reacted by forming a new government, legalizing the opposition and setting up a round table. The Round Table became the effective government and included the Communist SED (*Sozialistiche Einheitspartei Deutschlands*), the bloc parties of the National Front, mass organizations, church organizations, and the newly founded independent parties and citizens' movements (East 1992: 82).

Revolutionary ČSSR

Up to the mid 1960s, the Czechoslovak Communists were even more orthodox than their East German neighbors. Their leader, General Secretary Novotný, had the great dishonor of being the only East European leader[11] to hold new trials *after* Stalin's death.

After two decades of political and economic suffocation, reformers came to power in 1968. During the "Prague Spring," they allowed some fresh air into the country. Independent organizations blossomed as critical voices spread throughout the country. At the end of the summer, however, Warsaw Pact tanks trampled on the budding society. Gustaf Husák eventually replaced Alexander Dubček as general secretary. At first, Husák inspired hope that some reforms would continue. But soon the new leader slammed the door shut, drew the "iron curtain" over the windows again, and announced a policy of "normalization." The new leadership expelled around a third of the members of the Party (Pelikan 1976: 43; cf. Kusin 1978: 85). It fired more researchers and silenced more cultural personalities than any other government in Czechoslovak history (cf. Kundera 1985: 128). Moreover, despite the founding of the human rights group Charter 77 in 1977, dissidents remained largely isolated from the populace.

When Miloš Jakeš replaced Husák as general secretary in 1987, the situation did not change much. Jakeš had hardly any reform credentials. He had openly supported the Soviet invasion in 1968. Then, as head of the Party's control commission, he was responsible for the

---

11. Some citizens of the four countries studied in this book may take offence at being labelled East European. After all, one of the reasons they rebelled against the *ancien régime* was to return to Central Europe. For the sake of simplicity, however, I am retaining the cold-war geopolitical usage of the term, since these countries not only belonged to the Soviet bloc, they were also geographically to the east of every member state of the European Community (with the notable exception of Greece). If I were to use the more specific term "East-Central Europe" now in vogue to refer to these four countries, I would cause confusion when speaking of the USSR's satellite states in general, since the area in question would include countries to the east of East-Central Europe as well.

mass purges during the normalization period. So it seemed the ČSSR would continue as a bastion of stability.

On Friday, November 17—One week after the Berlin Wall came down—the recently formed (but not yet legal) independent student organization STUHA ("Ribbon") held a demonstration together with the official youth organization SSM (*Socialistický svaz mládeže*). It was in memory of a student, Jan Optel, whom the Nazis had murdered 50 years earlier. Since the SSM participated, the students received official permission to hold the demonstration. Nevertheless, the police brutally attacked the students when they tried to approach the main square, Václavské náměstí. Rumors then spread—via foreign radio reports from the Voice of America and Radio Free Europe—that a student had died in the confrontation (Fleyberk 1990: 19).

On the following day, November 18, drama students from the Drama Academy of Musical Arts (DAMU) organized a student meeting at the Academy's theater. They announced that they were going on strike. They even suggested that a nationwide general strike be held on Monday, November 27. Later on that same day, various theaters announced that they too were going on strike. On Sunday, November 19, the dissident playwright, Václav Havel, summoned dissidents from Charter 77, together with other politically interested persons, to a meeting at the *Činohrdadý klub* theater. Thus was the future governing "party,"[12] *Občanské forum* ("Civic Forum," or OF), founded.

On Monday, the first mass meetings took place at Václavské náměstí. The following day, about 200,000 demonstrators gathered there. OF gave its support to the general strike. That week students and OF activists went out into the countryside to organize support for the general strike. On the following weekend, Havel and Prime Minister Ladislav Adamec held negotiations for the first time, up to 750,000 persons attended a rally at Letná park, and the entire Politburo resigned.[13] The crowds greeted Adamec as a hero when he spoke at this mass rally on Sunday, November 26. The cheers quickly turned into boos, however, when he started using traditional Communist phraseology, and tried to persuade the audience not to participate in the general strike (cf. Ash 1990c: 46). The general strike one day later was a success. The following week, Prime Minister Adamec proved too inflexible to meet the new situ-

---

12. Actually, OF did not consider itself a political party, "but an open association of citizens" (Wheaten & Kavan 1992: 76).
13. Cf. Wheaton & Kavan (1992: 88). Konůpek (1990: 18–19) puts it at 500,000.

ation. He presented a new cabinet in which 16 of the 21 posts were filled by Party members. Rather than consider changes in the cabinet, he resigned. A new government was quickly formed, in which OF and its Slovak sister *Verejnos proti násiliu* (VPN) furnished the majority of ministers, including the important economic ones.[14]

As in East Germany, then, the impetus for change came from a highly mobilized, broad-based mass movement engaged in non-accepted means of collective action. The general secretary of the Communist Party in each country resigned after hundreds of thousands of citizens had taken to the streets to protest against the regime. In contrast to the negotiations between the regime and a demobilized population in Poland and Hungary, the negotiations between regime and opposition in the GDR and ČSSR occurred under the constant pressure of mass demonstrations.

Some theorists claim East Germany was more revolutionary than the ČSSR.[15] The revolutionary process, however, was much quicker in the ČSSR than in the GDR. It took over five weeks for the size of the East German demonstrations to surpass the 100,000 level (cf. Mason 1992: 60). By comparison, the demonstrations in Prague reached the six-figure level after just four days. A few days later, moreover, anywhere from 500,000 to 750,000 people participated. This demonstration was much larger than any in the GDR during the entire transitional period. Similarly, while it took around six weeks for Honecker to retire, and several months for most of the other members of the old guard (including Krenz) to leave office (cf. Cipkowski 1991: 40), it took exactly one week for the Czechoslovak Politburo to tender its resignation.[16]

CONVENTIONAL EXPLANATIONS

Now that I have given the reader a brief description of events, I shall discuss the most common explanations for the collapse of the regimes of Eastern Europe.

---

14. However, the OF advisors—Economics Minister Vatr Komárek and Planning Minister Vladimír Dlouhý—were officially Party members.

15. For example, Huntington (1991: 113) claims that East Germany experienced a revolution (which he terms "replacement"), while Czechoslovakia only underwent "transplacement."

16. Ironically, Huntington (1991: 144) also claims that students are the universal opposition. They play an important role in revolutionary countries, although they do not bring down the regimes. Yet, as my description makes clear, students were much more important for the Czechoslovak than for the East German revolution. Students actually sparked off the Czechoslovak revolution, by organizing the demonstration on November 17 and declaring a strike the following day. In contrast, the East German students never organized against their regime.

The dominant explanations for the collapse of the Soviet-type regimes are

- the existence of an economic crisis,
- the loss of legitimacy,
- Gorbachev's policies, and
- the emergence of a civil society.[17]

Much of the academic literature concentrates on just one or two of these factors, and limits itself to one country. Those works that discuss the causal link between two elements often emphasize one aspect, and essentially take the other for granted. More importantly still, the theoretical works addressing these issues normally fail to account for either a) the possibility that the Communists could have maintained power notwithstanding the problems, or b) the wide divergences in the process of transformation that obtained despite the similarities. I give an extremely brief account of these types of explanations below, in order to support my claim that they cannot identify the sufficient conditions for the collapse.

Economic Explanations
There are basically six reasons of an economic character given for the collapse of the Soviet-type system: 1) the inefficiency of the economy, 2) the modernization process, 3) the failure of particular economic policies, 4) the increase in military spending, 5) changes in technology and the world economy, and 6) the inability to reform the economy.

There is a broad consensus that the Soviet-type economies suffered from organizational inefficiencies. This includes everyone from reform Communist economists and critical Marxists to Western Sovietologists.[18] Yet, since these economies have supposedly *always* been inefficient, this type of explanation cannot in itself explain why the system collapsed in or around 1989. If economic inefficiency did not cause the regimes to collapse in 1959, why should this problem increase in importance in 1989? Perhaps the economies became even less efficient in the 1980s. This could *partially* explain why the regimes collapsed in 1989, but then the question remains of *why* the East

---

17. All of these notions are included implicitly or explicitly in such popular books as Ash's (1990d) *We The People*, and Schöpflin's (1993) *Politics in Eastern Europe*.
18. For reform Communists, see for example Brus (1971) and Šik (1972a&b and 1973). Critical Marxists include Ticktin (1992). Western Sovietologists include, among others, Nove (1984), Hoffman (1966) and Åslund (1990).

European economies performed more poorly. As Hechter (1994: 160) observes, "none of these critiques casts much light on the reasons why at certain times and in certain places state socialism succeeded, why it did better in some places than others, and why it collapsed when it did." Moreover, even if these economies performed less well in the 1980s, that does not mean it would have been impossible for the Communists to maintain power. Kontorovich (1993: 35) reflects: "Poor economic performance is commonplace in the world, while the peacetime collapse of a political system is quite rare." Finally, since critics consider all the East European economies to be inefficient, this cannot account for differences in the process of collapse.

Similarly, theorists relying on modernization theories have trouble explaining why the regimes could not have survived longer. Nor do they even attempt to explain why the process of change varied so greatly among East European countries. One of the most well-known representatives of the modernization school, Samuel Huntington (1991: 69), provides a model in his book *The Third Wave*, in which he claims a higher level of economic development gives rise to a more highly educated public, the development of civic-cultural attitudes, and a larger middle class. A larger middle class and a more highly educated public also improves civic-cultural attitudes. Civic-cultural attitudes in turn lead to support for democracy. Where the Soviet bloc is concerned, however, it is hard to see this correlation. Most West European countries became democratic after World War II, while the regimes of Eastern Europe remained authoritarian until 1989. Consequently, if Huntington were correct, we would expect the East European countries to have become relatively more modern in 1989 than in 1948. Of course, all the Soviet-bloc countries were more modern in 1989 than in 1948, but—at least in East Germany and Czechoslovakia—they were *relatively less modern* in comparison with the democracies of Western Europe. In 1948 these two countries were among the most advanced countries in the world, but by 1989 they appeared hopelessly unmodern by Western standards.

Huntington has acknowledged this previously. In 1984 he wrote: "In terms of cultural tradition, economic development, and social structure, Czechoslovakia would certainly be a democracy today (and probably Hungary and Poland also) if it were not for the overriding veto of the Soviet presence" (1984: 214). The obvious conclusion is that it takes more than economic development to bring down a regime. In addition, even if it were true that no authoritarian regime can survive after a certain level of modernization, nothing in Huntington's modernization model gives any clue as to why the processes of collapse differed.

While economic development and the persistence of an inefficient economic system might not be enough in themselves to bring down a regime, the other economic factors listed above might conceivably provide part of the explanation for the collapse. Poor economic policies, increases in military spending, and technological developments could have caused an economic crisis.[19] However, Kontorovich's objection that other regimes have survived economic crises still casts doubt on the proposition that an economic crisis is in itself enough to bring down a system. Moreover, nobody has argued so far that differences in the degree of economic crisis led to differences in the process of change.

The failure to implement economic reform successfully might provide a clue as to why the regimes did not collapse earlier: as long as the elites did not believe that economic reforms had been given a chance to prove their merits, they could maintain faith in the system. The disappointing results of the various reform attempts might have convinced the Communist leaders that they could not save the Soviet-type system. Unfortunately, most of the literature on economic reforms concentrates on the *reasons* why the reforms failed, rather than on how their failure affected the thinking of the regimes.[20] But even if one accepts the hypothesis that the failure of the reform process caused the regimes to lose faith in the system, it does not explain why the various Soviet-bloc regimes behaved differently once they lost faith.

Loss of Legitimacy

Some authors claim that the various crises (economic, ideological, etc.) caused the regimes to lose their legitimacy among the population (Swain 1992: 13), or at least among certain sectors of society, e.g. the intellectuals (Chirot 1991: 10–11). Others have claimed that the regimes never enjoyed any legitimacy among the populace, but were able to maintain power as long as there were no feasible alternatives (cf. Przeworski 1986 and Rychard 1992: 141). The most common claims have been that the Communist leaders never based their legitimacy on popular support for the system, but rather on their goals, as well as on their conviction that

---

19. For literature dealing with the question of military spending, see for example Collins & Waller (1993) and Janos (1991). Those writing on the role of technology include Bates (1990), Chirot (1991), Reykowski (1994) and Szelenyi & Szelenyi (1994).

20. See, for example, Korbonski (1989), Wasilewski (1990) and Winiecki (1990a&b).

they were the true representatives of society (cf. Di Palma 1991 and Fehér & Heller & Márkus 1983). Consequently, the change in convictions among Party and union members (Rychard 1992) or ruling elites (Ash 1990a: 19, Di Palma 1991, Schöpflin 1993: 216–7) ultimately brought down the system. This is not to say, of course, that these authors neglect the remaining population. When the leaders' "self-legitimization" (Schöpflin 1993) deteriorated, this made the rulers appear weaker, encouraging the populace to protest against the system. These discussions on legitimacy have led to interesting hypotheses. Yet, so far as I am aware, none of these researchers have even tried to explain the differences in the process of collapse. They focus either on a single country or on the similarities among the countries. But if both the East German and Polish Communists suffered from a lack of legitimacy, why did they behave so differently?

Gorbachev's Role

Gorbachev has received much of the credit for the collapse of the East European regimes. Stokes (1991: 21) remarks that, if his "Brezhnevian rival" Viktor Grishin had come to power, developments would likely have been very different. Various authors emphasize different aspects of Gorbachev's influence on the collapse. Rush (1993: 19) claims that Gorbachev's economic policy hastened the downfall. A more orthodox policy could have preserved the system for "another decade or two." In other words, the system would have functioned better without any reforms at all than under the particular reform mix that Gorbachev chose. Other authors have concentrated more on the Soviet leader's influence on either the regimes (Roskin 1994: ch. 7) or the opposition (Tarrow 1991). While one certainly cannot ignore Gorbachev's role, his actions alone are not sufficient. First, a model that explains the collapse of the Soviet-type system must consider the factors that made it possible for him to come to power, the factors that encouraged him to launch his reforms, the reasons for their failure, etc. Second, explanations that focus on Gorbachev's decision to "let go" Eastern Europe (cf. Stokes 1991: 21) cannot explain why this policy induced the regimes and opposition in the satellite countries to react differently.

Civil Society

Ironically, many mainstream political scientists followed the totalitarian school in claiming that change in Eastern Europe was impossible due to the lack of a civil society. *After* 1989, suddenly, it has been in vogue to claim that the emergence of a civil society was the *cause* (or at least one of the major causes) of the collapse.[21] For example, Weigle & Butterfield (1992) claim that civil society in all of the East European countries went through several stages. These countries "experienced an emergent civil society that would quickly mobilize to overthrow the debilitated Communist regimes" (1992: 13–14). Such hypotheses cannot, however, explain the differences in the process of change. Instead, they must exaggerate the similarities of the countries to the point of not distinguishing between such radically different cases as: 1) Hungary, where several hundred dissidents who were active when the regime started contemplating negotiations and 2) Czechoslovakia, where millions of demonstrators forced their Politburo to resign after just one week.

EXPLANATIONS FOR THE DIFFERENCES IN THE PROCESS OF CHANGE

I have suggested above that, while the conventional explanations might be able to indicate some of the necessary conditions for the collapse of the system, they are not sufficient for understanding the different processes of collapse. The next task is to see how effective more specialized theorists are in dealing with this question. I claim that most of these theorists only concentrate on one aspect of the change, while neglecting others. Theorists of revolution have tended to work within a dichotomy between revolution and a regime maintaining power. Similarly, theorists of democratization have often used a dichotomy between institutional compromise (democratization) and the continuation of authoritarian rule. That is, the regime either reaches an institutional compromise with the opposition or it maintains power.

A second group of theoretical studies has interesting explanations for one of the two outcomes (revolution or democratization). Even though I disagree with their arguments, they are worth discussing in the later empirical chapters, because I cannot criticize them based on the commonly accepted facts. Rather, a closer look at the empirical evidence is necessary to support my skepticism. So I return to these explanations in the later chapters. Some of them become part of my analytical framework, others become competing explanations.

---

21. See, for example, Kirkpatrick (1979) for an argument about the inability of "totalitarian" systems to change. Some theorists writing after 1989, such as Arato (1991), deny that a truly civil society existed in Eastern Europe. Others, such as Lewis (1992: 6) warn against exaggerating the role of civil society. He notes: "It is too easy, in retrospect, to interpret all signs of opposition to communist rule and the serious examples of regime instability as signs of the growth and progressive development of an East European civil society."

Since many trees have been hewed in order to make it possible to print the enormous body of publications dealing with the collapse of the Soviet bloc, I must introduce some limits on the sources used.

First, I concentrate on works specifically devoted to the collapse of the Soviet bloc. This is not to deny the *possibility* that other theories could be usefully applied in the East European context, but for the sake of space, I assume that if representatives of a particular school of thought believed that they could apply their theoretical models to Eastern Europe, then they would have attempted to do so. That does not mean they will not do so in the *future*, but for the moment it suffices to note that they have not done so.

Second, I refrain from discussing authors who only explain developments in one particular country, without making any claims in regard to the applicability of their model to other countries. This is especially pertinent in the case of the East German revolution, where several illuminating articles have appeared which emphasize that country's uniqueness.[22]

Finally, I leave out the discussions on political culture. The few authors who have discussed political culture in the context of the collapse of the Soviet-type regimes have reverted to other theoretical models to explain the differences in the process of change. Thus, the political culturalists themselves do not believe their approach is fruitful for explaining these differences.[23]

---

22. For example, the notion of "spontaneous coordination," in which the claim is made that the level of repression was so high that the opposition did not dare organize revolts in the beginning. Instead, people went to places where they knew people would congregate (Opp 1993 and Opp & Gern 1993). Another example is the description of the East German events as an "exit" revolution, sparked off by the mass emigration to West Germany (Hirschman 1993, Offe 1993: 293 and Reißig 1993: 58).

23. For example, Szabó (1991) compares the relationship of political culture to social movements in Poland, Hungary and the GDR. In comparing Poland and Hungary, he notes that, after repeated uprisings, Poland developed a "protest culture." Yet he does not explain why Hungary and Poland followed nearly the same process of democratization despite their rather different political cultures. Nor does this provide a clue as to why revolutions in fact took place in the ČSSR and the GDR, even though they did not share Poland's protest culture. In the East German case, he reverts to the "voice-exit" paradigm, rather than relating the revolution to that country's culture. Another example is Lemke, who limits her study to the GDR. Although she pays a lot of attention to the change in cultural values among East German citizens, she uses what she calls a "critically reflected modernization theory" to explain these changes in values (1991: 55–57). Not only does she revert to a different school to explain the change in values, she does not even try to explain the mechanisms that caused the dissatisfied population to rebel. This lack of attention to the question of differences in the process of transformation is not surprising. As Eckstein (1988) admits, culturalist approaches are less useful for explaining change than for explaining the absence of change.

I limit this section to the few attempts at actually explaining the differences in the process of change. In the following section, I review theories explaining the revolutions. I then devote the next section to theories of institutional compromise (i.e., democratization).

Political Society

Ekiert (1991: 307) offers an explanation for the differences in the process of collapse based on the notion of political society:

> The events of 1989 show that where political society was stronger and pragmatic forces within the party-state were more influential, there were negotiated openings, as in the case of Poland and Hungary. A weaker political society and a more ineffective reformist faction within the party-state facilitated popular upsurge in East Germany and Czechoslovakia.

I agree with this observation, but it does not tell us *why* political society was stronger in these countries or *why* the leaders decided to negotiate in 1989.

EXPLANATIONS OF REVOLUTIONARY CHANGE

Several authors have tried to apply theories of revolution or of social movements to the events in Eastern Europe. Unfortunately, they postulate a dichotomy between revolution and no revolution (or between rebellion and no rebellion), and exclude the possibility of institutional compromise. Nevertheless, if they explain the Czechoslovak and East German revolutions, they may furnish an answer to part of the puzzle.

Rationalist Explanations

Several rational-choice theorists have used Granovetter's (1978) notion of participation thresholds to explain the sudden willingness of citizens to participate in mass collective action in Eastern Europe (Hermansson 1992, Kuran 1991, and Karklins & Petersen 1993).[24]

---

24. It may be no coincidence that rational-choice theorists writing about the East European revolutions have abandoned the more stringent public-choice assumptions of rational egoism, since, as Hough (1993: 353) remarks in his article on these revolutions: "If 500,000 people are demonstrating in the center of town and it is safe to join them, the 500,001st person will not worry about the lack of impact of his or her participation, but will join for the sheer excitement and novelty of the 'happening.'" Even supporters of the rational-egoist assumption, such as Taylor (1988: 86), admit that demonstrations are problematic, because in contrast to many other forms of collective action, they can actually give pleasure.

The basic idea is that different groups of people have different preferences. Some dissidents may be altruists who are willing to demonstrate regardless of how many others join them. Others might only be willing to participate when the number of demonstrators reaches such a high level that they are certain the revolution will succeed. Consequently, the "thresholds" for participation will vary between people and groups. Only a slight change in thresholds—caused for example by changes in preferences or a decrease in perceived costs—is enough to increase the number of participants radically.

According to Hermansson, this is exactly what happened in Eastern Europe. He notes (1992: 231): "All of the Eastern European states had civil rights organizations which continuously decided to protest despite hard repression." Yet, these were not enough to spark off revolts, because: "As long as most of the citizens have significantly higher threshold levels than those of the civil rights movement's core group, the majority of the citizens will most likely remain passive, keeping the opposition rather small and weak." As citizens changed their perception of the costs of participating, their threshold fell (1992: 231–2). Many were suddenly willing, therefore, to participate. Within a short period, this caused a "snowball effect" in both East Germany and Czechoslovakia in 1989, as the size of the demonstrations grew exponentially.

This approach leaves out the most important questions. If the main causes of revolutions turn out to be the original *preferences* (thresholds) and the *changes in the costs* of participating, then it is these two factors which need explaining. Usually, however, rational-choice models take preferences as a given rather than trying to explain them. Furthermore, it is better to develop theories about what types of factors cause the necessary changes in costs by carrying out traditional empirical comparative studies, rather than by devising special rational-choice models. One could combine theories about preference formation and lowered costs with Granovetter's rationalist model. Yet, these first two issues must be the focal point of empirical research even if one uses his model. Nevertheless, I can keep the threshold model as a partial hypothesis to be discussed in the empirical chapters. The point at issue is whether or not participation actually steadily increased until the Communist regimes fell.

Neo-Tocquevillian
Tarrow (1991: 14) offers a possible answer to the question of when thresholds change. He follows Tocqueville by claiming "revolts occur not when people are most oppressed or best represented, but when

a closed system of opportunities has begun to open up."[25] His four variables that can cause a political opening[26] include:

- the opening of access to institutional participation,
- disarray among political alignments before the formation of new ones,
- conflicts among political elites which the opposition can take advantage of, and
- offers of help from influential allies from within or without the system.

Surprisingly, Tarrow does not cite any of these factors in describing the actual openings that took place in Eastern Europe. Instead, he rightly emphasizes "Gorbachev's well-publicized refusal to use military force." So the real political opening did not come from action, but rather the refusal to act. Thus, one should add a fifth factor to Tarrow's list, or at least one should modify the fourth point to allow for the neutralization of a foreign power (i.e., the USSR) rather than require the *active* support of an outside ally. As Opp & Gern (1993) note, however, the liberalization of Poland and Hungary also influenced decisions to participate. Surely, these events should also qualify as political openings. So perhaps the best solution is in fact to add a fifth factor: encouragement from events in other countries.[27] In a more generalized form, one can speak of rising expectations: the events in the neighboring countries were important, because they encouraged citizens to believe that change was possible in their country as well. In this form, Tarrow's explanation can be incorporated into my framework.

---

25. The original quote by Tocqueville (1856: 141) is as follows: "The regime which is destroyed by a revolution is almost always an improvement on its immediate predecessor, and experience teaches that the most critical moment for bad governments is the one which witnesses their first steps towards reform. A sovereign who seeks to relieve his subjects after a long period of oppression is lost, unless he be a man of great genius." Thus, the concept of political openings is an expansion on the idea that revolutions are encouraged by political reforms. Tocqueville's thought, in turn, has its origins in Plato's *Republic*. In that book, Plato (1970: 268) declares that a ruling class cannot lose power as long as it is "of one mind."

26. Tarrow's term, in turn, comes from Kitschelt's (1986) notion of political opportunity structures.

27. Cf. Stone (1966: 172), who claims that rising expectations can lead to revolution. Nevertheless, he believes that frustrated expectations (when liberalizing regimes revert to their previous repressive practices) are the cause, rather than expectations coming from changes in neighboring countries. Elster (1990) also writes on the East European's disillusionment with the Soviet-type regimes: "Drawing once again on Tocqueville, one can argue that to raise expectations without fulfilling them is a recipe for revolution."

Yet, much more is needed to understand the underlying causes of the revolutions in the GDR and ČSSR. For example, Tarrow never discusses under what conditions a revolt will succeed or fail, if it will be large or small, which groups are likely to participate, and so on. Nor can one use the concept of political openings by itself to explain why revolts did not take place in the countries with the widest political openings: Hungary and Poland. As discussed above, both countries fulfilled several of Tarrow's criteria for political openings. There was an opening of access to institutional participation in Poland via the referendum and various councils. In Hungary, the Patriotic People's Front, headed by Politburo member Pozsgay, supported the founding of the Endue Bajcsy-Zsilinsky Fraternal Society. The Front also sanctioned a critical report written by radical economists. Furthermore, there were clear conflicts among political elites in these countries, but not in revolutionary Czechoslovakia and East Germany. In sum, all four countries experienced political openings in the modified form of rising expectations and the neutralization of an outside enemy. Yet Tarrow presents no hypothesis concerning the possible causes for such openings.

It should be said in Tarrow's defense, however, that he is not interested in answering these questions. Moreover, I believe that, in a modified form, political openings provide a useful tool for analyzing the revolutions in the ČSSR and GDR. A political opening then might be a necessary condition for a revolution. Nevertheless, a political opening is certainly not a sufficient condition. Although I incorporate Tarrow into my analytical framework, then, I believe my basic framework is much more comprehensive than his.

J-curve

Another approach has been to concentrate on the interplay between economic performance, expectations and revolution. Davies (1962) discusses the idea of rising expectations for revolutionary action in his famous "J-curve" analogy, which he bases on Marx and Tocqueville. His goal is to find a synthesis between Marx's assertion that revolutions occur during economic crises and Tocqueville's claim that they take place during periods of economic improvement.[28] He writes (1962: 216):

---

28. Interestingly, although Tocqueville is often credited with claiming that revolutions occur after periods of economic improvement, he makes the opposite claim in *Democracy in America*: "Among civilized nations, only those who have nothing to lose ever revolt..." (1848: 140).

Revolutions are most likely to occur when a prolonged period of objective economic and social development is followed by a short period of sharp reversal. The all-important effect on the minds of people in a particular society is to produce, during the former period, an expectation of continued ability to satisfy needs—which continue to rise—and, during the latter, a mental state of anxiety and frustration when manifest reality breaks away from anticipated reality.

Dix (1991: 234) argues that Davies's J-curve goes a long way towards explaining the collapse of the regimes in 1989, on account of the "relatively good economic performance" of these countries in earlier decades, together with "the rather precipitate decline in that performance in the 1980s, as well as increasing awareness of and attraction to the consumer goods available in the West but not to them...." Similarly, Mason (1992: 110) claims that the J-curve applies to the collapse of the East European regimes, since they "had experienced economic decline after a long period of economic improvement."

This is an interesting explanation which I shall examine in the empirical chapters. If the J-curve hypothesis is correct, we can expect two outcomes: 1) the economic reversal will be sharper in revolutionary Czechoslovakia and East Germany than in Hungary and Poland; and 2) the "prolonged period" of economic development will be much longer than the "short period of sharp reversal." I am skeptical of this explanation, but it is not possible to refute it without more empirical data.

In the chapters that follow, then, I incorporate the concept of political openings into my framework. By contrast, I refer to the J-curve in later chapters as a competing hypothesis.

EXPLANATIONS OF INSTITUTIONAL COMPROMISE

While theories of revolution are usually bound to the dichotomy between revolution and no revolution and, therefore, cannot explain institutional compromise, theories of democratization are usually bound to the dichotomy between authoritarianism and democratization and, thus, cannot explain revolutions. This means that such theorists can only explain the process of institutional compromise in Hungary and Poland, but not the revolution in Czechoslovakia and East Germany. Moreover, many of these authors tend to concentrate on the strategies of the reforming elite that sought to maneuver between the opposition and the hardliners. Thus, they take the existence of an opposition for granted, without specifying the conditions under which a strong opposition will emerge.[29]

The best-known analyses of the Soviet-type regimes from the democratization school are those of Bova (1991) and Przeworski (1991). Both authors use O'Donnell & Schmitter's *Transitions from Authoritarian Rule* as the basis for their models.

Bova

Bova (1991) focuses on the contradictory pressures which the "centrist" Gorbachev faced from the hardliners in the regime, who tried to block all changes, and from the opposition, which wanted "a complete and immediate break with the past" (1991: 121). He sees the reformist leader and the regime hardliners as the main actors, and hardly mentions the opposition. Following O'Donnell & Schmitter, he begins with liberalizing reformers. Once they begin liberalizing, pressures arise for the reformers to go further than they had originally intended (1991: 115). The further the reforms have come, the less credible are threats to reverse them. A reversion strengthens the hardliners, who could use the opportunity to replace the reformers. Eventually, the opposition realizes that the reformers are only bluffing when they threaten reversal; accordingly, the reformers' leverage with the opposition is reduced. As the opposition increases pressure for further liberalization, the hardliners retrench. The highly motivated hardliners become more powerful, which weakens the reforms. Thus, society becomes paralyzed between the hardliners and the opposition (1991: 124–5). Since the reformers become weaker, they must gain the support of the hardliners in order to insure a democratic transition. They can do this either by allowing the hardliners to maintain some political influence in the new system or by securing an opportunity for the hardliners to exchange political for economic power (1991: 128–9).

This framework is more fruitful for analyzing the thinking of the Hungarian and Polish reform Communists than for explaining the process of democratic change in the ČSSR and GDR. In the latter two countries, there were no reformers attempting any type of

---

29. Cf. McSweeney & Tempest (1993): "Elites are the principal actors in the literature of transition [to democracy]. Mass activity and demands are almost invisible according to some authors who explicitly deny their significance."

glasnost-like liberalization.[30] Yet, Bova's hypotheses do not always hold up even in the Polish and Hungarian cases. For example, rather than retrenching and becoming stronger during the reform process, the hardliners within the Hungarian Communist Party became much weaker. In contrast to Bova's claim, therefore, the reformers had no reason to placate the hardliners. Indeed, the former actively worked to expel the latter. I can state already here, therefore, that I am skeptical of Bova's hypotheses, although I return to them in the later empirical chapters.

Przeworski
In his book, *Democracy and the Market*, Przeworski (1991) uses several different analyses of the democratization process in general, and that in Eastern Europe in particular. Even though, in contrast to most theorists of democratization, he leaves the *possibility* of revolutionary change open, he devotes his main analysis to the usual dichotomy between democratization and the maintenance of authoritarian rule. More specifically, he is interested in discovering the conditions under which rulers will agree to a "democracy with guarantees." This term implies that rulers are only willing to reach an institutional compromise when they are given guarantees of being able to maintain some power. Like Bova, consequently, Przeworski is better able to explain Hungary and Poland than the ČSSR and GDR.

In chapter Two, Przeworski analyzes the options of the reformist leaders, who wanted to liberalize the system. He uses an extended game-theory model to scrutinize the situation. Since it would require a great deal of space to describe the technicalities of his model, I limit myself here to his main conclusions. He maintains that if the Liberalizers move first, and both the regime and opposition have perfect information, the result will be either the *status quo* or a broadened dictatorship. Which of these two outcomes emerges depends on the preferences of both sides (1991: 62). What is important for our purposes is that, regardless of their preferences, democratization is not possible. He furthermore concludes that, if all actors are rational, democratization is only possible if either a) Hardliners play no role, b) the regime is not divided, or c) Liberalizers control the weapons.

---

30. A moderate form of *perestroika* was being introduced in the ČSSR.

Przeworski (1991: 63–4) admits, however, that democratization is also possible if the main actors miscalculate the situation. Liberalizers may begin by opening the regime to some previously excluded groups. They do so because they expect society to be satisfied with cooptive arrangements that broaden the dictatorship. They do not believe that society will reject these offers and demand full democracy. But society might believe that the Liberalizers will not be willing to repress it. So society organizes itself against the regime rather than entering into cooptive agreements. Once Liberalizers observe that society is continuing to organize, they downgrade their estimate of successful repression to the point where they prefer a transition to democracy over repression. "Hence, civil society organizes, and Liberalizers update their beliefs about the effectiveness of repression as they watch the streets." Przeworski's suggestion is intriguing, since it emphasizes a dynamic process in which actors on both sides are continuously forced to change their calculations.

In the section on democratization, Przeworski considers once again the relations between the regime and the opposition—this time using game-theory models. He divides the regime into Hardliners and Reformers, and the opposition into Radicals and Moderates. His basic reasoning is that an agreement on democratization ("extrication") is possible if "(1) an agreement can be reached between Reformers and Moderates to establish institutions under which the social forces they represent would have a significant political presence in the democratic system, (2) Reformers can deliver the consent of Hardliners or neutralize them, and (3) Moderates can control Radicals" (1991: 68). Next, he looks at the possibilities for democratization with guarantees when the regime is relatively weak, and when it is relatively strong.

If the Reformers are too weak to do well in any type of competitive elections, Przeworski concludes that their dominant strategy will always be to align themselves with the Hardliners (1991: 70). An example is Poland in 1980–81. Przeworski writes (1991: 70–71):

> If the party had been getting 35 percent, it would have been child's play to invent an electoral system that would be competitive and give it a good chance of winning. But not at 3 percent. ...Under such conditions, Reformers could not venture into a democratic alliance with Moderates.

Under these circumstances, Przeworski finds the 1989 compromise solution of free elections to the senate "a stroke of genius"

(1991: 71).[31] He does not explain, however, why a compromise of this kind did not emerge in 1980–81. Perhaps he would propose an actor-based explanation: it could have emerged if the same genius had proposed it then.

Although his aim is to present a rationalist model, he also admits the possible pertinence of psychological and sociological explanations in certain cases. A psychological explanation is applicable when the actors "let their desires affect their beliefs and screen out undesirable information" (1991: 65). He continues: "Popular mobilization may be uncontainable, as it was in Poland. Under such conditions, the Liberalizers are likely to persuade themselves that the opening will be successful, even that they will win competitive elections if they proceed all the way to democracy."

Przeworski's (1991: 64–5) sociological explanation is that:

> As the organization of the civil society crystallizes, its leadership becomes known, and personal contacts become established, the Liberalizers learn that the opposition is not as threatening as they had thought.... Negotiations show that the opposition is willing to listen and to make concessions; personal contacts bring rapprochement among individuals. Gradually, transition appears as less of a chasm, and repression seems simply uncivilized. Liberalizers change their preferences endogenously as a result of bargaining with the opposition.

Thus, although Przeworski only devotes a few pages of his book to these alternative explanations, and never tries to apply them to Eastern Europe, it might be worthwhile to see whether his alternative hypotheses can better explain these events. For example, a plausible hypothesis is that the psychological explanation more accurately describes the behavior of the Polish Communists. Even if the actors had been rational in appraising their true popularity, and even if they could really have gained 35 per cent, their electoral proposal was far from optimal. Since the opposition stood united behind *Solidarność*, the simple-majority rule virtually guaranteed the Communists would be greatly underrepresented in the Senate. Theoretically, it would even have been possible for them to lose every single seat (as in fact they did) while still obtaining 35 per cent of the national vote (which, of course, they did not). Since they faced a united opposition, they could

---

31. Despite his actor's approach, ironically, he does not state *whose* proposal this was, nor the reason why he/she proposed it. He does not even say which *side* proposed it.

have expected to do much better under a system of proportional representation. Apparently, the Polish leaders irrationally filtered out information during their negotiations with *Solidarność*.

The Hungarian Communists apparently behaved much more rationally than their Polish counterparts in pushing for the maximal use of the simple-majority rule in parliamentary elections. In contrast to the situation in Poland, for one thing, some public-opinion polls in the early stages actually did show them gaining around 35 per cent of the vote. Moreover, rather than facing a united opposition, their opponents were divided into several competing groups. If the opposition vote had been spread fairly evenly among the MDF, the SZDSZ, the FIDESZ, and the Social Democrats, then 35 per cent of the vote might have been enough to obtain a majority of the single-member districts. In the end, they had to compromise with the opposition (who for their part favored proportional representation, and for just the same reason). Not even this form of institutional compromise really corresponds, however, to the "democracy with guarantees" predicted by Przeworski. At the very least, though, both sides behaved relatively rationally during the negotiations. One could claim, therefore, that Przeworski's hypothesis is still worth examining more closely in the empirical chapters.

If it appears, at first glance, that Przeworski's rationalistic explanation works better for Hungary, while his psychological one fares better for Poland, it will be necessary to develop a framework for discussing hypotheses regarding the conditions under which rulers behave more rationally, and those under which they behave less rationally. I shall attempt, in the following chapter, to develop such a framework. However, I use the term "strategic" instead of "rational." Many actions, after all, can be interpreted as rational, but not all actions make sense strategically. I keep Przeworski's notion— that the rulers in fact behaved strategically in all four countries—as a competing hypothesis (I return to this in the empirical chapters). Finally, even if Przeworski's rationalist explanation is correct, it should be placed within a larger analytical framework. Such a framework should consider three questions: 1) Under what conditions do rulers undertake liberalization? 2) How do the economic consequences of these measures influence further political developments? And most importantly, 3) when do revolutionary outcomes arise, rather than institutional compromise or continued authoritarian rule?

SUMMARY

I began this chapter by stating the problem: how can we explain the differences in the process of collapse in Eastern Europe? I then gave a brief summary of these events, in order to give the reader a reference point for understanding the theoretical discourse.

Subsequently, I claimed that the conventional explanations (the economic crisis, loss of legitimacy, Gorbachev, and the emergence of a civil society) might provide the *necessary* conditions for the collapse, but they are not *sufficient*. On the one hand, the regimes might have been able to survive in spite of these problems. On the other, even if they were doomed to collapse, these hypotheses cannot explain the significant differences in the process of change. Therefore, one must develop a model which shows why a revolution took place in the ČSSR and in the GDR, while an institutional compromise was reached in Hungary and in Poland.

In the next section, I looked at various theoretical attempts to explain the different processes of transformation. I noted that, to my knowledge, Eikert is the only person who has offered an explanation for the differences in the process of change. I concluded that Eikert is correct in stating that the reformist regimes in countries with stronger political societies were more willing to negotiate. However, to understand the underlying causes of the collapse, one must investigate the reasons why some countries had stronger political societies and more reformist regimes than others. Moreover, this explanation by itself cannot tell us why these regimes decided to negotiate in 1989 in particular.

Except for the political-society argument, the other approaches have limited themselves to simple dichotomies that can either explain 1) the presence or absence of revolutions, or 2) the presence or absence of institutional compromise. None of these, by themselves, seriously consider the trichotomy between revolution, democratization, and continued authoritarian rule. For this reason, they can only provide a partial explanation for the differences in the process of collapse.

When examining theories of revolution, I concluded that the J-curve and threshold models present hypotheses that I cannot reject based on the empirical data provided so far. In the empirical chapters, therefore, I will consider them as competing hypotheses. The J-curve approach predicts that revolutions will occur in the countries having the sharpest downturns. Moreover, the period of decline should be much shorter than the period of economic improvement. If the threshold model is correct, the number of people demonstrating should have continually increased until the Communist regime fell. The concept of political openings, by contrast, is worth incorporating into my model (although in a slightly modified form). That is, I believe that the political opening did not consist in the factors Tarrow lists, but rather in a fifth one: changes in neighboring countries. I have in mind the changes that took place in the USSR, Poland and Hungary, as well as Gorbachev's decision not to intervene. Moreover, the main impact of these factors was not necessarily to change the rational calculations of citizens as to whether or not they should oppose the regime; rather, it was the rising expectations of change that encouraged the East German and Czechoslovak citizens to struggle against their rulers. Even this provides but a partial explanation, since it does not indicate why changes occurred in the first place in neighboring Poland, Hungary and the USSR. Nor can it explain the behavior of the national regimes in the GDR and ČSSR.

While authors using theories of revolution have neglected institutional change, theorists writing about democratization have neglected revolutionary change. I have indicated that I am skeptical of Bova's model for the Hungarian and Polish cases. For in contrast to his expectations, the reformers defeated the hardliners rather than placating them.

Przeworski tries to develop a rationalist model. Yet he also admits briefly that psychological and social explanations might be better for explaining some situations. I prefer the term "strategic" to the term "rational," since the theorist can almost always find a rational explanation for behavior after the fact. For example, one could claim it is perfectly rational for a ruler simply to give up everything without a fight because he or she has grown tired of ruling, yet one could hardly call such behavior strategic. In contrast, it is easier to develop criteria for possible strategic behavior (such as when leaders believe they can increase their prospects for maintaining power or for shaping outcomes in a desired direction, or at least go down in history as someone who democratized the system). I argue that the Hungarian rulers acted more strategically than did their Polish counterparts. Furthermore, both groups acted more strategically than the leaders in East Germany and Czechoslovakia. Since Przeworski does not present any hypothesis about the circumstances under which rulers will behave less strategically, I shall present one in the final model which I develop in the course of this study. In the empirical chapters, meanwhile, I can examine the competing hypothesis that the elites actually behaved strategically in all four countries.

DISPOSITION AND MORE SPECIFIC QUESTIONS

I divide this study into three parts. In Part I, I concentrate on theoretical questions. This part encompasses chapters 1 (where I discuss the theoretical discourse) and 2 (where I develop a framework for pursuing my questions further). Then, in the empirical chapters that follow, I develop a model designed both to show the underlying causes of the collapse and to explain the trichotomy between revolution, democratization, and continued authoritarian rule. In each of the empirical chapters, I use my framework to carve out a piece of the model. I devote Part II to the general underlying causes of the collapse. I take up these issues in chapters 3, 4, and 5. In Part III, finally, I pose my main questions about the differences in the process of collapse. I discuss this in chapters 7, 8 and 9.

A more detailed account of each chapter follows below:

Part I: Theory
I began Part I by posing my main questions, and examining what other social scientists have written on these issues. In the next chapter, I develop a framework for analyzing my three questions further.

Part II: The Underlying Causes of the Collapse
In chapter 3 I examine the economic situation. Some authors claim the economic crisis was instrumental for the collapse, while others deny the existence of an economic crisis. I seek to ascertain here, therefore, whether or not these countries really suffered from an economic crisis. If, moreover, a crisis actually existed, I believe one must understand the *causes* of this crisis. This makes it easier to decipher the mechanisms that set the crisis in motion. If the rulers had succeeded in reforming the system, they might have been able to gain popular support. In chapter 4, therefore, I determine the reasons for their failure to carry out successful economic reforms.

In chapter 5, I look more closely at the relationship between economics and politics, in particular the connection between a diminished economic performance and the loss of ideological legitimacy. I take up the "Gorbachev factor" in this chapter as well, because I assert that he came to power as a result of the economic crisis. Moreover, his attempts at reforming the USSR obviously influenced the relationship between Moscow and its East European allies.

As already discussed, these general factors were important as underlying causes for the collapse. Yet they cannot explain differences in the process of collapse. That is the topic of Part III.

Part III: The Differences in the Process of Collapse

In chapters 6 and 7, I cover developments prior to 1988. I examine the events of 1988–89 in chapters 8 and 9. I deal with the regimes and society separately for the pre-1988 years, because the two topics belong to different theoretical discourses. In chapters 8 and 9, I combine the two discourses and examine the interplay between state and society during the collapse.

I devote chapter 6 to the discourse on the behavior of the regimes, and chapter 7 to the development of society. Eckstein points out that the reformist regimes took the initiative for negotiations with the opposition, but he does not explain why some regimes were more reformist than others. I consider this question in chapter 6. In addition, I concentrate on the relationship between the East European regimes and the Soviet Union, and on the relationship between these regimes and society before 1988.

Then, in chapter 7, I look more closely here at the civil society explanations of change in Eastern Europe. These explanations are then compared to explanations that emphasize the change in atmosphere caused by liberalizing regimes.

In chapter 8, I review the pre-1989 revolts to develop a framework that can help understand the successful resolutions in 1989. First, I ask why some groups have been willing to revolt under certain conditions. Does any pattern emerge from a review of these pre-1989 uprisings? I note that none of the theorists writing about the revolutions of 1989 have tried to explain why different groups have continuously behaved differently. Here I propose a partial model that addresses these issues. Since intellectuals have played such an important role in opposing the system, I also investigate the emergence of dissident groups. If one wants to avoid a static, deterministic model, one must do more than look at repeated patterns of behavior. One must also examine the thinking of opposition groups, since this affects their behavior. After discussing dissident movements, I return to the debates on civil society. Although I have stated already that these theorists do not propose an explanation for the differences in the process of change, they still have some interesting points to make about the relationship between the Communist-led regimes and the East European societies. Accordingly, I evaluate these contributions to see if I should incorporate any of their perspectives into my model.

After developing partial models for the behavior of the regimes and societies, I combine these ideas into an integrated model designed to explain the differences in the process of collapse. In chapters 9 and 10, therefore, I investigate more directly the interaction between the regimes and society during the actual collapse in 1988–89. I focus in chapter 9 on the institutional compromises in Poland and Hungary. In chapter 10 I turn to the non-violent revolutions in the GDR and ČSSR.

In the concluding chapter, finally, I lift the veil and present the model in its completed form. Since these outcomes took place in the context of various general crises (such as the economy, legitimacy, Gorbachev's rise to power, etc.), I describe 1) the causes for these general factors, and 2) the interaction between these general factors and the various actors in the four countries. By studying the inter-action between general causes and particular actors and institutions in the four countries, I explain why similar general causes issued in different transformational processes.

Chapter 2

THE MAIN FRAMEWORK

In chapter 1, in reviewing some of the theoretical work on the collapse of the Soviet-type regimes, I concluded that while some authors have interesting hypotheses about specific aspects of the collapse, almost none of them have tried to explain the differences in the process of collapse. The one person who presents such an explanation does not posit a hypothesis for the underlying causes of the breakdown. This chapter presents the main framework for analyzing these events. First, I discuss my choice of countries and my comparative method. Then, I propose a neo-Marxian framework which I believe provides useful tools for understanding the underlying causes of the collapse. In the upcoming empirical chapters, I will incorporate some concepts from other authors into my framework. I have already stated, for example, that the notion of political openings can be readily incorporated into the framework if used in a modified form. Within each empirical chapter, I add more pieces to my construction. At the end of the study, the pieces are integrated into a more comprehensive model. Although the model is expanded in various ways, it rests firmly on the framework presented in this chapter.

CHOICE OF COUNTRIES

The main reason for choosing these particular four countries is that they fit in best with John Stuart Mill's "method of difference."[1] According to this method of comparison, one isolates the independent variable by choosing countries which are as similar as possible, yet which display varying outcomes. These four countries are indeed rather similar in certain respects, but the outcomes within them differ (revolution in the ČSSR and in the GDR; institutional compromise in Hungary and in Poland).

The first step is to examine the similarities, which also serve to indicate that it is best to exclude the other East European countries (Bulgaria and Romania) from this study. I then discuss the differences

---

1. See Skocpol & Somers (1980), von Beyme (1990459–460), Hages & Meeker (1988: 45–6) and Lijphart (1971: 687). Przeworski & Teune (1985) call this "most similar systems."

in outcome. Among the major similarities displayed by the four countries are the following:

- The four countries have traditionally considered themselves to be "Central European" rather than "East European." In fact, the term Eastern Europe is used here only in the strictly political sense. That is, these countries belonged to the "Eastern" rather than "Western" bloc in the formerly bi-polar world.
- Geographically, these countries also lie more in Central Europe than do Romania and Bulgaria. The latter two do not share any borders with Western countries. (I consider Poland's border with Germany to be "Western," since social scientists usually consider Germany as a nation to be *geographically* and *culturally* Western, in spite of its eastern part, the GDR, having temporarily belonged to the "Eastern" political bloc).
- Religiously, the four countries selected are dominated by the "Western" Catholic and/or Lutheran religions, while in Bulgaria and Romania the "Eastern" Orthodox church reigns.
- Economically, the four countries were the most industrialized in the Soviet bloc.

The four countries were rather similar to each other in these respects, but the process of change differed. The ČSSR and GDR exprienced revolutions, while Hungary and Poland reached institutional compromises.

The Number of Countries
If these four countries fall into two different categories, one might wonder why I do not simply limit myself to two countries instead of four. First, my goal is set up a model that can explain the processes of collapse in Eastern Europe. If my model can explain the developments in four countries, it is obviously stronger than one which is only valid for two. Furthermore, by relating my model to four countries, I can show that it functions well for countries that have slight variations in their behavior. Even though Poland had a reformist regime, its economic reforms did not go nearly as far as Hungary's in the direction of market pricing and enterprise autonomy. Moreover, while the East German and Czechoslovak regimes were rather orthodox, the former regime greeted Gorbachev with a neo-Stalinist re-ideologization policy, while the Czechoslovak regime cautiously carried out moderate reforms. The value of the model is enhanced if it proves useful in providing explanations for the variations among the countries within each of the categories.

Second, by choosing two examples for each category, it is easier to isolate the underlying causes. For example, if I had chosen only the GDR as the example of revolution, then perhaps I would have concentrated on the "exit" option (by which East Germans escaped to the West via Hungary). A model would have been developed which was completely inapplicable to the Czechoslovak case.

Materials

The collapse of the Soviet-type system will probably be a central topic for social scientists for many years. It will also in all likelihood remain a popular topic for historians, who will continuously gather more information about the actual events and developments. With the passing of time, more and more formerly secret archives will become accessible to researchers. Newly emerging documents may alter our picture of 1989. Consequently, all of my conclusions in this study are tentative. I am fully open to the possibility that new evidence might call into question portions (or even the core part) of the theoretical model that I develop in this study.

Since much of the information I require is not presently available in documents, I have relied to some extent on interviews. Not only do interviews enable us to fill some of the gaps left by the available documents, they also help us to gain some insight into issues which probably do not appear in any documents. This includes such questions as what participants were thinking, how they perceived the situation, etc. Of course, problems can always arise here also, since participants may lie to make themselves appear more positive, or their memories might have become fuzzy by the time they grant the interview.

I have followed a common-sense rule in evaluating my interviews. *The more the merrier.* That is, the more people who confirm something, the more likely it is to be true. This is especially the case when the "opposing" sides have the same recollection. That can either be the case when leaders of the regime and of the opposition agree on the course of events, or it may be the case within the regime—i.e., when both hardliners and reformers have similar recollections. My interviewees exhibit, to a large extent, far-reaching agreement on all important issues. In cases where they disagree on minor points, I leave these discussions out (for reasons of space). For example, although the independent Czech students all agree there was a long debate on whether or not to allow the official Socialist Youth Organization (SSM) to join their demonstration on November 17, 1989, they disagree on exactly which students voted for or against. These details are more interesting for a focused case study than for a comparative study such as this one, so I merely state that the students all agree that the vote was extremely close. For reasons of space, I have also refrained from mentioning those cases in which I judge an interviewee's statements not to be credible (on the grounds that they conflict with the recollections of several other interviewees). I have for purposes of this book relied on interviewees whom I judged to be credible (because they have been confirmed by other interviewees or by documents). In order to keep the book at a reasonable size, I have preferred to present only reliable statements from interviewees.

Finally, there is the problem of memories becoming less reliable over time. This seemed to be more of a problem when I asked interviewees for the exact details of a particular meeting than when I asked them to recall their general attitudes and opinions at the time of an event, or the attitudes and opinions of other participants. Some interviewees had no problem with the details because they had taken notes. For example, former *Rudé pravo* editor Zdeněk Hoření was allowed to take notes at the Politburo meetings, since he was in charge of the Party's newspaper. He referred to his notes during my interview to remember exactly who said what. Michal Horáček, who acted as a go-between for the regime and opposition, kept a dairy which he later published in book form. Several others, such as Miroslav Štěpán and Oskar Krejčí, kept notes which they used to write their memoirs. Moreover, the negotiations in the ČSSR were published in book form, so all the participants could refresh their memories about particular details.

TOWARDS A NEO-MARXIAN APPROACH

The previous chapter contended that, while many valuable ideas have arisen in the discourse on the collapse of the Soviet-type system, none of them, by themselves, have succeeded in accounting for the differences in the process of the collapse.[2] My task in this chapter is to

---

2. The one exception is Eikert (1991), who makes the observation that, in the countries where political society was stronger and the rulers more pragmatic, negotiated openings came about. Meanwhile, in countries where political society was less developed and reformists within the Party-state were weaker, popular upsurges took place. As mentioned in the previous chapter, however, he does not tell us much about the mechanisms behind these developments. His explanation leaves many of the most interesting questions unanswered: Why, for example, were reformist factions weaker and political society less developed in certain countries? Why did the reform Communists suddenly decide to negotiate with the opposition, and why did they decide to do this in 1989 in particular? Why were millions of people suddenly willing to join demonstrations in 1989, but not in previous years? And so on.

present an eclectic framework based on Marxian traditions. It is not my intention to enter into a polemic with other Marxists over the "correct" interpretation of Marx. There are many interpretations of Marx. For my purposes, it is irrelevant that other interpretations may come closer to what Marx "really thought." My goal is to develop a Marxian-inspired model which can help us understand the mechanisms behind the collapse of the Soviet-type regimes, rather than to prove the truth of any particular Marxian dogma. Theoretical tools in Marx and among neo-Marxian writers can help us to unravel the hidden mechanisms behind the surprisingly rapid collapse of the Soviet-type regimes in 1989. As Elster (1989b: 7) states: "By concentrating on the mechanisms, one captures the dynamic aspect of scientific explanation: the urge to produce explanations of ever finer grain."

In subsequent chapters, I show that these instruments are fruitful for analyzing the process by which the Soviet-type regimes in Eastern Europe collapsed. Moreover, the book demonstrates that certain aspects of the Marxian framework are particularly helpful for understanding the complex dynamics behind the events of 1989 (although it must be combined with the insights of non-Marxist theorists). In the empirical chapters, I develop the Marxian framework further, allowing me to develop my own synthesis of Marx and non-Marxist theorists.

Of course, I am not excluding the possibility that other theoretical schools can account for the collapse as well. Nevertheless, there are several reasons for choosing a neo-Marxist approach. As long as the framework proves more fruitful than the explanations which others have offered, this book will mark an advance for social science theory. Moreover, since there are many theoretical analyses of the collapse, I have included a number of the mainstream schools within my theoretical discourse. Third, since the regimes professed to be "Marxist," many commentators have proclaimed that Marxism as a viable social theory died with the fall of the Berlin Wall. Although those more sympathetic to Marxism are quick to point out that there is a difference between Marxism as a *scientific* social theory and Marxist-Leninism as a state-supported dogma, few Marxist theorists have devoted themselves to analyzing the Soviet-type states. Consequently, the collapse of the Communist-led regimes presents a critical case (Yin 1989: 47) for Marxian theory. If I can show that a Marxian analysis can generate a *plausible* model for explaining the collapse, I can also show that at least certain theoretical ideas of Marxism did not fall with the Berlin Wall.

CLASS ANALYSIS

I claim throughout this study that, in the Soviet-type system, different groups of people reacted differently. In certain situations, some groups have revolted against the regime; in other situations, other groups have done so. By looking more closely at "class antagonisms" between the regime and various groups in society, I believe we can more clearly understand the underlying causes of the revolts that took place during the four decades of Communist rule in Eastern Europe. It also helps understand the dynamics of the failed reform attempts, and the willingness of the Hungarian and Polish regimes to transform the economic system in the late 1980s via "*nomenklatura* capitalism." Of course, class analysis by itself is not enough to understand these problems. It is merely the starting point; it helps us go deeper into the problems. The course of events was also greatly influenced, however, by institutional structures, and by the interplay between economic development and political decision-making.

My starting point is Fehér & Heller & Márkus' (1983) study, *Dictatorship over Needs*. They claim that the Soviet-type system constitutes a system in itself. It is a new mode of production which is neither capitalist nor socialist. In contrast to a socialist system in which the workers have taken over the means of production, they note (1983: 45):

> The working majority of the population in Eastern European societies has no control over the conditions, process or results of its own labour. Not only the technical organization of the process of production, but also all the social-economic decisions concerning what to produce and how to employ the gross product socially are actually established and made by a distinct and separate social group (the bureaucracy).

The members of this bureaucracy do not, however, own the state property in the way that capitalists own private property. Rather, the bureaucratic apparatus itself is the possessor of the means of production (1983: 55). Those working within the Party apparatus or state bureaucracy do not have the right to appropriate the surplus; however, as *members* of the ruling corporate entity, they have the power to *dispose* over it (*Verfügungsgewalt*). In Fehér & Heller & Márkus' words (1983: 68):

> They act in their function as fiduciaries and trustees, as representatives of the institutional interests of the apparatus as a corporate entity. Their role is

reduced (at least in principle and in norm) to this function of trusteeship primarily (though not exclusively) by the actual power relations within the hierarchically and functionally articulated and differentiated apparatus itself....

The material basis of this corporate rule is the "appropriation of social surplus by the apparatus as a corporate entity" (1983: 126). Furthermore, this form of social domination is "effected through the control its members exercise over the whole process of social production and the distribution of its results." Corporate domination "stands in sharp conflict both with the immediate material concerns and the long-term social interests of the productive workers themselves, and more generally of the whole ruled majority of the population."

Not only are there conflicts of interest between the corporate entity and the workers. The separation of production from the needs of consumers in the command economy also leads to a contradiction between the "administrative use-value of the product as the form of its social recognition and its real social utility" (1983: 32). The corporate entity's main interest is not to improve the value of consumer goods. Rather, it is to maximize the material basis of its domination over society (1983: 88–9). Since the enterprises are dependent on satisfying bureaucratic demands for production rather than the needs of consumers, much of production is "wasted" on goods that nobody wants, or that are of such low quality as to be useless. The corporation exercises, then, a dictatorship over the satisfaction of needs.[3]

Critiques of the Ruling-Class Argument

Some Marxists have denied that a ruling class existsed under the Soviet-type system. Most of these authors claim that the USSR and its satellites comprised transitional societies, which were undergoing a transition from capitalism to socialism. Since these countries had not yet reached the socialist level of development, they did not have a distinct mode of production, and so could not have a ruling class. This type of reasoning implies an adherence to historical determinism. The next stage of development after capitalism must be socialism (or its higher phase: communism). There is no possibility of another type of socio-economic system emerging. Obviously, if the Soviet-type

---

3. Gulcyñsi (1992) goes even further, claiming that the power of the Communists was based on their control of distribution.

countries really found themselves somewhere between capitalism and socialism, and if they were moving toward the attainment of a class-less society, then this higher stage could not be reached through the creation of a new, historically unique ruling class. Therefore, advocates of the transitional theory usually claim that the rulers comprised a "layer" (Mandel 1991), an "elite" (Ticktin 1992) or a "ruling stratum" (Trotsky 1937, Eklund & Reichard 1976).

If, however, one rejects historicism—as most neo-Marxists now do (see Isaac 1987)—then it possible to analyze the Soviet-type system as a special mode of production with a ruling class. Even if one sticks to the transitional argument, however, it makes little difference for my purposes here. Whether or not the ruling group comprised a layer, an elite, a ruling stratum, or a class, the point is that this group of people had power over the rest of the population, and that any systemic change required the removal of this group's monopoly on power. So while the above authors deny the existence of a ruling class, they still describe a struggle between the members of the working *class* and the rulers—in other words, a class struggle.

The other point at issue among Marxists has been whether or not the rulers really have control over the surplus product in the Soviet-type system. This is a basic requirement if the rulers are to constitute an economic class. Ticktin (1992: 63), for instance, asserts that the rulers do not have control over the process of production, because they do not have the mechanisms to compel workers "to work as required."

His argument is not convincing. Of course, the rulers do not have *complete* control over the process of production. In the Soviet-type system it is not generally possible to force workers to work as hard as the rulers wished. Yet this is true of any class system. In Western capitalist societies, for example, unions and government labor legislation restrict in some degree the control exercised by capitalists over their employees. Other factors, such as the level of unemployment, may also limit the control which capitalists have over workers. The lower the rate of unemployment, the greater is the bargaining power of the unions. As in all industrialized societies, the *size* of the surplus product (or "the rate of exploitation") might vary, depending on several factors (including the ability of the dominant economic class to weaken the workers). The point is that, in the Soviet-type system, *the surplus product which the workers produce is controlled by the ruling class.*

Ticktin (1992) himself indicates that the ruling group controlled the process of production. He notes that workers in the Soviet-type system were indeed exploited—as in class societies. Workers "alienate[d] their labor power" in order to produce "the surplus product" which the elite controlled (1992: 14). Ticktin furthermore agrees that, as in all class societies, workers and the ruling group had conflicting interests (1992: 179).[4] Yet, in contrast to the situation in Western capitalist countries, the workers were prevented from organizing around their interests because they are kept atomized (cf. 1992: 16, 38, 117). If he admits workers were more atomized under the Soviet-type system than they are under capitalism, how can these same workers be so successful in preventing the elite from controlling the production process? It seems that Ticktin, in his critique of class analysis, provides ample evidence that the Soviet-type systems in fact were class societies.

In addition to the above criticisms, one could also reject Fehér & Heller & Márkus' insistence that property can be collectively owned by a ruling class. Even under capitalism, however, property is often owned by a collective (such as a family enterprise). The dominant form of business today in the West is the stock company, which can have thousands of owners. Of course, in contrast to the members of the corporate entity, each individual stockholder of a capitalist company is free to sell his or her shares. Members of the corporate entity cannot sell their shares, although they can lose their position if they are purged from the ruling group. This difference presents no great problems, though, for applying class analysis to the Soviet-type societies. It is only natural to expect ownership forms to differ under different socioeconomic systems.

Another objection to the class argument could be that a true ruling class would not be willing to give up its power without a fight as was the case in Eastern Europe. Such a claim would be based on an extremely deterministic interpretation of Marx. This is rejected in my study. Marx is not fruitful if seen as the creator of iron laws of behavior, such as the principle that the ruling class will use force to maintain power under all circumstances. Not even the transition from feudalism

---

4. Actually, Ticktin only writes of a conflict of interests between workers and managers, and thus does not make it clear if he includes the rest of the ruling group. However, it is hard to imagine that he would claim that managers have different interests than the workers, while the rest of the ruling group has the same interests as the workers. It would not be logical to claim that a group which shares the workers' interests would appoint managers who have opposing interests to the workers.

to capitalism occurred at all moments and in all countries through the violent overthrow of regimes. Although most European countries went through periods of revolutionary upheaval, more often than not the aristocracy finally gave up its political monopoly without a fight. In Great Britain, for example, Cromwell's anti-feudal revolution was eventually overturned, and the monarchy came back to a position of considerable power. However, the aristocracy went through an evolutionary process of granting more and more rights to non-aristocratic property holders, until voting rights were eventually extended to the workers as well. The workers did not have to shoot any aristocrats in order to gain universal suffrage after World War One. In Sweden, for example, there had never been a Cromwellian revolution, and yet the ruling elite eventually agreed to universal suffrage without firing any shots against the workers.

Besides the regimes in Soviet-type countries *have* used force numerous times to defend their class interests. Communist-led regimes have—alone or with help of the Soviet Union—successfully repressed rebellions in the GDR (1953), Poland (1956, 1970, 1976 and 1980–81), Czechoslovakia (1968) and Hungary (1956). Most recently, China violently repressed the student protests in 1989, while the Romanian regime sought unsuccessfully to defend itself with violence that same year. Even in the East German and Czechoslovak cases, moreover, the regime used force against the opposition at first, but then caved in when the demonstrations continued to grow. By using force in some situations and refraining in others, in fact, the ruling class in the Soviet-type society behaved in a manner recalling that of the feudal aristocracy.

It has often been the case, furthermore, that members of the Soviet-type regimes have supported the transition to capitalism, seeing in such a change the opportunity to take over state enterprises and become wealthy capitalists. After all, many landowning aristocrats were also able to become successful entrepreneurs. When a socio-economic system starts crumbling, members of its ruling class often accept the fact. Rather than fighting the transition to another socio-economic system, they strive to join the ruling class of the new order. Just as aristocrats used their wealth to invest in capitalist enterprises, for instance, members of the Soviet-type ruling class used their position to gain control over privatized enterprises.

Rather than criticizing the existence of classes, some authors question the value of class analysis in understanding the collapse of the system. Higley & Pakulski (1992: 198), for instance, criticize class analysis for leaving out the consumer. They claim that East Europeans revolted more because of their dissatisfaction over consumption levels than because of workplace exploitation. They claim, accordingly, that the only applicable antagonism is the "us" versus "them" division between society and the Party-state.

However, if all citizens outside of the regime were motivated by consumption questions, and class relations completely lacked importance, then we would expect workers, intellectuals, professionals and other groups to revolt under the same circumstances. In the following chapters I argue, in contrast, that these groups have consistently behaved differently. Moreover, even if one adheres only to the consumption question, the levels and types of consumption differed for these groups. This implies that, at the very least, class relations affected consumption, which in turn affected behavior. Furthermore, class analysis does not disregard the importance of consumption. On the contrary, as Fehér & Heller & Márkus (1983) note, the relations of production under the Soviet-type system account for the poor level of consumption. They show that this system gives the ruling Party-state members a "dictatorship over needs" (which is also the title of their book). I maintain in later chapters, however, that there were also important conflicts at the workplace, which influenced political and economic developments. Finally, by adding an institutional analysis, I show that the various classes had institutional incentives to behave differently. I enumerate the classes which are relevant for this study below.

Economic or Political Class?

I have already argued that the Party-state apparatus fulfills the usual Marxian criteria for a ruling class. The next question to investigate is whether it is fruitful to see this as a classical Marxian economic class, or whether it would be more appropriate to call this group a "political class." Supporters of the political-class line might claim the uniqueness of the Soviet-type system lay not in the near-total state control over the economy, but rather in the state control over society and the near-complete destruction of civil society, which gave the system a "totalitarian" or semi-totalitarian character.

To begin with, it is certainly not strange from the classical Marxian perspective that the ruling class does in fact rule. Traditionally, Marxists expected those with economic power to have political power as well. What is important for Marxian class analysis is that the corporate entity's usurpation of the surplus product created by the workers provides a *material basis* for its rule. The fact that its rule could only be guaranteed through an extremely repressive state apparatus is not stranger for classic Marxian class analysis than the fact that feudalism (in its absolutist phase) or "oriental despotism" was maintained in this way. What may be unique in the case of the Soviet-type system is the fact that a group of people took political power first—before changing the economic system. This development stands in contrast to the scenario envisioned in traditional Marxian theory, according to which an economic class emerges before political change takes place.[5] Such a turn of events admittedly causes problems for orthodox Marxism; however, it is not at all problematic for studies such as this, which reject a historical-deterministic approach. Once one rejects historical determinism, it is only important whether a group of people fulfill the criteria for being an economic class. The manner in which a class comes to power cannot form part of the definition of what a class is.

If the focus is on the role of the ruling class rather than on how it came to power, it becomes clear that economic-political relations are in many ways parallel under the Soviet-type system and under feudalism. As Therborn (1980) shows, the aristocratic landowners under feudalism were both the dominant economic class and the political decision-makers. During the pre-absolutist period of feudalism, moreover, they were also the main implementers of state policy. Aristocrats led armies, kept their own prisons, acted as judges and interpreters of the law. Under the Soviet-type system, similarly, the members of the Party-state apparatus play the three roles of economic usurpers, political decision-makers, and implementer of policy. In contrast to the case under feudalism, however, a more rationalized division of labor is necessary in industrialized Soviet-type societies. Economic ministers cannot serve as judges, therefore, as feudal lords had done.

It is in reference to capitalism that the greatest problems are created for Marxian class analysis by the idea that the political elite could be to some extent separate from the dominant economic class. In modern, highly industrialized capitalist societies, wealthy entrepreneurs do not

---

5. Of course, in classical Marxism, the transition to socialism begins with a political act—the revolution, in which the working class takes power and then takes control over the means of production. However, I claim throughout this book that a socialist revolution never took place in the Soviet-type societies. Instead, an new-type of class society emerged.

usually become politicians (although their children do choose political careers at times, as we see in the case of Rockefeller and Kennedys families). Running a business is a full-time activity. In the early phase of capitalism, the entrepreneur typically worked full-time at administering a single factory or enterprise. Today, entrepreneurs are more likely to spend their time administering several different investment funds, and sitting on the board of directors for several different firms in which they or their investment firms hold stock.

Due to the division of labor required by capitalism, moreover, being a politician has become a profession in itself—thus Weber's "Polik als Beruf." Along with specialization came the liberal ideology differentiating between the private and public spheres. The institution of private property under a market economy was traditionally considered part of the "private sphere," making it more difficult for politicians to justify state intervention in the economy. Consequently, the state and the market grew apart somewhat, although state regulation of the economy increased dramatically after World War Two. In the postwar era in liberal Western democracies, citizens have sometimes been able to organize successfully and to pressure politicians into making decisions that the business community opposes. This has particularly been the case in countries where strong labor unions and social democratic parties have arisen. Consequently, a debate arose among neo-Marxists in the 1970s about the "relative autonomy" of the state under capitalism (see, for example, Block 1977, Dahlkvist 1978, Miliband 1969 and Poulantzas 1978). The main conclusion of this discussion was that, despite the huge structural pressures which the liberal state faces from capitalists, the state is still able—under certain circumstances and in the short run—to carve out a degree of autonomy from the business community on certain issues.

In the 1980s, "neo-institutionalists" have gone even farther than the neo-Marxists, claiming that the capitalist state is not just *relatively* autonomous from the dominant capitalist class; it has, in fact, become autonomous (cf. Skocpol 1979 & 1985). According to this argument, the members of the state bureaucracy have their own interests, which can run counter to the interests of the bourgeoisie. The neo-institutionalists were influenced by the growing literature in public administration, which shows that "street-level bureaucrats" rarely implement policy exactly as envisioned by policy-makers.

If the dominant economic class, the political decision-makers, and the implementers of policy are the same individuals (as under feudalism), or if they are comprised of the same group of people (as under the Soviet-type system), then the whole problem of state autonomy disappears, and it is no longer necessary to discuss the possible existence of a political class separate from the dominant economic class. So it is actually much simpler, ironically, to apply Marxian class analysis to the supposedly "Marxist" dictatorships in Eastern Europe than to apply it to capitalist societies. As under feudalism, there is no recognized dividing line in the Soviet-type society between the private and the public, or between the political and the economic sphere. In Therborn's (1980: 62) words, "under feudalism the state is privatized, while under [the Soviet-type society] the private sphere becomes public." Furthermore, when the market is replaced by state ownership, policy-making and policy-implementation tend to "melt together" (1980: 67). So the whole notion of a political sphere autonomous from the economic sphere becomes nonsensical in the Soviet-type system.

Although the three areas of economic class rule, policy-making and policy-implementation "melt together," this does *not* mean that policy is implemented exactly as planned. In fact, it is quite rare that policy is implemented just as the Politburo wishes. The point is that the Soviet-type society cannot be understood as a society in which three separate groups exist: one group that owns the means of production, another comprised of professional politicians, and a third group made up of professional state bureaucrats. Instead, the people doing all three activities belong to the same group. In a typical case, a university graduate starts his or her career as an engineer at a factory, later joining the factory management. Then this person gets a job at one of the economic ministries and eventually becomes a minister. As a minister and party member, said person also becomes a member of the Central Committee. In some cases, finally, the individual eventually acquires a seat on the Politburo.

In such a system, there is no clear line between property-owners, policy-makers and policy-implementers. To be sure, the Politburo and the Secretariat are the most important decision-making bodies; they are at the top of the ruling hierarchy. However, the lower levels are involved both in the designing of policy and in its implementation. In the planning process, for example, the Politburo might decide that the productions of cars should increase; however, they normally do not make such decisions without first consulting with the economic ministries and the relevant Party organizations. The relevant ministers are likely to try to convince the Politburo to lower its expectations. After

these negotiations, the various economic ministries must then negotiate with the managers of various enterprises on how to fulfill the
details of the plans. At this stage, the managers will typically argue for
lower plan targets than the ministry officials want, just as the ministers
typically try to get the Politburo to lower its original output goals.
Once the plans are made, finally, they must be implemented. Again,
the various levels of the Party-state apparatus are involved in making
sure the plans are fulfilled. A manager of an automobile enterprise
might complain to a regional secretary that certain parts are not being
delivered. The regional party secretary may then contact a minister in
an effort to find a solution, either by renegotiating the plan targets or
by asking the minister to put pressure on the managers of the enterprise that was supposed to deliver the parts. If this does not work, the
minister might turn to the Politburo or Secretariat in order to get the
total planning target changed, etc.

The above examples indicate that conflicts arise within various
levels and different *organizations within* the ruling corporate entity,
rather than between the dominant economic class and the state as
under capitalism. Consequently, rather than discussing state autonomy
from the dominant economic class, it is more fruitful to analyze the
conflicts between the levels of the ruling corporate entity. This does
not make for any problems in applying class analysis. Any sophisticated class analysis takes into consideration the conflicts among
groups within the dominant class. Such analyses of advanced capitalist
societies normally emphasize conflicts between the "petite bourgeoisie," middle-sized enterprises and "monopoly capital," while such
analyses of capitalist "Third World countries" traditionally emphasize
conflicts between national and international capital. As will be seen in
chapter 4, conflicts of interest in Soviet-type societies arise between
the Party and the state, between different levels of the Party-state, and
between the national corporate entity and the Soviet Union's corporate
entity.

These conflicts cannot lead to the economy becoming autonomous
from the state, but they could potentially cause the state to become relatively autonomous from the Party. However, even if the state became
truly autonomous from the Party, there would not be—as long as the
state maintained control over the means of production and the
country remained non-democratic—any important change in the functioning of the system. It would simply mean that a portion of the
ruling class (the Party functionaries) would be expelled from the cor-

porate entity. If, on the other hand, the state privatized its enterprises, thus giving up its control over the means of production, the economy would once again become relatively autonomous from the state. Such a system would no longer, however, be a Soviet-type system; rather, it would be capitalist.

Defining The Ruling Class

So far I have agreed with Fehér & Heller & Márkus in claiming that, in the Soviet-type system, the corporate entity is the ruling group. The next task is to determine the membership of this entity. Many authors, such as Michael Voslensky, claim that the *nomenklatura* comprises the ruling class.[6] In his book, *Nomenklatura: Anatomy of the Soviet Ruling Class*, he asserts (1980: 113-4)—in a manner reminiscent of Fehér & Heller & Márkus—that the *nomenklatura* own the means of production as members of a group. Secondly, he notes that the *nomenklatura* class lives—like its capitalist counterpart—on the surplus labor of workers (1980: 119).

Although Voslensky and others have tried to limit the ruling class to those holding relatively high positions,[7] a Marxist definition of class should include all members of the Party-state down to the level of *factory manager* or *head of the factory Party organization*. These are the ones given responsibility for making sure that the workers carry out their productive tasks; these are the ones who organize the process of production at the workshop level; and these are the ones who provide the information to the ministries and the planning commission which makes planning possible.

If all members of the Party-state at and above the level of factory director (and leader of the Party factory organization) belong to the ruling class, then it is not clear whether the corporate entity is synony-

---

6. Actually, Fehér & Heller & Márkus (1983: 114ff.) conclude that the Soviet-type system was a classless society. This really amounts, however, to a semantic question, because they claim that in *some texts* Marx reserved the phrase "class" for capitalist societies, and considered feudal societies to be ruled by "estates." If the history of non-communist societies is really a history of class struggle, however—as Marx and Engels (1848: 31) write in the *Communist Manifesto*—then slavery, feudalism, capitalism and the Soviet-type society are all class societies. Of course, the *types* of classes and the *manner* in which their power is exercised differs in each of these societies. So one could speak, if one insists, of "estates" under feudalism and "classes" under capitalism; in that case, however, "estate" and "class" both become subsets of "Class"—for Marx certainly did not deny the existence of class conflict under feudalism.

7. Cf. Nove (1982: 588-9) and Israel (1982: 177).

mous with the *nomenklatura*. Different Party organizations and different levels of the Party have responsibility for different *nomenklatura* positions. This makes it difficult to ascertain whether all positions within the Party-state above the factory level fell under the *nomenklatura* lists. It is clear, however, that whether or not all these positions belong to the *nomenklatura*, the Party organizations always have the right to veto appointments to these positions. Therefore, I suggest it is more fruitful to define the corporate entity as *all members of the Party apparatus and state bureaucracy at or above the level of factory manager or head of the factory Party organization.*

A case could be made for calling Party functionaries the ruling class, since the state bureaucracy under the cadre type of administration is supposed to be merely a transmission belt for Party decisions.[8] It is questionable, however, if the actual situation corresponds enough to the ideal-type of cadre administration to allow for such a strong differentiation between Party and state. In reality, it is difficult to distinguish between the Party and state apparatuses, because most of the members of the state apparatus are also Party members, and it is fairly common for members of the state apparatus to hold Party positions or to leave the state administration for the Party apparatus (and vice-versa). Furthermore, members of the state bureaucracy also have some control over the means of production, since the Party delegates much of the decision-making authority to the state economic apparatus on detailed questions of resource-allocation.[9]

Defining the Remaining Classes

Normally, in the literature on the Soviet bloc, the remaining groups are divided into three classes: the working class, white-collar workers (or professionals, or officially "the *intelligentsia*") and the peasantry (cf. Słomcyński 1994). For the sake of simplicity, I leave the peasantry

---

8. For discussions of the cadre administration, see Balla (1972) and Lipp (1978). Although no one has directly argued that Party functionaries comprise the ruling class, several authors have implied it. Cf. Djilas (1957: 47–56) and Šik (1981: 159). The idea of the Party functionaries as a ruling class also fares well with much of traditional Marxist theorizing; as Poulantzas (1978: 333–4) notes, a bureaucracy cannot itself become a class, it can at most *serve* a class. According to this notion, the members of the state bureaucracy cannot—even if they are part of the *nomenklatura*—be members of the ruling class.

9. See Saxonberg (1997: 39, footnote 10) for details of interviews with former economic minister in Hungary and Czechoslovakia which confirm the notion that the state bureaucracy did indeed have great influence over resource-allocation.

out of my analysis, since their role in the systemic change was relatively minor. Not only did they decline in number as the countries became more industrialized (as in the West), they were also politically passive. The only time they engaged in oppositional policies in any noteworthy numbers was during the *Solidarność* uprising in Poland, but even then their role was minor. Furthermore, since observers have not considered peasants to have been an important factor in these uprisings, there is virtually no information available about their participation.

If the peasantry is left out, that leaves the workers and the professionals. According to Słomcyński (1994: 169), "the core of the working class is composed of skilled and unskilled factory workers." Although factory workers are the focal point of this study, in my definition of working class I also include those belonging to other professions based on manual labor. This includes all professions that do not require higher education such as waiters/waitresses, sales personnel in stores, etc.

While my definition of the working class is rather uncontroversial, my definition of the *intelligentsia* flies in the face of mainstream praxis. Originally, the *intelligentsia* in Eastern Europe comprised the intellectual vanguard of society. The Communist-led regimes, however, use this term to denote *all* professions that require higher education. Both artists and civil engineers, therefore, fall under this category. In contrast, I differentiate between "professionals" and "intellectuals." I define intellectuals here in the way Gella (1989: 131) claims the term intelligentsia is defined in the West—as referring to the "social strata of educated people who in different ways and degrees contribute to the creation, development, maintenance, and distribution of cultural goods." This includes artists, writers, musicians, church leaders, etc. Professionals are comprised of all non-manual laborers who do not belong to the corporate entity or to the intellectual strata. In the productive sphere, this includes those whom Ticktin (1992: 61) defines as the intelligentsia, i.e.: "Those who are in charge of others but also alienate their labor power." In Wright's class model (cited in Holtmann & Strasser 1990: 5), this includes advisory managers and supervisors, while managers are part of the corporate entity. Thus, such professionals as civil engineers and accountants belong to this class. In the non-productive sphere, this includes groups like doctors, nurses and lawyers.

I have both theoretical and empirical reasons for wanting to differentiate between intellectuals and professionals. Many social scientists have observed that, as an empirical matter, intellectuals are usually the first to criticize and to organize against regimes (cf. Huntington 1968: 290 and O'Donnell-Schmitter 1986: ch. 5). I contend below that this generalization not only holds true in the Soviet-bloc countries, but also that professionals represent the opposite extreme. That is, they are normally the group that participates *last* in an uprising—after both the intellectuals and the workers. In theoretical terms, I also claim below that the position of the two groups in the process of production differs, as do their institutional incentives.

INTERESTS

I maintained above that the Soviet-type society was divided into classes. The members of these classes have different interests which affect their behavior. I follow Isaac (1987) in dividing interests into three different levels. He divides them into objective, real, and subjective interests. For reasons that will become apparent, I refer to these levels as postulated interests, institutional interests, and the subjective perceptions of interests.

Postulated Interests
The concept of objective interests is important for many Marxian approaches to revolution, because it emphasizes that, even if the members of an exploited class do not rebel against a system, they have the *potential* of so doing under more favorable circumstances. Relations of exploitation can exist even if the actors are not aware of it at the moment. Furthermore, even if the exploited classes are aware of their exploitation, they might not rebel unless the circumstances are right. So the idea of objective interests is not that these are observable interests which one can read off from the behavior of actors, but rather that there is an objective relationship of exploitation. *Under certain circumstances*, the exploited will act in accordance with their objective interests.

A basic tenet of Marxian class analysis is that a group of people which owns the means of production and employs others is an exploiting class. Members of this class exploit those working under them (whether they are wage-workers, feudal serfs, or slaves). Members of the exploited classes carry out the productive labor which creates a surplus product. Members of the ruling class, in turn, control this surplus. Some Marxists consequently claim that the members of the exploited class have an objective interest in obtaining control over their surplus product. If they become aware of their objective interests, they will potentially rebel against the system during a systemic economic crisis.[10]

I discuss these economic aspects in greater detail later on. For now it suffices to claim that, although the concept of objective interests might seem normative in nature, I do not use it in such a way. Of course, almost everyone—including non-Marxists—would probably agree that exploited peoples *should* rebel, although non-Marxists might disagree with Marxists on which groups (if any) constitute an exploited class. There are two important aspects of objective interests. First, they imply a philosophical theory of human nature—namely, that most people would prefer to be empowered rather than dominated. Second, it is true that the existence of objective interests cannot be empirically tested any more than the existence of workers, slaves, power, etc.—all such things are theoretical constructions. However, theoretical predictions based on this analysis are in fact testable. One can investigate whether or not subjugated classes follow their objective interests in overthrowing the socioeconomic system during an economic crisis.

Regardless of how I define objective interests, many readers will still associate them with a dogmatic, deterministic form of Marxism. Since the term "objective interests" has become so infected, I have decided to use "postulated interests" instead.

Since the theorist postulates these interests, they cannot be tested empirically. Only the results can be tested. This is not a weakness in my framework, however, for every framework must rest on some assumptions that cannot be tested empirically. Rational-choice theorists, for example, take choice as their starting point. This assumes that we can in fact make choices. They implicitly postulate the existence of a free will. They do not try to prove that we can really chose. B.F. Skinner, the behavorist psychologist, might be correct in claiming that the environment completely determines our behavior. This debate belongs, however, to a different level than that of rational-choice theorists. Similarly, one cannot prove the existence of objective interests, although one can debate the question on a philosophical level. Such a level lies beyond the task of this book, however. What is important is

---

10. I.e., when the forces of production come into conflict with the relations of production. Marx presents this thesis in his introduction to the *Critique of the Political Economy* (1859). I discuss it further in chapter 3.

that I can use this notion in a fruitful manner for analyzing events in Eastern Europe.

A word of caution is in order here. Since I am not advocating a deterministic, structuralist interpretation of Marx, the above hypothesis suggests necessary but not sufficient conditions for social revolution. Thus, if a revolution fails to break out, this does not refute the theory. On the other hand, if a social revolution had broken out in Eastern Europe and the Soviet-type system had collapsed during a period of economic prosperity for the common people, this would refute the theory, or at least make it necessary to revise it.[11]

Since I use postulated interests here in accordance with the Marxian notion that the economically exploited have an interest in obtaining control over their surplus product, the next question is: what form would such control take for the exploited classes? Marx himself maintained that it would be utopian to discuss what a future society would look like. Nonetheless, in the Soviet-type context, one can deduce certain hypotheses as to what this would entail. For the workers, gaining control over their surplus product would entail some sort of "socialist" solution. In its most centralized form, this entails state ownership of production, in combination with democratic elections. Under such a system, workers would gain control over their surplus production indirectly, through their democratic voting rights. In its most decentralized form, workers could gain control over their surplus production through direct ownership of their enterprises. If the choice

---

11. Since I am using objective interests in a manner that poses a hypothesis about human behavior, my usage diverges from the common non-Marxist usage of the term, which implies a normative theory. In the non-Marxist philosophical discourse, an objective interest is something that is for our own good, whether we want it or not; while subjective interests reflect our actual wishes. Hence, there is a difference between our needs and our wants (cf. Benditt 1975, Benn 1960, Flathman 1975, Karlsson 1993, Reeve & Ware 1984 and Swanton 1980). According to this line of thought, anorexics *need* food and thus have an objective interest in being force-fed, although subjectively, they do not *want* any food. In this extreme case, one can even empirically investigate objective interests, since we know empirically that people die if they do not eat food. In contrast, according to my usage, objective interests do not reflect any objective needs which one can empirically investigate. They simply reflect a structural relation of domination. From this philosophical construction comes the expectation that the dominated will potentially rise against their domination during a period of systemic economic crisis. Of course, relations of domination are theoretical, and thus are not empirically testable. But my understanding of objective interests does not reflect the normative presumption that the exploited *need* to revolt, or even that they should. Rather, it is based on the notion that, during an economic crisis, objective interests can be causal, in the sense of being a necessary but not sufficient reason for a large portion of a class or stratum to join a revolt.

is between the Soviet-type system and capitalism, it is not clear which system will lead to greater exploitation. It depends on how Stalinist the Soviet-type regime of that particular country is, as well as on how market-oriented or social liberal the capitalist form becomes (and how well-organized and politically powerful the workers prove to be after the transformation). However, my study of postulated interests indicates it will be much more difficult to mobilize workers in a Soviet-type system around an openly neo-liberal program than around most other revolutionary programs.

For the professionals, it is less clear what kind of solution leads to greater control over their surplus product. Theoretically, they would not be exploited under either a centralized democratic state socialism or a decentralized "market socialism" based on worker self-management (since they too would have voting rights at their firm). Still, many professionals could become private entrepreneurs under capitalism. Lawyers and psychologists could open up private practices. Engineers and economists could become managers of large-scale productive enterprises, etc. These professionals would have control over their own surplus product under capitalism as well. Furthermore, professional state employees under the Soviet-type system would likely obtain much higher salaries in the private sector under a capitalist regime (assuming they do in fact find employment there). In the words of Bauman (1987: 179–80)

> Before communism, education [sic] professionals boasted an elevated position on the income scale. Now, except for small privileged minorities inside each of these professions, this is no longer true. Communist industrialization has drastically downgraded the relative standing of the intelligentsia and redirected the available surplus product into areas of the economy seen as more "productive."

One could argue, then, that the greater income inequality under capitalism might drive their salaries to a level at which they are fully (or almost fully) compensated for their production, thus leaving the workers as the main exploited group.

It is a difficult question as to what type of system would give intellectuals control over their surplus product. Bauman (1987: 180) claims that: "Attaining greater control over 'cultural policy' and strategic decision-making would then be an indirect path to a change in the pattern of surplus distribution." Where non-capitalist economies are concerned, however, it is not fruitful to talk about economic surpluses in the cultural sector, since culture belongs to the ideological rather than the economic sphere. The ruling class is interested in controlling culture to legitimize its rule, rather than in earning any economic surplus. Thus, the conflict of interests between the corporate entity and the intellectuals is over control of the *content* of their production rather than over control of the surplus. It is likely that, under Soviet-type regimes, cultural enterprises lose money rather than earn any surplus. Under capitalism, by contrast, enterprises such as Hollywood film companies normally do try to maximize profits. Since the intellectuals do not produce a surplus product, it is more fruitful to classify them as a stratum rather than an economic class.

My analysis asserts that *all three groups* are exploited under the Soviet-type system. Workers and professionals do not have control over their surplus production, while intellectuals do not have control over the content of their production. They all have, therefore, postulated interests in changing the system.

Traditional Marxian theory predicts that the members of the exploited classes will only succeed during periods of economic crisis in carrying out a social revolution that transforms an international system. So one must look at the factors that prevent them from revolting under normal times. My claim in the next section is that much of the answer can be found in an analysis of institutional interests.

Institutional Interests

Although the exploited classes have postulated interests in working for a different system, I argue in this study that actors can have institutional interests which dissuade people from taking such action. Thus there are conflicts between levels of interests. My formulation draws upon Jeffrey C. Isaac (1987), who claims in his book *Power and Marxist Theory* that there are interests below the objective/postulated level. He calls these "real interests" (although I refer to them as "institutional interests"). He defines real interests (1987: 98) as "those norms, values, and rationalities implicit in the practices of social life and associated with social roles as their principles of action." Furthermore, these interests are real, "because they are causally effective in practice in the sense in which objective interests are clearly not. While objective interests may very well be ends that agents *should* subscribe to, real interests are those ends instantiated in their practice."

Already a difference in our understanding of interests is clear. Isaac implies that objective/postulated interests are normative and never causal, while I maintain that postulated interests are not normative, and that they can affect behavior (especially during periods of economic crisis). In contrast to subjective interests, he suggests, "certain interests are real, and causal, even if they are not avowed by social agents, and ... these interests shape and limit (thought they do not unequivocally determine) the development of subjective interests."

Unfortunately, the term "real interests" conjures up an image of arrogant social scientists telling people, notwithstanding what they think, that their interests *really* are something else.[12] Consequently, I prefer the term "institutional interests," since it implies that actors have certain interests which *derive* from institutional structures. It would be more accurate to use the term "institutionally derived interests," since it is the actors rather than the institutions that have the interests, but the term is rather awkward.

This definition allows one to examine more closely the relationship between institutions and actors. It also makes it possible to combine the insights of Marx with neo-institutionalism. If actors derive interests from institutions, and if these interests exert their strongest influence on behavior during normal times, then it becomes necessary to examine the institutional structures of society. Such an analysis helps us understand why certain groups behave the way they do during normal times.

Although Isaac includes norms in his definition of real interests, I limit my definition to institutional incentives. The reason is that it is extremely difficult to measure norm systems. By contrast, much more has been written about informal incentive systems under the Soviet-type regimes, i.e., *nomenklatura* lists, patronage, personal networks, etc.

In concrete terms, the notion of institutional interests implies that, by looking at different groups' incentives, one can get an indication as to how these groups will act during normal times. This implies some degree of stability, since it deals with a situation in which most people basically know the rules of the game. Moreover, even if some people do not know the rules, the rules still affect them anyway. Yet no society is static; a dynamic process is going on continuously. Consequently, actors are sometimes able to change institutions without changing the socioeconomic system. For instance, economic

---

12. To some extent, Steven Lukes (1974) and the Frankfurt school use the term this way (see Geuss 1981: ch. 2).

reforms can be carried out which change institutions by reducing the number of ministries or shifting the weight of various institutions.

I also argue, though, that among the exploited groups, institutional interests can encourage some groups to become dissidents, and to restrain others from participating in collective action. Institutional interests can bring some groups closer to their postulated interests in overthrowing the system, while the institutional interests of other groups can hold them back from their postulated interests. Many authors have observed that different classes and strata have differing propensities to revolt, but rarely do they tender theoretically based *reasons* as to why this is so. With the aid of this analytical instrument, I aim to move beyond observing patterns. This instrument should enable me to present a fruitful hypothesis regarding the underlying causes.

When discussing workers under capitalism, Isaac notes this potential conflict between real/institutional interests and objective/postulated interests during normal times. He writes (1987: 98–9) that

> while the proletarian may prefer to make more money in order to buy a Sony television set, and may have an objective interest in the transformation of capitalism into socialism, as a proletarian in a capitalist society she has a real interest in finding and keeping a job. The satisfaction of her preferences must be tailored to this; and as her objective interest potentially threatens this (by engendering economic dislocations in the process of change), she is unlikely to challenge the system.

Moreover, one should not separate institutional interests from the subjective motives of actors, since actors are able to change institutional structures and thus their institutional interests. Or as Saiedi (1988: 796) puts it:

> Individuals are not passive embodiments of social roles and the followers of clearly defined and determining rules. On the contrary, rule-following is accompanied by rule-defining, rule-redefining, and rule-exploiting practices of individuals in their concrete conflictual interactions.

Thus, institutional rules give people certain incentives to behave in certain ways within the existing institutional framework. These institutional interests can constrain actors from behaving in accordance with their postulated interests. Yet people interact continuously with the institutions and change the formal and informal rules. This in turn alters the institutional interests of the members of different social classes. My claim is that, except for some intellectuals, most members of the subjugated classes are effectively hindered by their institutional interests from following their postulated interests during normal times. During periods of economic crisis, however, these institutional interests can break down, thus making it easier for the actors to revolt.

Finally, adding the institutional level to the class analysis makes it possible to analyze the conflicts between sub-groups of the *same class*, as well as between different classes. This is especially important for analyzing the dynamics of the ruling corporate entity. For while members of the corporate entity have an interest as a class in maintaining their control over the process of production, different groups within the Party-state might have different institutional interests on particular policy issues. I contend in chapter 4 that these contrasting institutional interests within the corporate entity made it very difficult to reform the economy effectively. For now, it is enough to note that the introduction of institutional interests allows the theorist to incorporate the recent neo-institutional trends of "disaggregating the state" into the Marxian framework.[13]

Subjective Perceptions of Interests
It should be clear from the above discussion that, although structures and institutions are extremely important, they do not *determine* the behavior of actors. As many authors point out (Cerny 1990, Isaac 1987 and Rothstein 1988), there is a continuous interaction between actors and structures in which structures influence actors, who in their turn influence structures. In Marxian terms, there is a "dialectical relationship" between the two. As Marx (1885: 90) observes in his *18th Brumaire of Louis Bonaparte*: "People make their own history, but they do not make it just as they please; they do not make it under circumstances chosen by themselves, but under circumstances directly found, given and transmitted from the past." It becomes important, therefore, to look at the subjective level as well.

Instead of the usual phrase "subjective interests," I discuss the subjective perceptions that actors have of their interests. This makes it easier to avoid the revealed-preference tautology. According to this logic, the social scientist merely has to observe actual behavior to find out the preferences of the actors. The actors *reveal* their preferences

---

13. I discuss this in chapter 4.

through their behavior. This becomes tautological, inasmuch as the theorist claims actors have an interest in doing something *because they did it*.

In addition, I prefer the term "subjective perception of interests," because it emphasizes the possibility that psychological factors influence perceptions of interests. Moreover, even if such an approach portrays actors as relatively "rational" and free from the influence of psychological factors, it points to a constellation of postulated and institutional interests which exist simultaneously, and which may contradict one another. This runs counter to rational-choice approaches, which postulate the existence of clear preference-rankings. In my framework, it is not a question of actors favoring institutional interests over postulated interests or *visa-versa*, but rather of their tendency to give priority to institutional interests during normal times and to postulated interests during periods of economic crisis.

In one sense, this model is fairly rationalist: during periods of stability, most members of the exploited classes follow their institutional interests. Since postulated interests are relatively unimportant under such conditions, the conflict between interests is not as strong as during economic crises. However, this is a study about political change, and it is precisely when institutions become unstable and change approaches that the behavior of members of the exploited classes is less guided by their institutional interests. During uprisings, moreover, psychological factors such as emotions may count more heavily than cool calculations when it comes to inducing individuals to take part in protest actions. Furthermore, some actors behave irrationally even during normal times. The importance of such deviation increases with the importance of a post that somebody holds. For example, if local Party secretaries have an institutional interest in blocking reforms, it does not matter much if one of them advocates radical change. It has a great impact, on the other hand, if the General Secretary deviates from his or her institutional interests.

POLITICAL ECONOMY

One can understand the collapse of the Soviet-type system without investigating the relationship between economic and political developments. Some actor-oriented theorists emphasize the maneuverings of politicians between different political factions. Although this is important, it is necessary to place these political actions in a socioeconomic context, for economic structures both constrain and enable the policy decisions available to leaders, and they influence the strength of various political factions (including the strength of the opposition). When economic problems arise, a politician might try to appease certain political groups with some economic reforms, but these reforms in turn will affect the economy, which in turn will affect the relative strength of these groups.

Today, many actor-based theorists have realized the need to put actors in a socioeconomic context. Yet this leaves unanswered the question of how to do so. I believe it is fruitful to use Marx' distinction between the economic base and political superstructure.

There is a tendency to dismiss the base-superstructure paradigm as outdated. This is certainly understandable, since many theorists have interpreted Marx as claiming that economic developments completely determine political outcomes. Every political decision has an economic cause. I believe this to be an incorrect interpretation of Marx. My task here, however, is not to prove that my interpretation of Marx is *the correct* one. I intend, rather, to combine a *possible* interpretation of Marx with the insights of certain neo-Marxists in an effort to establish my analytical framework.

This study follows Manicas' (1987) interpretation of the base-superstructure relationship. Manicas notes that Marx uses the verb *bestimmen* to describe the relationship between the base (which Manicas calls the "foundation") and the superstructure. Unfortunately, *bestimmen* does not translate well into English. Most often, translators have used the word "determine." However, Manicas (1987: 101) claims that *bestimmen* really implies "direction, influence, constraint, or 'conditioning.'"[14] Manicas therefore concludes (1987: 101–2) that the metaphor of base and superstructure "implies, at a minimum, that not any superstructure can be built on any foundation, but rather that the foundation constrains or limits the possible superstructure."

---

14. Some theorists try to solve this translation problem by using the word "decides," rather than determines. This sounds awkward in English, however. It gives the impression that the economy is a conscious being that can make decisions. I might add that there is a German verb—*determinieren*—which directly corresponds to the English "determine." So it is at least possible that, if Marx had really interpreted the relationship between the base and the superstructure in a deterministic manner, he would have chosen *determinieren* rather than *bestimmen*.

I shall argue that this interpretation of the base-superstructure relationship provides a fruitful framework for analyzing the interplay between the economy and political decision-making in the countries in this study. It points to the importance of understanding the general economic situation. The economy and social system emerging from the Soviet-type of production mode becomes the most important structural background for examining the political actors. In addition, the base-superstructure model generates the famous hypothesis that a socioeconomic systemic collapses during an economic crisis. As Cohen (1990: 167) puts it: "There is, after all, a neat Marxist explanation of the collapse of Communist regimes [in 1989]: the base undid the superstructure." I develop this theme in the following chapters. Finally, Manicas' non-deterministic interpretation of the base-superstructure relationship yields a fruitful framework for analyzing the dialectical relationship between actors and structures, as I described in the section on interests.

THE NEXT STEPS

Part I of this book has formulated the problem and briefly discussed previous attempts at answering my questions. It concludes that nobody, to my knowledge, has sufficiently considered my particular question regarding the reasons for the differences in the process of collapse. This chapter has presented an analytical framework for investigating the matter further. The chapters that follow undertake a comparative analysis based on Mill's method of difference. The basic framework is a non-dogmatic neo-Marxian approach. This includes class analysis, a division of interests into three levels, and a non-deterministic approach to the relationship between the economic base and the political superstructure.

In these empirical chapters, this framework is used as a basis for incorporating other insights. Each chapter conducts a partial analysis of the collapse of the regimes, and tries to find the best explanations for the particular problem that I am investigating. In the concluding chapter of the book, I repeat my basic findings in an integrated model. This model is based on a neo-Marxian framework.

In Part II, I examine the causes of the collapse in general. This is a precondition for finding the underlying causes of each particular process of collapse. For if the system had not collapsed, it obviously would not be possible to discuss the different processes of collapse.

Thus, I concentrate here on the *similarities* among the four countries. Then, having ascertained in general the reasons for the collapse, I examine the differences in the process of collapse more closely in Part III.

Part II:

THE UNDERLYING CAUSES OF THE COLLAPSE

Chapter 3

THE ECONOMIC SITUATION

Most observers agree that the economic situation was one of the main factors in the collapse of the Soviet-type regimes. However, there are differences in judgement over the extent of the economic difficulties and the degree of their influence over events. I begin this chapter by briefly discussing these issues. Since so much literature is available on this topic, I do not go into much detail. The greater part of this chapter deals with the causes of the economic decline.

ECONOMIC DECLINE

At the very least, there is virtually unanimous agreement that living standards in the East European countries fell farther behind Western Europe during the 1980s. Even those who defend the performance of the Soviet-type economies usually agree on this point. For example, Arrighi (1991) admits that the Soviet-type countries were falling behind their West European neighbors. He also agrees that the citizens of these countries were, in fact, dissatisfied with the economic situation. He claims, however, that it was unrealistic of them to compare themselves to Western Europe. Instead, they should have compared themselves to the Latin American and African countries, which also found themselves on the periphery of global capitalism. Whether or not Arrighi is correct is beside the point here. What is important is that even defenders of the economic performance of the East European countries admit that these countries fell behind the West, and that the citizens of these countries were subjectively dissatisfied with this state of affairs.

Not only were the East European countries faring poorly compared to the West, most experts agree they were also faring poorly compared to their previous performance. According to official statistics, for example, growth rates in all four countries declined steadily during the last two decades of Communist rule (see Diagram 1).

The one partial exception is Poland, whose economy grew slightly after the three-year period of negative growth in 1979–81. This does not show up so clearly in Diagram 1, because it only shows 5-year averages, and these three years are divided into two different five-year periods. Despite the higher growth rates in the post-*Solidarność* era, by 1989 the net material product was still 1% below the 1978 level (Simatupang 1994: 219). Furthermore, negative growth returned to the country in 1989 (UN 1991: 441).

Already, we can safely discard the J-curve hypothesis about revolutions. The four countries had not experienced "a prolonged period of objective economic and social development" which "is followed by a short period of sharp reversal." These countries had all experienced a long period of declining economic performance before the regimes finally collapsed. At best, one could claim that the *Solidarność* uprising of 1980 followed the J-curve pattern, whereby rebellion takes place after a long period of economic upswing and a subsequent sudden decline.

There is also widespread agreement that Poland and Hungary entered the fatal year of 1989 with negative growth, an increasingly threatening debt burden, and either hyper-inflation or threatening hyper-inflation. Moreover, statistics made available after 1989 show that rising East German debts were also bringing that country nearer to financial ruin.

Elsewhere, I have even gone further and showed that living standards in all four countries were probably decreasing in absolute terms as well (Saxonberg 1996, ch: 3). For example, if the Czech economist Kosta (1990: 805) is correct in claiming that the "hidden inflation" in the ČSSR was over 2%, then even the most stable of the four econ-

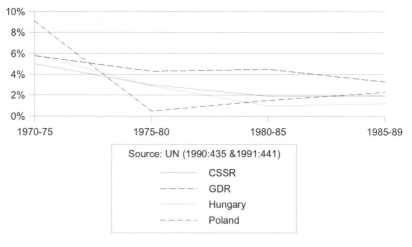

Diagram 1: Real Per Capita Growth Rates (Official Statistics)

omies actually had negative growth rates throughout its last decade of Communist rule. The former ministers for planning (Potáč) and finance (Lér) both admit, as does the former economic advisor to prime ministers Štrougal and Adamec (Navařil), that the official statistics underestimated the real rate of inflation by more than 2%.[1]

For our present purposes, it is not necessary to go into such details. The important matter is that these countries faced long-term economic problems. More than a decade of declining performance showed that these problems were clearly structural rather than cyclical. In other words, they were facing an economic crisis.

Below I briefly discuss the impact of the economic crisis on the thinking of the East European rulers. I do so to show that the economic situation influenced their behavior to a greater or lesser extent in 1989.

SUBJECTIVE INTERPRETATIONS OF THE ECONOMY

Poland

In Poland, the leaders clearly perceived the country was in the midst of a serious economic crisis. There was wide agreement among the elites that economic reforms were necessary. Their disputes centered on the type of reforms, not their necessity.[2] In fact, most observers claim that when the rulers realized that they lacked popular support for carrying out economic reforms, they began reappraising their attitudes towards the opposition. Stanisław Gebethner (1992: 51), the Communists' main advisor on political questions during the Round Table talks, writes that both the regime and the opposition were united by "the awareness that, faced by the dangerous and rapidly worsening economic situation, and the building up of tensions which could lead yet again to an uncontrolled outburst of social revolt, there existed the necessity to achieve some agreement which would prevent mass protest with consequences which might lead to a national tragedy."

Former General Secretary Jaruzelski makes clear in his memoirs that the Polish leadership was keenly aware that the country faced an economic crisis. Writing about his decision to have a referendum in 1987 on economic reforms, he states: "We had understood, for a long time, that

---

1. In a personal memo to Prime Minister Adamec a few weeks before the revolution, Nevařil estimated hidden inflation at 2–3%. He also claims that the economy had stagnated since the beginning of the 1980s, especially after 1984 (Document: Některá fakta....). I interviewed Lér on 3 March 1993, Potáč on 9 July 1993, and Nevařil on 30 March 1993.
2. Staniszkis (1991) divides the two main factions into "populists" and "globalists."

only a far-reaching economic reform would enable us to come out of the crisis which we had suffered from for many years" (1992: 322). In an interview with *Time Magazine* (31 December 1990) he admits that the failure of this referendum was a turning point for him. When asked when he realized "there was no future in communism," he responded:

> A very significant moment for me was in 1987, when in a referendum Poles rejected proposals for painful but necessary economic reforms. I realized then that without popular support we would be unable to follow the communist route any further.

Former Politburo member, Janusz Reykowski (interviewed 23 April 1993), adds that the economic crisis was so deep that even the leaders were dissatisfied with their living standards. They realized that, although they lived slightly better than average citizens, by Western standards they were only lower-middle class.

Public-opinion surveys show that citizens were also extremely critical of the economic situation. Ramet (1991: 352) recapitulates a poll by the Polish Television and Radio's Center for Public Opinion Research taken in February 1989.[3] When asked: "Is the economic

---

3. This was reported in *Trybuna Ludu*, 20 Feb. 1989. She does not give any information about the number of respondents or the survey methodology. For all surveys cited hereon in this study, the reader can assume—if no information is given on the methodology—that the information was not available in the source cited.

   I am aware that survey data collected under a dictatorship presents some problems of validity. If participants do not trust the anonymity of their answers, they will be afraid to give critical responses. Consequently, one must expect that to some extent the results will always underestimate the degree of dissatisfaction. As long as the fear factor remains constant, however, it is possible to compare changes over time. Thus, in the cases of the hardline East German and Czechoslovak regimes, there is no reason to assume that increasingly negative responses reflect greater trust in the surveyers. On the contrary, since the regimes took either no steps or only symbolic ones towards greater political liberalization, the participants were probably as mistrustful of surveyors in 1989 as in previous years. The Hungarian and Polish cases are more problematic. As Sułek (1994) notes, surveys taken in Poland during periods of greater openness (such as during the *Solidarność* uprising) were much more reliable than surveys taken during periods of increased repression (such as the first years of martial law). Thus, a survey from 1989 showing greater dissatisfaction with economic performance than a survey from 1985 may reflect greater trust in the surveyors, rather than an actual change in opinion. For once censorship was lifted and the Communists had recognized *Solidarność*, there was less reason to fear reprisals than during the height of martial law. However, since we can assume that *all* surveys taken under the period of Communist rule underestimate the degree of dissatisfaction, we can still safely assume that surveys showing that a majority of the population in Hungary and Poland was unhappy with the economic situation actually indicates a high level of deprivation. Although I might not be able to show in these cases that the populace became more critical towards the end of the decade, I can at least show that, at the subjective level, most citizens believed their country was in the midst of an economic crisis.

situation good?" only 4% replied "yes," while 95% answered "no," and 1% had no opinion. To the question: "How would you describe the supply of foodstuffs?" 57% replied poor and 30% mediocre. Only 10% claimed it was good, while 3% gave other replies.

A study one year earlier gives rather similar results. In March 1988, 81.3% of the respondents described the economic situation as "bad" or "very bad," while only 2.3% claimed it was "good or fairly good," and 15% said it was "neither good nor bad." An additional 0.7% did not know.[4]

Hungary

Like their Polish counterparts, the Hungarian elites were in wide agreement that the country was undergoing an economic crisis requiring radical reforms. The main point at issue was whether or not political democratization was a prerequisite for gaining public support for such reforms. General Secretary Grósz was known for advocating "one-party pluralism," while more radical reformists argued for a multiparty democracy (cf. Bruszt 1990 and McDonald 1993). Prime Minister Németh summed up the attitude of many reformers by stating publicly in December 1988 that "the market economy is the only way to avoid a social catastrophe or a long, slow death" (McDonald 1993: 219).

Fear that continued economic decline would lead to social upheaval is usually given as the main reason for the regime's decision to negotiate with the opposition. The architect of the economic reforms, former Politburo member Rező Nyers (interviewed 8 April 1983), supports this thesis.[5] He freely admits that the system was going through a process of collapse. The Communist rulers could no longer govern because the necessary economic measures required sacrifices from the population. Yet the population would not be willing to make these sacrifices without a legitimate government.

Györffy Tibor (interviewed 12 March 1993), former editor of a special newspaper for the *nomenklatura*, echoes this. He claims that

---

4. Cited by Kolarsko-Bobińska (1990: 169). The results were taken from a survey conducted by the government office for public opinion polls.

5. As the Central Committee economic secretary, he was the architect of the 1968 economic reforms. In 1988 he joined the Politburo. In the summer of 1989 he joined the Party's four-person ruling committee, which was set up to circumscribe Grósz's attempts at preventing full democratization. When the Party changed into a social democratic organization, he became its first leader.

the leaders had realized their economic policy had failed. In addition, they were afraid that an economic collapse would lead to a social upheaval. So it was better to negotiate with the opposition before this happened.

Unfortunately, it has become difficult to find public-opinion surveys about the Hungarian economy. Schöpflin, Tőkes & Völgyes (1988: 27), however, cite a survey taken in the fall of 1986, which shows that already by that time, 61% of the population described their position as hopeless or continually worsening. Since real wages continued to drop for most of the following years, there is littlr reason to assume that the population became more positive toward the economic situation in 1989.

Hankiss (1989a: 57) cites another survey from 1989 indicating that the Hungarians at least were aware of their relative decline. Fully 80% of those surveyed thought people live better in Austria, while only 13% believed that people were better off in Hungary.

Even though there is not enough available public-opinion research to prove that the population believed the economy was in crisis, everything indicates that Hungarian citizens were unhappy with their economic situation. Moreover, the Communist elites clearly believed they faced an economic crisis, and there is no reason to expect the population would have been less critical than its leaders. That would only have been the case if the elites had had access to some special economic information of which the rest of society had no idea. But the problems of high inflation, decreasing real wages, and a mounting debt crisis were all well-known.

East Germany
The former economic secretary of the GDR, Günter Mittag (1991: 40), was certainly himself aware of the country's worsening economic situation. In his memoirs, he admits that the country was heading toward economic collapse. Honecker, Mittag and the economic bureaucracy were become increasing nervous that the country would become completely insolvent. Schürer, who was head of the Planning Commission, announced in May 1988 that the GDR was "finished," and that it was impossible to prevent bankruptcy (Janson 1991: 104–5). Carl-Heinz Janson (1991: 69), who worked under Mittag as head of one of the Central Committee economic departments, adds that paying back the debts became the main issue for economic policy. Mittag (1991: 83) admits that the leadership was so preoccupied with the debt crisis that

he and Honecker received *daily* reports on the payment situation! An expert commission headed by Schürer reported, in September 1989, that even if exports to the capitalist world could be doubled by 1995, while imports remained the same, the hard currency debt would still increase by 25% (from 41.8 billion to 52.6 billion East marks; the document is reprinted in Przybylski 1992: 362). A member of the commission, Polze, who was also head of the state bank, announced to the commission in early 1989 that Honecker's economic policy had definitely collapsed (Przybylski 1992: 74). The leaders of the *coup* against Honecker, Schabowski and Krenz are also critical of the economic situation in their memoirs, although they were not aware of the true extent of the debt crisis.[6]

Unfortunately, the GDR had the worst record for conducting public-opinion surveys of the four countries. This makes it difficult to know what the population was thinking. The haemorrhage of young East Germans leaving the country shows that many expected a better life on the other side of the wall. Yet that does not prove they left just for economic reasons—political reasons could have been important as well.

The only survey information available from the period before Honecker's resignation comes from the Leipzig Institute for Youth Research. Their surveys never discuss economic questions directly, indirectly. Nevertheless, one can assume that the economic developments influenced the answers which the East German youth gave. For example, one of the questions dealt with the belief that the world will become socialist. That would not happen without certain political developments, of course, but it is also clear that East Germans, indoctrinated with the notion that the Soviet-type economic system was superior to capitalism, would not have expected the world to become socialist unless the East European economies out-performed the West. As Table 1 shows, there was a drastic change in attitudes among East German youths.

After Honecker resigned, but before the first free elections, *Der Spiegel* (18 December 1989) conducted a poll showing that East German citizens believed the West German economy was healthier than their own. 94% felt that living standards were better in the FRG, 95% felt that industry was better, 92% that science and technology

---

6. For example, see Krenz (1990: 174–5) and Schabowski (1992: 116).

Table 1: East German Youths' beliefs about future socialist development

"I believe the world will become socialist"	Completely			With limits			Hardly/not at all		
	1970	1988	1989	1970	1988	1989	1970	1988	1989
Students	65%	–	15%	27%	–	39%	8%	–	46%
Young workers	35%	6%	–	41%	30%	–	24%	64%	–
Apprentices	46%	10%	3%	36%	32%	27%	18%	58%	70%

Source   Friedrich (1990: 29) n = 3,080 apprentices, 2,480 students and 1,730 young workers for 1970. The survey in 1988 was taken in May for apprentices and October for young workers. In 1989 the survey was taken in October for apprentices and in May for students. No data on the age limit for young workers or for the number of responses for 1988 and 1989.

were better, and 80% that environmental protection was better. Of course, this only shows relative differences.

Thus, the results of the two surveys show that citizens were dissatisfied with the state of the economy.

Czechoslovakia

Within the former Communist leadership, there is widespread agreement that the country faced economic problems, although there are differing opinions on the extent of the crisis. The more critical group centered around former prime ministers Štrougal and (later) Adamec, and included economic ministers as well.

Oskar Krejčí (interviewed 13 April 1992), formerly the main political advisor to Prime Minister Adamec, claims that Adamec's economic advisors supported more radical economic reforms than those which the Politburo was considering. He adds that they claimed there was no future without reforms. This is confirmed by a memo which the economic advisor František Nevařil sent to Adamec slightly more than a week before the revolution broke out (Document: "Některá fakta k přípravě a hodnocení návrhu 9. pětiletky"). The memo begins: "Our economic level is excessively low and in relative terms continuously sinking." He goes on to declare that the economy had been stagnating since the beginning of the 1980s.

Among the economic ministers, former Finance Minister Leopold Lér (interviewed 10 June 1993) claims that, by the early 1980s, he was forced to "take the economic situation seriously." His colleague, former Planning Minister Svatopuk Potáč (interviewed 9 July 1993), claims that the Politburo tried to ignore the degree of the economic crisis. By 1988, though, it realized something had to be done.

As noted, Party leaders were less radical than state leaders. For example, former General Secretary Jakeš (interviewed 9 April 1992) does not say outright that the country faced an economic crisis. Yet he admits that the economy had problems, such as an overconsumption of raw materials and energy. He also mentions the environment, and adds that the leadership was preparing for a market-oriented economic reform that would have been more radical than that in Hungary during Kádár's reign. If the leaders had felt the economy were running smoothly, they would not have had any reason to contemplate such reforms—unless, of course, they were under pressure from the USSR to do so. But Jakeš (interviewed 9 April 1991) denies that Gorbachev pressured them to change their domestic policies. In a published interview (*Reportér* no. 17, 1991), moreover, he says he believes some sort of market economy is necessary. It is hard to imagine he would make such a statement if he did not believe the country had deep economic problems.

Former Politburo member Jozef Lenárt (interviewed 3 June 1993), who had enjoyed leadership roles within the Party and state since the late 1950s, acknowledges that the economy had been stagnating since the late 1970s. The most cautious statements from my interviews come from the hardline former Politburo member Miroslav Štěpán (interviewed 3 June 1992). He admits there was a growing economic problem, in that the younger generations were aware that the country was falling further behind the West. He adds that the Soviet Union's economic problems were beginning to affect the ČSSR, since its economy was so dependent on the USSR. Otherwise, he only mentions insufficient wage incentives as a major economic problem under the Communist regime. So although the leadership disagreed on the degree of the economic crisis, there appears to have been unanimous agreement that the economy had problems.

While the leadership varied in is perception of how serious the economic situation was, public opinion surveys leave no doubt. One survey taken from December 20–22, 1989, by the Federal Institute for Public Opinion Research shows amazing results, in which practically the entire population thought the environment, economy, and health care were great problems (see Table 2). Indeed, these were considered even

Table 2: Czech opinions on the severity of different problems
Survey conducted December 20–22, 1989

Issue/ opinion	Great problem	Small problem	Almost none	No prob/d.k.
Environment	98%	2%	0%	0%
Economy	92%	2%	0%	6%
Health	90%	7%	1%	2%
Political system	88%	8%	2%	2%

Source   Slejška & Herzmann (1990: 49). 401 Czech citizens participated.

graver than the question of democratization. The results become even more impressive if one remembers that, if anything, one should expect such surveys to *underestimate* the degree of dissatisfaction with the regime. For citizens probably still feared any institutes established by the crumbling Communist-led regime. Since only 401 Czechs participated in the survey, there is room for sampling error. Let us assume this margin of error more than compensated for the tendency of citizens to down play their dissatisfaction. Even with a unlikely 30% margin of error, the survey shows that over two-thirds of the population believed they faced an economic crisis.

Even though this surveys only includes Czechs, there is no reason to believe Slovaks were much more positive toward economic developments. Another survey taken by the same institute shows that the percentage of Slovaks who saw economic developments as "predominantly positive" fell from 76% in 1975 to just 17% in 1989 (Babůrková 1989: 14). The fact that these extremely negative results were nevertheless more positive than in the Czech lands may depend partially on the date of the surveys.[7] Although Babůrková does not make it clear what month in 1989 the institute carried out the survey, she presented her report in September. In contrast, the survey of the Czech population was carried out several weeks after the Communist leaders had resigned. Thus the Czechs had less reason to fear reprisals, even if they still might have remained suspicious of any surveyors left over from an institute that had existed under the previous regime.

---

7. Which is not to deny that the Slovaks, in general, were less negative toward the Communist regime than the Czechs (see for example Herzmann 1992: 166).

Summary

The Polish and Hungarian leaders clearly believed their countries faced economic crisis. Indeed, this is often given as their reason for deciding to negotiate with the opposition. The Czechoslovak leaders also realized the economy was stagnating, although opinions differed on the degree of the crisis. The last two prime ministers (Adamec and Štrougal) and their advisors, as well as the economic ministers were more critical of the economic situation than the conservatives in the Politburo. Yet there was a consensus that the country had economic problems. Similarly, the East German leaders were aware that their country had economic problems. However, only those with special access to information about the true nature of the debt crisis understood that the economy was coming close to collapse.

Concerning the citizens of the four countries, there are no indications they were particularly satisfied with the state of the economy. Unfortunately, relevant survey information is only available for Poland and the ČSSR. In both cases, the population was extremely critical of the economic situation. In the case of Hungary and the GDR, surveys show the population was aware they were falling behind the West, but they give no information as to whether or not they considered the situation critical. The rapidly rising emigration to the FRG shows that many East Germans were dissatisfied with the system. Economic reasons, presumably, offered the strongest incentives for leaving, but there is no way of knowing how much of their motivation was based on economic or on political reasons (i.e., the desire for more personal freedom).

Now that I have established that many citizens of the East European countries believed that they faced an economic crisis, the next step is to examine the causes of this crisis. I discuss the most common hypotheses below.

THE CAUSES OF THE ECONOMIC CRISIS

There are six common hypotheses for the collapse of the Soviet-type economies:

- the inefficiency of the economy,
- the failure of particular economic policies,
- the oil price increases,
- the increase in military spending,

- the modernization process, and
- changes in technology.

These hypotheses are examined below to see if they can explain the collapse of the system in general. I leave aside the hypotheses of economic inefficiency and modernization, since they were already discarded in chapter 2. I conclude that the changes in technology were the most important factor explaining the economic downturn that began in the mid-1970s. In Marxian terms, the development of the forces of production came into conflict with the relations of production. Finally, despite all these alleged problems, the system might have survived if it could have been successfully reformed. Chapter 4 deals, therefore, with the reform process.

THE FAILURE OF ECONOMIC POLICIES

Many economists writing about Eastern Europe, such as Simatupang (1994), concentrate on the events in a particular country, rather than on the collapse in general. Case studies of this type limit our ability to make generalizations. Discussions of differences in policies might be able to show why the economic crisis was more urgent in Poland and Hungary than in East Germany and Czechoslovakia. Yet this type of explanation cannot account for why the economic crisis hit these latter two countries, whose leaders pursued much more orthodox policies. Economic performance declined in all the Soviet-bloc countries during the late 1970s and 1980s, *regardless* of which policies were pursued. Honecker's orthodox policies of increased centralization (combining enterprises into larger branch "combines"), nationalization of the remaining half-private-half state firms, and continued reliance on a rigid command economy did not prevent the economy from falling into a crisis.[8] Nor could the Hungarian variant of "market socialism" avoid crisis. Between the two extremes, the Polish and Soviet hybrids fared no better. Meanwhile, the ČSSR's conservative strategy of "per-

---

8. For more detailed accounts of Honecker's policy, see Bryson & Melzer (1991), Cornelsen (1986), Ebel (1990), Janson (1991), Leptin (1986), Mittag (1991) and Voskamp & Wittke (1991).

fecting" the command economy succeeded only in avoiding the debt crises of its neighbors.[9]

These examples make clear that, *regardless of economic policy*, all of the Soviet-bloc countries suffered from economic stagnation or decline during the last 15 years or so.[10] So while actors are important, and poor economic decisions certainly added fuel to the fire, the question remains: why did the oil leak out in the mid-1970s, and why were a variety of different strategies not able to plug up the hole?

THE OIL CRISIS

Some authors, such as Ivan & Balazs Szelenyi (1994: 212), take the oil metaphor seriously. They blame the sharp rise in oil prices during the 1970s for much of the decline of the Soviet-type economies. Yet while the price rises hurt some of the countries, this can hardly be the main cause of the economic crisis. First, the Soviet Union (and at that time Romania) were *exporters* of oil. Consequently, they benefitted economically from the oil crisis. From 1976–1980, when the oil crisis was at its height, the USSR had a net fuel export of 44.2 billion dollars with the OECD countries (Wienert & Slater 1986: 228). Second, the members of the Soviet-bloc's economic organization CMEA (the Council for Mutual Economic Assistance) were less affected than the West European countries, because they could purchase Soviet oil below-world market prices. The CMEA also adopted a policy of basing its prices on the average world prices for the last five years. Therefore, the member countries had a longer period to adjust to the full price increases than did their Western counterparts. Finally, the CMEA countries could take advantage of these relatively lower prices by exporting petroleum products to Western Europe. This became a major factor in the GDR's export strategy (see Haendcke-Hoppe 1986: 55). An example comes from Central Committee employee Janson (1991: 99), who worked directly under Economic Secretary Mittag. He claims that his his boss decided to refine Soviet oil and then dump

---

9. For discussions of the strategy based on perfecting the planning mechanisms, see Altman (1980 & 1981), Kende (1982) Kosta (1985) and Levčik (1985).

10. Although Bulgaria and Romania have not been discussed in this study, the economy crisis at least in Romania was actually much worse than in any other the other countries. Energy was being rationed by the early 1980s, and electricity was only available during certain hours.

it on the world market in Rotterdam.[11] So while East European countries on the whole might have suffered more than they gained, the fact
that some countries gained, while all declined economically, shows
that oil prices cannot be the common cause of the economic crisis.
Similarly, Czechoslovak hard-currency exports of petroleum and
petroleum products increased from just 1.4% of total hard-currency
exports in 1970 to 5.9% in 1989 (my calculation, based on World
Bank 1991: 155).

MILITARY SPENDING

Collins & Waller believe that, while the crisis in the USSR in the late
1980s "presented itself as an economic crisis," the economic problems were in fact, caused by military spending, which was needed to
overcome difficult geopolitical problems (1993: 307). I have argued
elsewhere against this interpretation for the case of the Soviet
Union.[12] Even if this claim were true for the USSR, however, that
would not in itself suffice to explain the causes of the East European
economic crisis. If increases in military spending really brought about
the economic crisis of the Soviet bloc, then they should have caused
the economic crisis in the individual East European countries as well.

Unfortunately, it is impossible to find reliable information about the
true levels of military spending in the former Soviet-bloc countries. Yet
there is general agreement that the level was rather low in, e.g., in
crisis-ridden Hungary.[13] The ČSSR spent 43,784 million crowns on

---

11. The ability to obtain oil at below-market prices actually brought about some disadvantages to
East German society. Although the country earned a profit by re-exporting its cheap Soviet oil
imports, the GDR substituted its own oil usage with its infamous home-grown brown coal.
This led to further deterioration of the environment.

12. See Saxonberg (1996: 76f.). For example, Steinberg (1990: 675) cites CIA estimates that
Soviet defence spending only increased a few percent from 12–14% of GNP in the early
1970s to 15–17% in the 1980s. Steinberg (1990: 688) also calculates that total defense spending, taking into account hidden inflation, rose by only 12% from 1982 to 1988. In comparison, it rose by 14% during the last three years before Reagan's first defense budget came into
effect. Part of the increase between 1981–1982 could have been in response to the expectations that American military spending would rise the following year. Yet the fact that defense
spending rose by its greatest margin from 1979–1980—that is, *before* the American presidential election—indicates that the invasion of Afghanistan was the main cause of the military
build-up. In any case, military spending fell by an impressive 6% in 1989—the year in which
the "satellite regimes" collapsed.

13. Cf. Magas 1990: 92 and interviews with Farkas and Váss on 12 March 1993, as well as interviews with Nyers on 8 April 1993 and Simai, published in April 1992 on internet.

both defence and domestic security in 1989, according to previously secret information from the Czechoslovak Federal Statistical Office (Federalní statistický úřad 1990b: 29). Since the gross *domestic* product that year was officially 524,565 million crowns (Český statistický úřad 1993: 106), that means it only spent slightly more than 8% of GDP on defense and domestic security. The portion of gross *national* product spent on defense and domestic security was even lower. Moreover, if the costs of domestic surveillance of citizens are subtracted, then the actual share of defense spending of GNP was probably only around one-third of the Soviet total.[14] Even in the more militant GDR, the share of the budget going to defense spending actually *fell*—from 5.9% in 1980 to 5.8% in 1988.[15]

So while increased military spending in the USSR probably worsened that country's economic situation, the *underlying cause* was still the deteriorating performance of the Soviet economy. This made it harder and harder to keep up with the technological advances of the military-industrial complex in the NATO countries (cf. Cohn 1987: 158). I discuss the question of technology below.

CHANGES IN TECHNOLOGY AND THE WORLD ECONOMY

Some authors have blamed changes in technology for the decline of the Soviet-type economies, while others have denied its importance. Although not everyone who supports the technological explanation is a Marxist, such an explanation fits well into a Marxist framework. Before discussing the arguments for and against the technological explanation, therefore, I briefly present a possible Marxian framework for interpreting technology's role.

In his *Forward to the Critique of the Political Economy*, Marx (1859: 9) asserts: "At a certain stage of their development the material forces of production in society come into contradiction with the present social relations of production...." The relations of production

---

14. That is, the ČSSR probably spent around 5–6% of GNP on defence, compared to around 15–17% in the USSR (see footnote 12 for figures on the USSR).

15. My calculations are based on Statistiches Amt der DDR (1990: 299 301). Since this yearbook came out *after* the fall of the Communist regime, its figures are much more reliable than official statistics from the Honecker era. As I discuss later, at times the statistics from this yearbook deviate radically from previous ones—which strengthens my confidence in the reliability of this particular yearbook. They would not have taken the effort to drastically change some of the previous data if they were not serious about presenting more reliable information.

become a "fetter" on the forces of production. The development of the forces of production includes the opening of new sources of energy, changes in technology and science, in the technical division of labor, and in the education of the productive classes.[16]

In my adaptation of Marx, this means that while the Soviet-type economies might have functioned relatively well in the era of heavy industry, they were not able to adopt to the techno-scientific changes that became predominant in the 1970s. Marx (1859: 9) believed that when the relations of production are no longer able to adapt to the forces of production, the resulting economic crisis brings down the system. "With the changing of the economic base, the entire enormous superstructure collapses slower or faster."

Of course, there are many interpretations of Marx' statements, and many possible ways of adapting them to Eastern Europe. I do not see the base-superstructure relationship deterministically. Rather, the economic crisis at the base presents a structural framework within which the rulers at the political level must make decisions. The same holds true for members of the exploited classes. A crisis at the base of the system influences their perception of the situation. Furthermore, a crisis caused by the development of the forces of production is systemic rather than cyclical. This too affects the thinking of the rulers and the ruled.

Since the question of changes in technology (i.e., changes in the forces of production) is central to my model, this section is longer than the others. First, I examine a critique of this view. I then present some proponents of this view and seek to assess their arguments. Finally, I present the available evidence.

Against

Kontorovich (1993: 43) argues that the technological changes of the last two decades could have been an important factor in the collapse of the Soviet Union:

> The spread of radio, telephone, T.V. and the international combustion engine earlier in this century changed the world as radically as the computer changes it now. The Soviet response to technological change was always slow, incomplete, and uneven. In the 1980s, the Soviet economy was still struggling with the diffusion of the automobile and the telephone. It

---

16. See Bottomore (1983: 178), Haffner (undated: 103) and Kolakowski (1978: 337).

lagged even in the adoption of relatively old products and processes, and the microchip would not have been the first technological challenge unmet by the Soviet economy.

For

In contrast to Kontorovich, several social scientists contend that the Soviet-type of command economy functioned better for large-scale heavy industry, and worse for the newer "high-tech" industries that require greater innovation and flexibility (cf. Reykowski 1994: 233 and Ivan and Balazs Szelenyi 1994: 223). In Bates' (1990: 27) words:

> When firms that used high proportions of plant and machinery relative to human skill formed the basis of economies, then centrally directed systems tended to work; [by] mid-century, the Soviet Union competed successfully with capitalist nations as measured by rates of economic growth. But as the economies of nations have moved toward forms of production that require a high level of human capital, these forms have proved increasingly inefficient. Forms of organization where those who control the most essential factor—human capital—make the key decisions themselves become more appropriate and effective.

Similarly, Chirot maintains that the root of the economic crisis of the Soviet-bloc countries came from what he terms the "fifth stage of industrialization." The "age of electronics, information, and bio-technology," he estimates, began in the 1970s (1991: 7). This stage of world economic development is characterized by "[s]mall firms, very open to change, extreme attention to consumer needs, reliance on innovative thinking—all [of which] were exactly what the Stalinist model lacked" (1991: 8). In the Soviet-type economies, the large, heavy industries, "protected by the party and viewed as the very foundation of everything that communism had built, were able to resist change, at least for another twenty years." Coming close to the Marxian notion of a contradiction between the forces of production and the relations of production, he concludes,

> the struggle to keep out the world market, to exclude knowledge about what was going on in the more successful capitalist world, became more and more difficult. It also became more dangerous because it threatened to deepen backwardness.

According to this view, Kontorovich may be correct to stress the long-standing inability of the USSR to keep up with the West in technological change, but he does not account for the *qualitative differences* between the telecommunications revolution and previous periods of radical technological change. For while a five-year lag in automobile technology would not be so devastating for a country's ability to compete internationally, a five-year lag in computers is a very different story. The same is true of military technology: a five-year difference in the technology of fighter jets or missiles in the 1960s is not comparable to a similar lag in precision weapons based on computer technology.

In addition, the new technologies not only required industry to react more quickly in adapting more advanced technology, they have also changed the manner in which national economies operate. During the previous two decades, all advanced countries have become much more dependent on international trade for getting the necessary inputs for modern technologies. As Ladislav Russmich (interviewed 29 May 1991), a former economist at the Czechoslovak Planning Commission put it, the quantity of necessary inputs from the West increased every day during the 1980s. Without such imports, products using modern technologies were not only of much lower quality than in the West, but also much more expensive (as the great failure of the massive East German investment in the microchip attests).

Finally, Ebel (1990: 185) notes that the micro-electronic revolution of the 1970s was more far-reaching than previous post-war technological developments:

> Microelectronics had the function of sparking off the explosion that affected all branches of science. It revolutionized especially the technological usage of four sciences which are decisive for determining productivity: mathematics, physics, chemistry and biology. From this, it developed the preconditions and basis for the revolutionary change of all engineering and economic sciences. In a truly breath-taking tempo it encompassed all areas of society, the productive process, the information and communication systems, office technology, trade, medical technology, techniques of scientific experiment and learning, military and space technology, the entire supply of goods for industrial consumption, everything from household appliances to entertainment electronics to optics, electronic tools to cars and motorcycles.

Or in the words of the Hungarian economist Gál (1987: 55):

> The growth in the developed countries [since the mid-1970s] has been basically technology intensive. The technological development clearly manifested itself in electronics and its complicated usage in the economy, the

usage of interactive technologies, new technologies for raw materials, which greatly reduced the material requirements of production, energy saving productive processes, and bio-industrial technologies. The technological regeneration lowered the value of economic structures, which had been efficient in the 1950s and 1960s.

Moreover, he adds, these technologies were more difficult to obtain through international trade (in the form of goods or licences). So they required direct capital investment.

Below I examine the evidence for the forces-of-production view.

Evidence 1: Capital Productivity
The inability of the Soviet type of productive relations to adapt to the changing forces of production manifested itself statistically in four areas: 1) decreasing capital productivity, 2) large sums spent on research and development (R&D), 3) declining exports of capital-intensive goods, and 4) increasing dependence on the import of capital-intensive goods from the West.

First, the decreasing capital productivity indicates the East European countries were unable to replace old machines fast enough. Nor were they able to incorporate the new technologies into their production efficiently. Brand (1992: 241) remarks about the inability to replace outdated machinery: "the service life of the Soviet stock of industrial capital averaged an estimated forty-seven years, compared to seventeen years for the United States." Once new machines replace old ones, furthermore, the problem remains of using them efficiently. New technology, under Soviet-types of production relations, actually raises costs, rather than lowering them as in the West:

> This is because ... new technology leads to the use of new fuel or more fuel in many instances, higher maintenance costs (even if less time is spent, it usually requires more skill), a higher depreciation cost, more breakdowns in the initial learning and development stages, and more auxiliary costs... [In addition, such investments] are all exacerbated to a considerable degree and above all not compensated by a reduction in the work force, higher output, and the greater reliability and precision of the new machines.... [Therefore,] it will cause the continued hypertrophy of the repair sector, which in turn will require still more labor and more spare parts. Unless the auxiliary aspects are mechanized, the demand for labor actually increases (Ticktin 1992: 143).

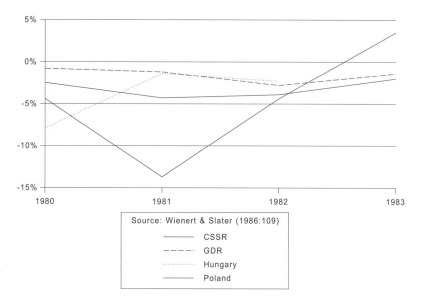

Source: Wienert & Slater (1986:109)
——— CSSR
— — — GDR
············ Hungary
——— Poland

Diagram 2: Changes in Capital Productivity

The decline of capital productivity caused by these developments can be seen in Diagram 2. Unfortunately, this data only goes up to 1983, but the trend is clear. Poland is the only country with a positive growth of productivity during any one year. That slight increase of 3.5% occurred after a cumulative 21% loss during the previous two years (Shen 1993: 61). Shen (1993: 60) calculates that the increase occurred after a 5.5% decline from 1976 to 1980. Moreover, even this slight increase in capital productivity in the post-1981 period occurred as "the direct result of government action streamlining investment allocation, as well as sustained investment retrenchment." Thus, it was caused by decreased rather than new investment. In 1987, the change of capital productivity was negative again. So by the 1989 elections, capital productivity was still lower than in 1975. Shen also calculates that the change in capital productivity in the ČSSR averaged –1.9% from 1976–80, and then continued falling during the remainder of the decade.

Short (1990: 32) has data for Eastern Europe as a whole up to the year 1986. She calculates that industrial capital productivity growth declined for the Eastern European countries by 2.7% from 1982–85, and then fell an additional 0.7% in 1986.

Table 3:

R&D as a % of GDP or NMP		R&D personnel as % of total non-agricultural employment
ČSSR (1978)	2.9%	1.8%
GDR (1979)	—	2.2%
Hungary (1978)	2.5%	1.4%
Poland (1978)	1.6%	1.4%
USSR (1977)	3.4%	—
FRG (1979)	2.3%	1.0%
Sweden (1979)	1.9%	1.0%
USA (1979)	2.4%	0.8%

Source Winiecki (1987: 41). Note: for the CMEA countries, NMP (net material product) was used, while GNP was used for the OECD countries.

Evidence 2: R&D

A second indication that the relations of production hindered the adaptation of the modern productive technologies is the fact that the CMEA countries spent at least as much on R&D as the OECD countries. As Table 3 shows, the ČSSR, Hungary and the USSR all devoted greater resources on research than the FRG, Sweden, and the USA. Unless one believes East European scientists are much less capable than their Western counterparts, one must conclude that the Soviet-type economy was not organized in a manner that could incorporate their results efficiently into the productive process. Gomulka (1985: 13) sums up the situation:

> Despite its large size, equal to at least one-quarter of the size of world R&D, the contribution of Soviet and East European R&D activity to the world flow of new inventions is negligible. In the 1970s, member countries of the CMEA were importing about ten times more licences in terms of dollars paid than they exported, the exports representing merely 1 per cent of the estimated total of world exports.

The prime example of this inability to utilize research efficiency is the East German attempt at developing its own computer industry. Ebel (1990) claims that investments in microelectronics caused the collapse of the East German economy. First, they came at the expense of investment in other fields. From 1976 to 1988, investment declined in all four major categories: construction, agricultural and forestry, transport and infrastructure, and domestic trade (1990: 194). Meanwhile, investment in computers and office machinery increased more than four-fold (1990: 196). Not only was the cost tremendous, the investments were extremely inefficient. Former Politburo member Schabowski (1992: 126) remarks that the first 256-kilobyte chip cost 536 marks. Society subsidized them with 520 marks. The enterprises only had to pay 16 marks, but this was still more than twice the world market price! Likewise, Janson (1991: 82) calculates that the growth of national income produced per mark invested in science and technology fell by 38% between 1985–1987.

Evidence 3: Trade Patterns
The continued fall in competitiveness also manifests itself in the decline of capital-intensive export goods. As diagrams 3 and 4 show, exports both of capital goods and of engineering and metal-working goods to OECD countries started dropping in all of the countries except Hungary in the early to mid-1970s. In Hungary, it dropped during the early 1980s. While their products were becoming less competitive, the East European countries had to increase their import of

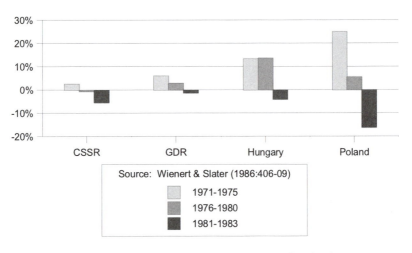

Diagram 3: Change in Exports to OECD Countries: Engineering and Metal-Working

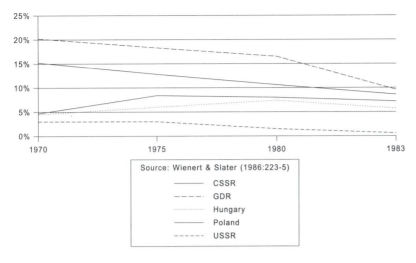

Diagram 4: Exports of Capital Goods as % of all Exports to OECD Countries

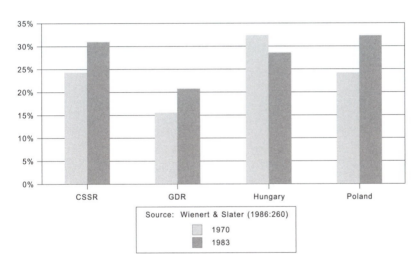

Diagram 5: Imports From OECD Countries % of Highly & Moderately R&D-Intensive

research-intensive goods in order to improve the quality of their own goods.[17]

As Diagram 5 shows, Hungary is the only country which did not increase its import of highly research intensive goods and moderately

---

17. To some extent the decline in exports was due to the period of stagnation that arose in the West, but that in itself cannot explain why the composition of exports changed from higher to lower tech goods.

research intensive goods from 1970 to 1983. However, its import of *highly* research intensive goods actually increased from 1970 to 1983 (Wienert & Slater 1986: 260). Moreover, the fall in Hungary's technological imports does not imply a sudden ability to develop its own modern high-tech industries. It reflects, rather, a decision to cut back on hard-currency imports in order to pay back debts. By the end of the decade, moreover, Hungary's import of high-tech goods had radically increased. Between 1986 and 1989, non-ruble imports of telecommunications machines and products rose from 77.9 million to 125.1 million dollars. During the same period, non-ruble exports fell from 79.2 to 19.8 million dollars (*PlanEcon Report* 13 April 1990).

This pattern held as well for Hungarian imports and exports which were less technologically intensive. For example, the share of non-ruble exports accounted for by machinery, transport equipment and other capital goods declined from 14.9% in 1982 to 10.4% in 1989. Meanwhile, Hungarian hard currency imports of these items increased from 13.8% to 17.2% (my calculations, based on *PlanEcon Report* 13 April 1990). Likewise, the OECD (1991: 89) reports that the share of hard-currency export goods accounted for by raw materials and semi-finished goods rose from 30.2% to 37.8% between 1986 and 1990, while the share accounted for by machinery dropped from 31.1% to 20.1%.

In the remaining three countries, this trend toward Third World trading patterns was also strong. Barłomiej Kamiński (1991: 110) calculates that, between 1978 to 1987, Poland's machine exports as a percentage of its total exports declined (and to both the developed West and the Third World). Müller (1987: 15) adds that Polish hard-currency exports of electrical engineering products? plunged by 36% between 1980 and 1985.

An analysis of East Germany's trading patterns shows that this country was having economic problems as well. Unfortunately, the extent of the country's technological problems were not known, since its statistics were so unreliable. According to the last statistical yearbook of the Honecker regime, for example, the share of exports to the industrialized West as a share of all exports increased by only 0.1% between 1980 and 1988—that is, the share of exports to the West of total exports fell from 27.4% of total exports to 27.5% (my calculations, based on *Staatlichen Zentralverwaltung für statistik* 1989: 240). In contrast, the first yearbook after the collapse showed that, between 1980 and 1985, exports to the West as a total of all exports had more than doubled—from 24.1% to 48.5% of all exports (*Staatlichen Zentralverwaltung für statistik* 1990: 277). This shows how unreliable official data was. During the rest of the decade, exports to the West maintained a similar portion of East German exports. Thus, the GDR had become more dependent on trade with the West. Although a greater percentage of GDR exports went to the West, the country did not actually increase its trade with the West. Instead, its exports to the West decreased by 4% from 1985 to 1989. In other words, the GDR actually exported fewer goods during the latter half of the decade, and it also exported less to the West. The country's decrease in exports indicates that its products had increasing difficulties to compete on the world markets. Meanwhile, the country's increasing dependence on trade with the West (which was done without increase the volume of exports) shows that the country was secretly redirecting its trade from the East to the West in order to pay back its debts.

The question still remains about the *quality* of East German exports to the West. Was a third-world pattern emerging, in which the country had to increasingly export low-tech products in order to pay for high-tech imports? According to official statistics, the country's exports of finished goods and machines increased from 1985 to 1989 as a share of total exports, which by itself might indicate that the quality of exports were actually improving. On the other hand, these increases were rather small (around 5%). Meanwhile, exports of fuels declined radically, from nearly 35% of total exports to the West to 15% (*Staatlichen Zentralverwaltung für statistik* 1990: 279). Since total exports to the West had decreased by 4%, and exports of finished goods and machines increased by 5%, then it seems the volume of these exports was nearly unchanged. Thus, there was little change in the quality of exports. The main difference was that, once Gorbachev had stopped subsidizing fuel exports to the GDR, the country was no longer profitable for the GDR to re-export the fuel to the West.

Since the GDR was able to maintain similar levels of exports of finished goods to the West throughout the decade, one might conclude that the country was not facing any major technological problems. Information from the first post-Honecker yearbook, though, indicates that the country was *not* able to compete on the world markets with its finished goods. Instead, the GDR was only able to export these goods by selling them under production costs. Thus, subsidies to non-agricultural industry increased by 114.5% from

1980–1988.[18] If it is true, as Janson claims (1991: 69), that paying back the debt had become the main issue for all economic policy, then it makes sense to support enterprises that export goods at a loss. Of course, the end result is even greater imbalance in the economy, since inefficient firms can prosper by garnering subsidies rather than by improving production techniques. So short-term debt relief is paid for by long-term technological decline. Since the regime had to sharply increase subsidies to the non-agricultural industry in order to maintain export levels of finished goods, one can assume that the country was having increasing problems to compete on the world markets for finished goods.

The ČSSR also had problems with high-tech exports. It was the only country to avoid a debt crisis. Yet it did so by cutting down on trade. According to Štouračová (1989: 55) Czechoslovak trade with developed capitalist countries decreased by 5% from 1975 to 1987. In general, the country was losing its importance on international markets. Štouračová (1989: 297) shows that the country's exports as a share of world trade dropped from 1.21 % in 1970 to 0.93% in 1987, which implies a 23% drop.[19] By lowering trade with the West, the regime could keep down its debts, but it was also less able to purchase new technology.

The declining quality of Czechoslovak goods compared to those of its capitalist competitors was also reflected in the drop in prices for Czechoslovak goods on the world market. By 1986, they were only 66.6% of their level in 1970 (Štouračová 1989: 66). Vintrová (1989: 15) claims this drop was caused in part by the lower quality of Czechoslovak goods, although some of it was also due to the rise in prices for raw materials. Another way of measuring declining comparative quality is to look at the per-kilo prices of exports. Štouračová (1989: 67) notes that, in 1985, Czechoslovak exports to the FRG only brought in an average of 2.99 DM per kilo, as compared to an average of 14.12 DM for all countries and 11.39 DM for neighboring Austria.

---

18. My calculations, based on *Staatlichen Zentralverwaltung für statistik* (1990: 301). Although this does not include inflation, open inflation was extremely low: in 1989, prices were 12.3% higher than in 1980, according to the *Staatlichen Zentralverwaltung für statistik* (1990: 308). Even if hidden inflation is taken into account, the rise in subsidies was certainly several times higher than the rise of prices. This can also be seen by the fact that the share of the state budget going to these subsidies increased from 24.6% in 1980 to 31.4% in 1988.

19. I.e., $(1.21 - .93)/1.21 = .23$.

Finally, many statistics show a decline in exports requiring modern technology. During the 1980s, the ČSSR tried to increase its export of engineering products, machines and high-tech goods to the West (Voráček 1987: 9 and Žabža 1984: 2). This strategy was clearly unsuccessful. The Czechoslovak economist Czesaný (1989: 88) complains that the share exports to capitalist countries from industries that require a high level of scientific research sank from 11.9% in 1975 to 9.4% in 1985. By 1980, Czechoslovakia's share of exports as a percentage of total world exports of engineering goods to developed market economies had fallen by 44% from its 1965 level (calculation based on Levčik 1986: 101). Levčik & Skolka (1986: 49) point out the disparities between imports and exports of high-tech goods in trade with industrialized Western countries. Their statistics show that while exports of communications equipment and electronic components fell by 50% from 1972–1982, imports increased by more than 4% (my calculations). More dramatically, the export of office and computing products fell to only 13% of its 1972 level, while imports rose by 66%.

CONCLUSION ON THE CAUSES OF THE ECONOMIC CRISIS

My conclusion is that changes in technology were the most important reason for the economic crisis. I have not found much support for any of the other common explanations. Perhaps the Soviet-type economies were always inefficient, but that cannot explain why they suddenly became less efficient. Of course, the economic crisis became even worse after the introduction of certain misguided economic policies, but that cannot explain why all of the countries suffered from an economic crisis regardless of their policies. The rise in oil prices did hurt some of the countries, but it also helped others. The USSR, for example, was an exporter of oil. The remaining Soviet-bloc countries had the possibility of re-exporting Soviet oil at higher world prices. They could even export finished petroleum products. In addition, although the East European countries had to pay more for Soviet oil imports, they still paid significantly less than world prices. Meanwhile, there is no evidence that military spending increased in the other Soviet-bloc countries, although they too suffered from economic crisis. Modernization theories cannot explain why the Czechoslovak and East German economies, which in the 1940s were among the most modern in the world, suddenly entered into a crisis.

Instead, I conclude, changes in production technology were the main cause of the economic decline. History shows it is easier to make a five-year plan for coal production than for computers. In Marxian terms, the relations of production prevented the economy from adapting efficiently to changes in the forces of production. This manifested itself in several respects. First, capital productivity declined. Second, statistics indicate that this decline occurred despite large-scale investments in research and development. Thus, the economy was incapable of utilizing the domestic research results. Third, as a consequence of the Soviet-bloc countries' inability to adopt the new technologies, these countries behaved increasingly like Third World countries. They could no longer export finished goods to the industrialized West. Instead, they relied increasingly on exports of raw materials. Meanwhile, since they could not develop the required modern technologies at home, they had to import them from abroad. Their high-tech imports increased, consequently, while their exports fell.

Even if, however, these countries suffered from an economic crisis, and even if the crisis was due to changes in the forces of production, this does not mean the system had to collapse. First, if the rulers had succeeded in reforming the economies, they might have been able to maintain power. Second, even if they had failed to make the economy function better, they might have retained power had they been willing to repress the opposition at all costs. I discuss the failure of economic reforms in the next chapter. The reader must wait patiently until chapters 8 and 9 for a discussion of the reasons why the leaders did not violently repress the opposition.

Chapter 4

A DIALECTICAL MODEL

Notwithstanding the economic problems faced by the Soviet-type countries, the Communist rulers might have been able to stay in power, if they had succeeded in reforming the economy. So the question remains: why, after so many decades of attempted reform, were the results so meager?

I begin by presenting a dialectical model that represents the interaction between economics and politics in the reform process. This partial model forms a part of the complete model that I present in the conclusion of this study. In this chapter, I concentrate on the similarities between the countries. The exact course of events varies in each country for a given period; nevertheless, this simplification goes a long way in explaining the base-superstructure dynamics. I briefly present some empirical descriptions of the four countries to demonstrate that this partial model captures the actual behavior of the regimes. In the

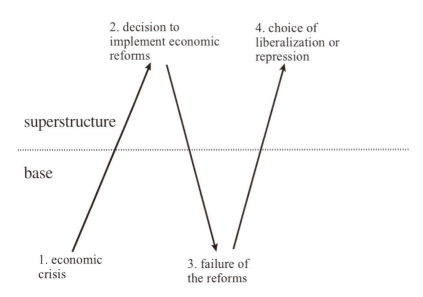

Diagram 1: The Dialectics of Reform Attempts

following sections, I look more closely at the mechanisms which induced this pattern of behavior. However, I do not devote much space here to describing the actual reform proposals in detail. My main concern in this chapter is not to analyze the reform proposals, but rather to look at which groups tended to support reform and which ones tended to fight it.

My partial model has four stages. First, at the economic base the regime faces an economic crisis (stage 1). To alleviate the situation, the regime might decide to introduce economic reforms (stage 2).[1] If the regime chooses the reform path, groups within the ruling corporate entity (including the Soviet rulers) or workers oppose the reforms. Thus, the reforms fail to reach their desired results (stage 3). This leaves the rulers with the choice of either liberalizing the system or reverting to repression (stage 4).[2] By liberalizing the system, they might hope to gain the support of workers and other groups outside of the corporate entity. Furthermore, such steps allow them to remove some of the conservative members of the corporate entity who prefer the status quo. This involves risks, however, since liberalization opens the regime to demands for democratization, which in turn would threaten its power monopoly. Below I give one brief example of this cycle for each of these countries.

Economic Reform in the ČSSR

In the ČSSR in the 1960s, the leaders faced an economic downturn which was not as acute (in terms of structural maladjustment) as the one in the 1980s, but which was nevertheless cause for concern (stage 1 in the diagram). The reform economists worked out a series of measures which they intended to introduce step-by-step, starting in 1968. The original proposal included three main points: 1) price reform, in order gradually to bring most goods to "market equilibrium levels,"[3]

---

1. I am not arguing that the regimes *must* attempt to reform the economy. The cases of the GDR, Albania and Romania in the 1980s show that the regimes at stage 2 can attempt to deal with potential unrest by increasing repression, rather than by reforming the economy. Regimes can also choose to revert to more orthodox, centralized economic policies.

2. The idea of using arrows to show the connection between the base and superstructure comes from Dahlqvist's (1975: 59) theoretical diagram, which shows the chain-reaction between economic and political causes.

3. See Havlik & Levčik (1985: 20), Holesovsky (1970: 15–18), Kosta (1984: 157), Moreau (1965), Šik (1966a: 32) and Typolt (1966). During the first stage, there were to be three price groups: fixed, limited and free. In 1967, before implementing the reform, the authorities decided to recalculate the prices for 25,000 groups of consumer goods. Eventually prices were to be set free and supposedly prices would reach a level in which supply equalled demand.

2) the replacement of mandatory planning with indicative planning at the enterprise level,[4] and 3) measures to increase the connection between wages and productivity.[5]

When General Secretary Novotný tried to slow down the pace of reform, the reformers rebelled and replaced him with Dubček (stage 2). The new leaders were dissatisfied with the country's economic performance, and blamed it on bureaucratic opposition to the implementation of the economic reforms (stage 3). They planned, therefore, to take steps towards greater political liberalization and even democratization. These measures included the removal of censorship, so that the mass media would be able to criticize anti-reformers. They also planned to have a new, democratically elected Party Congress that would replace the hardliners in the Central Committee with reformers (stage 4). In order to gain more support from workers, who were skeptical of marketization, the Czechoslovak leaders also worked out various proposals for setting up worker councils. Before the Czechoslovak regime could take further steps toward democratization, however, the Warsaw Pact countries invaded and put an end to the "Prague Spring."

The post-invasion leadership in the ČSSR had an institutional interest in preventing a new wave of reforms, since it came to power to prevent reforms. By the late 1970s, though, economic problems had re-emerged, so the leaders found themselves back at stage 1. When Gorbachev began emphasizing the need for economic reform, the Czechoslovak leadership felt forced to propose some moderate reforms (stage 2). In 1988 and 1989, for example, the staff of the central planning commission was reduced somewhat. Some attempts were also made at decentralizing some of the decision-making. Some export industries were also freed from most—but not all—centrally determined plan indicators. In 1989, some other enterprises also had the number of plan indicators decreased (see for example Wolchik 1991: ch. 4). These reforms failed to improve economic performance (stage 3). Hence the leaders faced a dilemma in regard to their next

---

4. Kýn (1972: 173–7). However, the state would still influence enterprise behavior through control over investment and taxes. All investments above a certain level would need the approval of the state bank. See Holesovsky (1970: 20), Moreau (1965: 19) and Taborsky (1968: 44).

5. Kosta (1984: 161–2). Šik's original reform package was published as early as 1963; see *L'Express*, 9 Jan. 1967.

move (stage 4). Once the Communist regimes had fallen in the neighboring countries, rising expectations for change encouraged intellectuals to mobilize against the regime. When they had succeeded in gaining the support of the workers, and Gorbachev had refused to intervene, a revolution was under way.

Economic Reform in Hungary

During the economic downturn of the 1960s in Hungary (stage 1), the Kádár regime decided on a wide range of economic reforms known as the "New Economic Mechanism" (or NEM) (stage 2). According to the original reform plans, the state was to limit itself to setting the main national economic objectives. Economic planning would still exist at the ministerial and branch levels. However, the branch directors would no longer disaggregate the plan down to the enterprise level. That is, enterprises would be relatively free from detailed regulation by higher-level authorities. Enterprises were to maximize profits. The enterprise manager would be made responsible for technological development, product patterns, the introduction of new commodities, making new investments, raising credits, and distributing personal incomes. Furthermore, supply and demand would play a greater role in determining prices. Prices for about 30% of all goods would be freely determined. Prices for another 40% would float freely within certain maximum and minimum limits set by the state. Prices for the final 30% would still be fixed by the state (Swain 1992: 100–103).

At first the NEM was fairly successful. The economic problems became much worse, however, in the late 1970s. This was caused in part by developments in the forces of production that adversely affected all the Soviet-block countries. Policy decisions—such as borrowing money from the West—also intensified the crisis. These policy decisions help explain why the crisis was more acute in Hungary than in neighboring Czechoslovakia. During the first half of the 1980s, the authorities tried further economic reforms that increased enterprise autonomy and allowed for the creation of small private firms. These measures, however, failed to improve the economic situation. By the mid-1980s (stage 3), the debt crisis was getting out of control. Encouraged by Gorbachev's policies, the reformists undertook a campaign of political liberalization (stage 4); this ended in an evolutionary, negotiated transition to democracy.

Economic Reform in Poland

The Polish case was in many ways similar to the Hungarian case. While Kádár came to power after an *actual* Soviet invasion, Jaruzelski's rise to the top coincided with a *threatened* invasion. The entire crisis culminated in the *Solidarność* uprising. Although one might argue that Jaruzelski started his economic reforms for political reasons (i.e. to consolidate his power after imposing martial law), the uprising itself was set off by the deteriorating economic situation (stage 1).[6] After declaring martial law, Jaruzelski announced that the reform process would continue (stage 2). The blueprint for radical reform had been worked out several months before the declaration of martial law. According to these plans, enterprises would maximize profits instead of filling plan quotas, and worker councils would run the enterprises. Prices, furthermore, would be brought to market clearing levels. Central planning would only remain to correct market failures and to influence the general structure of the economy.

However, these reforms were only implemented in a watered-down version following the declaration of martial law. The regime suspended the laws on state enterprises and worker self-management. But the authorities did enact some less radical reforms. They increased the price of consumer goods nearly to market levels, although they kept administrative control over prices. They reduced the number of branch industries from nine to four. And they eliminated the middle level of industrial administration (the enterprise associations, that is). Shortly afterwards, they passed new legislation compelling some of the enterprises to recreate their associations, while other enterprises were encouraged to form voluntary associations. The middle level therefore survived (Bartłomiej Kamiński 1991: 51–4).

As the debt crisis grew (stage 3), Jaruzelski concluded that more radical economic reforms were necessary. He also realized that these reforms (such as bringing prices into line with costs and reducing subsidies to industry) would mean deteriorating living standards for most citizens in the short term. Since he lacked the popular support needed for such measures, he tried in various ways to coopt the opposition into sharing responsibility for the economy (stage 4). This liberalization process ended with the semi-free elections of June 1989, which *Solidarność* won.

---

6. I discuss this in later chapters.

Economic Reform in the GDR

In contrast to the other countries, the GDR had only a short period of experiments with reform. The reforms in question, moreover, were comparatively mild. During the economic downturn in the mid-1960s (stage 1), Günter Mittag developed a package of reforms known as the New Economic Policy (stage 2). Although central planning was kept intact, there were some changes in the organization of the planning bureaucracy. The state plan only set targets for finished goods. Enterprises were grouped together in branch organs called *Kombinaten*. These *Kombinaten* took over the responsibility for planning material balances. They were to make sure the necessary inputs were available to meet production goals.[7] In addition, the number of planning indicators decreased. The reforms gave meager results, however, as the economy continued to slide (stage 3), and started coming increasingly out of balance besides. Rather than support more radical reforms, however, Ulbricht tried to placate the populace by pursuing a more independent foreign policy *vis-à-vis* the Soviet Union. This included an attempt to place re-unification with the FRG on the political agenda. This combination of economic failure and a growing foreign-policy independence encouraged Moscow to support Honecker's challenge. With Honecker at the helm, the country returned to orthodoxy (stage 4).

CONFLICTS OF INSTITUTIONAL INTERESTS

A key to the above partial model is the opposition to reform encountered by the regime (stage 3). I analyze this situation by looking at the conflicts of interests on five levels: 1) between the Soviet elite and the East European elites, 2) between the Party elite and the workers, 3) between the Party and the state, 4) between the various levels of the Party apparatus and state bureaucracy, and 5) within the same level of the bureaucracy (both among ministries and between large and small to medium-sized firms).[8]

---

7. See Brus (1981: 186). Sometimes, if they controlled a dominant share of the production of a certain type of good, the enterprises themselves took over responsibility for the material balance.

8. For the sake of simplicity, I leave out the question of the military and the secret service. Very little has been written on this subject, after all, and interviewees are less likely to be completely honest about it. In general, however, since the military belongs to the "military-industrial complex," I expect it to behave similarly to other large industrial organizations when seeking to gain funds. Thus, the military industrial complex comes under the fifth level of conflict described in this chapter (i.e., conflicts within the same level of the bureaucracy).

Diagram 2 shows the first three conflicts. The thicker lines indicate greater influences than the thinner ones. The numbers correspond to the numbers above. ("1," for example, indicates the conflict between Soviet and East European rulers.) For the sake of simplicity, I divide the state and Party hierarchies into three levels:

- The top level of the Party includes all voting and non-voting members of the Politburo and Central Committee, all the secretaries of the Secretariat, and the department heads of the Central Committee. The top level of the state includes all ministers, vice-ministers, department heads, and advisors to ministers.
- The middle level of the Party includes all employees of the Central Committee departments, and all regional and district[9] Party functionaries. The middle level of the state bureaucracy includes all employees working in the national, federal and local administrations. That is, everyone above the level of enterprise manager.
- The lower level of the Party includes all Party functionaries at the workplace and neighborhood level. In the state bureaucracy, all directors of factories and enterprises belong to this level.

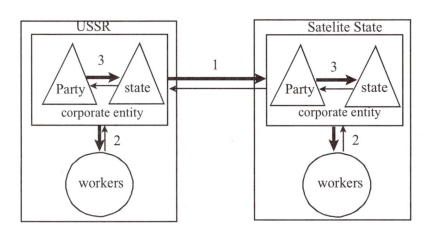

Diagram 2: Conflicts of Institutional Interests

---

9. For cities, the district and municipal levels coincide. The first secretary of the capital city was almost always a Politburo member, and thus a member of the Party elite according to my definition.

In this part of the chapter I concentrate on institutional interests, since most of these conflicts are at the institutional level. The exception is the section dealing with the conflict of interests between workers and the corporate entity. Here I also briefly discuss the workers' postulated interests in gaining control over the productive process. The other sections deal with conflicts *within* the ruling class.

Due to space limitations, I leave out most of the empirical evidence for all cases except the conflict between the Party and the state. For all the other conflicts, there is widespread agreement among researchers. In addition, my interviews with members of the Party-state have confirmed the hypotheses of most theorists for each of the spheres. I believe, therefore, that readers will be more interested in seeing my empirical material for the one conflict which has been essentially neglected by researchers. Moreover, my conclusions on the conflict between the Party and the state might be surprising to many readers— they certainly were to me!

In the other chapters, I concentrate on the incentives which the various groups have in opposing reform. Although there is widespread agreement on these issues, there is less agreement on theoretical approaches. As long as the others discuss the existence of incentives to block or support reforms, their theoretical terminology can readily be translated into terms of institutional interests.

My approach to analyzing the economic reforms differs in two ways from mainstream political-science research on this question. First, it emphasizes the relation between economics and politics. This becomes especially clear in the concluding section of this chapter. Most research in recent years has been actor-oriented. It has concentrated on the decisions of reformist leaders who must balance the demands of hard-liners with the those of the opposition.[10] These divisions are indeed extremely important, and I analyze them in the following chapters. However, many of the actor-based approaches fail to incorporate the interplay between economics and politics. Since they do not make this connection, they do not develop any hypotheses as to *why* the reformers would want to introduce reforms. More importantly still, by concentrating on the reactions of various actors to the reforms, they leave out the effects of the reforms on the economy. Yet the results of these reforms are likely to influence the attitude of all actors towards the reforms.

---

10. Cf. Åslund (1989a: 10), Lewin (1988: 62) and Sakwa (1990: 20, 27).

Second, there has been a tendency for political scientists to view the state as a single institution, while my analysis here follows the more recent trend of "disaggregating the state."[11] Authors using actor-based approaches to democratization have usually concentrated on the ruling factions within a *unitary* state. Normally, they limit their disaggregation of the state to discussions about the need to placate the military. Similarly, many institutionalists have emphasized the role of the state as a unitary actor with its own interests.[12] As Davidheiser (1992: 464–65) remarks, however, the state is comprised of many units, and the degree to which these different units penetrate society affects the pattern of politics.

In this chapter, I disaggregate the Party-state in Eastern Europe by emphasizing the conflicting institutional interests between its different segments. Since the Soviet corporate entity ruled over the leaders of the East European corporate entities, I consider this conflict of interests to be within the Party-state as well. Such an approach does not contradict the use of class analysis. Virtually every sophisticated study using class analysis of a particular society admits that, while the major classes have conflicting interests, they also have conflicting interests within themselves. It is quite common, for example, for class analyses of "Third World" countries to include discussions of the conflict between "national" and "international" capital, while studies of advanced capitalist countries analyze the conflicts between small, middle and large capital.

I go beyond a simple dissection of the state below. I also include the conflict of interests between the Party-state and workers. Since workers comprise a majority of citizens in these societies and since the Communists claim to be ruling on their behalf, the corporate entity needs the passive support of the "proletariat" in order to remain in power. As noted in chapter 2, the corporate entity also has a conflictual relationship with the professionals and intellectuals. For the sake of simplicity, however, I leave out these conflicts in this chapter. These groups are less interesting than workers in a discussion of opposition to economic reforms. As compared to workers, for example, professionals

---

11. In the words of Migdal (1994: 8): "We need to break down the undifferentiated concepts of the state—and also of society—to understand how different elements in each pull in different directions, leading to unanticipated patterns of domination and transformation."
12. A classic example is Skocpol. In her dissertation, *State and Social Revolutions* (1979), she emphasizes state breakdown as an encouragement to rebellion.

have much less reason to oppose reforms. In fact, they may be the major beneficiaries of measures that increase income inequality within society.

For the rest of this chapter, I ignore the GDR. The country only had a short period of economic reforms (in the mid-1960s), and scarcely any information is available about its failed reform attempts.

The main task of this chapter is to show that, *even if* the Politburo had been completely unified in its support for radical reforms, the reformers would still have faced the difficult task of juggling many contradictory interests based in various levels of the Party-state, as well as in society.

THE CONFLICT BETWEEN THE NATIONAL AND SOVIET RULING ELITES

Western literature on Soviet-East European relations is filled with examples of conflicts of institutional interests between the Kremlin and its "satellite states." The most obvious manifestation of the differences in institutional interests between the two sides are the open interventions, such as the Soviet invasions of the GDR (1953), Hungary (1956) and the ČSSR (1968).

If one accepts the logic that leaders have an institutional interest in keeping or increasing their power, then the conflict of institutional interests is clear. National leaders can increase their power by building their own national power base and leaving the Soviet bloc, as the Yugoslav leader Tito did.[13] Such moves obviously decrease the power of the rulers in the Soviet Union, who have an institutional interest in keeping these countries under their control.

It would be a simplification, however, to say that the national and Soviet leaders have diametrically opposing institutional interests. For without the aid of Soviet tanks, none of the East European Communists would have come to power in the first place. Similarly, problems arise for the Kremlin if the East European rulers are faithful Soviet puppets but completely lack popular support. The greater the hatred felt by the populace for its leaders, the higher the costs are for the Soviet Union to repress the people and to keep its stooges in

---

13. Actually, he did not leave the Comintern voluntarily. Rather, the organization voted to expel his country. Although he would have preferred to remain within the organization, he nevertheless *chose* national sovereignty (and thus increased personal power) over subjugation to Soviet dominance. I should stress that this was Tito's choice in the end; after all, he could always have accepted the Comintern's conditions and thus remained a member.

power. At times, therefore, the Kremlin is willing to give some degree of independence to the national Communists.

Nevertheless, a potential conflict is always looming, and it can break out as soon as national and Soviet leaders perceive their institutional interests differently. National leaders might perceive that their country would be better off by pursuing policies of which Moscow does not approve. Or the Soviet authorities might fear that, after having been given a degree of autonomy, these marionettes will becoming popular enough to want to leave their masters and to rely on their own national power base.

Taras (1990: 6ff.) recognizes these tensions. Comparing Poland and Hungary in 1956, he notes that Gomułka and Kádár came to power under different circumstances, which caused the USSR to treat them differently. The new Polish leader, Gomułka, posed a potential threat, since he came to power on a wave of popular support during anti-Stalinist demonstrations. Consequently, his superiors in Moscow forced him to retreat from radical reform and to purge liberals from the Party. As a result, he became less popular and more dependent on Moscow. While Gomułka was a threat because of his popularity, Kádár posed the opposite problem for the Soviet leaders. Since Kádár came to power on the backs of Soviet tanks, he lacked of course Gomułka's popularity. Therefore, the Kremlin allowed him to take reformist measures that could make this "traitor" somewhat more bearable to the populace. According to Taras, this explains why Gomułka progressively withdrew portions of his reforms (including the establishment of workers' councils), while Kádár could steadily increase his dose of reforms over the course of the next decade.

While Taras recognizes the balancing act which the Soviet leaders engaged in, Antoni Kaminski notes that the national leaders had to do some similar juggling (1992: 296):

> The role of a peripheral [general][14] secretary was loaded with conflict. He often had to choose between his loyalty to the Soviet leadership and to the

---

14. Note: Kaminski uses the term "first secretary" rather than general secretary. I have changed it to "general secretary" in order to avoid confusion. In some countries the former term was used, although the latter was used in most. For similar reasons, I have chosen to call the highest Party ruling body the "Politburo" for all of the countries, although in many countries it was actually called the "presidium" instead. The same is true of the name "Communist." In East Germany, the Party actually changed its name to the Socialist Unity Party (*Sozialistische Einheits Partei Deutschlands*), while the Hungarian party was called the Hungarian Socialist Workers' Party. The Polish party was known officially as the Polish United Workers' Party.

society he ruled. The dilemma confronted him not only at the symbolic level but also at the level of strategic economic and political choices. If not kept within limits, the conflict could threaten the integrity of the Soviet block but was alleviated by the awareness of most Communist leaders that they owed their position to factors other than popular support and that they could rely on such support only under exceptional circumstances.

THE CONFLICT BETWEEN THE PARTY ELITE AND THE WORKERS

In my analysis, workers are assumed to have an interest in obtaining control over their surplus production. For the sake of simplicity, lets us also assume that, at the subjective level, all workers are "class-conscious." The workers are aware, that is, of their exploitation. Furthermore, they conclude they would be better off if they could gain control over their production. Now the interesting question is: what are the workers' institutional incentives?

Where the members of the corporate entity are concerned, let us assume the following: they wish to keep control over the surplus product. The question is: how can incentives be structured, at the institutional level, so as to allow the ruling entity to keep control during periods of economic reform? Of course, there are usually differences among the rulers in their perception of the need for reform. For the sake of simplicity, however, let us assume that all Politburo members agree on the necessary economic reofrms. In this case, they face potential working-class opposition in several areas.

First, reforms are likely, at least in the short run, to lower workers' living standards. Workers rebelled openly against rice increases in Poland (in 1956, 1970, 1976 and 1980). In the GDR in 1953, they revolted against increases in productin norms that would have lowered living standards. Other studies have shown that workers engaged in work slowdowns to combat economic reforms which gave management the power to lower wages (Lomax 1990: 54).

Second, market reforms might bring about unemployment. In a society with guaranteed employment, such reforms go against the interests of the potentially unemployed, unless they have a good chance of finding other work (see, for example, Antoni Kaminski 1992: 330–331).

Third, market reforms that give enterprises more autonomy have a special dynamic in Soviet-type societies. For giving mangers complete power would result in them becoming the owners. This would deprive the elites of the corporate entity of much of their power. Thus, the obvious solution for combining a market economy and enterprise autonomy with socialism is some form of worker self-management. In addition, moves in this direction might increase worker support for market reforms that otherwise scare them (since they cause increased insecurity). Steps in this direction represent a trade-off, in which these elites give up some economic power in return for being able to maintain their monopoly on political power. This trade-off, however, is not easy to accomplish, because economic reforms can spark off demands for political reform.

Several authors have noted the connection between economic reforms and increased demands for poltical democracy. In the Polish case, Brus (1988) discusses the dialectics between the need for political leaders to introduce reforms to improve economic preformance and the fear that greater enterprise autonomy and democratically elected worker councils would threaten their power monopoly. Thus, cycles arose in which the regime introduced and then took back reforms. Quite sijmply, it is hard to defend democratic elections to the boards of enterprises while denying these same people the right to elect their political leaders. In Mujżel's words (1989: 14): "A man deprived of the right to co-determine the destiny of his society should not be expected to want and be able to involve himself actively in managing an enterprise."

Again, even if the regime can gain worker support for reforms—by introducing some sort of participation in enterprise deciion-making, for example—the economic reforms cannot go so far as to raise the wrath of the Soviet Union. How far the Soviet rulers will let them go varies over time, but it is always an important constraint that may prevent them from going as far as they would like to.

THE CONFLICT BETWEEN THE PARTY AND THE STATE

In the original Stalinist model of "cadre administration," the state was supposed to be a transmission belt for Party decisions, without any institutional autonomy in decision-making (Balla 1972, Glaeβner 1993, Lipp 1978, and Therborn 1980). The basis for this immense poewr was the Party-state system, in which employment for all important positions within the government and state required the approval of the appropriate Party committee. Beck (1961: 290) provides an example of this power in the ČSSR, where the Party had dismissed entire local governments for having deviated too much from the official line. As Lowenthal (1983) maintains, mass-mobilization regimes tend to be based aroudn the power of one leader, whose death forces the Party to find mechanisms for institutionalizing its power. In his study of cadre administration, Balla concludes that, once the regimes become institutionalized, they have an increasing need to hire experts for managing the technical aspects of the economy. This dilutes ideological vigor; previously, the state had followed Party commands unquestioningly. The institutional interests of the Party and state come into conflict in complicated ways, which vary among levels and ministries. Therefore, I divide this section into two parts. In the first I only deal with the ministers, while in the second I deal with the state bureaucracy.

Finally, since I devote the rest of the chapter to institutional conflicts *within* the Party-state, I concentrate on the realm of institutional interests. Again, there will certainly always be differences among individuals in each institution, but if they have certain institutional interests, then *most* of them will usually act in accordance with these interests. The subjective level becomes more important in later chapters, in which the actual decision-making of certain leaders comes into focus.

The State Ministers versus the Politburo and Central Committee Secretaries

One interesting phenomena about which no one has theorized, to the best of my knowledge, is the tendency for prime ministers to be among the strongest reform advocates in the Soviet-type regimes. During the Brezhnev era, Prime Minister Kosygin was the main reform advocate within the regime.[15] In Hungary in the latter part of the 1980s, Prime Minster Grósz began criticizing General Secretary Kádár for the slow pace of economic reforms. Once Grósz took over Kádár's position, he in turn fell prey to the new Prime Minister Nemeth's criticisms for opposing more radical reforms.[16] In the ČSSR, Prime Minister Štrougal was the most radical reformist within the Politburo. When he resigned, his replacement, Adamec, took over the role as the most radical member of the Politburo.[17]

---

15. cf. Åslund (1989a: 10), Lewin (1988: 62) and Sakwa (1990: 20, 27).

16. Interview with Váss (12 March 1993). See also Batt (1991a: 11–12) and MacDonald (1993: 217–19).

17. This view is also supported by insiders among the Czechoslovak Communist elites. I found this out through personal interviews with Čmejrek (interviewed 23 March 1992), Hoření (interviewed 30 March 1992), Krejčí (interviewed 13 April 1992), Lér (interviewed 3 May 1993), Nevařil (interviewed 30 March 1992), Poledník (interviewed 9 July 1993) Pavel (interviewed 29 April 1993), Sedlák (interviewed 11 May 1992) and Štěpán (interviewed 3 June 1992).

Zdenek Hořeni (interviewed on 30 March 1992), the former editor of the Czechoslovak Communist Party's official daily newspaper *Rudé pravo*, suggests that prime ministers were pro-reformist because, as the official heads of government, they were held responsible for economic failures. Yet they were not responsible for forming the actual economic policies. One can say that prime ministers and important economic ministers have an institutional interest in increasing state autonomy from the Party, so to be able to gain control over their policy decisions. Put in more general terms, if the members of the state bureaucracy want to maximize their control over the distribution of resources, then they have an institutional interest in gaining as much autonomy as possible from the Party apparatus.

Many reform attempts in Soviet-type societies aimed at improving economic efficiency by increasing the state's autonomy from the Party. Even Party elites believed they could boost economic performance by allowing the more capable economic experts at the various economic ministries greater influence over policy. Too much state autonomy, however, threatens the power of the Party elite. Antoni Kaminski (1992: 161) describes this dilemma:

> The problem of the autonomy of the state in a Soviet type of political system is both critical and insoluble. On the one hand, the relative autonomy of the state is functionally indispensable for the efficient exercise of authority. On the other, because of the nature of political controls, autonomy can be achieved only to a limited degree. To this, one important point should be added. In the absence or weakness of all forms of democratic control over the state, should the fetters of party controls be eased, the only outcome would be neither an increase in effectiveness nor an improved efficiency of state activities, but disintegration and disorder countered to some extent by a growing importance of the army or the security police, the obvious reason being that the whole institutional setup that is needed for a responsible government controlled by and accountable to the population is absent.

It is not clear, though, that the army or security police must necessarily step in to fill the void. Why could not the state simply become the center of power and take control over the police and army? It is clear, however, that state autonomy from the Party *by definition* decreases the sphere of the Party's control over the state—and with it the basis of the Party's political and economic power. Thus, while state elites have an institutional interest in increasing their autonomy from the Party, the Party elites have an institutional interest in hindering the state elites from getting out of their grasp. If Party elites decide to give the state more autonomy—in the making of detailed decisions, for example—then they have an incentive to compensate for this loss of micro-control by increasing their macro-control over the state's general decision-making. In this case, the Party leaders give up a bit of the quantity of their control over the state bureaucracy in order to improve the quality of their control. If the Party leaders behave in this manner, the state does not become more autonomous from the Party; instead, the content of its dependency on the Party changes.

Although the Party and state have conflicting institutional interests, the members of both organizations are in a variety of positions. Members of the state bureaucracy *always* have an incentive to carve out more autonomy from the Party. The situation of the Party leaders changes depending on the economic situation. If the economy is performing relatively well, Party elites have no incentive to give the state more autonomy. If living standards are stagnating, however, Party elites must balance contradictory institutional interests. On the one hand, they have an incentive to maintain as much control over the state as possible. On the other, they have an incentive to improve the living standards of the potentially rebellious working class. Yet reforms that improve economic efficiency and raise living standards might require Party elites to hand over more power to the state.

I argue below that these conflicts of institutional interest between the Party and the state hindered the state from becoming more autonomous when the most radical market reforms were carried out in Hungary, as well as when less radical reforms were attempted in Czechoslovakia. I also assert that the Hungarian and Czechoslovak ministers perceived this conflict. I leave out the GDR, since it has minimum experience of economic reforms (except for a few short-lived moderate changes in the mid-1960s). Poland falls somewhere between Czechoslovakia and Hungary. The secondary literature on Poland describes the same problems as in Hungary and the ČSSR. I concentrate on the Hungarian and Czechoslovak cases, because there is no sign that Poland experienced any marked differences. Besides which, I did not interview any former Polish economic ministers.

a) State Ministers: State Autonomy and Market Reforms
A comparison of the Czechoslovak and Hungarian cases shows, that in Soviet-type economies, increased marketization does not necessarily bring about increased autonomy. My interviews with former economic

ministers in the two countries indicates that the Hungarian Party apparatus actually had greater control over decision-making than its Czechoslovak counterparts. The main reason is that the decision to abandon mandatory planning in Hungary meant that the ministries no longer had to make such detailed plans. Instead, they relied more on indirect influence over enterprises through taxation, subsidizing and pricing policy. Since they had less to decide over, the Party apparatus had an easier time controlling them.

Thus, the former Planning Minister in Czechoslovakia, Potáč (interviewed 9 July 1993), claims that although general directives came from the Party, he had immense influence in working out the details of the plans. Furthermore, the government corrected the one year plans. His former assistant, Šťastný (interviewed 28 July 1993), adds that the planning commission had great leeway in deciding over the distribution of funds. He claims Planning Minister Potáč had to work withing the framework of the central plan, but within this framework the planning minister had a lot of space to maneuver in. For example, he could agree to give some enterprises more money without asking the Politburo for permission. Former Vice-Minister and Minister for Heavy Industry Ladislav Gerle (interviewed 17 August 1993) agrees that the Party could not control the detailed decisions. He notes that the Central Committee had two departments which monitored him: the economic department and the industrial department. Together these two departments had around 80 employees plus two deputies, while his ministry and the planning commission alone had around 6,500 employees.

Interestingly, the Hungarian ministers to whom I have spoken claim to have had more autonomy from the Party than their Czechoslovak colleagues. Yet, when I have asked these Hungarians detailed questions about these relationships, the opposite picture has emerged. For example, former Hungarian Finance Minister István Hetényi (interviewed 8 April 1993) claims there was a committee for coordinating economic policy. Its members included the prime minister, the finance minister, the head of the national bank, the head of the Party Central Committee's Department for Economic Affairs, and the economic secretary. After the meetings, the economic secretary decided on the statement to present to the Politburo. Interestingly, the economic secretary never signed the statements himself, but rather had the head of the Party's department for economic affairs sign it, in order to give the economic secretary greater flexibility in his negotiations with the

Politburo. Thus, the economic secretary was clearly the most important person in formulating daily economic policy.[18] If any of the ministers disagreed with the economic secretary, they had the formal right to present their proposal to the Politburo. In practice, though, Hetényi was never able to persuade the Politburo to change its opinions. Hetényi adds that although he mostly agreed with the economic secretary on policy decisions during Hetényi's first four years of holding office, during the last one-and-a-half years he often disagreed with the economic secretary. Eventually, the economic secretary pressured Hetényi into resigning because of their differences. So it was clear who was the boss.

Mátyás Timár (interviewed 17 March 1993), who was finance minister, deputy prime minister and finally chair of the Hungarian national bank, claimed that the initiatives on economic policy still usually came from the Politburo. Moreover, he was only able to communicate with the Politburo via the economic secretary, with whom he met every other week.

Lajos Faluvégi (interviewed 11 March 1993), who was finance minister and then later president of the planning commission, also claims that the state enjoyed more room for maneuver after the initiation of economic reforms. Yet his description of the policy-making process is similar to that given by his Czechoslovak colleagues. He notes that the Politburo made the main decisions, while the government worked out the details. He adds that most ministers were Party members who followed the main Party line, so only details remained. The Politburo kept its veto power over the details of the plans. It normally forced the government to rewrite its plans two or three times before giving its final approval.

One area where the Hungarian ministers seem in fact to have gained more autonomy was in the appointment of new employees. Faluvégi says that management had been a political question previously; later on, however, the ministries appointed managers directly. Hetényi's version is a little more complex. He claims that the Party-state system still existed, but that it became more decentralized in the mid-1980s. Consequently, many decisions now took place at the local and county level of the Party apparatus. This implies that the Party still had power over the state, but that the power had spread to more levels. But

---

18. This view is also supported by former Economic Secretary Nyers (interviewed 8 April 1993).

Hetényi also claims that, later on in the decade, the Party no longer had any clear ideas in practice, so the Party organs normally accepted the ministers' proposals.

Even here, however, it is not clear that the state gained as much autonomy as these former ministers claim. Nyíró Sándor (interviewed 9 April 1993), the former Party secretary for a middle-sized enterprise,[19] claims that in general, the regional, city or district Party appointed the directors to the enterprises. At his firm, the general director had been the first secretary of the municipal Party for the past 17 years. He "chose" this job, because he only had three years left until his retirement. Since he had not worked in business for nearly two decades, he did not have any professional competence. Sándor adds that, in practice, the city government hardly existed; only the Party apparatus was important.

This story shows there were still limits to the economic ministries' control over the appointment of directors. Of course, it is difficult to reach conclusions from only one case. Sándor's critical appraisal of the situation is more believable, though, because rather than remaining in the Party after it transformed itself into a social democratic organization, he joined the hardline splinter group that still claims to be "communist." One would not expect a more conservative Communist to claim that appointments were based more on politics than on skill unless he honestly believed it was true.

Sándor's version also finds support in Csanádi's (1991: 1092) case study of a Party district in Budapest. After the reforms of 1985–86, which decentralized decision-making, enterprise boards were to chose the managers in open competition. The employees in turn were to elect the enterprise boards. In practice, however, Party candidates won up to 80% of the seats of these enterprise boards. The employees calculated rationally that Party members would wield more influence than non-Party members over decisions, for Party members had contacts with people in higher positions within the Party-state hierarchy. Since the Party cell always held sessions within the enterprise before the enterprise board meetings, the Party was able to control the board meetings. Not surprisingly, the boards re-elected around 90% of the former managers. So again, it appears that even on the question of appointing managers, the Party was able to keep its grip over the state.

---

19. The firm's name was Miskolc; it was located in Diósgyőr. It employed approximately 2,000 people.

So far, I have hypothesized that the Hungarian economic ministers might have actually enjoyed *less* independence from the Party apparatus than their Czechoslovak colleagues. Since much of my material comes from interviews, and since the number of interviews is so low, it is difficult to draw any certain conclusions. But at the very least, my findings call into doubt the hypothesis that market-oriented reforms *within* the Soviet-type system bring greater state autonomy. It is also rather clear that the Party had difficulty keeping its hands off the state bureaucracy. Thus, the leaders never found the right balance between their conflicting interests in keeping power and achieving greater economic efficiency.

b) State Ministers: Consciousness of Institutional Interests
Regardless of whether or not the Hungarian state gained greater autonomy from the Party, my interviews with economic ministers in both countries[20] suggests they felt that their interests conflicted with the Party apparatus to some extent. In both countries, these economic officials believed they were more pragmatic than the Party. They claimed that they were fighting for greater realism and balance in the economic development, while the Party was more interested in keeping up consumption levels, even if it meant greater economic imbalance.[21]

Gregory's (1990: 34) extensive interviews with former members of the USSR's central planning authority, Gosplan, basically confirms my finding. These officials were aware that they were often forced to construct unrealistic plans. There were even cases of employees being fired because they insisted on setting realistic targets.

In the Hungarian case, former Minister for Planning Faluvégi (interviewed 11 march 1993) says that he tried to convince the Politburo in the late 1970s to allow prices to rise by 10–12%. The Party elite insisted, however, that inflation remain under 8%.[22] Similarly, former head of the Hungarian National Bank Timár (interviewed 17 March 1993) explains that, in 1984, the Party said that living standards had

20. This also includes the head of the Hungarian national bank.
21. The one exception was Gerle. Not that he denied this; unfortunately, however, I did not have time to ask him about this issue.
22. In a system with controlled prices, this lower rate of inflation meant that there would be shortages and that the imbalance between supply and demand in the economy would increase, as would the imbalance between investment and consumption. Holding down prices, then, meant keeping them below their equilibrium levels.

to increase. He and the finance minister opposed this proposal, but the Politburo refused to change its opinion. Finally, as noted above, former Finance Minister Hetényi claims that the Economic Secretary Havasi eventually pressured him into resigning. He adds that he does not think Havasi was representing his own opinion, but rather that of the Politburo. The top party organ had been pressuring him to give political considerations precedence over economic ones.

The Czechoslovak economic ministers also experienced this conflict of institutional interests. Former Planning Minister Potáč (interviewed 9 July 1993) recollects that the Politburo wanted to increase living standards at all costs. But the social investments involved would be a brake on other economic spheres which he considered important. The Politburo forced him to change the plan. He adds that, during the last five-year plan, the Politburo finally understood how serious the economic situation was. So in 1988 it made changes in the government, and criticized the very same five-year plan which it had forced Potáč to draw up.

Former Finance Minister Lér (interviewed 10 June 1993) also observed tensions between the Party and state over economic policy. He headed a governmental economic commission that was to propose moderate reforms. He reflects that everyone knew that the system must change, but the question was how and when. The Politburo, except for Prime Minister Štrougal, took a wait-and-see attitude. One example he gives was a suggestion to allow individual firms to conduct their own foreign trade. Economic Secretary Jakeš opposed the idea. Štrougal supported it, but for tactical reasons he was not willing to fight for it. Eventually, Lér resigned when one of his reform proposals did not receive any Politburo support.

Bohumil Sucharda (interviewed 4 June 1993), who served as finance minister from 1965 to 1969, asserts that the situation improved during the Dubček era. Still, he claims, the economic secretary, Šimon, was much more powerful than he was. It was usually necessary to get Šimon's support in order to obtain Politburo approval. Sucharda does not remember the Politburo ever endorsing a minister's proposal that did not have Šimon's support. He adds, though, that he and Šimon usually had similar opinions during the reform era.

Judging from the particular persons I interviewed within the state bureaucracy, the perceived conflict of institutional interests between Party and state increased in intensity according to a) the degree to which members of the state organs identified with the state over the

Party, and b) the degree to which they had a "technocratic" educational background. All of my interviewees have in common career routes which they had followed entirely within the state bureaucracy. None of them had ever held any office within the Party apparatus. All of them except Hetényi had been members of the Central Committee at the height of their careers, but they had done so as representatives of the state. Moreover, all of them agreed that Central Committee membership was a honorary title that conferred no institutional influence.[23] The Central Committee merely rubber-stamped Politburo decisions. None of the ministers whom I interviewed had joined this highest organ. Among the Czechoslovak ministers, Potáč actually claims to have refused the offer to join the Politburo *precisely* because he wanted to maintain some independence from the Party. If he had joined it, he would have felt more bound to tow the Party line. He considers himself a rather apolitical technocrat, who came to the planning office directly from the state bank. Similarly, Lér says that he worked his way up the finance ministry's hierarchy. He was not even a Party member when he joined. This was possible because the ministry needed someone with his language skills (he speaks Russian, English and German). Gerle, in contrast, was a Party member at an early stage. Yet he too worked his way up the state machinery, starting at the shop-floor level as an engineer. The three Hungarians were also technocrats; they came from the Karl Marx University[24] rather than from the Party apparatus.

I have gotten the impression, in general, that at least the economic ministers normally come from the state bureaucracy or the research institutes, rather than from the Party apparatus. Former Politburo member Lenárt (interviewed 3 June 1993) goes so far as to claim that one of the arguments used for choosing Jakeš over Štrougal in the succession battle for general secretary was that Jakeš came from the Party, while Štrougal represented the state! This is not to say the Party and state were totally separated. Nonetheless, it appears to have been uncommon for Party functionaries to take over ministerial posts.

Not only did these ministers identify more with the state than with the Party, they also had a more technocratic background. All of them had university degrees in economics or engineering. Politburo

---

23. As former Central Committee employee Hajdu (interviewed 12 March 1993) notes, the Central Committee meetings were formal affairs in which pre-written speeches were given; rarely was anything discussed.
24. Now called the Budapest University for Economic Sciences.

members, in contrast, tended to lack such university educations. In the ČSSR, for instance, Politburo members Lenárt and Jakeš had their training at the shoe factory Bat'a.[25]

For Hungary, Nyírő (1992) calculates that, in 1983, only 4 of the 15 Politburo members were university graduates. Within the Central Committee apparatus, however, over 90% of members were university graduates. Among the university graduates within the Central Committee apparatus, though, by far the largest number held degrees in philosophy (36.2%)—a field that helps little in understanding the practical side of running the economy. Only 12.8% of employees within the Central Committee were economists. Falus (1991: 86) cites a study showing that, while 73% of the heads of central state administration bodies between the years of 20 and 34 years old were university graduates. Among those above 35, slightly more (77.4%) were university graduates. Furthermore, only 47.9% of the heads of party and mass organizations were university graduates. Among those between 20 and 34, the percentage of university graduates drops to a mere 34.5%. Thus, the Party apparatus did not have the same technical skills in economics that the heads of the economic ministries possessed.

The Middle Levels of the State bureaucracy versus the Party Apparatus
Even if the political leaders and the economic ministers might have supported reforms at times, the question is whether they could rely on the state bureaucracy to carry out their program. Here I look at what institutional interests the bureaucrats might have in blocking reforms.

a) Middle Levels of the State: Institutional Interests in Blocking Reforms
Kornai (1986), among others, blames state economic bureaucrats for sabotaging Hungary's "New Economic Mechanism." He complains that, once mandatory planning ceased, they continuously intervened in the operations of individual enterprises. They arbitrarily raised the taxes of profit-making firms and increased subsidies to loss-making firms. In addition, they tried to control prices as much as possible,

---

25. Jakeš studied later at the Communist Party school in Moscow, but its academic level is lower than that of a normal university.

even though the official policy was to move toward free price-setting. Consequently, Hankiss (1990a: 201) complains, managers were more dependent on connections with state bureaucrats than on their ability to perform on the market.

For the Polish case, Wasilewski (1990) suggests that the state bureaucracy had become "relatively autonomous"; after all, it succeeded in foiling the Party's efforts to recruit "loyal experts" to the state administration. The political opinions of loyal experts were not to be a matter of the appointment procedure, as long as they declared loyalty to the constitution.

In both the USSR under Gorbachev and the ČSSR in the late 1950s and during the Prague Spring, the state bureaucracy was also blamed for slowing down reform attempts.[26] Although the state could block reform, it was less successful in asserting a more *positive* autonomy, in the sense of being able to pass its own reforms. Gazsó (1992: 79) concludes that, although the state administrators in Hungary tried to limit the scope of competence of the party functionaries during the 1980s, their "efforts resulted in only minor changes."

Myant (1992: 115) claims as well that the economic bureaucracy usually opposes reforms. In his words: "Planning officials might be the first to feel their interests threatened and also be the best placed to 'sabotage' unpalatable measures." Similarly, Antoni Kaminski (1992: 213) argues that many economic planners would lose their jobs if genuine market reforms were enacted. Winiecki (1990b: 200) also asserts that market-oriented reforms threaten jobs within the economic bureaucracy. Many other authors have also detected bureaucratic opposition to reforms.[27] If economic bureaucrats stand to lose both power and jobs, then they have institutional interests in blocking such market-oriented reforms.

b) A Special Case: Middle Levels of the State and Support for Privatization

Finally, one can question why these same state bureaucrats who supposedly sabotaged all reforms during Communist rule were so willing

---

26. See James (1969: 3) for the Czechoslovak reform attempts in 1958, and Åslund (1989a: 31) for the USSR in the 1980s.

27. See for example Hill & Löwenhardt (1991: 231), Åslund (1989a: 31) and Batt (1991b: 372–3). Zhang (1992) goes even farther and claims that in the Soviet Union, the entire economic bureaucracy—including the ministers—blocked reform attempts, because they would have lost too much power.

to accept much more extreme market reforms after the collapse. Perhaps the answer is that they were not against all reforms. It depends on the *type* of reforms. For example, Gazsó (1992: 87) presents statistics showing that, in Hungary, the state bureaucrats at the middle to high level had much more "convertible skills" (which they could use to gain top jobs in the private sector) than did their counterparts at the same level of the Party apparatus.[28] While 71.4% of the state bureaucrats had "convertible skills," only 28.5% of the members of the Party apparatus fell into that category. In addition, 92.8% of the state bureaucrats had university or college degrees and 26.5% had Ph.D.s, as compared to 57.1% and 7.8%, respectively, in the case of the members of the Party apparatus. Similarly, 69.4% of the state bureaucrats knew a foreign language, as compared to 19.2% of the members of the Party apparatus. The gap increases when knowledge of a second foreign language is included (43.6% versus 7.1%). Thus, state bureaucrats have greater institutional interests in reforms that allow for *private* enterprise than in reforms that allow for greater *autonomy* for *state* enterprises. For if private businesses are allowed, state bureaucrats are likely to take advantage of this, either by starting such enterprises or by finding employment in them. On the other hand, if reforms limit state influence over the economy by giving greater influence to local firms, they restrict the bureaucrats' power and even threaten their jobs, without giving them anything in return.

Hence, Tőkés (1990: 63) remarks that, after the privatization process began in Hungary, nobody "had to be dismissed from the Ministry of Finance when the new government took over because most of the top experts had already left for the private sector." So while state bureaucrats might try to block reforms that limit their control over enterprises without giving them anything in return, *they are more likely to support reforms that can give them direct economic benefits, such as privatization of industry or laws allowing the formation of private enterprises.* Accordingly, Walder (1994: 315) observes:

> As a separate and lucrative private sector emerges, officials find both that these sectors are important new sources of revenue (through rights to tax and impose levies) and also of personal income (by extracting incomes from

---

28. Although Gazsó (1992: 77) writes that his statistics are limited to "persons in leading positions," that fact that his data base includes information on almost 6,000 persons implies that most of the officials fall into my mid-level category.

the regulative powers of officials that affect the incomes of entrepreneurs). They therefore turn away from former allegiances to bureaucratic superiors in favor of new economic activities in their localities.

It is likely, however, that even within the Party apparatus, some of the most talented members supported privatization. For example, some Hungarian researchers to whom I have spoken doubt that there was much difference in convertible skills between members of the state economic bureaucracy and the Party's economic experts in the Central Committee organs, although they admit that such differences might exist among those in non-economic branches. Bunce & Csanádi (1993: 243–4) assert, "in *all* cases, the ex-Communists have managed to convert their political capital in the old system in to economic capital during and after the fall of state socialism." I take this to mean both those from the Party and those from the state. For the Hungarian case, Fellegi (1992: 138–9) observes that, in 1988 and 1989, when it became clear that the system was collapsing, members of the Party apparatus[29] "flocked" into state positions, where they had a better chance of surviving. Many of these people became school principals, factory directors and so forth.

Similarly, Ivan and Balazs Szelenyi (1994: 219) claim that the second economy in Hungary attracted members of the corporate entity to private wealth. They "began to believe it is better to be rich than communist." Once members of the state and Party organs get involved in the "second economy," Staniszkis (1991: 66) reasons, the situation changes. These cadres become willing to support systemic changes that might reduce their profits, but which also provide them with greater security (in the form of legal rights) and free them from the arbitrariness of their superiors.

Nevertheless, to the extent state bureaucrats have more in the way of convertible skills, they have a better chance of surviving on the open market. If the above statistics are true, then a member of the Party apparatus is less likely to have the requisite skills for private-sector work. That means that, even if they use their position to acquire businesses, their businesses are less likely to perform well. In addition, if they are perceived as being less qualified, their appointment to positions within the public sector and newly privatized enterprises is

---

29. He also includes members of the Party's transmission belts (unions, the youth organization, etc.).

more likely to meet with protest. Accordingly, Fellegi (1992: 139) reports that, in Hungary, there were "a relatively large number of strikes" in protest against this tendency of the regime to appoint Party *apparatchiks* to leading positions in enterprises.

Finally, shaping market reforms to meet the material interests of the corporate entity raises moral questions for society. "Political capitalism" (Staniszkis 1991) rewards the most unscrupulous members of the regime and often leads to large-scale corruption as in China. If society does not see the new capitalists as legitimate, the lack of popular support for the reforms may mean the persistence of political crises.

If Party radicals are serious about reform, if they discover the state bureaucracy blocks market socialist measures, and if they find *"nomenklatura* privatization" too unpopular or morally too noxious, then the alternative is for the reformists to appeal outside the regime— to the populace—for support. Strong societal support can act as a counterweight to attempts by conservative cadres to reverse radical reforms. As Csaba (1989: 22) points out:

> All meaningful reforms imply a relevant redistribution of power at the cost of the political centre and of the bureaucracy. On the other hand reforms are changes that are by definition initiated and managed from above. Thus a reform is always a *contradiction in adjectio*, as the political centre must act in an 'enlightened' way, against at least some of the former bastions of its own power.
>
> Therefore the ability to gain new allies, to *rally truly social support* [my italics] behind its project is crucial for the overall outcome of a reform.

THE CONFLICTS OF INTEREST BETWEEN DIFFERENT LEVELS OF THE PARTY-STATE

In the previous section, I discussed differences in institutional interests between the state economic bureaucracy and the Party elite. In so doing, I disaggregated the state into two levels: the ministerial level and the middle level of the state economic bureaucracy. At both levels, there are conflicts between the state and the Party, although the conflicts sometimes differ. I will concentrate now on conflicts of institutional interest between different *levels* of the Party-state complex. I already went into detail above about the institutional interests of mid-level state bureaucrats in blocking reforms, although I put this conflict in the perspective of the state having different interests than the Party. In this section, I concentrate on the middle level of the Party apparatus, since I have already discussed the middle level of the state. The reader should keep in mind, however, that the middle level of the state bureaucracy also has similar institutional interests in blocking reforms. In theory, moreover, one should expect members of the lower levels of the Party-state to have different institutional interests than members of the middle and upper levels. Unfortunately, I have not found much material on this matter, so I leave it out of my analysis.

Many theorists have pointed out that members of the middle level of both the Party and the state have incentives to block market reforms.[30] For example, Winiecki (1990b: 200–1) claims that the middle levels of both organizations tend to oppose economic reforms. When parameters (such as interest rates) replace commands, the number of employees needed by the economic bureaucracy decreases. For it takes many more administrators to plan such details as the volume and prices of millions of goods for thousands of enterprises than it does to set a global interest rate for borrowing money. Reforms hurt mid-level members of the Party apparatus as well. In the Soviet-type system, these people often have influence over the appointment of "their people" to well-paid jobs in the state bureaucracy. This type of patronage can give them some amount of wealth and power. Market-oriented reforms reduce these apparatchiks' pool of well-paid jobs in the bureaucracy. Thus, they suffer from a decline both in job opportunities for themselves and a decrease in the number of jobs whose appointments they can influence.

Although members of the middle layers in general have incentives to oppose market reforms, members of the Party apparatus are hit harder than members of the state bureaucracy. For even if a Western-type of market capitalism were to be instated, the state ministries would still need to keep many of their employees. In contrast, the positions of the mid-level members of the Party apparatus become obsolete during a transition to a capitalist economy—especially if it is accompanied by political democracy. If the dictatorship disappears, a state bureaucracy is still necessary and powerful, but being the district or regional secre-

---

30. See, for example, Batt (1991b: 372–3), Brus (1989: 264), Csaba (1989: 23), Hill & Löwenhardt (1991: 231), Kargarlitskij and Staniszkis (1991: 129). According to my knowledge, Mandel (1991: 63) is the only theorist who claims that the members of the middle layers support reforms. He contradicts himself, however, later in the same text (1991: 156) and admits that large groups within the Party-state are hostile to reforms that threaten their positions.

tary of a party in a normal political democracy does not bring much power.

As Gregory (1990) notes, the regional and district Party secretaries have an important function in the planning process. Since state planning is on the branch level, local Party secretaries must assume responsibility for the regional balance. They also have the function of making sure that the plans are fulfilled (interview with Potáč 9 July 1993). Often, moreover, they are involved in the choosing of managers, which gives them even more power (interview with Hoření 30 March 1992). All of these tasks disappear with the introduction of market reforms. In addition, as discussed above, members of the state bureaucracy are in a better position to get involved in private enterprise than are members of the Party apparatus—not least because they have more marketable skills.

THE CONFLICTS OF INTEREST WITHIN LEVELS

Conflicts of institutional interest did not just exist between levels of the Party-state. They also existed *within* levels of the state apparatus. In particular, there were conflicting interests between functional and branch ministries, and between large and medium-to-small enterprises.

Conflicts of Institutional Interest between Ministries

Swain (1992: 153) points out there is a conflict of interests between functional and branch ministries. Market-oriented reforms take power away from branch ministries (that is, ministries for a particular industry) and give them to functional ones (such as the finance ministry). Swain (1992: 134) notes, for example, that the 1981 Hungarian economic reform abolished the three industrial ministries and replaced them with a ministry of industry. According to von Czege (1987: 132), this new ministry had only had half as many employees as the previous three combined. The abandonment of planning means that the branch ministries lose their importance. Meanwhile, the finance ministry and the national bank gain in importance. These organizations control the most important mechanisms for regulating a market economy (taxes, subsidies, credit policy, etc.).[31]

---

31. Adam (1987: 623) says the same thing indirectly: "The reform has increased the role of fiscal policy." Obviously, the finance ministry controls fiscal policy.

Conflicts of Institutional Interest between Enterprises
Much more has been written about conflicts of interest between enterprises than about conflicts of interest between ministries. The basic
argument has been that large enterprises have much greater bargaining
power than small or medium-sized enterprises. Therefore, they are
more likely to get subsidies and access to inputs from the state. Thus,
they have institutional interests in opposing reforms that would make
them more dependent on the market. For the same reason, smaller
firms have stronger institutional interests in supporting increased
enterprise autonomy, since they would not be at such a disadvantage
on the market as they are in the bargaining process.

Here is a rather long quote from Short (1990: 26) on the matter in
Hungary after the abolition of mandatory planning:

> Although smaller firms had some success [in lobbying], the power and pres-
> tige interests associated with large firms put increasing pressure, especially
> through members of the Central Committee, on the government to provide
> greater protection for large firms. Large firms, both through direct relation-
> ships with the political leadership and by virtue of their significant share of
> output and employment in the overall economy, therefore had sufficient
> bargaining power to increase subsidies and tax exemptions granted to them
> from the center. Investment retained most of its inefficiencies: dependence
> on the center continued as funds for large investment projects were still
> allocated by the state.

Thus, in spite of attempts at giving enterprises more autonomy, large
firms could utilize their bargaining power to keep up their economic
position regardless of their market performance.

Winiecki (1989: 375) also provides the rationale for economic
bureaucrats and members of the Party apparatus to give priority to
the large firms:

> bureaucrats and apparatchiks accord privileged access to scarce resources to
> those enterprises with the highest aggregate political clout, that is to say,
> overwhelmingly to large enterprises in priority industries. The rationale for
> such a pattern of resource allocation is that it is in their own interest to do
> so. Their colleagues, representatives of the same ruling stratum, who have
> been appointed managers, benefit materially from their position directly
> (best paid jobs, 'perks' associated with their position) and indirectly (acqui-
> sition of goods and services in short supply at below market prices), while
> bureaucrats and apparatchiks benefit from having their colleagues there
> indirectly (from the flow of goods and services arranged by their manager

colleagues). Let us add in passing that both managers and bureaucrats and apparatchiks benefit also from the opportunities for the firm to appoint their relatives to relatively well paying non-*nomenklatura* jobs with great scope for shirking.

CONCLUSION

In this chapter I have claimed that at the institutional level of the Soviet-type system there are five areas of conflicting institutional interests: 1) between the Soviet elite and the East European elites, 2) between the Party elite and the workers, 3) between the Party and the state, 4) between the various levels of the Party apparatus and of the state bureaucracy, and 5) within the same level of the state machinery—i.e., between different ministries and between large and medium-to-small firms. As a result of these conflicts of interest, reform proposals normally reflect many compromises between groups. Thus, the proposals themselves are often inconsistent. Once the leaders submit these proposals, moreover, they usually face once again the resistance of the various groups in implementing them—especially the middle levels of the Party apparatus and of the state bureaucracy.

I do not go so far as to claim that successful reform would have been impossible altogether. Instead, I take the less deterministic line that it would have been extremely difficult. The Hungarian case shows that Communist leaders and members of the middle level of the bureaucracy can support radical transformation when they no longer believe the system can be saved. Yet, it is interesting that the Hungarian leaders concluded it would not be possible to gain bureaucratic support for *within-system* reform. Rather, they decided it was better to scrap the entire system and to reward the bureaucrats by giving them the possibility of taking over formerly state firms. It is easier to get members of the corporate entity to support political capitalism than to get them to support democratic market socialism. The former system gives them the opportunity to become private entrepreneurs, while the latter threatens their position.

Finally, I should add that, while conflicts of interest exist in Western capitalist societies too, the institutional conflicts are greatly intensified in the Soviet-type system. The reason for this is that the leaders of Soviet-type regimes were never able to find legitimate ways of channeling these interests. In Western democracies, citizens are able to organize around their interests. This includes forming political parties, unions, employers associations, and other organizations that promote their interests. This does not mean, of course, that all organizations have *equal* influence. In fact, many critiques have claimed that capitalists enjoy much greater influence than do members of other interest groups. Nevertheless, by allowing citizens to participate in multiparty elections and to organize freely, these regimes have won a much greater degree of legitimacy than the Communist-led regimes did. Under a system in which one group enjoys monopoly power and claims to be the sole representative of society, all attempts at organizing around group interests ultimately question the system itself.

Chapter 5

THE RISE OF GORBACHEV AND THE FALL OF LEGITIMACY

So far I have emphasized the economic causes for the collapse of the Soviet-type regimes in general. Some authors have concentrated either on the loss of legitimacy which plagued the Communist-led regimes, or on Gorbachev's role. While agreeing with these authors on the importance of legitimacy and of Gorbachev, I will maintain in this chapter that both aspects are heavily connected to the economic crisis. Not only did economic decline eat into the regimes' legitimacy, it also made it possible for Gorbachev to come to power. Furthermore, once Gorbachev did come to power, the economic crisis probably induced him to introduce more radical reforms than he had originally contemplated. Once in power, however, the actual decisions which Gorbachev made were in no way predetermined. Thus, I do leave room for the influence of actors. Perhaps my most controversial assertion is that Gorbachev did not try to promote reforms in Eastern Europe. In fact, he did much to hinder the reformist groups from gaining power in the ČSSR. Nor did he encourage reforms in the GDR. He was basically passive toward the East European states. Given these regimes' lack of popular support, though, Gorbachev's passivity in the end came close to actual support for change.

Below I examine these two political aspects of the collapse in general. As in the previous two chapters, I concentrate on the similarities between the four countries. Just as the economic crisis hit all four countries, Gorbachev's rise to power and the loss of legitimacy also affected all four. It is first in Part III that I discuss the causes for the differences in the process of collapse. I begin this chapter with Gorbachev's role. Then I discuss the loss of legitimacy.

THE GORBACHEV FACTOR

Everyone agrees that Gorbachev was instrumental in the collapse of the "satellite regimes" in Eastern Europe. For instance, Stokes (1989: 21) postulates that letting Eastern Europe go "was not a socio-economic imperative or a structural necessity...." Rather, it "was the outcome of a policy conceived and introduced by a particular individual, representing a significant strain of Soviet thought...." Rush (1993: 23–4) goes even further in stressing Gorbachev's role. He labels the former Soviet leader "a remarkable figure" and claims there were no other potential Gorbachevs available at the time. He adds that if Gorbachev's supporters had known the extent of his dissatisfaction, they never would have elected him to the post of general secretary.

Although few deny Gorbachev's importance for the collapse in 1989, there is less certainty over his actual behavior toward the East European regimes. Was Gorbachev an active player pushing his teammates in Eastern Europe into following his reforms? Or was he a passive bystander, who helplessly watched the satellite countries drift out of orbit? Of course, whichever view one chooses, one still cannot deny Gorbachev's importance. For even if he was passive, the mere decision *not* to prevent the changes in Eastern Europe separates him dramatically from his predecessors. Yet, even if he strongly influenced the process of collapse, he did so in a certain socioeconomic context. This context made it easier for him to come to power in the first place. Then it influenced the policy options open to him. I examine his foreign policy, therefore, within this context.

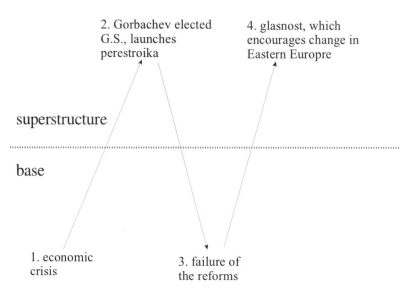

2. Gorbachev elected G.S., launches perestroika

4. glasnost, which encourages change in Eastern Europre

superstructure

base

1. economic crisis

3. failure of the reforms

Diagram 1: The Dialectics of Reform in the USSR

Certainly, the economic crisis was extremely important. Without an economic crisis, the conservative Soviet Politburo probably would have not been willing to risk its future by choosing an unorthodox person like Gorbachev for the post of general secretary. At the institutional level, the various groups with different institutional interests hindered Gorbachev's efforts to carry out the intended economic reforms. He had to go further, therefore, than he had originally intended. When he faced opposition within the corporate entity, he decided to liberalize the political system. By opening up the conservative elements to pressure from the media and populace, he tried to purge his conservative opponents.

The base-superstructure framework from chapter 4 captures the dialectics of the situation. Diagram 1 shows this framework once again, although modified for the specific Soviet case. The Soviet Union faces an economic crisis (stage 1). The leaders realize that some changes are necessary to fight the economic stagnation, so they elect Gorbachev. The new leader launches a moderate economic reform, *perestroika* (stage 2). This fails, partly because of resistance within the Party apparatus and the state economic bureaucracy (stage 3). To fight this inertia, he embarks upon political reform, *glasnost*. This, in turn, influences developments in Eastern Europe (stage 4). Actually, he announced political reform simultaneously with economic reform, but he did not begin emphasizing *glasnost* until the first economic reforms had failed. Since I discuss the economic situation (stage 1) in chapter 3, I begin here with stage 2.

Gorbachev's Election (Stage 2)
It was by no means predetermined that Gorbachev would come to power. If Brezhnev's health had been as good as Dieng Xiaopang's, or if Chernenko had miraculously recovered from his sickness and lived for another 10 years, then the outcome might have been very different. For example, at the trial of the Communist Party in 1992, several witnesses testified that, shortly before Chernenko died, the Party was planning to revive the Stalin cult and to start a big wave of arrests (*DN* 19 October 1992). Nevertheless, even if events would not have run the same course without Gorbachev, *without the economic crisis there probably would not have been a Gorbachev phenomenon.*

There are several indications that the leaders were extremely divided when they elected Gorbachev. They knew he represented change, even if the elites had no idea that the changes would be so radical. So it is unlikely the conservative Politburo members would have supported him if they did not also feel that society was stagnating. Already three months before his election, Gorbachev had made his reformist leanings clear at a Central Committee ideological conference by using terms such as *perestroika*, "self-management," "democratization" and *glasnost* (Åslund 1989a: 26 and Sakwa 1990: 6). The mere fact that the conservative, sick and ageing Chernenko defeated Gorbachev in the struggle for the throne after Andropov's death indicates how divided the leadership was. Gorbachev's election to the post of general secretary was highly disputed.[1] According to some rumors, Gorbachev was elected by just a single vote in the Politburo.[2] Hough (1989: 5) cites Ligachev's speech at the 19th Party Conference, where he openly stated that Gorbachev did not at first enjoy the support of the majority of the Politburo. He would not have become general secretary without the support of several non-voting members of the Politburo—including the KGB chief Viktor Chebrikov and some regional secretaries.[3]

The mere fact that the KGB supported Gorbachev indicates the degree of the crisis. For the KGB was the organization with the most

---

1. For example, Bialer (1986: 110) reports that, before Chernenko died, members of the "old guard" (including Gromyko and Grishin) "made a last stand against Gorbachev." They launched Romanov as a counter-candidate. Knight (1988: 62) indicates as well that the vote for Gorbachev was close; he writes that KGB chief Chebrikov "initially supported Gorbachev and his vote was crucial to the latter's election as general secretary in March 1985." If one person's vote was *crucial* for the election, then it must have been an extremely close vote.

2. See for example Seiffert in Kuhn (1993: 15).

3. Hough sees this as proof that the Central Committee does in fact have power over the Politburo. I will maintain in the following chapters that at least in Eastern Europe, the Central Committee was normally just a rubber-stamp organization. But even in the case of Gorbachev's election, the fact that non-voting members had some influence does not necessarily mean that the Central Committee had much influence. It is more likely that the KGB as an organization was able to sway the vote. Everyone was afraid of the secret police in all of the Soviet-type countries. Since the KGB held the leaders under constant surveillance, they could at any time be accused of corruption or of holding deviating opinions and thus conspiring against the regime. Finally, although the Central Committee *normally* was a rubber stamp organization, the Central Committee always existed as an organ that under certain circumstances could exercise the influence that it formally held. This could happen when the Politburo was extremely divided and some leaders were willing to risk the sacred Party unity. However, such occasions rarely arose. If the Central Committee on a rare occasion asserted itself, however, this does not mean it was a powerful organization. The support of the various organs of the Party apparatus was probably much more important for Party policy than was the support of the Central Committee. While the Central Committee was a large organization that only met a few times a year, the Party organs connected to the Secretariat functioned all year long, with their own research institutes. These organs suggested policies to the Central Committee secretaries, and they had the resources for monitoring the state administration, enterprises, mass organizations, etc.

detailed information about the seriousness of the crisis. Thus, its leaders were more aware than most elites about the necessity for change. Yet the KGB was also one of the organizations with the most to lose from radical political liberalization. Much of its power came precisely from its surveillance of citizens. Any steps towards creating a legal-rational *Rechtsstaat* based on the rule of law and respect for human rights would curtail the KGB's power. The organization felt, apparently, that the socioeconomic problems were so urgent that it was worth taking the risk.

Not only did the economic crisis make it possible for Gorbachev to become general secretary, it also strongly influenced his agenda. Improved economic performance immediately became the new general secretary's main policy issue. While Gorbachev's own attitude toward economic policy was decisive, he would have had difficulty obtaining support for economic reforms—regardless of his private opinions—if the economy had been in a better condition. So again, there was a dialectical interaction between structures and actors, between economics and politics. The economic crisis (a structure) made it more likely for Gorbachev to get elected. It influenced his thinking on policy-making and made it easier to gain support for some reforms. Yet the exact type of reforms which he supported was not predetermined, and the decision to support reforms set off a new dialectical dynamic.

Gorbachev's Foreign Policy during this Period
Gati (1990: 65) detects an "early Gorbachev" from 1985 to 1988 who had a more conservative foreign policy than the Gorbachev of 1989. The early Gorbachev wanted to maintain stability in Eastern Europe. Thus, he was content to allow the conservative regimes in the GDR and ČSSR to continue their orthodox policies. At the same time, he had a favorable attitude toward the Polish and Hungarian regimes. Their experiments in economic reform made good laboratories for Soviet policy makers. This does not mean he encouraged them to take more radical measures. Rather, he gave them great flexibility in deciding their own policies. As Gati (1990: 70) observers:

> While by 1988 the Soviet Union had begun to be tolerant toward and even supportive of Polish and Hungarian experiments..., it was still reluctant to pressure either its Brezhnevite allies elsewhere in Eastern Europe or the Stalinist Ceauşescu regime in Romania to undertake serious reforms. ... [Gorbachev] was concerned that radical change would spark persistent instability.

Gorbachev's cautious attitude comes out in his behavior toward Czechoslovakia in 1987. This was a crucial year, because a battle over the general-secretary post broke out within the Party. The two main candidates were Prime Minister Štrougal and Economic Secretary Jakeš. Štrougal was the most radical reformist within the leadership, while Jakeš was an uncharismatic and uninspiring conservative. As former head of the Party Control Commission, he was responsible for the post-invasion normalization purges of the 1970s. Over half a million members had to leave the Party for the crime of having supported the Prague Spring. When Gorbachev visited Prague that spring, expectations were quite high among the populace that the Soviet leader would try to rehabilitate the Prague spring and pressure the Czechoslovak leadership into making radical changes. The Czechs and Slovaks were disappointed.[4] Gorbachev praised the Husák regime. He even recalled his visit to Prague in 1969, one year after the invasion, when the country had 19 youth organizations. In Gorbachev's opinion this showed that chaos had reigned in the consciousness of the country's youths![5] To make sure that nobody would think he was actively promoting reforms in the country, Gorbachev said in one speech during his visit "we are far from intending to call on anyone to imitate us" (Saskwa 1990: 340).

Everyone whom I interviewed agrees that Gorbachev showed no signs of supporting reforms during his visit in 1987. The historian Viliam Plevza (interviewed 6 March 1993), the official biographer of former General Secretary Husák, claims that both Husák and Politburo member Colotka wanted to speak to Gorbachev during his visit about re-evaluating the Warsaw Pact invasion of 1968. The Soviet leader refused to speak about this subject. In addition, Gorbachev sat near to Jakeš and made a toast to him. His hosts interpreted this as support for the future Czechoslovak general secretary, because such behavior deviated from normal protocol. Others have told me that Gorbachev could defend the action because both Jakeš and Gorbachev had known

---

4. Cf. Gati (1990: 69), Mlynář (1988: 122–129), TAZ, 13 April 1987 and Smith (1992: 326). Smith claims that huge crowds chanted "Gorby! Gorby!" and then implies that Gorbachev used his influence to replace Husák with "a more reform-minded party secretary, Milos Jakeš." I will make it clear that most reformists in Czechoslovakia believe that, to the extent Gorbachev intervened on Jakeš' behalf, it was not to support radical reforms, but rather to prevent them.
5. See for example Mlynář (1988: 127–8).

each other from their studies at the Party school in Moscow. They had further contact during their time as agricultural secretaries. These observers agreed, however, that his toast was also interpreted as possible support for Jakeš.[6] Plevza adds that, during Jakeš's visit in Moscow in December 1987, he spoke to Gorbachev's advisor Smirchov about re-evaluating 1968. Again, the Soviet side refused to speak about this hot subject. Plevza concludes that a change in the evaluation of 1968 was a precondition for real change in the ČSSR, but that the Soviet leadership made such a transformation impossible.

After Gorbachev's visit, the struggle for succession to the Czechoslovak throne intensified. Sedlák (interviewed 11 & 12 May 1993), formerly Štrougal's main political advisor, claims that the reformists had planned to put forward either Štrougal himself or the younger Pitra as their candidate for the post. They would have been happy with either one, but they believed Pitra lacked experience. Husák had promised Štrougal he would kick out the hardliners such as Bil'ak and Jakeš from the Politburo and bring in new people. Štrougal also pressured Husák into resigning, so that he or Pitra could take over. They expected help from Gorbachev and sent him a message about their plans, but he refused to support them. Their contact man in Moscow, Oleg Bogomolov, from the Institute for Socialist Countries, hinted that Jakeš would be elected and that Štrougal's people should be willing to work with him.

Almost everyone with whom I have spoken confirms aspects of Sedlák's story. For example, Plevza agrees that Husák tried to gain Soviet support for Štrougal. He met with Gorbachev at the end of October, during the celebrations of the Russian Revolution. Gorbachev replied that he had already promised Jakeš and Bil'ak that Jakeš would become the new general secretary. Plevza also agrees that Husák wanted to remove Bil'ak and Lenárt from the Politburo, but that they had the support of Moscow. According to Plevza, both of these hardliners, as well as Jakeš and Indra, worked for the KGB.

Former Central Committee Secretary and non-voting member of the Politburo, Poledník (interviewed 6 April 1992), also agrees that Husák "strongly supported" Štrougal. He adds that as far as he knew, Gorbachev did not have any preferences for the post of general

---

6. Unfortunately, I have not written down these conversations in my notes, so I am not sure exactly who has made these comments, although I believe it was both Čmejrek and Sedlák.

secretary; it was clear, however, that he was not against Jakeš. He adds that Husák had discussed the issue both with Gorbachev and with the Soviet embassy in Prague, but he does not know the contents of these discussions.

Even Jakeš confirms much of Sedlák's story. He claims that Štrougal led the pressure on Husák to resign. He probably did so in the mistaken belief that he would become the new general secretary. Jakeš agrees that Husák was reluctant to hand over his position to him. Husák claimed that he was preparing Pitra for the post.[7] Jakeš also maintains that, although the Politburo kept Moscow informed on the debates of the Czechoslovak Politburo, Gorbachev did not try to influence the Czechoslovak Party on the leadership question.

Finally, Jakeš blames Gorbachev for blocking reforms even after 1987. For example. Jakeš alleges that he took up the question of Soviet troops in Czechoslovakia. Gorbachev replied that they would remain in the country as long as NATO had troops in West Germany. Former researcher for the Central Committee Institute for Foreign Affairs, Čmejrek (interviewed 23 March 1992), basically confirms this, but claims that Jakeš took up the issue indirectly via his foreign minister.

Gorbachev's cautious policy continued throughout 1988. Gati (1990: 75) quotes an interview with the Soviet leader from the *Washington Post* on May 22, 1988, in which he still defended the Warsaw Pact invasion of Czechoslovakia. Gati (1990: 93) adds that Gorbachev "could not yet decide what to do" in Czechoslovakia. Similarly, in the East German case, Gati (1990: 95) notes that Gorbachev did not "assert himself" until October 1989—several months after waves of mass emigration, and several weeks after the mass protests began.[8] Thus, there is no evidence that the "early Gorbachev" tried to induce his East European allies to pursue reformist policies.

The Failure of Economic Reforms (Stage 3)
At first Gorbachev was rather orthodox in his economic reforms. During his first year in office he emphasized the need for greater discipline. This included a campaign against alcohol, a stricter system of

---

7. Jakeš told me this in an interview on 9 April 1992. He has repeated the part about Husák supporting Pitra in a published interview appearing in *Reportér*, no. 17, 1991.
8. Actually, Gati does not give any dates on this page, but later in the book he makes it clear that Gorbachev's interventions came during the celebration of the 40th anniversary of the GDR, and in the days shortly thereafter.

quality control at enterprises, and a struggle against unearned income. Other measures included a restructuring of investments towards more modern technology and "technocratic fine-tuning"—such as the intro-duction of new wage scales (Åslund 1989a: 67). According to Gill (1991: 238), this policy shows that Gorbachev initially believed that, "fundamentally, there was nothing wrong with the Soviet politico-economic structure."

Perhaps Gorbachev did not really appreciate, originally, the extent of the country's problems. Then he underwent a learning process, in which he progressively realized that greater change was necessary. Yet *even if* he had secretly been a radical reformer from the beginning, it is not clear that another economic policy would have been politically feasible. Since his election was so close, he did not possess any mandate for radical change. Suggestions for radical economic reform would have certainly met stiff resistance. Thus, it was more prudent strategically to start with traditional measures aimed at "perfecting the economic mechanisms." Once he tried this and failed, it would be easier to convince some of the skeptical *apparatchiks* to support more radical measures.

As Gill (1991: 239) notes, Gorbachev became progressively more radical after the Party Congress in February–March 1986, emphasiz-ing greater enterprise autonomy and the like. Yet as Åslund (1989a: 180) observes, it was difficult to obtain the cooperation of the Party and state organs in carrying out these reforms. By 1987, Gorbachev's economic advisors had become convinced that "far-reaching democra-tisation" was "the only way of breaking the harmful power of the bureaucracy over the economy." Hence the need for more *glasnost*.

Glasnost (Stage 4)
Although Gorbachev first spoke of *glasnost* before becoming general secretary, he began emphasizing this aspect of the reform process after his first attempts at economic reform had failed. This is not to say he had made no attempts at political change before this. On the contrary, he had tried continuously to consolidate his power by replacing con-servatives in the apparatus with reformists. In the first stages, however, it was easier to replace cadres for being corrupt or too old. After his attempts at economic reform, though, he could begin attacking conser-vatives for sabotaging his program, and he could start replacing cadres for ideological reasons. Furthermore, to gain support for his economic reforms within the Party apparatus, it was necessary to invoke a sense

of urgency—that society was declining and that something had to be done. It was logical, therefore, to start a campaign for greater openness, so that the mass media could begin reporting about the actual problems in society. Without a critical appraisal of the situation in the media, it would be difficult to convince cadres that society really was facing important problems which required radical change.

Again, I am not claiming Gorbachev had no choices. His situation was not structurally predetermined. He could have decided in 1987 that it was better to ally himself with the conservatives, on the grounds that the bureaucratic resistance to radical economic reform was too strong. He did not need to risk opening Pandora's box by continuing with the reform process and fighting for political change as well. Nevertheless, as O'Donnell & Schmitter (1986) demonstrate, once leaders start wandering down the path of liberalization, they eventually reach a point where they can no longer make credible threats of retrenchment. If they retreat, they risk losing power to their hardline opponents within the regime. So if Gorbachev had suddenly decided to revoke *glasnost* a few years later, it is likely the liberals would have abandoned him, while the hardliners would already have become so angry with him that they would have tried to replace him with a true conservative.

O'Donnell & Schmitter base their model on the reformist leaders, who must balance between regime hardliners and the radical opposition. The model could also show Gorbachev's attempts to balance the reformist East European regimes against the hardliners in his own regime. After years of having preached *glasnost* and non-intervention, Gorbachev would have found the costs of using force in the satellite states to be immense. It would have forced him to line up with the hardliners at home—that is, precisely those who had blamed Gorbachev's policies for creating "chaos and disorder" both domestically and internationally. How could Gorbachev support democratization at home if it were dangerous abroad? Gorbachev would have had to retreat from *glasnost*, and thus economic reform at home as well. As stated above, his new alliance with conservatives probably would not have lasted long. They would certainly have tried to replace him with a someone more to their liking.

Gorbachev's dilemma was not limited to maintaining domestic support for his rule within the Party apparatus. He also wanted to solve the country's economic problems. He perceived that radical reforms were necessary obviously influenced his domestic policies. But since he believed the economy faced serious problems, he was less likely to intervene in Eastern Europe. On the contrary, he was certainly aware that military invention would have been costly economically. And not merely in terms of the military costs of fighting a war. As Smith (1992: 326) reasons, it was extremely expensive to continue controlling the satellite states. The East European countries received raw materials from the USSR at prices well below world levels, while the USSR paid inflated prices for East European manufactured and consumer goods. Furthermore, military intervention would have damaged relations with the West. Gorbachev believed his country needed Western technology to modernize its industry, which made him dependent on good trade relations with the NATO countries.

Gorbachev's policy of *glasnost* certainly influenced developments in Eastern Europe as well. Conservative leaders became afraid, while reformists became optimistic. Hopes and expectations of change rose among the populace as well. Once Gorbachev allowed semi-free elections in Poland and the formation of a non-Communist government, other East Europeans became increasingly hopeful that similar change could occur in their own country. When Gorbachev failed to prevent the opening of the Berlin wall, the Czechs and Slovaks realized he would not support a violent solution in their country either. After all, he had been willing to let East Germany go after his country had fought two world wars against a united Germany; he would hardly be more interested in keeping Czechoslovakia.

The question, however, remains: did Gorbachev actively support these changes in Eastern Europe in 1989, or did he remain as passive as he had been in the previous period?

Gorbachev's Foreign Policy in the Glasnost Period: Poland

Gorbachev might have been passive during his first years in power, but many observers claim that, by 1989, he was actively pressuring the Czechoslovak and East German leaders to undertake reforms (cf. Jowitt 1992: 256 and Schöpflin 1993: 235). Some day—when researchers have complete access to all of the archives—we might find support for these assertions. The available evidence so far, however, indicates that Gorbachev continued his passive neutrality. The irony of course is that, for the East European regimes, neutrality implied support for change. The East European regimes had been propped up by the Red Army. Consequently, the decision to withdraw this support made the satellite regimes so weak that it became easy for society to blow them out of the Soviet orbit. Under such circumstances, it was not neutral to be neutral. Nevertheless, my sources indicate that

Gorbachev's support for change was passive and indirect, rather than (as others have claimed) active and direct.

Poland was the first test for Gorbachev. Former General Secretary Jaruzelski (1992) speaks warmly about the Soviet leader in his memoirs, but gives no indication that Gorbachev tried to influence the negotiations with *Solidarność*. In an interview (published in *Aftonbladet/Kultur* no. 3/95), Jaruzelski claims that he never discussed the Round Table discussions personally with Gorbachev. Rather, he sent the Central Committee secretary Czyrek to Moscow to inform the Soviet leadership *after* the Polish leaders had already decided to start negotiations. Thus, the Polish Communists did not give Gorbachev a chance to interfere with their decisions.

Similarly, former Politburo member Reykowski (interviewed 23 April 1993) adds that, to the best of his knowledge, the Soviet Union did not try to influence the negotiations. As leader for the Round Table discussion group on political reforms, the Soviet Union would have certainly contacted him if the Soviet leaders had wanted to influence the negotiations. Reykowski claims, however, that although he met with many of the Eastern and Western embassies, he had no contact with the Soviet embassy. Gati (1990: 168) writes that, after the elections, Prime Minister Rakowski talked to Gorbachev on the telephone about the process. He does not know, however, what Gorbachev actually told Rakowski. For good reason, he assumes Gorbachev did not *object* to a non-Communist prime minister, but we do not know whether Gorbachev gave Rakowski any advice, or whether he merely acquiesced, saying it was Poland's internal affair.

Gorbachev's Foreign Policy in the Glasnost Period: Hungary
The next big test was Hungary, where the reform Communists advocated completely free elections even before the Polish agreement. Váss (interviewed 12 March 1993), a former advisor to Politburo member Pozsgay, relates the following story. Pozsgay was the main advocate of accommodation with the opposition, and well as being the Politburo member in charge of the negotiations; as his advisor, therefore, Váss came into contact with both the Soviet and American ambassadors. He claims that, before 1988, the Soviet embassy meddled constantly in the internal affairs of the Hungarian leadership. The Soviet ambassador was an oldtimer, and he did not understand the changes that had begun in that year. He therefore became passive. Rather than making demands as in the past, he merely tried to keep himself

informed. The meetings became less frequent than before 1988. When the ambassador did meet with Pozsgay and his staff, he asked questions instead of expressing his views.

The American ambassador, in contrast, was extremely active. He met Pozsgay quite often and was not afraid of making demands. At first, he was worried that the changes were going too quickly. He did not want radical transformation to destabilize Gorbachev's position in the USSR. Eventually, when he was more certain of Gorbachev's position, he began making demands for more radical change. Not only did he meet often with Pozsgay, he also had intimate contact with Prime Minister Nemeth. They were even tennis partners! The most ironic story that Váss recalls is the time when the American ambassador took the Soviet ambassador to a meeting of opposition leaders at a peace exhibit. The American ambassador introduced the opposition leaders to the Soviet ambassador. Thus, he assumes that through the efforts of the American embassy, the Soviet embassy kept in contact with the opposition. Váss concludes that Gorbachev did not try to influence developments in Hungary. If the Soviet leaders had really thought Hungary was important, they would have sent a stronger person to that post.

This does not mean the USSR did not influence the Hungarian Politburo. For example, Bruszt (1990: 381) observes that, in December 1988 (when it looked like Ligachev might take over), the hardliners in the Hungarian Politburo went on a counter-offensive. When it became clear Gorbachev had defeated the conservative challenge, the hardliners backed off. Again, this indicates that Soviet events influenced East European politics, but in an indirect manner rather than actively.

Gorbachev's Foreign Policy in the Glasnost Period: The GDR
The GDR provides the obvious exception. Or does it? Here Gorbachev "clearly" intervened by warning his East German comrades: "history punishes those who act too late!" Krenz (1990: 87) writes in his memoirs that he saw this as a signal to act. One week later, Krenz replaced Honecker as general secretary.

This story would do well in a Hollywood film. Reality, though, is often less heroic. In his interview book *Gorbatschow und die deutsche Einheit*, Kuhn discusses this statement with both former leaders. Gorbachev claims he was thinking about the USSR—*not* the GDR—when he made the famous statement (Kuhn 1993: 48). Krenz confirms this. When he visited Gorbachev a few weeks later in the USSR, the

Soviet leader claimed he had been misunderstood. He had meant the USSR when he made his famous speech (Kuhn 1993: 54).

In the best seller *At The Highest Levels*, Beschloss & Talbott (1993: 134) claim Gorbachev was active in the decision to open the wall. Their version is that Krenz, full of doubt and uncertainty, panicked and called Gorbachev. When he asked the Soviet leader what to do, Gorbachev replied that he should open the wall to let off some steam. Again, reality was less heroic. Krenz remembers that, already in his first statement as the new leader on October 24, 1989, he announced that he and his team would work for free travel. He added that they were working on a new law. This law did not go far enough to meet the population's expectations, so the Politburo asked Prime Minister Stroph and Interior Minister Dickel to work out a more radical version. Krenz read out their proposal word for word at the Central Committee meeting on November 9. The members approved it. Later that evening, Schabowski read the statement on TV, and East Germans immediately started their pilgrimage to the wall (Kuhn 1993: 62). All of these steps were taken *independently* of Gorbachev.

The East Germans did not inform the Soviet leader of this decision until *after* the wall had been opened! The following morning (on November 10), Krenz sent Gorbachev a telegram (Kuhn 1993: 66). Although Krenz did not call Gorbachev and ask him what to do before opening the wall, he did not have any reason to fear that Gorbachev would criticize the decision. During their meeting on November 1, Gorbachev had told Krenz that the renewal process would not succeed if Germans did not have the opportunity to visit each other (Krenz's version in Kuhn 1993: 57). Gorbachev's advice came far short, however, of suggesting that Krenz tear down the wall.

Falin, the former head of the Central Committee Section for International Questions, agrees that the Soviet leadership was basically non-interventionist on this question. He alleges that the East German leaders Krenz, Schabowski and Modrow came to the Soviet embassy in Berlin to discuss liberalizing border controls. The ambassador received the message from Moscow to tell the East Germans that it was their own affair what sort of border controls they should maintain (Kuhn 1993: 64).

Gorbachev's Foreign Policy in the Glasnost Period: The ČSSR
Czechoslovakia is another country where Gorbachev allegedly actively worked for change in 1989. Both Bradley (1992: 56) and *Time*

Magazine (11 December 1989) report that Gorbachev contacted the Czechoslovak General Secretary Jakeš in the summer of 1989. The Soviet leader demanded that Jakeš take three steps. First, Jakeš was to repudiate the Warsaw Pact invasion of the country. Second, he was to re-instate all the purged members of the Party. Finally, he was to remove all of the collaborators from the Politburo—except Jakeš himself.

Unfortunately neither Bradley nor *Time Magazine* reveal any of their sources. Nobody with whom I have talked has confirmed the Gorbachev story. Krejčí (interviewed 7 June 1993), a former advisor to the reformist Prime Minister Adamec, claims that if Gorbachev had written such a letter, the Adamec camp would have certainly found out about it. The closest thing I have come to a confirmation is a statement by former Politburo member Štěpán (interviewed 3 June 1993). Štěpán says nothing about Gorbachev's trying to influence Jakeš, but he claims there was a plan to purge the leadership of everyone tainted by collaboration in 1968–9. He says nothing in this context, however, about either Gorbachev or Jakeš playing any role in this. In addition, his account differs from *Time Magazine*'s where the dates are concerned. While *Time* alleges the purges were to take place in October, Štěpán speaks of the December Central Committee plenum.

Until the archives are opened for researchers, we can only speculate about Gorbachev's role. If Gorbachev had really wanted, though, to pressure Jakeš into creating a pro-reformist Politburo, it would have been logical for him to have cooperated with the reformist wing of the Party as well. The reformists were gathered around Prime Minister Adamec and former Prime Minster Štrougal. Yet the former advisors to these prime ministers deny that the Soviet leader took any such action. Krejčí (1991: 25) writes that Adamec sent his press secretary Pavel[9] to Moscow in May 1989, in order to obtain support from Gorbachev for Adamec's reform line. He left empty-handed, however. Pavel himself (interviewed 29 April 1993) verifies Krejčí's statement. He adds that the Soviet leaders were so busy with their own problems that they had already written off Czechoslovakia. Gorbachev might have had his reasons for distrusting Adamec, or Adamec's advisors

---

9. Even though he acted as a press secretary, his official title was "director of the press department," because the Central Committee never officially approved his appointment.

might have lied. Still, I have found no convincing evidence so far to believe that Gorbachev actually pressured Jakeš into making reforms.[10] Another time when Gorbachev allegedly intervened in the ČSSR was during the student demonstration on November 17, 1989. At that demonstration, the police viciously attacked the students. One of the injuries was reportedly fatal. It turns out that no student died. Instead, an agent of the Czechoslovak secret police, StB (*Statní bezpečnost*), faked the death. The parliamentary commission that investigated the event hypothesized in its preliminary report that the KGB had been behind the faked death. According to the conspiracy theory, the KGB wanted to encourage an uprising against the hardliners, so that reform Communists from the Prague Spring could come back to power.[11] The parliamentary commission reversed itself, however, after having investigated the events further. It concluded there had not been any foreign conspiracy.[12] The StB connection will probably be a hot debate topic for many years to come. Until all of the archives become available for researchers, the final parliamentary report remains the best documented and reasoned investigation of the matter. In addition, even if it turns out that the KGB was somehow involved in these events, that

---

10. There were also indications that the Soviet leadership was re-evaluating the invasion, because it allowed the press to question it. Thus, on September 17, 1989, the Soviet newspaper *Izvestia* published a letter from former Czechoslovak Foreign Minister Jiří Hájek supporting the Prague Spring leadership. Not only was Hájek one of the leaders of the Prague Spring, he was also one of the leaders of Charter 77. Later that month, a Soviet television interviewed former General Secretary Dubček. The interview was broadcast on Leningrad television in October and word of this spread throughout Czechoslovakia (Gati 1990: 179). Such actions do not necessarily imply that Gorbachev was trying to pressure the Czechoslovak leadership. It is just as possible that these Soviet journalists took these initiatives independently of the Soviet leadership. Gorbachev might have simply decided that it would go against the principles of *glasnost* to censor such reports.

11. The former ideology chief of the Prague Spring, Mlynář, was supposedly to be the new leader. He was an obvious choice, since he was one of the leaders of Charter 77, and he had been friends with Gorbachev from their student days at the Party college in Moscow. The versions I have heard of the story are that Mlynář either refused to play his assigned role, or that he was willing to become the new general secretary, but pulled back when he arrived in Prague from his Austrian exile and realized he did not have any popular support. For support of the conspiracy theory, see *DN* (31 May 1990), Schöpflin (1993: 235), interview with Zbořil (December 1990). Wheaton & Kavan (1992: 35) recapitulate the conspiracy theory, but add that the results of the parliamentary inquiry were inconclusive.

12. For a summary of the conclusions, see *Prague Post* 4–10 February 1992. The final report was published as *Závěrečná zpráva vyšetřovací komise FS pro objasnění událostí 17. listopadu*, Prague: Nakladatelství Futura. It was also published in the newspapers *Rudé pravo* (in three parts from 5–7 February 1992) and *Svobodní slovo* (on 4 February and 6 February 1992).

does not automatically mean Gorbachev was behind the plot. It could just as well have been a faction within the KGB.

Again, the issue is not whether Gorbachev influenced events in Eastern Europe, but rather whether he *actively* tried to promote change. My contention is that he was rather passive, deciding to let the East European countries solve their own problems. Since these regimes were unpopular and had come to power behind Soviet tanks, Gorbachev's neutrality obviously weakened these regimes and encouraged the opposition movements. Still, there is an important difference between portraying Gorbachev as an active reformer and portraying him as a passive retreater.

Not only did the economic crisis make it possible for Gorbachev to come to power, it also deepened the legitimacy crisis of the Soviet-type regimes. "Legitimacy" is a much less tangible concept than "economic crisis." It is not possible to measure legitimacy as one can do with economic growth. It is less clear, moreover, how to define it. As far as I know, no researcher has ever asked rulers the question: "on what do you base your legitimacy?" If ever one posed this question, one would likely receive different responses from the same leader at different times. In addition, no leader would likely admit to having, e.g., a "charismatic" legitimacy.

The case of the former Communist-led regimes becomes complicated, since several different types of legitimacy might be applicable, depending on *what* the theorist wants to explain, and in *which periods* in *what countries* the theorist is interested. For instance, Gill (1982) is undoubtedly correct in stressing the importance of charismatic leadership for establishing the Communist-led regimes in Russia and China. He points out that both Stalin and Mao purposely created a personality cult to legitimize their power. The same certainly holds true for other Communist leaders, such as Hoxa in Albania or Castro in Cuba. Even Tito in Yugoslavia meets the usual criteria for being a charismatic leader, although his cult of personality was not nearly as strong as those in the other countries.

Yet such a usage of legitimacy is not fruitful for my purposes here, for two reasons. First, charismatic leadership might have been important in *establishing* the Soviet-type regimes in some countries. However, once the Communists had consolidated their power and the original charismatic leaders had died or lost power, their successors were usually sterile, uninspiring *apparachniks*.[13] It is hard to imagine less charismatic leaders than Brezhnev and Chernenko in the USSR, Husák and Jakeš in the ČSSR, Honecker and Krenz in the GDR, Kádár and Grósz in Hungary, or Gierek, Kania and Jaruzelski in Poland.

Second, even the original leaders in the satellite states were rarely as charismatic as those in the countries where the Communists had come to power on their own. For example, the names of Mao and Castro often come up in discussions of charismatic leadership. But I have yet to hear anyone mention Ulbricht or Gottwald in this connection.

So, while some earlier Communist leaders like Stalin or Mao might qualify as charismatic leaders, a traditional Weberian analysis of legitimacy does not hold up well for the four countries in this study. Whether rational-legal, charismatic or traditional, a regime needs, according to Weber, the support of the populace if it to be legitimate. Citizens must believe the regime is rightfully theirs. In the East European countries, Communist rule rested on Soviet tanks rather than on popular support. The Communists lacked popular legitimacy, then, but are there other forms of legitimacy they might have possessed? This has been the question plaguing Sovietologists.

Some theorists, such as Przeworski (1986), agree that the regimes lacked popular legitimacy; they argue, therefore, that we should discard the term. Przeworski notes that regimes can maintain power for long periods even without enjoying popular legitimacy. He believes they can continue ruling until alternatives arise. The problem is that he does not define the term "alternative."

Heller (1982: 45) uses the notion of *alternatives* more clearly. She writes:

> According to one of Max Weber's formulations, a social order is legitimated if at least one part of the population acknowledges it as exemplary and

---

13. There are some slight exceptions. One could argue, for example, that since Stalin was Lenin's successor, it was Lenin and not Stalin was responsible for establishing the Soviet-type system. Against this, most Sovietologists would undoubtedly agree that the system was still in flux when Lenin died. Stalin was clearly instrumental in shaping the Soviet Union's institutional structures. Another possible exception is Ceaușescu, who was Romania's second Communist leader. He did establish a cult of personality, but the events of 1989 show he did not possess—at least in the latter years of his rule—the charismatic hold of a Stalin or a Mao over the population.

binding while the other part does not confront the existing social order with the image of an alternative one seen as equally binding.

Heller (1982: 46) goes on to admit that, in the Soviet-type societies of Eastern Europe, both of these requisites are absent. Basically, the only part of the population which acknowledges the system as legitimate is the ruling elite itself. At the same time, "the overwhelming majority of the population *does* have an image of an alternative order, namely that of the West European or North American liberal-legal state, which is acknowledged by them as exemplary." Obviously, the East European citizens had this image of an "exemplary" alternative system well before the collapse of the system. In fact, one could even claim they had this image from the very inception of Communist rule. Thus, the mere existence of alternatives in Heller's sense is not enough to bring down a system.

Rychard (1992) implies that oppositional organizations can supply the alternative. He claims that, in Poland, *Solidarność* did just that. Again, the problem is one of definitions. Does the mere existence of an oppositional organization imply an alternative? In that case, the dissident organizations KOR (Committee in Defense of the Workers) in Poland and Charter 77 in the ČSSR were providing alternatives more than one decade before the collapse. Moreover, the regime collapsed in the GDR, where no such organizations existed until *after* the mass flight from the country began. In Hungary, new political parties emerged during the last two years of Communist rule, but the opposition was actually encouraged by the reform Communists to form parties.[14] So they were more the *effect* than the *cause* of the Hungarian collapse. If the organizations must be strong and well-known, than only *Solidarność* meets Rychard's criteria. If one requires these organizations actually to offer an alternative vision of a society, then there is even less support for Rychard's argument. The anti-Communist coalitions that came to power in Poland, Hungary and the ČSSR won the elections more for their anti-Communism than for their ability to offer a plausible alternative policy. As Ivan and Balazs Szelenyi (1994: 228) note: "neither KOR, nor Charter 77, nor any Hungarian dissident movement churned out its political or economic alternative to the regime until they were handed over the reins to power." Habermas

---

14. I discuss this more in chapter 6.

(1990) therefore calls the transformations "rectifying revolutions," changes marked by a "total lack of ideas that are either innovative or orientated towards the future."

Legitimacy from the Top

I have noted above that several authors have claimed it was not the loss of legitimacy that was not important for the collapse of the Soviet-type regimes, but rather the existence of alternatives. I criticized this "alternative" argument, claiming it does not provide a fruitful alternative to the legitimacy argument. Or to play with words, the "alternative" alternative turns out not to be an alternative. I will now develop Di Palma's (1991) notion of legitimacy from the top. Most legitimacy approaches to describing the collapse of the Soviet-type regimes have in common some of the basic aspects of Di Palma's concept. The main elements of legitimacy from the top are the following:

- Legitimacy is based on fulfilling goals, rather than on obtaining popular support. Thus, outcomes rather than procedures (such as democratic elections) comprise the heart of legitimacy.
- At the same time, the leaders claim to be "guided by a superior truth" (1991: 57). Thus, the Party reserves the sole right to interpret its results.

Although the exact goals varied over time and—at least for the Soviet Union—might have contained some military elements, Di Palma sees the main goal as "overtaking and replacing the Western model." After the end of Stalinist terror, the leaders dropped their visions of world revolution. Instead, their goals translated into non-revolutionary phrases about superior economic performance.

Basing legitimacy on economic performance raised problems for the regimes. Di Palma (1991: 61) writes that "the more general abandonment of salvationist language and the adoption of more mundane middle-range goals opened the way for more articulate citizens to verify whether those goals had been met." This encouraged the opposition to become more critical, and it influenced the rulers as well. For when dissidents pointed out that the Communists had not reached their goals, the leaders began to lose confidence in their ability to rule. How could they believe themselves to possess a monopoly on Truth, when their policies were clearly failing? Consequently, the economic downturn in the mid-1970s set into motion two simultaneous processes: the rulers became weakened by increasing doubt in their own ability to rule, and the members of society were increasingly encouraged by the visible cracks in the regime's legitimacy from the top.

Ideological Legitimacy
Although I basically agree with Di Palma's argument, I prefer the term "ideological legitimacy" to "legitimacy from the top." It is a much less awkward phrase. Furthermore, legitimacy implies popular support. Most of the populace must believe the regime truly represents society. In a feudal system based on traditional legitimacy, the subjects might not like a particular king, but they support the monarch's right to rule because it is part of the nation's tradition. If support for a Communist or a king only comes from the top, then it is not a question of legitimacy, but rather of the pure exercise of power.

Even if the Soviet-type regimes never gained complete legitimacy in the sense of gaining popular support for the system, they certainly tried. How else can one explain the massive propaganda campaigns? Why have elections at all, if the regimes did not want to gain some amount of legitimacy? Why the mandatory courses in Marxist-Leninist or the May Day parades etc.? All of these legitimization attempts have in common their ties to ideology. They were attempts to convince the populace that in accordance with Marxist-Leninist ideology, the Party indeed represents society's best interests in general, and the working class' interests in particular. The claim to have a monopoly of interpreting Truth comes directly from ideology.

In addition, even if the Soviet-type regimes failed to gain complete legitimacy, at least in the beginning of their rule, they probably enjoyed the support of several segments of society. Most people who joined the Party before it came to power probably did it for ideological reasons. Opportunists who did not all believe in the ideology had no reason to join before it had a good chance of gaining power. Many workers also supported the Party at first. Except in Czechoslovakia, it is unlikely that a majority of workers in 1948 would have chosen the Communists as their first alternative. Yet many probably had the Party as their second alternative. In the years directly preceding the Communist takeovers, the Parties were able to mobilize workers for mass demonstrations in all four countries. Many of the other workers were probably willing to give the new regimes a chance at first. Finally, idealist intellectuals in all four countries flocked to the Communist organizations. Again, they might not have comprised a majority, but they included many of the most prominent intellectuals, including the playwright Brecht in the GDR, the philosopher Lukács in Hungary and the author Andrzejewski and film director Wajda in Poland. Thus, even if the system was never completely legitimate, one can still observe a loss of its partial legitimacy if these segments stop supporting the system.

Below I briefly discuss the support for the two main elements of ideological legitimacy: the monopoly of Truth and legitimacy based on meeting economic goals. I also assert that many authors have made similar claims, but in different phraseology. Then I proceed to examine empirical evidence for Di Palma's conclusions that society became more critical and that the regimes lost confidence in their ability to rule.

The Monopoly on Truth

The law on the "leading role of the Party," which was enshrined in the constitutions of the Soviet-type regimes, guaranteed the corporate entity the sole right to interpret truth. Fehér & Heller & Márkus (1983) assert that the doctrine of the Party's leading role is the "supreme principle" of Communist rule. It gives the Party the task of representing society's interests.

The anti-democratic attitude of Communist leaders, who really believed that they knew the Truth, comes out clearly in this interview with former Polish Politburo member Jakub Berman. From 1948 to 1956, he was the highest ranking member of the Politburo after the general secretary. The interviewer, Teresa Toranski (1987: 334) exclaims:

> What, then! Part of the nation spits on you, the other part curses you, and about 90 per cent doesn't want you.

Whereupon Berman replies:

> Well, let's say 90 per cent, I won't haggle about percentages. If we were wrong, or if reasons were dreamt up or plucked out of thin air, then of course someone could come along and say it was madness—I agree. But we are right, in the most rational way, and the prospects which I've already outlined for you several times were and are real ones, there's nothing I can do about it. And as to the fact that we were few, and still are, history teaches us that the minority always rescued the majority.

Brunner (1982: 30) cites a similar attitude expressed directly in an East German textbook from 1970:

> The party has the advantage over the masses of working people of its insight into the course of social development in accordance with scientific laws. It is the direct bearer of *Marxist-Leninist* theory. It not only has at its disposal knowledge of the laws of development of socialist society, but also possesses the best preconditions for pushing forward this development under the circumstances prevailing at any particular time.

Such quotes show that the leading role of the Party is based on the notion of the Communist elite having a monopoly on the interpretation of Truth.

Economic Goals

The above quote from the East German textbook also indicates the connection between the monopoly on Truth and legitimacy based on economic performance. For the "laws of development of socialist society" are nothing other than the doctrine of the inevitability of reaching a higher state of socioeconomic development. A society reaches the final goal of communism when the productive forces have become so well-developed that everyone lives in a constant abundance, and all goods are free. Hence, prices lose their function, scarcity disappears, and people engage in work for self-fulfilment rather than for income. At this point, people are able to reach their full "species being," about which Marx wrote in his *Philosophical Manuscripts* (1844). It is also easy to find many statements of Communist leaders stressing the superior economic performance of the Soviet-type system. The most famous is Khrushchev's speech claiming that the USSR would overtake the USA by 1970.[15]

Some theorists have implied the connection of the economy to legitimacy. For instance, Chirot (1991: 9–10) writes that, in the beginning, communism enjoyed a great deal of legitimacy among cadres and many young idealists. For in spite of the problems caused by Stalinist repression, there was "clear economic growth and extraordinary progress." Janos (1991: 108) states that the East Europeans suffered

---

15. Another telling example comes from an interview of Toranski's (1987: 24) with Julia Minc. Minc's husband had been the third-in-command during the original Stalinist regime in Poland. When Toranski asked her "What is socialism?" she replied: "A higher standard of living for everyone, free education and social security."

from "a sense of relative deprivation" when comparing their living standards with the West. The combination of relative deprivation and "cries of corruption went together to delegitimate communist regimes."

During the 1970s, it became more common for theorists to note the connection between economic performance and legitimacy. Some writers, such as Krisch (1982), proclaimed it outright in an article on the GDR. Others asserted this connection indirectly, when writing about of "social contracts." The type of social contract developed in each country varied. For example, Hankiss (1989a: 116) observes that in Hungary,

> the population renounced its rights to power and participation and, in exchange, got a relatively relaxed social-cultural atmosphere, a relatively tolerant administration (by East European standards), a cease-fire on the ideological front, a consensual rhetoric instead of an aggressive and inquisitive one, a kind of cultural pluralism, and the opportunity to build for themselves a more comfortable, West European style of material life.

In the case of Poland, the Bakuniak & Nowak (1987: 407) write, the Gierek regime entered into an unwritten "consumerist social contract" with the population:

> for the price of resigning from political concessions, society received the promise of visible improvements in its living standard in the immediate future. According to the new concept the growth of individual consumption was to be the driving force of development....The authorities, in turn, in shaping anew their own image, resigned from a number of ideological elements dominant in the previous period—these were kept only for more ceremonial occasions... The authorities presented themselves as a pragmatic administrator and distributor of goods, legitimized by rationality and the effectiveness of organizing socioeconomic processes.

Similarly, Meuschel (1992: 222) observes that, when Honecker became general secretary in the GDR in the 1970s, he based his legitimacy on improved living standards. This is clear in his slogan "unity of economic and social policy." This meant that East Germans would no longer be asked to sacrifice consumption for investment. Instead, living standards would increase as much as the economy grew. "Material equality and social security became central legitimizing principles for the Party's domination...."

So far, I have claimed that Di Palma finds support directly or indirectly from many other theorists. Some theorists support the notion that legitimacy was based on a purported monopoly on Truth. Others see the connection between legitimacy and the fulfilment of economic goals. Furthermore, I have maintained that Di Palma's analysis makes sense logically. The claim to have a monopoly on Truth results from the law on the leading role of the Party found in all of the East European constitutions. Moreover, it appears that the Party leaders had economic goals in mind when they proclaimed their belief that the Party used its knowledge to discover the "laws of development" of socialist society. For according to Marxist-Leninist doctrine, a society requires extensive economic progress to reach communism. Such a surplus of production must exist that money loses its value. Furthermore, as many authors have pointed out, the Communist rulers tried to placate their restless subjects with promises of economic improvement.

Below I examine some of the empirical evidence for Di Palma's claim that the loss of legitimacy caused two simultaneous developments: 1) the populations became increasingly critical, as they saw that the claims of superior economic performance differed from the reality; and 2) the elites lost confidence in their ability to rule, as they saw that they could not meet their goals. The rulers were also influenced by the increasing criticism coming from dissidents and other intellectuals.

Society Becomes More Critical: Dissidents

I divide this discussion into two parts. First I examine the dissidents, who articulated the public's criticism of the regime. Then I look at the available data on public-opinion research to see if the populations had become more critical.

Judt (1991: 255ff.) divides the development of dissident thinking in Poland, Hungary and the ČSSR into three phases:

- the revisionist period, from 1956 to 1968
- disillusionment, from 1968 to 1975
- catch-up, from 1975–1989

1956 was an important year. Khrushchev revealed Stalin's crimes. Then the USSR invaded Hungary. These events destroyed the myth of the Party uniting the proletariat on the wings of history (Judt 1991: 255–6). Those events encouraged some intellectuals to re-evaluate their support for the system. Yet the dissidents of that period were still under the influence of Marxist-Leninist ideology. These revisionists believed they could reform the system from within, by appealing to its own ideological premises. Some of the most prominent dissidents of the time either were members of the Party or came from families headed by Party members.

One of the most famous examples of a Marxian critique from this period is Djilas' *The New Class* in Yugoslavia. In Poland, famous Marxian critiques include the works of both the economist Brus and the philosopher Leszek Kolakowski, as well the "open letter to the party" authored by Jacek Kuron and Karol Modzelewski. In Hungary, the members of the "Budapest school" around Lukás were the center of Marxist criticism. Havermann's *Dialectics without Dogma?* in the GDR was also well-known.[16] Since the dissidents used a Marxist framework, they hoped to be able to influence their leaders directly. Schöpflin (1993: 120) asserts that, by using Marxist terminology, they kept the non-Marxist majority outside the conflict. Although the Marxist intellectual dissidents were isolated in this period, one should not underestimate the attraction which socialist ideals still held even for non-Marxist intellectuals. Some advocated democratic socialism, but others were willing to settle for less than completely unhindered multi-party democracy. During the Prague Spring, for example, not even Havel thought it was necessary to allow bourgeois parties. He advocated, rather, the creation of another socialist party that would run against the Communist Party in elections (Havel 1973: 135).

According to Judt (1991: 256), the dissidents became disillusioned in 1968 following the events in Poland and Czechoslovakia. First, students and intellectuals in Poland demonstrated against the closing-down of a play by Adam Mickiewicz. The regime responded by clamping down on these groups (see Adams 1992: 221–2). The Communist rulers also forgot Marx's background. They engaged in anti-Semitic purges, in which they removed almost everyone of Jewish heritage from the universities. In the same year, Warsaw Pact tanks put an end to the Czechoslovak reform movement. Judt believes it was the ease with which the reformist wing of the Party crumbled after the invasion, in combination with the Polish events, that convinced most dissidents the system was no longer reformable.

---

16. During this period, no well-known revisionist critiques were written in the ČSSR.

Finally, in the "catch-up" period, which began in the middle-1970s, the intellectuals abandoned their political ideology and embarked on a struggle to defend human rights. The Helsinki Accords on human rights, which the Communist-led regimes had signed, encouraged the dissidents to demand their regimes' compliance. For example, Czechoslovak intellectuals actually founded Charter 77 in response to the persecution of the underground rock group Plastic People of the Universe (see Gruntorád 1990: 7). Schöpflin (1993: 180) claims that the shift in emphasis from revisionism to the struggle for human rights made it possible for the dissidents to cooperate with other sectors of society.

Perhaps it would have been possible for the intellectuals to gain the support of society by *combining* support for human rights with a positive socioeconomic platform for democratic socialism. This may or may not have been possible, but in any case most intellectuals abandoned their previous socialist beliefs. For instance, the core of the neo-liberal Hungarian party SZDSZ consists of former Marxist dissidents (cf. Ivan and Balazs Szelényi 1991: 132–3). Many of the leaders of the liberal *Občanské hnuti* in Czechoslovakia are former Communist Party members. This includes such leading figures as the first post-Communist foreign minister, Jiří Dienstbier, and the first post-Communist prime minister of the Czech lands, Petr Pithart. Except in the GDR, there was a general trend among dissidents to become anti-socialist.

In the East German case, no prominent democratic figures like Havel or Michnik emerged. Nor did any oppositional organizations resembling *Solidarność* or Charter 77 appear until the uprising in 1989 (Offe 1993: 281). Those intellectuals who did appear on the scene during the revolution continued to support some version of democratic socialism. By this time, however, the public had become more critical of "real socialism," and so rejected their message (cf. Kühnel & Sallmon-Metzner 1991: 378–9).

Society Becomes More Critical: The General Population
Normally, the best manner to determine how critical the populace has become is by comparing data from public-opinion surveys over time. In the Polish and Hungarian cases, however, this is unreliable, because the regimes went through periods of greater and lesser political liberalization, which likely influenced the results. If respondents do not trust in the anonymity of their replies, they are more likely to give critical

responses during periods in which they are less afraid of reprisals for having given "wrong" answers.

Survey data from the GDR and ČSSR give more reliable indications of trends in public opinion, since the regimes in these countries were fairly consistent in their repressiveness. Of course, we would expect persons living under a repressive regime to be afraid of showing the extent of their anti-regime feelings to interviewers. So for any particular year, the percentage of the populace claiming to support the regime will probably be greatly overestimated in public-opinion surveys. Since the two regimes were fairly consistant in their degree of repressiveness, however, we would expect this bias to be equal for all years. These surveys can therefore tell us a lot about the direction of change in public opinion, even if we cannot be as sure about the actual *level* of support or discontent.

During the last years of Honecker's rule, in fact, it is likely that the degree of repression increased (during the "re-ideologization" campaign); surveys showing falling support for the regime may actually, therefore, greatly underestimate the increase in discontent. In the ČSSR, the regime paid some lip-service to reform, but there were no significant moves towards easing the level of repressiveness.[17] The amount of fear felt by the respondents was likely constant across the

Table 1: Identification with Marxist-Leninism (GDR Youths)

	Strongly	With limits	Hardly/not at all
Apprentices 1975	46%	40%	14%
1989 (May)	9%	35%	56%
Students 1975	61%	34%	5%
1989 (May)	35%	46%	19%

Source   Friedrich (1990: 27). For 1975 n = 4,000 apprentices and 2,400 students. Two sets of figures are given for the year 1975, but since data has been collected throughout the survey for the year 1979, *except* in the table showing the population sample, I assume that the second "1975" is a typographical error, and that it should instead read "1979." No data was given on the number of respondents for May 1989.

17. I discuss these matters in more detail in chapters 6 and 9.

Table 2: Identification with the GDR (Youths)

	Very strongly/ strongly	With limits	Hardly/not at all
Apprentices 1975	57%	38%	5%
1983	46%	45%	9%
1988 (May)	28%	61%	11%
1988 (Oct.)	18%	54%	28%
Young workers 1975	37%	53%	10%
1983	55%	38%	7%
1988 (May)	32%	61%	7%
1988 (Oct.)	19%	58%	23%
Students 1975	66%	32%	2%
1983	70%	29%	1%
1988 (May)	52%	45%	3%
1989 (Feb.)	34%	51%	15%

Source   Friedrich (1990: 30). Note: I give the data from 1983 as well, because starting in that year, the wording of the question differed. Until then, the respondents had indicated the extent to which "I am proud to be a citizen of a socialist state." From 1983 onwards, the question was whether "I strongly identify with the GDR." For 1975, n = 4,000 apprentices, 2,180 young workers and 2,400 students. For May 1988, n = 440 apprentices, 150 young workers and 550 students. For October 1988, n = 830 apprentices and 1,250 young workers. For February 1989, n = 3,860 students.

different measurement occasions; the credibility of their replies, accordingly, was probably consistent as well.

Again, the Leipzig youth surveys provide the only available public opinion investigations done under the Honecker regime. The two most relevant surveys were on the question of identification with Marxist-Leninism and with the East German state. Tables 1 and 2 both show a marked decrease in identification both with the official ideology and with the state itself. In both cases, students are more supportive of the system than other groups. Even their support, though, fell by nearly one-half in both cases.

There are two possible reasons why students expressed stronger support for the system in the polls. One is that they had stronger institutional interests in claiming to support the system, since they were more open to reprisals if their ideological purity came into question.

Students were the most vulnerable group, for while persons who had already completed a university education or an apprenticeship might have been able to come back to their profession, students who had been expelled from university would have had difficulty finding qualified work even if they were later rehabilitated by the authorities. Another possible reason why students expressed stronger support than other groups in the surveys is that they actually *were* more supportive. As Reißig (1993: 53) notes, by the 1970s the East German elite were recruited almost entirely from its own ranks. Thus, a large portion of the university students came from privileged ruling class families.

In the Czechoslovak case, survey data is available for the entire population. Unfortunately, the reports of the public-opinion surveys normally only have data for the last few years of Communist rule. Yet the results indicate the populace was becoming more critical of the system. A report delivered in November 1989 showed that the number of workers approving of the way the Party was implementing its leading role fell from 57% in 1986 to 26% in 1989. For other employees (i.e., mostly white-collar professionals), the number fell from 62% to 35%.[18] In a survey of the Slovak population, which generally was less critical of the system than the Czechs, the percentage of the population who saw the economic development as "predominantly positive" decreased from 76% in 1975 to only 17% in 1989. Attitudes towards political development were not much better: 79% saw developments as positive in 1975, but just 28% in 1989.[19] Another survey taken in 1988 showed that 59% of the population believed that reconstruction of the economy was "very necessary" and 30% believed it was "necessary." Meanwhile, 55% felt the democratization of public life was "very necessary" and 34% that it was "necessary."[20] These are quite impressive figures, since one would expect that, under a hardline authoritarian regime, the results will *underestimate* the degree of discontent. It is reasonable to assume that a large proportion of the respondents did not trust that their replies would be anonymous. A pollster at the Federal Institute for Public Opinion Research, Herzmann (1992: 107), accordingly concludes that, by the end of 1987, the majority of the Czechoslovak society was convinced that change was necessary.

---

18. Babůrková (1989: 30). For 1986, n = 1,850. For 1989, n = 2,041.
19. Babůrková (1989: 14). No information was given about the number of participants.
20. Mišovič (1988: 38). N = 3,364.

Although I have not recapitulated survey data here for the Polish and Hungarian cases, the dismal results attained by the ruling parties in the first elections indicate that an overwhelming majority in these countries too also favored change. The Polish Communists did not win a single freely contested seat. Their candidates did not even win most of the seats that were reserved for them, since more than half of the voters crossed out their name. The Hungarian Party changed its name and became social democratic, but it still received less than 9% of the seats in the first free elections. It is more difficult to prove, however, that Polish and Hungarian citizens were more critical of the system in the late 1980s than in the previous decade.

The Ruling Elite

It is quite common for observers to declare the "decomposition of ideology" among the ruling elites in Eastern Europe.[21] Ash (1990c: 19) echoes Di Palma's assertion that the East European leaders lost confidence in their ability to rule. Brzezinski (1989: 234), writing a few months before the *Solidarność* electoral victory, is a little more nuanced in his judgement. In his chart on factors indicating a crisis one of his variables is "Communist party dispirited." He claims this is "very true" for Poland, while it is "true" for Czechoslovakia and Hungary. East Germany is a special case. He believes that the ruling SED had not become dispirited. However, in spite of the widespread declarations that the leaders stopped believing in the system, it is difficult to find evidence to prove this. If, moreover, Brzezinski is correct in his assessment of East Germany, then perhaps some of the leaders did not lose confidence in their ability to rule until *after* the revolutionary mass movements emerged.

For the Hungarian and Polish cases, not much evidence is necessary. The very decision to allow elections—free or semi-free—indicates that the leaders no longer believed in the system. As Waller (1993) notes in his appropriately titled book, *The End of the Communist Power Monopoly*, the monopoly on power was the *basis* of the Soviet-type system. If the rulers base their ideological legitimacy on their monopoly on Truth, then allowing free elections delegitimizes the entire system. This is one issue on which true believers could not compromise. Similarly, if the Pope gave into public pressures and allowed the use of contraceptives, he could still call himself a Catholic. But if he

---

21.   This is the title of a section in Schöpflin's book *Politics in Eastern Europe*, (1993: 159).

reached a compromise with his atheist antagonists and denied the existence of Christ, he could not.

I have already noted that many of the Polish and Hungarian leaders felt that systemic change was necessary in the economic sphere.[22] As support for the lack of faith in the system, I can add some data about Party members. Rychard (1992: 141) cites statistics for Poland showing that, by early 1988, 38% of Party members and 41.6% of the members of the Communist union (OPZZ) supported the legalization of the opposition. Moreover, by August 1989, less than half of Party members approved of their organization's activities. Another indication that the Communists had legitimacy problems was the decline in Party membership. This indicates both that people were leaving the organizations and that the parties had more difficulty recruiting new members.[23] After the declaration of martial law in Poland, Party membership declined radically: from 3,040,000 in 1980 to 2,488,000 in 1982. By 1987, membership had dipped further to 2,129,000, although it increased slightly the following year. In Hungary, Party membership actually increased from 1980 to1985, but it declined from a height of 870,992 in 1985 to 816,662 in 1988.[24]

Statistics about declining Party membership might indicate a loss of legitimacy within the Party itself, but a legitimacy crisis can exist within the Party even without such a decrease, as the ČSSR shows. Although Party membership actually increased from 1,532,000 in 1980 to 1,705,490 in 1987,[25] public-opinion polls showed that the members were fairly critical of the system. For example, when asked what should be done to get non-Party members to help solve society's problems, both Party members and functionaries listed the following as the three most important steps: 1) giving non-members greater opportunities; 2) *glasnost*, open information and allowing criticism; and 3) greater democracy (Baburková 1989: 23).

---

22. See chapter 3.
23. This need not always be the case. If there are mass purges from the Party as in the ČSSR after the Warsaw Pact invasion, the decline in membership may simply reflect Party policy rather than a crisis of legitimacy. No such purges took place in Poland and Hungary in the 1980s, however. After the declaration of martial law in Poland, some top elites lost their positions, but there were no mass purges.
24. The data comes from Staar (ed.) *Yearbook on International Communist Affairs*, Stanford: Hoover Institution Press. For Poland I have used the following years and pages: (1981: 267), (1983: 291), (1988: 285) and (1989: 335). For Hungary I have used (1981: 259), (1986: 296) and (1989: 329).
25. For 1980, I use Staar (1981: 234). For 1987, I use Staar (1989: 305).

Table 3: Opinion on the possibility of people to openly express their
opinions about problems and faults in society in the ČSSR

	Great possibility	Limited possibility	Hardly any	Don't know
Party functionaries	45%	37%	18%	0%
Members & candidates	24%	52%	20%	3%
Non-members	9%	46%	40%	5%

Source Babůrková (1989: 21). n = 101 functionaries, 306 members and
candidates, and 1,637 non-members.

Nevertheless, the surveys show a radical difference in the degree of criticism between Party members and non-members. Table 3, for instance, shows that only a minority of Party functionaries thought citizens had a great possibility of openly expressing their opinions in society and only one-fourth of the members and candidates thought so. Yet, fewer than one in ten non-members shared this opinion. The results of the other questions in the survey were quite similar. So the obvious conclusion is that, while even Party functionaries and members were critical, they were less so than the rest of society. On the other hand, one should be careful in exaggerating this difference, because Party functionaries might have been more afraid of giving honest replies. Since the survey only includes 101 functionaries, these functionaries might have feared it would be relatively easy to track down the critical respondents. Thus, it appears that Prague-based political scientist Dvořáková (1993) is basically correct in claiming that not many Party members believed in the official ideology.

It was not just members and lower-level functionaries who had become relatively critical of the system. My interviews indicate that even many of the leaders were becoming critical of the system. When I asked former Vice Prime Minister Gerle whether he still considered himself a Communist, he replied "What do you mean by *Communist*? If you mean Communist as in the textbooks, then I have *never* met a Communist."[26] Jaroslav Čmejrek (interviewed 23 March 1992), who was formerly a researcher at the Central Committee's institute for

---

26. I interviewed him on 17 August 1993. Since I took notes rather than tape my interview, the citation might not exactly be word-for-word, but it certainly approximates what he said.

foreign affairs, explains that Bil'ak was the only Politburo member with any ideological convictions. The other members were not politicians but administrators—grey people without any ideas of their own. It was too dangerous to have any ideas and to try to fight for them.

Jindřich Poledník (interviewed 6 June 1992), who was formally a non-voting member of the Politburo, claims that he opposed Jakeš' election in 1987 to the post of general secretary, because he believed that the country was going through a difficult period, and therefore needed a stronger leader. "Real socialism," he adds, would not have succeeded anyway, but the collapse would have been different. Of course, it is hard to know if he really thought already in 1987 that the system might collapse. Still, if there is any truth to his statements, then he believed that the leadership suffered from a legitimacy crisis. Former Prime Minister Adamec's main political advisor, Krejčí (1991: 64) writes proudly that most of Adamec's advisors were non-Communists. He adds that the regime, in general, had lost its ideological orientation (1991: 10). To the extent he can be believed, this gives a further indication of the lack of ideological conviction in the leadership.

This is not to say all the members of the ruling elite had lost confidence in the system. Many of the more reform-minded leaders who opposed Jakeš' elevation to general secretary were forced out of the Politburo. This includes Poledník, as well as Jakeš' main competitor, Štrougal. In addition, former Politburo member Štěpán (interviewed 3 June 1992) admits that, although he thought some reforms might have been necessary, he believes they should have been done "within the framework of the constitution." This is synonymous with supporting the continuation of the Party-dictatorship. As in the East German case, the leadership lacked radical reformists or even less radical reformists who could offer a new vision for the Party. But signs that they had lost confidence in their ability to rule first came out clearly with the emergence of the protests in November 1989, when they became too paralyzed to take action. Logically, if they really believed that they should continue to rule, they would have taken all possible measures to ensure their continuance in power, rather than giving up so quickly. For within one week of the first demonstration, the entire Politburo resigned—and without having done a single substantial act that could have stopped the opposition.[27]

---

27. I discuss their inability to act in 1989 in greater detail in chapter 9.

In the GDR, those involved in the economist sphere have indicated in their memoirs that they were losing confidence in the system before the collapse (see Janson 1991 and Mittag 1991). The other leaders seem to have believed in the system until the emigration rush began in the summer of 1989. Schabowski (1990: 19), who was Krenz's co-conspirator against Honecker in the Politburo, admits that, during the large demonstrations in October 1989, "our thoughts were still determined by our firm belief in the complete power of the Party; the reaction of the people still lay far away." Schabowski's description of the situation indicates that most of the leaders truly believed in the system until confronted with the uprising. They were so shocked by this turn of events that they quickly lost confidence in themselves. But this happened *after* Honecker had already resigned.

Finally, although the Hungarian leaders were not as surprised about the collapse as the East German and Czechoslovak leaders, the mere fact that they supported a democratic transition implies they had lost confidence in the system. Former Politburo member Nyers (interviewed 8 April 1993) sums up the situation as follows: the system was going through a process of collapse, and the leaders wanted a peaceful transition. They no longer felt they could govern the country, nor could they maintain the one-party system.

Similarly, Hajdu Tibor (interviewed 12 March 1993), former editor of the corporate entity's secret newspaper, remarks that the leaders realized their economic policy had failed, and that they did not have enough police power for a Chinese solution. Thus, he believes, they were expecting an uprising to take place at a not-so-distant date, unless they pre-empted it by giving up earlier.

Laszlo Váss (interviewed 12 March 1993), formerly the main political advisor to Politburo member Pozsgay,[28] claims that, during the 1980s a significant minority of the Party apparatus understood that their market reforms would result in the emergence of different interests groups. They believed this would make some form of pluralism unavoidable. Even the hardliner Grósz understood this, but he wanted to keep the leading role of the Party intact. So although Grósz was conservative by Hungarian standards, he was a radical reformist in comparison with the leaders in the neighboring Warsaw Pact Communist countries.

---

28. Pozsgay was the politician who led the negotiations with the opposition.

McDonald (1993: 218–9) observes likewise that Grósz was against a multi-party democracy, but for radical economic reform:

> As a speaker, Grósz was not unlike Reagan or Thatcher. In his parliamentary address on the Development Program, for instance, he announced (albeit inaccurately) the size of Hungary's foreign debt, the disturbing result, he argued, of rewarding the lazy and penalizing the diligent. Here and elsewhere Grósz supported stiff income differentiation: "If we wish to further people's entrepreneurial spirit, to develop their creative strengths," he said, "then we must accept high incomes in proportion with achievements." Similarly, during this summer 1988 trip to the United States, he announced that foreigners could now own 100 percent of Hungarian companies. Despite the disruptive August miners' strike, he advocated the bankruptcy of loss-making firms even to the miners.

Such statements indicate that much of the Hungarian leadership at the very least understood the loss of legitimacy of the old system, since even the hardliners wanted radical change. This does not necessarily mean, on the other hand, that all of them had lost confidence in their ability to rule.

It thus appears that, in all of the countries except the GDR, the leaders were losing confidence in the system. Opinions differed, however, over whether it would be possible to maintain the one-party dictatorship while reforming the system. That is, the leaders were losing confidence in the system, but not necessarily in their ability to rule. The regimes which fought the most against reforms—the ČSSR and the GDR—lost confidence first when they were confronted by a large mass movement. The rapid manner in which they gave up power—without a fight—shows that they had lost confidence in their ability to rule by that point. It is probably no coincidence that the Polish and Hungarian regimes, which had the most urgent economic problems, were also the first to lose confidence in their ability to rule. Their ideological legitimacy had become weaker than that of the Czechoslovak and East German regimes.[29]

---

29. As mentioned in chapter 3, the GDR also had extremely serious economic problems. Its debt crisis was just as grave as that in Poland and Hungary. However, except for Honecker, Mittag and a few economic officials, the extent of this crisis was secret. (Stasi leader Mielke probably also knew about it). On the surface, the economy in East Germany was more stable than that in Poland and Hungary. Not only was the true debt situation unknown for the population and most leaders, the GDR did not show the open signs of economic collapse that Poland and Hungary showed, such as hyperinflation and officially falling living standards.

SUMMARY

I began Part II by claiming, in chapter 3, that the East European countries suffered from an economic crisis caused by the development of the forces of production which came into conflict with the relations of production. Nevertheless, if the regimes had succeeded in reforming the economic system, they might have been able to remain in power. In chapter 4, I asserted that it was extremely difficult to reform the economic system without bringing about systemic change. In the Soviet-type system, there are so many conflicting institutional interests between various groups that some groups will usually try to block the reforms. In addition, the existence of these contradictory institutional interests induces the regimes to make many compromises in the original reform proposals. Thus, the policy decisions are often contradictory and inconsistent. This makes it even less likely economic reforms will succeed.

Here in Chapter 5, I considered the political aspect of the economic crisis. Obviously, these internal dynamics took place within an international context. Without Gorbachev's policy of non-intervention, the results would probably have been very different. I claimed, however, that he was rather passive. Instead of pressing for reform, he was content to let the East European rulers make their own decisions. Finally, Gorbachev's policy decisions fit well into the base-superstructure model of this study. The economic crisis at the base made it possible for him to come to power in the first place. The crisis also induced him to introduce economic reforms. When the reforms failed, he realized that political reform would also be necessary, in order to muster support for his economic policies. His *glasnost* policy, in turn, encouraged reform Communists and the oppositional movements in Eastern Europe.

After discussing Gorbachev's role, I looked more closely at the legitimacy question. Here, I supported Di Palma's notion of legitimacy from the top, although I re-named it "ideological legitimacy." According to Di Palma, the legitimacy of the Soviet-type regimes was based on their alleged monopoly on Truth, as well as on their goal of surpassing Western living standards. I prefer the term ideological legitimacy, because the East European rulers tried to base their legitimacy on an ideological doctrine. Furthermore, rulers cannot base their legitimacy completely on their own perceptions of their right to rule. At least some segments of society must see the leaders as legitimate if a system is to have any legitimacy. I furthermore claimed that, although the regimes never achieved full legitimacy, they did at least enjoy some legitimacy among groups of workers and intellectuals when they first came to power. This deterioration in ideological legitimacy among their former supporters also played a role in the collapse of the system.

When it became clear that the leaders' economic goals were not reachable, it was easy for citizens to question the Party's monopoly on Truth. The Communist leaders began losing confidence in their ability to rule. In Poland and Hungary, this occurred before 1989. In the ČSSR and the GDR, this manifested itself in the inability of the Communist leaders to act when confronted by a mass movement. While the loss of legitimacy weakened the rulers, it also strengthened the opposition. In addition, the dissidents became increasingly critical of the system, as they lost hope that the system was reformable. Thus, the majority of dissidents changed from revisionist socialists into anti-socialists.

In sum, I concentrated in Part II on four factors that caused the collapse of the Soviet-type system in Eastern Europe at a general level. These factors include: 1) the economic crisis, 2) the failure of reforms, 3) Gorbachev's policies, and 4) the loss of ideological legitimacy. Although these four factors contributed to the collapse in general, they are not enough to explain the *differences in the process of collapse*. In addition, notwithstanding the radically changed structural conditions under which the East European leaders found themselves, it is still not clear that they *had to* lose power. If they had been willing to call out their armies, perhaps a Chinese solution would have been possible. Thus, one must look more closely at the developments in the individual countries in order to understand the collapse. That is my task in Part III.

Part III:

DIFFERENCES IN THE PROCESS OF COLLAPSE

Chapter 6

REGIME POLICY BEFORE 1988

I devote Part II to the similarities of the Eastern European countries. There I emphasize the general structural conditions for the collapse. None of these factors, however, can account for the differences in the *process* of collapse. I argue despite these structural conditions, the East European regimes still might have been able to remain in power if they had acted differently. Part III explains the differences in the process of collapse. In the present chapter, I concentrate on regime policy before 1988. Chapter 7 considers the debates about the civil society during this period. I also look at the general atmosphere in the East European societies. In chapter 8 I analyze in more detail the development of social movements and revolts under the Soviet-type system. I divide the regime and society into different chapters, because to a large extent there are different theoretical discourses around these two topics. So in these chapters I develop the partial model, which I use in chapters 9 and 10 to explain the actual handing-over of power to the opposition in the four countries. Since the relations between the Party-state and society are important, I combine these two aspects in the final two chapters. I divide these two chapters according to theme. In chapter 9 I examine Poland and Hungary, where institutional compromises took place. I have decided to save the revolutionary countries (East Germany and Czechoslovakia) for the grand finale in chapter 10. Finally, in chapter 11 I give a summary of the entire model that I develop throughout this study.

In this chapter, I look at regime policy before 1988. First, I consider the pragmatic manner in which the regimes tried to gain the acceptance of the population after Soviet invasions or threats of invasions. Then I examine the regimes' actual policies in light of their different modes of pragmatic acceptance.

PRAGMATIC ACCEPTANCE

Although the term "ideological legitimacy" introduced in chapter 5 is useful in explaining the general collapse of the Soviet-type system, it cannot explain the particular *differences* in the processes of collapse. This chapter focuses on the institutional level to explain the differences between the four regimes. My contention is that, although the regimes lacked full legitimacy and were losing their ideological legitimacy among the segments that had supported them, they still could convince the populace to accept their rule *pragmatically* until the late 1980s. The populace accepted these regimes on the pragmatic grounds that the Soviet Union would not allow a different type of regime. The assumption at the time was that freedom from Soviet domination was an impossible dream.

The pragmatic arguments of the Polish and Hungarian regimes differed from the Czechoslovak and East German regimes. These differences were institutionalized in ways that influenced their behavior in 1989. The regimes that came to power in each of the four countries after Soviet invasions or threatened invasions developed a pragmatic acceptance to defend their rise to power. They could not refer to ideological legitimacy, since it concerned change *within* the regime rather than a change *of* regime. So regardless of which Communist leaders came to the top, the regimes still claimed to have ideological legitimacy. Yet it was necessary, in this situation, to defend the fact that *they* were the ones at the top (rather than previous Communists).

Since the relatively "liberal" leaders of Hungary and Poland claimed to have come to power for foreign-policy reasons (to prevent Hungary from leaving the Warsaw Pact and to prevent a Soviet invasion of Poland), they obtained greater space for autonomy in domestic politics. Of course, the USSR's veto power constrained these rulers too. If they were to go against the wishes of the Kremlin, their position would be in danger.[1] Nonetheless, these leaders had much more room to carry out reforms than did Honecker or Husák. They could take advantage of the opportunities to utilize greater pragmatism in domestic policies. Hence, they developed reformist "identities."

---

1. In contrast to other Polish and Hungarian leaders, Kádár and Jaruzelski were also personally constrained by their previous roles in repression. Kádár had led the purges of rebels after the Soviet invasion in 1956. The younger Communists who overthrew him in 1988 did not suffer from these constraints. Similarly, Jaruzelski's reputation suffered from his role in declaring martial law. After he arrested *Solidarność* leaders, it was more difficult for him to advocate talks with the opposition than it was for the more liberal Communists who had not been involved in the military *coup* of 1981. These liberals actively supported negotiations with the opposition during the 1980s. Jaruzelski recruited some of them in the Politburo when he was ready to begin negotiations.

These identities became a form of institutional interest, on which they based their pragmatic acceptance.[2] Since these policy legacies become institutionalized, I refer to them synonymously as pragmatic acceptance and as institutional interests. The concept of institutional interests includes much more than pragmatic acceptance; institutional interests include all forms of institutional incentives. On the other hand, pragmatic acceptance, once institutionalized, becomes a form of institutional interest.

Put differently, the Hungarian and Polish rulers invested their political capital in reforms. They developed their pragmatic acceptance (which became a form of institutional interest) as leaders who could test the limits of what the Soviet Union would allow. Consequently, once the system starting breaking down, it was much easier for them to continue the process of institutional reform and take it one step further—towards democratization.

In the ČSSR and GDR, in contrast, the Soviet Union made it clear that it had invaded to prevent domestic developments that, it claimed, would have led to the reinstatement of capitalism. Thus, the leaders of these countries based their pragmatic acceptance on the notion that they were in power to *prevent* reforms, since reforms lead to Soviet reprisals. Their pragmatic acceptance based on their adherence to orthodoxy gave them institutional interests in opposing reforms. If they were to advocate reforms, their possession of power would immediately come into question. When Gorbachev came to power, he advocated reforms in his own country and removed many of the constraints on the regimes abroad. This changed the basis for the pragmatic acceptance of the Czechoslovakian and East German regimes. When their institutional interests in preventing reform collapsed, they had no guide in how to act. Therefore, they became paralyzed. Their Polish and Hungarian comrades, in contrast, experienced much more continuity in their institutional interests based on a reformist pragmatic acceptance.

Put in neo-institutional terminology, the Soviet invasions or threats of invasion were formative moments (Rothstein 1988 & 1992: 17).

---

2. This idea of reformist identities is similar to the neo-institutionalist notion of "policy legacies" (see Weir & Skocpol 1985). I prefer the term "pragmatic acceptance," because I am referring to a particular form of policy legacy: namely, the policy legacy that comes from the manner in which the Soviet-type regimes in Eastern Europe tried to justify their rise to power after Soviet intervention.

That is, they were periods in which actors enjoyed unusually large space for restructuring institutions. These new institutions, in turn, strongly influence later behavior. The Soviet invasions or threatened invasions were formative movements, in which actors could reshape institutions. It was not pre-determined how the Moscow leaders or the new domestic leaders would defend the seizure of power once the Red Army brought about a change of leadership (either by invading or by threatening invasion). During these formative moments, the leaders in Moscow and in the national capitals developed new forms of pragmatic acceptance. Once they had decided on a particular form, however, policy legacies/institutional interests were formed that strongly influenced future behavior. This is especially true for the leaders who had originally contributed to the creation of these mods of pragmatic acceptance. When new leaders come to power, they are less bound by these legacies and have more room for maneuver. A typical example may be seen in the battle over the pace of reforms in Hungary. Although Kádár had previously been the most radical leader in Eastern Europe, he was not willing to go as far as the younger reform Communists gathered around Pozsgay. These younger Communists felt themselves less constrained by Kádár's defense of the Soviet invasion in 1956. Thus, it was easier for them to recommend systemic change that would ultimately move them outside the Soviet orbit.

This notion of pragmatic acceptance can explain the behavior of the four regimes more clearly than, for example, theories of political culture. Otherwise, how can one otherwise explain, for example, the fact that Czechoslovakia, which had the strongest democratic traditions among the four countries, had an orthodox, hardline regime, while Hungary and Poland, which were run by dictatorships during most of the inter-war years, had reformist regimes? The repressive East German regime, with its militaristic, Prussian cultural heritage, was the only one whose behavior is easily explained in terms of political culture.

The pragmatic acceptance of each regime up to the year 1988 is discussed below.

Poland Under Gomułka

Poland was the only one of the four countries that did not suffer a Soviet invasion. Yet on two occasions the regime felt threatened. The first was during the worker protests in1956 which brought Gomułka to power. The second was during the *Solidarność* uprising in 1980–1.

In 1956, workers went on strike in Poznań. The strike broke out into mass demonstrations which the regime quickly repressed. Despite their victory, the leaders were afraid they might lose control on the next occasion. They had already lost control to such an extent that the USSR threatened openly with an invasion. Soviet tanks had approached the border, and Soviet warships had appeared at the coast. Meanwhile, Red Army units within Poland had left their barracks and begun approaching Warsaw. When the Polish Politburo met, the entire Soviet Politburo flew to Warsaw to help "bring order" to the country.

By this time Gomułka had already re-entered the Politburo. During the Stalinist era, he had spent time in prison for allegedly having been a bourgeois nationalist. His popularity and nationalist background frightened the Soviet leaders. They feared he might become another Tito. The Soviet Politburo tried, accordingly, to convince the Polish leaders to drop Gomułka and to maintain hardliners at their posts. Instead, the Polish Politburo elected Gomułka the new general secretary of the Party. After intensive negotiations, Khrushchev backed down, but he made it clear he was not pleased with the turn of events. Soviet pressure continued after the election.

Gomułka's fall-out with the hardliners gave citizens hope that he would liberalize the country. At the same time, the threatened invasion and the presence of the Soviet Politburo during his election highlighted external constraints. Gomułka himself had contradictory institutional interests. On the one hand, it was in his interest to be popular. On the other, it was in his interest to keep his Soviet masters satisfied, so they would not try to remove him.

At first Gomułka built on his reformist image. His initial acts as leader included stopping collectivization, easing censorship, creating multi-candidate electoral constituencies, reaching an accommodation with the Church, and supporting the formation of worker councils.[3] Thus, he created the image of a reformist pragmatic acceptance based on the notion that Poland would become a relatively open society by Stalinist standards.

After consolidating his power, Gomułka took an increasingly con-, servative position. The worker councils that symbolized the 1956

---

3. My account is based on Harman (1983: ch. 6), Taras (1986: ch. 2), and Waller (1993: 124–5). I also rely heavily on Syrop (1982: ch. 20) for the negotiations with the Soviet Union and (1982: ch. 22) for the accommodation with the Church. However, almost everything in this section is common knowledge and can be found in most textbooks on Eastern Europe.

rebellion eventually lost most of their power. Gomułka's first step was to convert them into self-management committees that included representatives from official organizations such as the Party committee and trade-union. Later, he extended the committees to include youth groups and technicians' and engineers' associations (Taras 1990: 8). Not only did workers lose their influence in the councils, other measures curbed the power of the councils. They became more hierarchical, as they lost power to the trade-union factory councils. Meanwhile, the unions themselves lost their autonomy from the Party (Gramatzki 1977: 128). The Gomułka regime also developed a progressively more critical attitude toward the intellectuals.

Although Gomułka did not live up to earlier expectations that he would play the role of a radical reformer, he still enjoyed a reformist image behind which he could hide. Despite an increase in repression, for instance, Poland continued to be the most open of the Soviet-bloc countries until the Prague Spring. Even Gomułka's more conservative turn could be justified to some extent on the assumption that he had to placate his Soviet superiors who had been skeptical about his rise to power.[4]

This does not imply that Gomułka's behavior was only determined by his reformist policy legacy and by Soviet pressure. Although he had more room to maneuver on domestic issues than his East German and Czechoslovak neighbors, he did not necessarily fully utilize it. Gomułka might have been able to pursue more radical reforms had he really attempted; however, it is probable that he was actually more conservative that the population had expected. Or perhaps he grew more orthodox with time. One indication of his anti-reformism is his stance toward the Dubček regime. His former interpreter claims that, among Warsaw Pact leaders, Gomułka was the main advocate of invading Czechoslovakia during the Prague Spring.[5] Another indication that

---

4. In chapter 5, I noted Taras' (1986) hypothesis that, since Gomułka came to power against the will of the USSR and enjoyed great popularity, he must have faced more pressure than Kádár to tone down his reformism.

5. Gomułka reportedly criticized Kádár for having too much patience with Dubček: "If you think, comrade Kádár, that you are helping the cause of socialism with your objections and reservations, you are making a big mistake, and you have no idea what will happen next. Once the American-West German imperialists have got Czechoslovakia in their control, then you will be next to go, Comrade Kádár. But that is something you cannot or won't understand" Erwin Weit (1971) *At the Red Summit: Interpreter behind the Iron Curtain*, New York: MacMillan pp. 193–217, quoted in Gati (1990: 85).

Gomułka had become anti-reformist is the anti-Semitic campaign which he sanctioned in 1968. Virtually everyone of Jewish heritage had to leave the universities. Nothing suggests that Brezhnev forced Gomułka to launch this campaign. Some authors conclude that Gomułka's turn away from reformism did not come just from Soviet pressure; it was also a result of his own beliefs (see for example Taras 1986: 54–5).

Nevertheless, Gomułka had created a reformist legacy on which his predecessors could build. His reformist legacy also made it dangerous for him to become too conservative, since the populace pragmatically accepted him on the grounds that they believed he liberalized society as much as the USSR would allow. Anti-reformist actions, such as his crackdown in 1968, cost him support among intellectuals. He caused more difficulty when he behaved like a traditional anti-reformist Stalinist leader, who could do whatever he wanted, without worrying about public reaction. As Gomułka arrogantly raised food prices right before Christmas in 1970, workers launched a violent protest, which forced him to resign.

Poland under Jaruzelski

In the midst of the *Solidarność* uprising in 1980–1, the USSR made its dissatisfaction clear. The official Soviet newspapers became increasingly critical of the Polish regime. General Secretary Kania attended four summit meetings in Moscow within 13 months. The Soviet Central Committee sent two letters to its Polish counterpart in June and September 1981. Both criticized the Polish leaders for their excessive cautiousness. They also condemned the increasing "anti-Soviet" atmosphere in Poland. Phrases like "counter-revolution" appeared in the letters.[6] Since everyone in Poland was aware of the previous Soviet invasions of Czechoslovakia, Hungary and East Germany, this open pressure by the Soviet leadership spread fears that their turn might be next. At the same time, *Solidarność* was becoming more radical and making demands for political democracy.

During the crisis, a formative moment emerged in which the decisions of the Polish and Soviet leaders would restructure the institutional structures. Either they would try to reshape the institutions, or the Party power monopoly would collapse and give way to radically

---

6. Again, most of the content of this paragraph is general knowledge. I have based this account mainly on Gerrits (1990: ch. 7).

new institutions. Since General Jaruzelski crushed the *Solidarność* uprising through a military *coup*, the Soviet Union had little reason to invade. Although it is still not certain whether the Soviet Union would have invaded if Jaruzelski had not carried out his *coup*,[7] virtually all Poles considered this a likely outcome. Thus, when Jaruzelski declared martial law, it was relatively easy for him to defend it by claiming he was preventing something even worse from happening.[8] Gerrits (1990: 22) summarizes:

> The Jaruzelski regime was the first loyal Soviet ally that tried to at least partly legitimize its rule on the basis of a perceived Soviet threat. The decision to declare a state of war was justified as a "lesser evil," a misfortune which was less drastic than anarchy, civil strife or a foreign military intervention.

Thus, as Gomułka in 1956, Jaruzelski came to power during a period in which there was widespread fear of a Soviet invasion. And in both cases a Soviet invasion was in fact rather near. Finally, in both cases, the new leaders (Gomułka and Jaruzelski) claimed that they would pursue reforms.

Jaruzelski continued the reformist pragmatic acceptance despite his declaration of martial law. While declaring martial law was necessary to prevent civil war, Jaruzelski stressed his commitment to reform (cf. Batt 1991a: 8 & 1991b: 371). Since he had inherited a reformist legacy, it was easier to build upon this form of pragmatic acceptance and to advocate reforms than it would have been had he succeeded an orthodox regime. Nevertheless, he could have utilized this formative moment to incorporate a hardline policy. He could have claimed that the economic crisis proved "revisionist" ideas had failed. If he had pointed to the GDR as proof that orthodoxy brings stability, he

---

7. After leaving politics, Jaruzelski (1992: 290) claimed that he discovered in 1992 that the Soviet Union indeed had planned to invade. A Czech parliamentary committee also reported in 1995 that the Warsaw Pact had prepared to invade Poland (ČTK 28 September 1995). In contrast, rumors have recently circulated that Jaruzelski actually asked the Soviet Union to invade, but the Red Army was afraid of doing so. This issue cannot be settled here. What is important is that the Jauzelski could credibly claim to have saved the country from an invasion.

8. In Wlicki's words, "the [martial-law] government wanted to be recognised as a 'lesser evil,' a geopolitical necessity, thus deriving its legitimacy from a certain understanding of the national interest at a given moment, and not from any universalist ideology" (quoted in McSweeney & Tempest 1993: 415). Similarly, Staniszkis (1991: 189) refers to the use of "geopolitical" arguments to justify the military *coup*.

certainly would not have met any opposition from Brezhnev.[9] In fact, Brezhnev would probably have preferred such a turn. However, once Jaruzelski chose to base his pragmatic acceptance on the need to carry out reforms while maintaining order, it became more difficult for him to bring about an about-face. It would have meant betraying his supporters within the Party. The Party's relations with the populace would have worsened. The *Solidarność* uprising had already shown that the Party enjoyed hardly any support from the workers it supposedly represented. After having given society some hope that reforms might continue, a sudden turn towards orthodoxy would have deprived the Party of any goodwill at all. The citizens might grudgingly have offered the regime their acceptance (on the grounds that Soviet constraints made democracy impossible), but they would not have been so tolerant of a Stalinist reversion. Thus, by the mid-1980s, Jaruzelski clearly had an institutional interest in continuing the reform process.

In sum, Jaruzelski did not base his acceptance on the need to stop reforms, but rather on the necessity of bringing order to the country before an eventual Soviet invasion did so with much harsher results. Since Jaruzelski sought to implement economic reforms during his entire tenure in power and tried continuously to coopt parts of the opposition, it was not difficult for him to take the reforms a step further by negotiating an institutional compromise with the opposition in 1989.[10]

Hungary

Less than one week after the Polish uprising brought Gomułka to power in Poland, the Hungarians took to the streets. On October 23, 1956, a crowd gathered in Budapest, waving banners, singing the *Internationale* and chanting their support for Nagy. The reformist Prime Minister Nagy had lost power in internal power struggles during the previous year. When the crowds that day grew to several

---

9. In chapter 3 I argue that the GDR underwent an economic crisis. The crisis was not nearly as deep, however, at the time of the *Solidarność* uprising. The greatest deterioration occurred in the following years. Moreover, the debt statistics were kept hidden, as were the real rates of inflation. Consequently, both the Polish leadership and the Polish population was unaware of the GDR's true economic situation.

10. I discuss his attempts at economic reform and cooptation of the opposition below. I give more details of the institutional compromise with the opposition in chapter 9.

hundred thousand, the Party leaders panicked. On the one hand, they asked the USSR to send in troops. On the other hand, they agreed to bring back Nagy to head the government. Meanwhile, several thousand insurgents took to arms. Rather than fight back, the Hungarian Communist organization evaporated. On October 25, Kádár replaced the hardliner Gerö as general secretary. A few days later the Soviet emissaries, Mikoyan and Suslov, arrived. They agreed to withdraw Soviet troops and security forces from the country. On October 30, Nagy set up a coalition government that included non-Communists. He enjoyed the support of the insurgents, so all fighting stopped. During a radio address, the new prime minister announced the formation of a multi-party cabinet and the intention to leave the Warsaw Pact. The next day he announced that the country had regained its sovereignty and independence. That same day Soviet reinforcements crossed the border. In the evening, Kádár announced that he had dissolved the old party and established a new one, entitled the Hungarian Socialist Workers' Party. In his first speech, he gave unequivocal support to the uprising and claimed that Hungary had to maintain its independence. Then he disappeared to the Soviet Union for a few days. When he returned, he set up a new government.[11]

Virtually all analyses of these events conclude that the Kremlin decided to intervene because of Nagy's intention to withdraw from the Warsaw Pact (see for example Waller 1993: 123).[12] Kádár learned his lesson afterwards: his country had to pursue a pro-Soviet foreign

11. I have based this account mostly on Molnár (1987: ch. 9 and the beginning of ch. 10).

12. Váli (1961: 364) criticizes this usual account. He maintains that Nagy announced that Hungary would leave the Warsaw Pact after the invasion had already started. Nagy said the USSR had violated the rules of the Pact, so Hungary no longer had to abide by it. Nevertheless, in contrast to Czechoslovakia in 1968, it was clearly a nationalist uprising that threatened Soviet dominance. At the first meeting of the students who started the revolt, a demand was put forth for a "re-examination of Hungary's relations with the Soviet Union under the principle of equality..." (Váli 1961: 266). The new Nagy-Kádár government declared, after the first Central Committee meeting on October 26, that it would "create a free country of prosperity, independence and socialist democracy." It would negotiate with the USSR "on the basis of independence, complete equality, and non-interference in one another's internal affairs" (Váli 195: 288). Such statements amounted to a declaration of independence from the Soviet Union, even if it left open the possibility of reforming the Warsaw Pact rather than leaving it.

policy regardless of what he thought personally.[13] Thus, Kádár built his pragmatic acceptance on the notion that Nagy could not remain in power, since he opposed Soviet security interests. Kádár came to power to guarantee that the country would remain a reliable Soviet ally on foreign-policy issues. Since the intervention was justified for foreign-policy reasons, the Hungarian leader enjoyed some leeway in domestic policies. That does not mean he utilized at once his relative freedom from the Soviet Union. During his first years in office, he concentrated on consolidating his position. His reform-concept crystallized first one decade later, although internal Party discussions had begun even earlier. Despite an occasional retrenchment, Kádár clearly led the most market-oriented of the Soviet-bloc countries. During the 1970s, moreover, he began liberalizing cultural life. By the 1980s, his country had the most liberal policies on travel and culture, and the most open political debates within the bloc.[14] As former Economic Secretary Nyers (interviewed 8 April 1993) puts it, Kádár was able to pursue relatively independent domestic and economic policies. The price was support for Soviet foreign policy. In this manner, Kádár established a reformist pragmatic acceptance upon which the new generation of radical reformers could build when they ousted him in 1988.

Again, Kádár's acceptance was pragmatic, because although the population certainly did not support the invasion, it was *pragmatically* willing—given certain geo-political realities—to accept a pro-Soviet foreign policy and continued one-party rule, in return for rising

---

13. He therefore reluctantly agreed to send troops to the ČSSR in 1968. He even met with Dubček beforehand to try to convince him to moderate his policies in order to placate the angry Russian bear. The Czechoslovak leader did not, however, take his indirect hint. As already mentioned, Gomułka's former interpreter claims that Kádár opposed intervention in Czechoslovakia in 1968. It was, allegedly, the Polish and East German leaders who were the most active supporters of intervention. On August 17, four days before the invasion, Kádár had a meeting with Dubček. Most Sovietologists have assumed Kádár tried to warn Dubček, so that the latter could avert an invasion by moderating his policies. Dubček himself (1993: 216) maintains that his Hungarian colleague gave no indication of the impending invasion during their talks. However, knowledgeable Hungarians to whom I have spoken assume that Kádár hinted at the problems, but could refer to them directly. They conclude that Dubček was so naïve about the USSR that he did not understand Kádár's hints. For example, both Tibor and Hajdu voiced this opinion during a conversation following my interview with them on 12 March 1993.

14. I discuss this in more detail below.

living standards and economic reform combined with a degree of liberalization. Thus, Kádár and his successors developed an institutional interest in supporting reforms. In addition, even though a pragmatic acceptance based on the need for a pro-Soviet foreign policy made it possible for him to pursue relatively independent domestic policies, that does not mean that he was bound to do so. If he had not supported liberalization personally, nobody would have forced him to follow such a strategy. Once he had instituted a reformist mode of pragmatic acceptance, however, it would have been more difficult to return to orthodoxy.

The GDR

After Stalin died, the new Soviet leaders were not certain what they should do with the GDR. Khrushchev claimed that Beria and Malenkov urged the East German leadership to abandon its "socialist" system (Harman 1983: 78). Whatever reservations they had about keeping control over the GDR evaporated, however, on June 17, 1953. On that day, hundreds of thousands of worker revolted to protest increased work-norms. The Red Army quickly crushed the uprising.

Even though Ulbricht remained in power, this was still a formative moment. Institutions were open for change. He had lost much of his support within the Party before the uprising. Without Soviet backing, he would probably have lost the support of the Central Committee. Even more importantly, without the aid of the Red Army the entire corporate entity would probably have lost power. As Harman (1983: 79) notes, the Party was so deeply divided at the time of the uprising that the East German security forces were passive, without any directions as to what they should do. Thus, Ulbricht had to defend his pragmatic acceptance on the basis of his remaining in power due to Soviet intervention. So the Soviet decision to invade, together with Ulbricht's defense of the invasion, resulted in new institutional structures.

Afterwards, the Soviet Union made it clear it was not going to tolerate any changes in the East German state. Throughout the postwar period, the Soviet press reminded the world of the 20 million Soviet citizens who were killed by Nazi Germany. After having fought two world wars against Germany, the leadership in Moscow was afraid of a united, non-allied Germany. It realized that any steps toward liberalizing society could lead to demands for reunification, and thus threaten Soviet security interests. It therefore supported Ulbricht, the most orthodox of the potential East German leaders.

Again, this outcome was not completely structurally determined. The Soviet Politburo could probably have decided to follow the wishes of some of its members and to let the GDR go. In addition, once the USSR intervened, the Soviet leaders could have decided to choose a less orthodox leader than Ulbricht. They could have blamed the uprising on his mistaken policies and replaced him with a more centrist leader. Once they decided to keep Ulbricht, however, the East German mode of pragmatic acceptance was set.

Throughout the period of his rule, Ulbricht based his pragmatic acceptance on two notions. First, the country had to become the Soviet Union's most faithful ally. Second, no experiments straying too far from orthodoxy could be tolerated. Thus, the country became a bastion of conservatism. Although Economic Secretary Mittag worked out some minor economic reforms, these reforms were much less daring than those in Hungary and Czechoslovakia at the time.[15] In addition, the "New Economic System" had an extremely short existence. Only a few years after the introduction of these reforms, Honecker removed most of them when he came to power in 1971.

In 1970, Ulbricht dared to act contrary to his institutional interests. He voiced his skepticism of Brezhnev's attempts at arranging a meeting between the prime ministers of East and West Germany, Stroph and Brandt. His critique of Brandt's Ostpolitik cost him his position. The following year, with the consent of the Kremlin, Honecker, replaced his former mentor as general secretary (see Griffith 1989b: 316, Neuman 1991: 145 and Simmons 1989: 5–6). To make it clear he would continue to pursue his institutional interests in upholding orthodoxy, Honecker quickly demoted Mittag, the man behind the economic reforms.[16]

---

15. Some of the main points were a decrease in the norms which the central planners assigned the enterprises. Rather than giving the firms more autonomy, these changes gave more responsibility for micro-planning to the combines. These combines were created to oversee all the firms in a particular industry. Thus, planning remained just as important as before, but the mid-level planners gained more influence. Furthermore, profits were supposed to become more important. Since the profit levels were planned, however, and since there was no connection between wages or salaries and profits, this reform did not give the enterprises more autonomy. See Brus (1981: 185–193) and Jeffries (1992: 18–9).

16. Mittag later repented. As his reward, he eventually became Honecker's economic guru. Although he developed a reputation as one of the most dogmatic economists within the Soviet bloc, he claims in his memoirs that he continued to favor reform, but was not able to advocate this openly during Honecker's reign (see Mittag 1991).

The ČSSR

The Prague Spring Communists began by acting much more like the Hungarian reformers of the late 1960s and 1970s than those of 1956. While the Nagy regime was swept quickly into power before it could work out a program for economic reform, both the Kádár and Dubček regimes started out with well-planned, technocratic economic reforms. Nagy panicked upon returning to office. Before he had much time to think about economic measures, he faced important decisions in the *political* sphere. Within a few days he decided to install a coalition government, while calling for free elections and a withdrawal from the Warsaw Pact. In contrast, the Czechoslovak Communists never questioned their allegiance to the Soviet Union, nor did they call for free elections. Systemic transformation was not on the agenda. The Czechoslovak reform economists gathered around Ota Šik began working out a package of economic reforms in the early 1960s. Thus, Dubček inherited a cautious reform program before taking over the leadership. At first, he continued to concentrate on economic measures. Except in its emphasis on worker self-management, his economic reform proposals differed little in its main points from the Hungarian New Economic Mechanism, which Kádár's economists had worked out during the same period (see chapter 4).

Despite the similar origins, in Brezhnev's eyes the Hungarian Communists had not loosened their grip over society, while the Czechoslovak Communists appeared to be losing control. Workers were distrustful of market reforms which threatened to raise prices and cause unemployment. To appease them, the leaders agreed to support the formation of worker councils.[17] Thus, the Party was willing to give up some of its monopoly power both to enterprises and to the enterprise workforce. This turn towards "humanism" contrasted with the Hungarian regime, which restricted its reforms to the technocratic issue of making the economy work more efficiently.

In the non-economic sphere as well, the Dubček regime discovered it was more difficult to calm down the population than it had been for Kádár. The Hungarians had already partly settled accounts with their

---

17. I mention this in chapter 4. See Lemân (1977: 152–3), Hejzlar (1976: 209), and Touraine et al. (1982: 30). For a discussion of the various proposals on worker councils during the Prague Spring, see also Golan (1973: 24, 44–5), Holesovsky (1970: 32), Kosta (1974: 193; 1978: 148–9; 1984: 147, 190–1) and Selucký (1969: 95–6).

Stalinist past. Rakowski lost his general-secretary post shortly after Stalin's death, Nagy became prime minister twice, and even Kádár openly decried the crimes of the Stalinist era. To emphasize the break with the Stalinist past, Kádár rebuilt the Party under a new name. In the ČSSR, by contrast, the Stalinist general secretary, Novotný, remained in power until 1968. In the early 1960s intellectuals led a drive to rehabilitate the victims of the show trials for which Novotný had been responsible. This process of rehabilitation had already begun prior to 1968.[18] When Dubček took over, the Czechs and Slovaks had much higher hopes, as well as a greater need to release pent-up energy, than did the Hungarians. The intellectuals broadened their demands to include free speech, political pluralism, etc.[19] The reform Communists responded by removing censorship, easing travel restrictions, and taking steps to set up due process of law within the judicial system. Although the Central Committee never discussed establishing a multi-party democracy, it did consider giving more power to the allied parties of the National Front. It encouraged these parties to shed their roles as rubber-stamp organizations. The non-Communist allies could now freely recruit new members and propagate freely within the confines of the Front. Members of the allied parties also became ministers in the new government. Moreover, the Communists began speaking about the need to "earn" their leading role. They also considered granting the allied parties ministries in proportion to the size of their

---

18. In the early 1960s Khrushchev started pressuring Novotný to rehabilitate the victims of the show trials. See Hejzlar (1976: 111–3).

19. Kleberg (1968b: 66) notes that the Slovak writers had become an important pressure group, whose actions were centered on complete rehabilitation of the Slovak "bourgeois nationalists," who had comprised the intellectual elite among Slovakia's Communists. Even though they eventually reached a quiet agreement that gave them cultural self-determination in exchange for agreeing not to criticize the Party publicly, many of them continued with their dissident activities.

    Eventually, the Czech authors took a more provocative line than their Slovak colleagues. Their union had its own press—as did the Slovak organization—and was therefore able to serve as a forum for ideas which were too radical to print in the official publications. During the first half of 1967, its literary magazine *Literární Noviny* had a weekly distribution of 135,000 copies (Kleberg 1968b: 71), and by June 1968 it had reached the level of 300,000 (Kleberg 1968b: 94). This journal consistently made demands for more radical political change; it irritated the Party leadership so much, in fact, that it was even forbidden in late 1967 (Kleberg 1968b: 85).

membership. Thus, a sort of membership-rather than vote-based competition between the parties would have emerged.[20]

As in Hungary in 1956, the Kremlin had reason to fear the Communists were losing their power monopoly. Even though Dubček, who grew up in the USSR and was loyal to Moscow, any national Communist Party that tried to obtain popular support eventually threatened the institutional interests of the Soviet Party in maintaining control over its satellites. For liberalization easily leads to demands for democratization, and it is unlikely any party would have been able to win democratic elections if its leaders were subservient to the USSR. The most the Soviet leaders could have expected from any democratic regime in Eastern Europe would have been neutralization, as the cases of Finland and Austria.

Thus, the reason for the invasion of Czechoslovakia was similar to that for Hungary in one sense: it was done to prevent the eventual independence of the subordinate country. Nonetheless, the *immediate* causes of the invasion were different. Since the economic reforms had gone further than the other reforms and since the Dubček regime had pledged loyalty to the Warsaw Pact, it was easier to justify the invasion as an attempt to save the country from "bourgeois" economic reform. Thus, during this formative moment the new leaders established their pragmatic acceptance on the notion that they had come to power to prevent a return to capitalism. In a speech in September 1969, for example, the new general secretary, Husák, accused the reform Communists of being "right-wing opportunists," of being "petty bourgeois," and of advocating class-based policies. He also spoke of "Rightist" movements.[21] Other common accusations were that the reformers were "revisionists," "opportunists," "right-wing,"

---

20. Kleberg (1968a) and Hejzlar (1976: 192–200). Dubček (1973) seems to have considered the possibility of allowing new parties into the National Front, as long as they adhered to socialist principles and did not question the leading role of the Party. No party should be allowed to exist outside of the Front in his opinion.

    Mlynář (1973), who helped write the action program, took a more open attitude and admitted there was nothing "anti-socialist" about a system with two competing parties. Rather than openly advocating multiparty elections, though, he favored incorporating new parties into the Front. In his memoirs over the Prague Spring, Mlynář (1980: 156–7) claims he had planned for a gradual transition to a completely pluralist, parliamentary democracy within 10 years. Of course, it is impossible to know whether or not he is being honest or simply trying to improve his image after the fact.

21. Originally printed in *Neues Deutchland* on 14 October 1969, reprinted in Crusius et al. (1973: 202–4).

etc. (Pelikán in Crusius et al. 1973: 220). One Czechoslovak book on political economy attacked the Prague Spring reformers for "idealizing the market" and being "against socialist ownership of the means of production" (Fremer et al. 1984: 439). Šik (1981: 114) concludes: "The entire campaign conducted against the revisionists in the CSSR is based solely on the accusation that these people wanted to eliminate socialism and reintroduce capitalism."

Since the new rulers based their pragmatic acceptance on the need to preserve the orthodox system from a reversion to capitalism, any attempts to introduce reforms put their right to rule into question. Even if the majority of the population did not believe that the Prague Spring reforms would have led to capitalism, they could pragmatically accept the fact that the USSR was not going to let them reform the system. As long as old, orthodox men sat in the Kremlin, and as long as the Husák regime could offer the populace increasing living standards as compensation, the system proved to be relatively stable. The ageing leaders could rely on their institutional interests in blocking reforms as a guide to their actions. This changed when Gorbachev came to power. The Czechoslovak regime's pragmatic acceptance evaporated when the new Soviet leader made it clear the Kremlin would no longer veto all reforms. The evaporation of institutional interests started slowly during the first part of the Gorbachev era, but sped up as the public's rage boiled over in 1989.

POLICY BEFORE 1988

In the last section, I discussed the pragmatic acceptance of the four regimes. I concluded that the Polish and Hungarian regimes had reformist policy legacies that gave them some room for flexibility. The East German and Czechoslovak rulers, in contrast, developed anti-reformist pragmatic legitimacies, which resulted in institutional interests in avoiding reforms. Yet within such structural constraints, these leaders had some room to maneuver. The following discussion examines how they utilized this room and focuses on the policy *decisions* that facilitated the subsequent collapse in 1989.

Poland: Failed Cooptation

Gomułka lost support by rescinding the worker-council reforms and repressing intellectuals in the 1960s. On December 11, 1970, he made a fatal mistake. That day, he completed plans for a large and immediate increase in food prices. From the viewpoint of the workers, it was bad enough that he wanted to increase food prices. Gomułka made the situation worse, however, by deciding to announce the increase one week before Christmas. When the minister of foreign affairs showed his skepticism at a Party meeting, Gomułka replied: "Whatever the position of the party, that will also be the position of the working class and society" (Laba 1991: 18). Reality proved to be different. Workers along the Baltic cost revolted immediately after the announcement. The following day, they showed their wrath by burning down the Gdańsk Party headquarters (Laba 1991: 35). Although the army eventually quelled the revolt, these actions cost Gomułka his job as general secretary.

His replacement, Gierek, still had a reform legacy upon which he could build. Gomułka's failure had highlighted the need for reforms. Gierek took some small steps to improve the cultural situation. This included giving "considerable autonomy ... for artistic endeavours" (Taras 1984: 135). Furthermore, Gierek believed that, "political culture had to be modern, it had to be modeled on advanced Western industrial societies, and it had to substitute repressive tolerance and popular consent for violent repression and coercion as the basis of rulers' legitimacy" (Taras 1986: 61). In addition, Gierek reestablished cordial relations with the Church which had marked the beginning of Gomułka's rule. "The state desisted from taking repressive measures against the church, as had occurred on the issues of taxation of ecclesiastical property and teaching of religion in schools under Gomułka" (Taras 1984: 128). While Poland was still relatively open compared to its neighbors, it was far from a pluralist democracy.[22]

Rather than radically liberalize the political system or decentralize the economy, Gierek decided to base his policy on the import of Western goods. He paid for these goods by taking credits. At first his policy succeeded. Growth rates were quite high. Real wages rose by 40% between 1970 and 1975 (Syrop 1982: 215). The regime used the credits both for buying consumer goods and for acquiring industrial goods, which it used in turn to produce more consumer goods domes-

---

22. Another example of Poland's relative openness was the existence of the newspaper *Polityka*, which was edited by Mieczyslaw Rakowski. Taras (1986: 57) writes, it "developed into an officially sanctioned organ of unorthodox views. The editor's own writings reflected a critical distance from the policies of the rulers." Such a newspaper would never have been allowed in the neighboring GDR or ČSSR.

tically. By 1976, however, the economy was tipping off balance. Still, Gierek believed that, after six years of "normalcy," he could get away with the same attempt at increasing food prices that had failed Gomułka. And he *did* succeed—in the sense that he was able to stay in power. By any other standard, however, it proved an equally serious mistake. Workers went on strikes at once in over 100 factories (Laba 1991: 104, cf. Curry 1988: 90 and Touraine et al. 1982). The very next day the regime rescinded its decree.

Since Gierek had a reformist pragmatic acceptance, he could have used the 1976 uprising to claim that some political or economic liberalization was necessary. But he was far too cautious to do so. Despite his bad experience in 1976, Gierek still shared his predecessor's conviction's that the public would accept Party policy. So on July 1, 1980, Gierek introduced price hikes once again. Again this sparked off a strike. The independent trade union *Solidarność* grew out of it. By the end of August, *Solidarność* had signed the historic Gdańsk accords with the Communist regime, which granted—for the first time in the history of the Soviet bloc—the right to strike, and also the right to form free trade unions.

The Party became divided over how to deal with the uprising. One month after the signing of the Gdańsk accords, Kania replaced Gierek as general secretary. Between August 1980 and December 1981, the Central Committee had 15 plenary meetings (Gerrits 1990: 26). Sandford (1983: 90–91) describes three different factions which emerged within the Central Committee during the autumn of 1980. Former Politburo member Kubiak (interviewed 25 January 1995) agrees. He names 5 Politburo members as "liberals" (including Kania and himself), 5 as "centrists" (including Jaruzelski), and 5 as "orthodox." Among the Secretariat, 3 were liberals, 3 were centrists, and 2 were orthodox.[23] Gerrits (1990: 27) observes that the divided Party leadership in this period had no "deliberate, well-defined reform strategy—it was a mixture of reform and retreat." Nevertheless, Kania

---

23. He gave me a list with the names the day after our interview. The liberals in the Politburo include: Barcikowski, Kania, Kubiak, Łabęcki and Opałko. The centrists include Czechowicz, Czyrek, Jaruzelski, Messner and Romanik. The orthodox include Grzyb, Milewski, Olszowski, Porębsk and Siwak. The liberals in the Secretariat include Barcikowski, Kania, and Kubiak. The centrists are Czyrek, Michal'ek and Woźniak. The orthodox are Milewski and Olszowski. Of course, *after* the transition to democracy, Kubiak has an interest in claiming he was a "liberal." Outsiders such as Taras (1992: 95), though, confirm his reformist credentials.

tried to utilize the Party's reformist legacy to renew the apparatus. He was willing to democratize the Party, but he also wanted to contain *Solidarność* (cf. Gerrits 1990: 26).

His steps towards internal Party democracy and his accommodation to *Solidarność's* demands alienated both Moscow and much of the Party apparatus. General Jaruzelski took advantage of the situation, and maneuvered himself into the post of general secretary. In December 1981, he declared martial law, banned *Solidarność*, and arrested its leaders.

By now the Party's ideological legitimacy had totally dissolved. The economic crisis contradicted claims to economic superiority. The emergence of an independent trade union with 10 million members, combined with the rapid decline of Party membership, falsified the Party's claim to represent the working class. Finally, the military *coup* made a mockery of the Party's claim to possess a monopoly on Truth.

Jaruzelski was not in an easy position. The Party had lost its remaining ideological legitimacy during the months before the *coup*. The Soviet Union made it clear that it might invade. Jaruzelski recalls that the Soviet Central Committee sent the Polish Politburo a letter in the summer of 1981 which was much more sharply worded than the letters to Dubček that had preceded the Warsaw Pact invasion of Czechoslovakia. Furthermore, he adds, Brezhnev told him directly that if they did not crush the opposition, then "everything was lost" (interview with Jaruzelski in *DN* 19 November 1995). While facing pressures from the book for reform, he also faced pressure from the USSR to take a tough stance.

So it was not clear in which direction Jaruzelski would go. Jaruzelski decided to use this formative moment to continue the Party's reform legacy. This was not such an easy task, since he had to purge many reformers from the apparatus in order to carry out the military *coup*. Yet, these were the very people he needed to push through a reform package. The hardliners thus strengthened their position. Jaruzelski admits that he lost control during the first period of martial law. The army interned people it should not have. Conservatives were able to use the situation to block reforms (interview in *Time* 31 December 1990).

Nevertheless, Jaruzelski continued to press for reform. The 9th Extraordinary Congress in 1981 decided to bring the government's economic policies under the control of the Sejm (the Polish parliament). Enterprises were to compete with each other and to maximize profit rather than fulfill plan quotas. They were to be run directly by worker councils and firmer would be allowed to suffer bankruptcy. These reforms, however, were never fully carried out (see Barłomiej Kamiński 1991: 51–7).

On the political front, Jaruzelski took measures to placate the public and to coopt the opposition. To gain public support, he disbanded the old Communist union in 1982 and set-up a new union (OPZZ), which he hoped would be less noxious to the populace. However, only around half the workforce joined it, as compared with the nearly 100% membership in the former union (Ziemer 1989a: 801). The fact that half the population dared to refrain from joining it shows that society had become more open. In the same year, he also set up the Patriotic Movement for National Rebirth (PRON). This was to be a platform for all "patriotic forces"—including non-Communists—to discuss society's problems. One of its leading members, Mil-kolaj Kozakiewicz, admitted that the public basically ignored the organization (Gerrits 1990: 98).

In addition, the Sejm became more independent and critical during the 1980s. Parliamentary elections were also fairer. While nearly 100% officially voted in previous elections, only 67% participated in the national council elections in 1984, and 78% in the Sejm elections one year later (statistics from Ziemer 1989a: 800).

Jaruzelski also established several new institutions to increase the appearance of legality. This included the establishment of a state tribunal (a law court elected by the Sejm) in 1982. In 1985, the Sejm added the Constitutional Tribunal, which was to make judgements on the compatibility of current legislation with the constitution. An ombudsman was installed in 1987 (Gerrits 1990: 87–9).

To coopt the opposition, Jaruzelski set up a consultive council in 1986. It included 56 members, most of them specialists on economic and social policy. About 70% of the members did not belong to any political party. Some were even close to *Solidarność*. It was an attempt at "consultative democracy." Non-Communist specialists had access to a forum for discussing problems with the Party. Thus, the Party leadership hoped to become informed of the problems and of the thinking of non-Party members. Yet the organization had no decision-making powers; the Party leadership was free to reject its advice. None of the *Solidarność* leaders joined it. It failed, therefore, to generate much public enthusiasm (cf. Ziemer 1989a: 801).

During that same year, the Polish regime took several other measures to gain opposition support. Holc (1992: 124) lists the following
steps:

- amnesties for political prisoners,
- reform proposals advocating privatization schemes and extensive
  use of the market,
- the establishment of closer relations with the Church,
- looser censorship.

He adds that none of this succeeded in giving the regime any credibility.

The next step in trying to gain popular support was to hold a
referendum on economic reform; this took place in 1987. It had the
potential for being an ingenious move. It was a way of mobilizing the
support of society against the conservatives in the apparatus who were
blocking reforms. At the same time, it placed *Solidarność* in an embarrassing position. All opposition leaders were aware that the country
was in an economic crisis which required economic reforms. It would
be irresponsible, therefore, to campaign against reforms. But if they
supported the referendum, they would be granting legitimacy to the
regime. The opposition interpreted the vote as a referendum on the
regime. *Solidarność* therefore encouraged citizens to boycott the referendum. Despite the boycott, two-thirds of those taking part in the
referendum supported the regime's reform proposal.

This *should* have meant the Communist regime defeated *Solidarność*
and increased its legitimacy. However, Jaruzelski was so certain of
victory that he decided to require a majority of the *entire electorate*,
rather than just a majority of those voting. Thus, the referendum was
narrowly defeated (cf. Sanford 1992: 9). The leadership further
lowered its chances of winning the referendum by using an extremely
complicated voting procedure. The questions were formulated using
extremely difficult wording which made them difficult to understand.
To make matters more confusing, an "x" on the yes-box meant a
"no." Furthermore, for the first time in the history of the Communist-
led regime, the authorities counted unmarked ballots as invalid, rather
than as "yes." On one of the questions, 6% of the ballots were invalid
(see Ziemer 1989a: 804). If, as in previous elections, these votes had
been counted as "yes" votes, then the regime's proposal would have
won. So although it was perfectly rational to hold the referendum, the
manner in which the regime carried it out was an invitation to defeat.

Jaruzelski himself has admitted this was a turning point for him. After this defeat, he realized the Soviet-type system had exhausted its possibilities.[24]

Hungary: Embourgeoisement

Kádár's pragmatic acceptance gave him more room than most other leaders for domestic reforms. In contrast to its behavior after the interventions in the ČSSR and GDR, the Soviet Union emphasized the foreign-policy aspect of its invasion of Hungary. So Kádár had to be a faithful supporter of Soviet foreign policy, he could pursue certain domestic reforms. Of course there were limits. At no time could Kádár allow a re-assessment of 1956, since that would call into question his own ascension to the throne. Before Gorbachev came to power, furthermore, he had to convince the Kremlin that the Party was not losing its power monopoly and that market reforms were not leading to the reinstatement of capitalism.

Although he could not introduce political democracy, Kádár did open up society parallel with his economic reforms. In the 1960s, the regime announced a general amnesty. It also became possible to travel to the West, and the most important modern works of literature became available in Hungarian translations (Varga 1991: 172). Schöpflin (1992: 97) sums up Kádár's strategy as an attempt to depoliticize society and to keep it satisfied through economic concessions.

> Instead of being forced to stand up and proclaim, as they had been in the 1950s, that "socialism was the most marvellous system in the world," [intellectuals] could say, in effect, "the system that we have here in Hungary is full of defects, it does not work very well, it is open to criticism on a whole variety of grounds; but it is the best that we can hope to have." This formula completely demobilized crucial intellectuals and built self-censorship into their public utterances.

Kádár's policy was summed up by his motto: "Those who are not against us are with us" (Molnár 1987: 203). Or in Molnár's words (1987: 200): "the régime tries to safeguard its tolerant not to say 'liberal' reputation by overlooking oppositional activities confined to mere words, except for certain street demonstrations or commemorative ceremonies."

---

24. I quote his interview with *Time Magazine* (31 December 1990) in chapter 3 of this study.

In the economic sphere, the regime launched the NEM in 1968. It resembled the Czechoslovak proposals in its market orientation. In contrast to Dubček's "socialism with a human face," Kádár's "goulash communism" was more technocratic. For example, there was no major discussion about workplace democracy or humanizing the workplace. Nyers (interviewed 8 April 1993) admits that the Communist leaders were afraid of worker councils because of their role in supporting the 1956 uprising.[25]

Throughout the 1970s and 1980s, the Kádár regime continued its relatively tolerant policy toward society. By the 1980s, Budapest had become a cultural center, to which East Europeans would pilgrimage to see films or buy records forbidden in their home countries.[26] The capital had become an immensely commercialized city, but Brezhnev still prevented Kádár from carrying out all of the economic reforms which he had intended.[27]

By the early 1980s, the economy had weakened to such an extent that the regime started experimenting with more reforms. It took steps in two directions. State firms were to operate more like private firms. Thus, they could sell bonds and eventually even stocks to other state-owned firms (especially banks). So "pseudo" stock and bond markets emerged. But since these firms still were state-owned and lacked "hard budget constraints," they could always count on state help to bail them out. The enterprises kept their soft budgets, therefore, and never behaved like private firms (cf Kornai 1990: ch. 1).

Second, the Kádár regime encouraged the "second economy." Small private firms could operate in the service sector. Between 1975 and

---

25. In the mid-1980s, the regime did enact a law allowing for the formation of worker councils. These remained a formality, however, and the workforce did not gain any control over management (see Swain 1989: 14).

26. Many Czechs in this period told me that they saw Miloš Foreman's film "Hair" in Budapest. Although the film was "Leftist," in the sense that it criticized America's participation in the Vietnam war, Foreman had committed the crime of emigrating from the ČSSR during the normalization period. Another personal anecdote concerns a visit to a record store in Budapest. The employees were very surprised that I was interested in contemporary *Hungarian* music. I was an unusual customer. They were used to two kinds of tourists: Westerners in search of cheap Bartok records, and Easterners in search of Western pop music unavailable in their home countries.

27. See chapter 4. The commercialization of the city was clearly visible. During my trips to Budapest in 1983 and 1987, for example, I saw a Coca Cola banner hanging over the main shopping street and Michael Jackson advertisements for Pepsi in the windows of many stores. Both t-shirts and sweatshirts with the names of American universities and sports teams abounded in the clothing stores.

1985 the number of self-employed shopkeepers and private caterers increased from 10,000 to 25,000. Even more important were the mixed forms of cooperative enterprise and cooperation between private and state firms. Within agriculture, households could utilize resources at state and cooperative farms. The number of state shops and catering units leased to private entrepreneurs rose from just over 2,000 in 1981 to almost 12,000 in 1985 (Berend 1988: 284). Another important decision in 1981 allowed the establishment of "intra-company economic working partnerships." Workers could establish private work teams that utilized enterprise facilities. They were able to function as private, profit-maximizing firms, without state regulation. This work could only be done, however, *after* the normal working hours at the enterprise. By 1985, there were over 13,000 work teams inside companies with approximately 168,000 employees involved (Berend 1988: 287).

These measures affected society and the corporate entity in several ways. First, they led people to believe that the private sector was more efficient than the state sector. Workers would try to save as much energy as possible during their normal working hours at state firms, so as to be able to produce more at their second job. Second, this development had consequences for the health of the population. Hankiss (1990b: 21) reports that, in 1989, Hungarian adult males worked 14 hours a day, 6 days a week. As a result, they had high rates of early death and of heart attacks. Third, many of the members of the ruling corporate entity became convinced that they could make more money in the private sector than by remaining a member of the ruling clique. Thus, Ivan and Balazs Szelenyi (1994: 219) remark:

> Eventually the cadres themselves became attracted to private wealth, they began to believe it is better to be rich than communist. Their willingness to accept market reform cannot be totally separated from their desire to become personally wealthy, to use their political office to accumulate private wealth.

As it became clear that goulash Communism had failed to alleviate the country's economic problems, younger technocrats within the regime started pressing for more radical change. Unlike that of Kádár, their pragmatic acceptance was not tied to the 1956 uprising. They tried to build on the corporate entity's reformist orientation and to go further with democratization and marketization. Kádár, fully aware as he was of his responsibility for Nagy's execution, fought against all attempts to re-evaluate the 1956 uprising. Although he allowed some independent candidates to stand in the 1985 elections, he also continued to resist political democratization.[28] In a famous speech, Kádár warned there would be "no reform of the reform" (Schöpflin 1993: 217).

The younger softliners decided to gather support by going outside the regime to the public. On May 17, 1986, the Patriotic People's Front, headed by reform Communist Imre Pozsgay, suggested founding the Endre Bajcsy-Zsilinsky Fraternal Society. This organization later participated in the Opposition Round Table.[29] Then the Patriotic People's Front sanctioned a critical report written by radical economists. Even though the Central Committee rejected the report, it could not prevent Pozsgay from publishing it through the Patriotic People's Front. Thus, the reform economists were able to make their proposals known. Then, on September 27, 1987, a group of dissidents founded the Hungarian Democratic Forum (MDF), and Pozsgay attended their meeting (Swain 1989: 17 & 1992: 16–7, cf. Körösény 1990a: 2–3 and interview with Laszlo Váss 12 March 1993). Prime Minister Grósz conveyed his greetings through Pozsgay (Schöpflin, Tőkés, & Völgyes 1988: 36). Starting in December 1987, Nyers and other reformers inside and outside the Party began talking about forming the New March Front, an umbrella group of reform Communists and non-Communists devoted to unifying the nation (cf. Swain 1992: 18). Thus, the Party entered 1988 clearly split between conservatives around Kádár and his ideological chief Berecz, and reformers around Pozsgay and Nyers.

Interestingly, the dynamics of this split among elites differs substantially from mainstream theory about democratization. Most theorists such as O'Donnell & Schmitter (1986) start their analysis with an authoritarian regime that begins liberalizing. During this first step of liberalization, softliners are the dominant force within the regime. These softliners must contend with opposing demands advanced by the hardliners within the regime and by the opposition. In Hungary, by contrast, the centrists and conservatives around Kádár and Berecz were in charge. Thus, the reformers did not play the opposition and con-

---

28. In the 1985 elections, independents gained 10'% of the seats in the Hungarian parliament (see Hankiss 1990b: 21).

29. The Opposition Round Table was an organization within which the main opposition groups met to work out a unified strategy for dealing with the regime in 1989.

servatives against each other. Instead, they appealed to the opposition in order to gain support against the ruling centrists and hardliners.

Re-ideologization in the GDR

When Honecker replaced Ulbricht, he built heavily on the SED's anti-reformist pragmatic acceptance. Ulbricht had paid the price for upsetting the USSR. After having opposed Soviet foreign policy on the German question, he did not have to wait long before the Kremlin replaced him with Honecker. The new leader made it clear that he would revert to orthodoxy. He demoted Mittag and cancelled the economic reforms. He led the country still further down the orthodox road by nationalizing the remaining half-private firms.[30] Rather than liberalizing the cultural sector or attempting economic reforms, he tried to gain support by increasing living standards without any institutional changes. He chose, therefore, to increase investment in the social and consumption sectors, under the motto: "unity of economic and social policy."[31]

Within the apparatus, Honecker made Party discipline the ultimate principle. In Neumann's (1991: 160) words: "Towards the end of his reign, Honecker ruled almost alone." Economic Secretary Mittag and Stasi[32] chief Mielke had special access to Honecker. Apparently, Honecker made his decisions alone with the two of them, and then presented the result to the Politburo for confirmation.[33] However, even Mittag (1991) claims in his memoirs that he did not believe in the

---

30. See chapter 3. Previously, the GDR had allowed some private firms to retain 50% ownership, with the state owning the remaining share.
31. See chapter 5.
32. STASI is the abbreviated form of *Staatsicherheit*, meaning state security.
33. Both Krenz (1990: 123) and Schabowski (1992: 159) claim that Honecker always met alone with Mielke after Politburo meetings. They add that nobody else knew what they spoke about. Concerning Mittag's special relation with Honecker, Przybylski (1991: 123) claims there were two Politburos, one with the economic functionaries gathered around Mittag, Kleiber and Schürer, and then the other official Politburo. Former Prime Minister Sindermann (interviewed in *Der Spiegel* 19/1990) confirms Honecker's special relation with Mittag, and asserts that he felt he had to accept Mittag as his first vice prime minister responsible for economic questions. If he had refused to accept him, Honecker would have chosen Mittag over himself. Mittag's former employee Janson (1991: foreword) claims that Mittag made all of the important economic decisions. Interestingly, Honecker himself claims that he did not have much control over state security (interviewed in Andert & Herzberg 1990: 363–77). Furthermore, he denies that he had any special powers, and sees himself as having been an "equal" member of the Politburo. Yet he admits that he always get along well with Mittag, Mielke and Herrmann (Andert & Herzberg 1990: 361). This indicates that, indeed, he had a special relation with Mittag and Mielke.

economic policies he was proposing. He dared not go against Honecker's wishes, although he realized prevailing policies were leading to economic catastrophe. Przybylski (1991: 124) provides another example. In 1980, Politburo member Krolikowski sent a letter to Moscow. In it he informed the Soviet leaders of a conversation which Prime Minister Stroph had had with Mielke about Honecker's absolute power. Stroph complained that the other Politburo members were uninformed about important issues. They were forced to follow their leader blindly. Mielke added that "everyone is afraid of Erich Honecker."

Former Politburo member Schabowski (1990: 24–5) describes Honecker's divide-and-rule tactics. He claims Honecker tried to isolate the individual Politburo members, in order to prevent them from building factions. No group in the Politburo (not even two persons) ever had any discussions over fundamental or principle issues. Everyone was afraid that any doubts or deviating views expressed could be passed on to the "wrong addresses." If even two people got along especially well, that was reason for Honecker to distrust them. So Honecker played the one against the other by criticizing the one and praising the other. In another book, Schabowski (1992: 115) claims that Honecker had such control over the mass media that he read the layout of the Party newspaper *Neues Deutschland* the evening before it came out. Not only would he approve the contents of the newspaper in advance, he did the same for the evening news program "Aktuellen Kamera." He played, then, the role of "super censor" (1992: 92).

If the top leaders did not dare break Party discipline, those at lower levels were even less willing. Meuschel (1993: 102–3) concludes that reformers within the Party were too weak to force any discussion. Nor could they turn to the public outside the Party.

When Gorbachev came to power, Honecker faced a dilemma. His pragmatic acceptance rested on two pillars. First, he was a guardian of orthodoxy. Since the USSR considered the GDR vital for its security, it would not allow any experiments. Second, East German leaders had to show total allegiance to the Kremlin. Ulbricht lost power to Honecker precisely because he had challenged Moscow's control over East German foreign policy. Accordingly, the most famous slogan in the GDR was arguably "learn from the Soviet Union." Yet, this same Soviet Union was now advocating radical political and economic reform. So the second pillar of pragmatic acceptance collided with the first. When Honecker opted for the first pillar, his sudden switch to slogans about each country's right to choose its own path sounded rather hallow.

Honecker responded to Gorbachev by initiating a "re-ideologization" campaign. He strayed so far from the Kremlin's position that he even banned Soviet publications on several occasions.[34] The regime considered *Glasnost* so dangerous that it organized groups of Party militants to go to stores and buy out brochures of Gorbachev's speeches. It also tried to limit the circulation of Gorbachev's book *Perestroika* (Wielgohs & Schultz 1990: 16). Meanwhile, Honecker increased his tough stance toward the opposition. In 1987, for example, the police raided East Berlin's Zion Church. This church was a center for alternative organizations, and had a famous environmental library. The police arrested activists there and confiscated environmental pamphlets (cf. Pond 1993: 82).[35]

As Honecker would soon discover, society was only willing to accept the first pillar of pragmatic acceptance (orthodox policies) as long as the second pillar (allegiance to the USSR) held firm. Once the second pillar fell, the house caved in. For in the absence of Soviet pressure, East Germans felt they had no reason to accept strict orthodoxy as the only pragmatic alternative to a democratic system. Meanwhile, the country's ideological acceptance had also collapsed. In the 1980s, it had become easier for Western tourists to visit the GDR, and Party militants no longer checked TV antennas to make sure people were not watching Western TV Thus, East Germans realized—from watching West German TV and meeting West German tourists—that their living standards had fallen much farther behind those of their Western relatives. The constant reports in the mass media on the alleged economic advances completely lacked credibility in the eyes of the populace.

Buying Time: The ČSSR

When the Warsaw Pact invaded the ČSSR in August 1968, it assumed it would be able to install a puppet regime quickly. Brezhnev

---

34. See for example Wielgohs & Schultz (1990: 16 fn. 7).
35. Although Honecker cracked down on the opposition and stepped up the ideological warfare, he did ease up on some policies. It became a little easier for East Germans to travel to the West; however, this was mostly restricted to pensioners, who would no longer be a burden on the East German budget if they chose to emigrate. It also became slightly easier for West Germans to visit East Germany.

originally wanted the dogmatic hardliner Alois Indra to build a "revolutionary worker and peasant government." But his government failed to gain any support from either the populace or the Central Committee. Hence, the Soviet leaders reluctantly agreed to negotiate with the very Prague Spring reformers whom they had arrested and brought to the Soviet Union for possible imprisonment or execution. An additional group of negotiators came from Prague; they included hardliners such as Jakeš and Bil'ak. Among these extra negotiators was Husák. He had originally opposed the invasion, claiming that he stood and fell with Dubček, but in Moscow he became suddenly more "understanding" of Moscow's view. During the negotiations, Brezhnev made it clear he did not consider the ČSSR to be a sovereign country. He demanded that they initiate a "normalization" process. Yet he allowed Dubček to remain in power, although some of the most radical reformers such as Kriegel and Císař had to retire from politics. In addition, supporters of the invasion, such as Bil'ak and Indra, had to remain in the top leadership.

As the normalization process began, the Kremlin looked for an alternative to Dubček, whose continuation as general secretary was embarrassing to them. In April 1969, Husák replaced Dubček.[36] Husák gained the support of the Politburo by presenting himself as a pragmatic alternative to the naïve Dubček. Before the election he promised he would try to save as much of the reform program as possible. Being less naïve than Dubček, he would know how to deal with the USSR. He would be, in short, a Czechoslovak Kádár.

Meanwhile, Husák was palatable to the Soviet leadership for several reasons. First, he was not as strongly identified with the Prague Spring, since he had not been a member of the Politburo or Secretariat before the invasion. Yet, since he had supported reforms, he was much more popular among Czechoslovak citizens than the "traitors" who had welcome the invasion. Second, since Husák was a reformer, who had turned opportunist, the Kremlin could always threaten him if he got out of line, by bringing up his former "sin" of having opposed the invasion. Third, having demanded that hardline supporters of the invasion be given top positions, Husák now had to work with a noose

---

36. For details of the invasion and its aftermath, see Dubček (1993), Engman (1969), Hejzlar (1976: ch. III&IV), Mlynář (1980) and Szulc (1971: ch. VIII-X).

around his neck.[37] For the unpopular Soviet stooges wielded great power, while Husák bore responsibility for their decisions.[38] With the continuous presence of hardliners in the Czechoslovak leadership, the Kremlin could be certain that nothing would remain of the "capitalistic" reforms. To remain at the post of general secretary, Husák had to criticize his former reformist colleagues for wanting to re-instate capitalism. So although Husák would reportedly have liked to pursue Kádár's brand of "goulash socialism,"[39] he had to go back to the old, tainted cans of Russian borscht—without anything to spice them up. Still, as a "moderate," Husák had greater pragmatic acceptance than the hardliners, for he could always claim he was preventing something even worse from happening. He used the room for maneuver that the USSR gave him, but he enjoyed much less room than did Kádár.

The "cultural cemetery" (Böll 1985: 15) of the normalization period is well-documented.[40] During the ensuing purges, around 500,000 members (about 1/3) either were expelled from the Party or left voluntarily (Pelikan 1975: 43, cf. Kusin 1978: 85). In the schools, about 1/3 of the teachers who were Party members lost their jobs; 42% of the functionaries in the teachers unions, 48.6% of the members of the regional school committees, and 60% of the chairs of the district committees suffered the same fate (Kusin 1978: 98). At the same time, the Journalist Union dismissed approximately half of its 4,000 members

---

37. For example, Hoření (interviewed in *Mosty* no. 32–33, 1991), a former *Rudé pravo* editor, member of the Secretariat, and non-voting member of the Politburo, recalls that Bil'ak seemed to have had more influence than Husák in questions of cadre policy. Plevza has stated that Husák would have liked to purge Bil'ak from the leadership, but could not because of the Kremlin's support for him (interview with Plevza, 6 March 1993). He adds that, in 1970, both Bil'ak and Indra sent a petition to the USSR which implied criticism of Husák for being a "bourgeois nationalist." Plevza writes in his book (1991: 136) that Husák wanted Bil'ak to leave the Politburo, but Brezhnev wanted him to stay. Sedlák (interviewed 11 May 1992) agrees that Husák wanted to drop Bil'ak, but was unable to gain Soviet support for the step. Furthermore, Husák was afraid of Bil'ak because he had controlled the *nomenklatura*.

38. Piekalkiewicz lists a public opinion survey showing that nearly seven months after the invasion (March 11–18, 1969), 76% of the population still had confidence in Dubček, as compared to 8% for Husák, while Bil'ak and Indra were not named by any of the respondents (1972: 265; in this survey, the respondents were asked to identify the five individuals in public life whom they trusted most.

39. Cf. Batt (1991b: 375–6), Hejzlar (1978), interviews with Plevza on 6 March 1993 and Sedlák on 11 May 1992.

40. Aragon (1985) uses the equally unflattering term "cultural Biafra" to describe the cultural climate during the normalization period. See also Milan Kundera (1985: 128) for a similar denunciation of "normalization."

(Kusin 19778: 101), and the Czechoslovak radio network fired 1,500 employees (Hejzlar 1976: 354).

After "successfully" carrying out normalization, the Czechoslovak leaders proudly entered the 1980s knowing they had destroyed almost all opposition. The price was cultural stagnation. During the 1980s, furthermore, it became clear that economic stagnation accompanied cultural stagnation. Since economic reforms were taboo, the regime embarked on several attempts to "perfect" the not-so-perfect economic mechanism.[41]

By 1985, Gorbachev had come to power and started talking about reforms. As in the GDR, Gorbachev's advocacy of reforms destroyed the Czechoslovak regime's pragmatic acceptance. The regime was even more dependent on the USSR than was the GDR, since its most influential leaders had come to power as passengers on Soviet tanks. If Gorbachev were serious about reforms, than the Czechoslovak rulers could no longer claim they were in power to prevent reforms; nor could they still claim that all reforms lead to capitalism. So the Czechoslovak leaders tried to shrug off talk of reforms, hoping that there would not be any substance behind Gorbachev's words. And when they could no longer avoid the issue, they tried to make sure there would not be any substance behind *their own* words. The economic restructuring they announced in 1987 was belittled by Western observers as "minimalist" (*Czechoslovak SR/1*, 17 Jan 1987) and it was not to take effect until 1990, except as an experiment in a few enterprises (*FAZ*, 6 Feb. 1987). Some Czechoslovak economists also criticized it openly for not going far enough (*SvD*, 5 Oct. 1989). The leadership's tactic was to buy time with symbolic reforms.[42] The majority of the Politburo believed that, if they waited long enough,

---

41. Cf. Hatschikjan (1987: 59). For a discussion of the failure of these steps, see Blaha (1985 & 1986). For relatively critical appraisals among Czechoslovak economists, see Kaspárek (1985), Filip & Valach (1986), Halík (1986), Dvořak (1986), Bukač (1985), Sourek (1986, and Čap & Rybnikár (1985).

42. See Vlačil (1992). Albæk (1988: 86) defines symbolic policies as decisions which serve the symbolic function of making it appear that the decision-makers have taken some problem into consideration, although their real objective is to make the issue disappear from political debate.

Gorbachev would lose power. Then it would be the USSR's turn to undergo "normalization."[43]

Although reforms would undermine the regime's pragmatic acceptance, there was still one chance to change the regime's course in 1987. Husák was coming under increasing pressure to resign. The hardliners never liked him because of his previous condemnation of the invasion and support for the Prague spring. Yet, because he had become synonymous with normalization, he had little backing among reformists, who thought they could utilize Gorbachev to change the course of the sinking ship. The Štrougal camp thought the time had come to strike. Prime Minister Štrougal stepped up his attacks and became a more outspoken supporter of reforms. He tried to convince Husák to resign and support his candidacy to the general-secretary post, or at least to support Pitra. By then, the leadership had basically become non-ideological. As former Adamec advisor Krejčí (1991: 10) observes, the regime had lost its ideological orientation. Several insiders note that most of the infighting at the top was non-ideological.[44] Instead, Politburo members fought to gain more privileges and more investments for their regions. Nevertheless, Krejčí and everyone else agrees that Bil'ak was an ideological hardliner and that Štrougal basically supported reforms.

Although there were no open ideological struggles until 1987, there were potential divisions under the surface. On one hand, there were the hardliners gathered around Bil'ak. Since they had supported the invasion, their power was completely bound to the regimes' anti-reformist pragmatic acceptance. This orientation was based on the

---

43. The following Politburo members have told me this: Štěpán (full member, interviewed 3 June 1992) and Poledník (non-voting member and member of the Secretariat, interviewed 6 April 1992. In addition, Krejčí, who was an advisor to Prime Minister Adamec, agrees (interviewed on 13 April 1992), as does Sedlák, who was an advisor to Prime Minister Štrougal (interviewed on 11 May 1992). Hořeni (non-voting member and member of the Secretariat, interviewed 30 March 1992) maintains that anywhere from 1/3 to 1/2 of the Politburo was against Gorbachev. Jakeš' replacement as general secretary, Karel Urbanek claims in an interview that Jakeš supported reforms, but conservatives such as Indra convinced him that Gorbachev would not hold out (Mladý svět no. 37, 1991).

44. Those interviewees agreeing with this include: Čmejrek (interviewed 23 March 1992), who had been a member of the Central Committee organ for foreign policy, Krejčí (interviewed on 13 April 1992), who had been an advisor to Prime Minister Adamec, and Sedlák (interviewed on 11 May 1992), who had been an advisor to Prime Minister Štrougal. Neveřil, former economic advisor to Adamec and Štrougal, claims that after 1968, ideological issues did not play any role, they were only ceremonial (letter to the author on 12 April 1993).

notion that they were put in power by the USSR in order to prevent all reforms. On the other hand, there were the opportunists, such as Husák and Štrougal, who had originally condemned the invasion. They were less bound by the pragmatic acceptance, since they could claim they had always tried to make the best of a bad situation. The problem was that, after so many years in power, the populace identified them with normalization; they did not, therefore, enjoy much popular support. Finally, there were the younger politicians, who had joined the elite after the invasion; they were even less bound by the anti-reformist pragmatic acceptance.

Bil'ak was a front runner among the prospective hardline candidates. There is widespread agreement that Bil'ak would have liked to have become general secretary.[45] Since he was hated by the population, however, the hardliners decided not to back him. Officially, he decided not to run for the office because he was too old. Furthermore, after the long reign of the Slovak Husák, it was time for a Czech. Eventually the hardliners agreed to launch Jakeš as their candidate. As a supporter of the Soviet invasion and the leader of the Party purges during the 1970s, he had clear hardline credentials. Yet, as a late comer to the Politburo—he joined in the early 1980s—he was not as well known and hated as the older hardliners. Furthermore, since the hardliners considered him a weak person, they thought they could hold the real power and use him as a front-man.[46]

At the fateful Politburo meeting on November 19, 1987, Adamec proposed Jakeš to replace Husák as general secretary. Although Adamec would later emerge as the most reformist member of

---

45. Published sources include Anonymous (1991: 65) and Plevza (1991: 149). Those who have spoken in interviews about Bil'ak's aspirations to become general secretary include Plevza (interviewed 6 March 1993) and Lenárt (interviewed 3 June 1993, Hoření (interviewed 30 March 1992) and Poledník (interviewed 6 April 1992).

46. Ironically, Poledník (interviewed 6 April 1992) claims that one of the arguments used for supporting the weak Jakeš was that there was already a precedent for a weak general secretary, meaning Dubček! Jakeš himself (interviewed 9 April 1992) confirms this claim indirectly—and without him realizing it. When I asked him why he was asked to be a candidate, he asserts that his supporters told him he was a "team player," whereas Štrougal went his own way. In other words, the weaker Jakeš would agree to their policies, while the stronger Štrougal would likely try to push through his own program.

the Politburo, he was still willing to support orthodoxy at this point.[47]

With the support of moderates like Adamec, the hardliners had expected an easy victory. In addition, the Kremlin had already assured them it did not oppose Jakeš. To their surprise, the opposition was much greater than they had anticipated. In fact, the opposition was so great that they were forced to have two meetings before the final decision was made. Hoření (interviewed 30 March 1992) reports that he, Poledník, Harlín, Pitra and Beňo opposed Jakeš. In addition, Colotka and Kempený were neutral. Poledník (interviewed 6 April 1992) claims that he, Kapek, Colotka, Herman, Haman and Hruškovič supported Štrougal. Most of those who opposed the hardliners had joined the elite after normalization had begun. They were less bound, therefore, by the pragmatic acceptance based on the invasion. If Štrougal and Husák are added, then a majority supported Štrougal.[48] Unfortunately for the Štrougal camp, most of his supporters were not full members of the Politburo. Thus, they had no voting rights. Among the six whom Poledník lists as Štrougal supporters, for example, only the first two were full-fledged Politburo members with voting rights. None of those mentioned by Hoření were voting members except for Pitra. Virtually all of Štrougal's supporters were demoted in the following year. Colotka, Kapek, Kempený and Štrougal left the Politburo, while Harlín and Beňo lost their positions in the Secretariat (and with it their observer status in the Politburo). Herman, Haman and

---

47. There are several reasons for Adamec's support for Jakeš. Obviously, it furthered his career. Shortly afterwards, he replaced his rival Štrougal as prime minister. In addition, Adamec was never as radical as Štrougal. While Štrougal had supported the Prague Spring, Adamec was skeptical. Dubček demoted him at the time for his attitude. Neveřil (interviewed 30 March 1993 and personal letter to the author on 12 April 1993), former economic advisor to both former prime ministers, asserts that while Štrougal honestly believed in the necessity of reforms, he had to persuade Adamec of the severity of the economic crisis before the later was willing to support them.
48. There are two probable reasons why Hoření and Poledník do not name the exact same people. First, Hoření told me who *opposed* Jakeš, while Poledník told me who *supported* Štrougal. Thus, they were not really describing the same thing. Second, no former vote was ever taken. Instead, the members chose their words carefully at Politburo meetings, knowing that a slip could cost them their career. Since the members often spoke indirectly, it was difficult to know exactly where everybody stood. The desire not to clearly state ones preferences was probably strengthened by the advanced knowledge that a majority would support Jakeš, so it was pointless to protest too loudly. Nevertheless, the Jakeš-Bil'ak camp seems to have been genuinely surprised at the opposition they faced.

Hruškovič remained in purgatory as candidate members, without voting rights. They were passed over in the promotions to the Politburo in favor of Štěpán, Urbanek, and Knotek. All three newcomers were either hardliners or at least much more conservative than the Štrougal group. Among the remaining Štrougal supporters, Poledník was demoted to the newly created Czechoslovak Physical Education Association, and he lost his observer status in the Politburo. Hoření kept his post, but he told me that he had merely supported Štrougal *personally*. He never indicated that he had made his position clear at the Politburo meetings. So the only Štrougal supporter who remained unscathed was Pitra. Even he moved downward to the position of Czech prime minister, which gave him less influence than his original post of agricultural secretary.[49] So in the end, the Czechoslovak leaders tried—like their counterparts in the GDR—to continue their anti-reformist pragmatic acceptance, even after Gorbachev had removed the basis for it.

CONCLUSION

In this chapter I identify the different policy directions chosen by the four East European regimes before 1988. My main argument is that their behavior was strongly influenced by the pragmatic manner in which the leaders defended their rise to power as a result of of a Soviet invasion or threat thereof. During these formative moments, the new leaders usually lacked popular support. Gomułka in 1956 is the only exception. Still, despite their lack of popularity, citizens were willing to accept these regimes pragmatically — as the best possible alternative given the Soviet constraints.

In Poland and Hungary, Soviet intervention occurred in a manner which made domestic reforms possible. In Hungary, Kádár based his pragmatic acceptance on the question of foreign policy. The Red Army had invaded the country to prevent it from leaving the Warsaw Pact and installing a multiparty democracy. Consequently, Kádár had to pursue a pro-Soviet foreign policy; he had room to maneuver, however, in shaping domestic policy. Of course, he still had to convince Brezhnev that he was not going to re-install capitalism and that

---

49. Wightman (1989) and Wolchik (1991: 126–31) mention the names of those promoted and demoted in 1987–8.

the Party would maintain its political monopoly. But he was still able to pursue more radical policies than his other colleagues in the Warsaw Pact. When Gorbachev came to power, his pragmatic acceptance became weaker. For much of the populace *and* many Party activists no longer believed that the Soviet Union demanded that the Party maintain its monopoly on power. The younger generation of leaders could build on the Party's reformist orientation, which was based on the notion that they would test the borders of what the USSR would allow. Now they felt that the USSR would allow more radical reforms than before. In addition, their personal pragmatic acceptance was not tied, as Kádár's had been, to the suppression of the 1956 revolt. They could therefore be more flexible than the ageing and increasingly rigid general secretary. The Party entered 1988 more split than at any time since 1956.

Similarly, the Polish regime was able to build a reformist pragmatic acceptance, because of the manner in which Gomułka and Jaruzelski came to power during periods of Soviet threats. Gomułka rose to the top as a reformist with the support of worker-led demonstrators. He won the election to the post of general secretary during an election that was directly monitored by the skeptical Soviet Politburo. On the one hand, he came to power with a reformist reputation and with substantial support from the populace. On the other hand, he had to convince his Soviet superiors immediately that he would not go against their institutional interests. Thus, although he could create a reformist pragmatic acceptance he had a good alibi for restricting the reach of reforms. When Jaruzelski carried out the military *coup* a new formative moment arose, which gave the general a change to change the regime's reformist pragmatic acceptance. Rather than switch directions, he claimed that the *coup* was to prevent a Soviet invasion rather than to prevent reforms. He declared that the reform process must continue. Once Gorbachev came to power, he was able to utilize his reformist position even further, with various attempts at coopting the opposition. But his various attempts at "consultative democracy" and authoritarian liberalization failed to satisfy the populace. After losing the 1987 referendum, Jaruzelski entered 1988 facing a deep crisis.

In contrast with their counterparts in Poland and Hungary, the East German and Czechoslovak regimes built anti-reformist pragmatic legitimacies. Ulbricht was only able to maintain power after the Soviet army had lent him its support during the 1953 uprising. The Kremlin made it clear it considered the GDR a vital security interest, and that no experiments would be tolerated. When Ulbricht dared to show his disloyalty by questioning Brezhnev's policies towards the FRG, the Kremlin supported Honecker's campaign to replace the ageing leader. Honecker proved even more orthodox than Ulbricht, quickly cancelling the modest economic reforms of the 1960s. Despite the growing economic crisis of the 1980s, the Party remained unified under Honecker's tight control. The Party's unwritten motto was: *Disziplin über alles!* Gorbachev's rise to power undermined the regime's mode of pragmatic acceptance, since it could no longer claim that the Soviet Union would punish all deviations from orthodoxy. Slogans about learning from the Soviet Union changed to tirades about the necessity for each country to find its own way of "building socialism." The Red Prussians entered 1988 more prepared for increased discipline than for the looming threat of a spontaneous anti-Communist revolt.

The dilemma faced by a regime losing its pragmatic acceptance was probably most severe in the ČSSR. For the rulers in that country had clearly come to power to prevent reforms. With Soviet guns trained on them, the new leaders had claimed that the previous reforms were leading to capitalism. Thus, they were in power to prevent such deviations. They set in motion a normalization process which cost many people their positions. A cultural dark age set in. When Gorbachev launched his *glasnost* and *perestroika* policy initiatives, the Czechoslovak leaders could no longer claim that the Soviet Union equated all reforms with capitalism. This dilemma was highlighted when Western reporters asked Gorbachev's spokesman, Gennadi Gerasimov, what the difference was between the Prague Spring and the present Soviet reforms. His short reply was: "Nineteen years."[50] Although the shift in Soviet policy caused the collapse of the foundations of the Czechoslovak regime's anti-reformist pragmatic accept-

---

50. This quote has appeared in many news reports and books. See for example, Gati (1990: 178). Since Gorbachev's spokesman made such a statement while Gorbachev was in Prague, it might seem strange that I argued that the Soviet leader did not encourage reforms in the ČSSR. It should be noted, however, that Gorbachev did not make this statement. Rather, it was his spokesman. Moreover, he said it to the Western media, rather than to the Czechoslovak media or Central Committee. This is in line with Gorbachev's general tendency of presenting a reformist image to the West, and behaving cautiously when dealing with the Eastern leaders behind closed doors.

ance, the hardliners tried to increase their stranglehold on the Politburo by electing Jakeš over the reformist Štrougal in 1987. After his election, Jakeš succeeding in demoting all of Štrougal's supporters. Thus, the Politburo became more unified and conservative than it had been before the Gorbachev era. Nevertheless, the Czechoslovak leaders tried to appease the populace through a series of symbolic reforms. Later events would show that appeasement worked no better for Jakeš than for it had for Chamberlain.

Chapter 7

CIVIL SOCIETY AND THE DEGREE OF LIBERALIZATION

In the last chapter I discussed the policies of the regimes before 1988. In this chapter I discuss the interaction between these policies and society. It has been common for observers to discuss this interaction in terms of civil society versus the state. In contrast, I consider it more fruitful to consider the degree of liberalization reached by a society.

TERMINOLOGY

The term "civil society" is currently in vogue. However, there are many different definitions of the term. Each of them implies a different result. There is wide agreement, however, among many of the authors who use this term in explaining the collapse of the Soviet-type system. Most of the authors writing on this topic use definitions similar to that employed by Frentzel-Zagórska & Zagórski (1990), who define civil society as "a structure of the self-organisation of society, located outside, though not disconnected from, the institutional framework of the state." Since my ambition in this study is to limit myself to the discourse on the collapse of the Soviet-type system, I accept Frentzel-Zagórska & Zagórski's definition, rather than discuss other definitions that have been used in other discourses. Authors writing on Eastern Europe define civil society as separate from the state because they believe that, by opposing the state, civil society can bring it down. They concentrate, then, on the civil society/state dichotomy.

I believe it is more fruitful in the East European context to discuss the degree of liberalization of society in general, rather than civil society in particular. "Society" includes the entire aggregate of individuals in a country, *including* those in or engaged with the state. "Liberalization" refers to the degree of political and cultural openness in a particular society. The degree of liberalization rises if an authoritarian regime increases its tolerance of critical opinions and previously unacceptable cultural styles. This includes such measures as easing or eliminating censorship and encouraging more open debates among Party leaders and in academic journals. Although liberalization is often the first step toward democratization, they are not identical. Democratization requires that decision-making institutions be opened up to people outside the regime (cf. O'Donnell-Schmitter 1986 and Przeworski 1991).

I prefer the term "degree of liberalization" to "civil society" for three reasons. First, by using this term, one avoids the sticky problem of deciding where to draw the line between civil society and the state, or between active and passive members of civil society. It is especially difficult to find the cut-off point between civil society and the state in Soviet-type societies, since virtually all citizens are employed by the Party-state, and virtually all organizations except the churches are officially run by or under the direct control of the Party or the state. Even the churches were subject to varying degrees of control and penetration by the Party-state apparatus, although the degree of state control varied. In countries such as the Soviet Union and Romania, the Orthodox Church became *de facto* an extended arm of the Party, while in Poland after 1956 the Church enjoyed relative freedom from Party-state control (which did not prevent security agents from murdering several outspoken priests in the 1980s). Some of the church organizations (especially certain branches of the Lutheran Church in East Germany) were eventually able to open themselves up and to allow dissidents to carry out activities under their protection.

Second, if one limits the concept of civil society to *legal* organizations outside the state, then civil society in Eastern Europe before 1988 consisted mainly of the Catholic Church in Poland and certain branches of the Evangelical Church in the GDR. In 1988, some independent organizations were allowed in Hungary, and by 1989 *Solidarność* was legalized in Poland, but these organizations did not *cause* the collapse of the system; rather, the regimes decided to allow them because they realized it was necessary to change the system. Nevertheless, these organizations played significant roles in negotiating the transition to democracy. Except for their churches, the GDR and ČSSR had little or no civil society before the collapse—at least, if one defines civil society as legal, non-governmental organizations, that are autonomous from the state. If one includes *illegal* organizations, on the other hand, then the only country with a large-scale civil society was Poland, where *Solidarność* once had 10 million members. (In its underground years between 1982 and 1988, the union still had a potentially large following, but it was much smaller and its activities were more limited.) So regardless of whether or not one chooses to include illegal organizations, civil society in Eastern Europe was far too weak to bring down the regimes.[1] Although the number of dissident groups grew in Eastern Europe during the late 1980s, except for the leaders of *Solidarność*, none of them enjoyed much popular support until 1989. These groups were potential catalysts for revolution, then, but they were not strong enough to put the regimes under much pressure until the revolutions actually broke out.

Third, the manner in which the public influenced the thinking of Communist elites should be emphasized. The state/civil society dichotomy implies an opposition between the two, especially if one defines civil society as exclusive of the state—which, to the best of my knowledge, writers explaining the collapse of communism always do. I believe, in contrast, that the degree of liberalization was even more important than the existence of independent organizations. In comparatively open Poland and Hungary, the leaders were able to read critical discussions of current affairs by intellectuals and researchers, who most often were themselves Party members. These journals arguably influenced the elites as much as the writings of dissidents who stood outside the system. Since all legal journals were either state- or Party-owned, again the problem emerges of drawing the line between civil society and state. It is especially difficult to maintain a clear division between the two if one keeps in mind that the authors of these articles were usually employed either by state universities and research institutes or by newspapers owned by the Party-state.[2]

Universities themselves present another ambiguous case, as far as drawing the border between civil society and the state is concerned. Social scientists often place universities in capitalist societies under the heading of civil society. In Soviet-type societies, however, all universities are owned by the state, and all teachers must be approved by the Party committee. Under the most orthodox regimes, university teachers and researchers risk losing their job and being imprisoned if they dare to diverge from official dogma. Yet, under liberalizing regimes as

---

1. However, their potential to bring down the regime was increasing in most countries. In the case of Hungary, this was partly the result of regime policies which encouraged these organizations.

2. Which does not mean, of course, that these authors had complete freedom to write as they wished. They often had to weigh their words carefully, and those who went too far sometimes lost their job. The main point here is that official authors writing in official journals were able to criticize the system to such an extent as to influence the thinking of the Party-state elite, so that the elite became more critical of the system.

in Poland and Hungary in the 1980s, universities could and did become centers for critical opinion. The term liberalization describes this change better than the phrase "emergence of a civil society." Nothing new emerged, since the state-run universities existed under both orthodox and reforming regimes, and no new institutions emerged in Poland and Hungary. The important change under liberalization is that the institutions which already exist became more open. Once the universities become more open, researchers there were able to influence the thinking of ruling elites by publishing critical articles, becoming advisors to reformers, and having private meetings with high-standing members of the ruling corporate entity.

My main argument in this chapter is that the regimes with a reformist pragmatic acceptance took advantage of their reformist legacy in order to liberalize their societies. As a result, liberalization proceeded much further under these regimes than under those with an anti-reformist pragmatic acceptance. This difference in social climate led in turn to a different dynamic between members of the regime and other citizens.

In Poland and Hungary, the reformist regimes allowed relatively open discussions already as early as the 1960s and 1970s. As the economies deteriorated in the 1980s, the critical debates among economists, sociologists and other social scientists influenced the elites. In addition, given the relatively open atmosphere, some of the elites also read the underground *samizdat* publications. As the economy deteriorated further, and attempts at economic reform failed, many of the elites opened up to both the legal and forbidden critical writings that were circulating. This caused a further erosion of the regimes' ideological legitimacy. The reformist leaders in these countries were quicker to lose confidence in their ability to rule than were the hardline leaders of the anti-reformist regimes. As a result, the reformists became more open to change of a systemic character

In addition, since the opposition was not as repressed in the reformist countries as in the remainder of the Soviet bloc, some of the elites established contacts with dissident leaders. Thus, both sides were able to build up greater trust for each other. When the time came to negotiate, the opposition had already established political organizations that were ready to negotiate. This made it easier to negotiate institutional change.

In the GDR and ČSSR, where the regimes had an anti-reformist pragmatic acceptance, it was more difficult to achieve a negotiated change. In the closed atmosphere of these countries, the elites were not confronted by articles authored by critical social scientists. Nor did they listen to the voices of the isolated dissidents. Consequently, it was easier for the rulers to maintain the belief that problems go away if they buried their heads in the sand like ostriches. Furthermore, their confrontational attitude toward the dissidents made it more difficult for the two sides to trust each other once the time to negotiate arrived. In addition, the opposition did not have established organizations which could prepare for negotiations as in Poland and Hungary.[3] In what follows, I examine the development of society before 1988 in the reformist and anti-reformist countries.

Some theorists have claimed it was the emergency of civil society that caused the collapse of the Soviet-type regimes. Once civil society emerged, the opposition could mobilize the populace against the system and force the regimes to resign (see, for example, Weigle & Butterfield 1992). In contrast, Szakolczai & Horváth (1992: 16) write:

> The struggle of the civil society against the state would imply a certain degree of confrontation, some mass organisation and mobilisation for positive goals. Nothing like that happened in the [East European] countries. Quite the contrary; one could perhaps say that the changes occurred at a point where any type of mobilisation was at its lowest ebb...

Although it is an exaggeration to claim that "mobilisation was at its lowest ebb," Szakolczai & Horváth are certainly closer to the truth than Weigle & Butterfield. While Polish and Hungarian society were more mobilized in the mid-to-late 1980s than in previous decades, they were not nearly as mobilized as Polish society had been during

---

3. In the ČSSR, Charter 77 did exist as an organization that might—potentially—have negotiated with the regime. Yet, the organization was unprepared for this. In contrast to MDF in Hungary or *Solidarność* in Poland, the organization was never recognized by the regime. Thus, its members had never established contact with the leaders until the actual negotiations began in 1989. Some of its members had some brief contacts with Krejčí (the prime minister's advisor), a few months before the negotiations began, but that was limited to shaking his hand and delivering a letter to the prime minister. I discuss this more in chapter 10. As I show in chapter 9, the Polish and Hungarian regimes had established contact with the opposition several years before actual negotiations began.

the *Solidarność* uprising, or as the societies of East Germany and Czechoslovakia proved to in 1989. Rather, both the small underground organizations *and* the non-dissident intellectuals (who worked for the state) were particularly important for the influence of their ideas on the Party elite in Poland and Hungary. Moreover, these organizations may have been *potential* threats, given the precarious condition of society.[4]

The first task is to decide which groups in society could have been important. There are four possible alternatives. 1) A Hegelian definition of civil society would stress the emergence of market actors. 2) One could also concentrate on legal organizations that are independent from the state. 3) More common approaches include illegal organizations as well. 4) Finally, one stops thinking in terms of civil society versus the state and instead emphasize the manner in which certain liberalizing regimes created an atmosphere in which both official and unofficial criticism could emerge and in turn influence the judgement of the rulers.

If one looks at market actors, one discovers that, indeed, that the "second economy" grew in Hungary. The regime allowed small private enterprises during the 1980s. In addition, Poland private farming continued during the entire era of Communist rule. Most observers conclude, however, that these private owners were among the most politically *passive* groups in these countries.[5] Once the regime had given up trying to collectivize farming in the 1950s and decided to leave the farmers basically alone, it was unlikely that private farmers would cause any significant political problems for the rulers. In Hungary, there were no organizations for private owners until 1988—legal or otherwise. To the extent that these private owners influenced the rulers, it was by impressing them through their accumulation of wealth. In the words of Ivan and Balazs Szelenyi (1994: 219):

---

4. I discuss this in previous sections of this chapter.
5. A typical example is Frentzel-Zagórska & Zagórski (1989: 105), who write, "the owners of private nonagricutural small business in Poland constituted the least politically active group in Polish society. They were often even afraid of Solidarity. Moreover, they were ... the only group taking advantage of the continuing economic crisis and of the persistent inefficiencies of the centrally planned economy. The greater the inefficiencies of the main, state-owned part of the economic system and the greater the resulting gaps between demand and supply, the greater the opportunities for small business to fill some of these gaps and to make a profit."

Eventually the cadres themselves became attracted to private wealth, they began to believe it is better to be rich than communist. Their willingness to accept market reform cannot be totally separated from their desire to become personally wealthy, to use their political office to accumulate private wealth.

Similarly, Ost (1990: 201) notes that reportedly 25% of those seeking a license to run a private enterprise in Gdańsk in mid-1987 came from the corporate entity.

Another possibility is to look at the legal organizations that are independent from the state. Before 1988, the only organization that would qualify as somewhat autonomous was the Church.[6] Indeed, the Church was important, because its mere existence provided an alternative value system to the official Marxism-Leninism. In Poland especially, the Church helped pave the way for the original *Solidarność* uprising. Not only did it provide a value system that competed with the party-state's official Marxist-Leninist dogma, it also provided several fora for the expression of such views. One movement within the Church established summer camps for children. In addition, the Church was able to establish and maintain the only independent university in Eastern Europe (the Catholic University of Lublin). The Church also had its own press (Szajkowski 1983: ch. 2). At times, the Church criticized the regime publicly. After the party-state violently crushed the 1976 workers' revolt, the Church gave indirect support to KOR. As will be discussed in the chapter 8, a group of intellectual dissidents set up KOR in order to help imprisoned workers with their legal defence. This was the first successful attempt to bridge the gap between workers and intellectuals, and it sowed the seeds of the *Solidarność* uprising a few years later. The Church did not want to support any oppositional organization openly, since it saw itself as a mediator between the party-state and society. In practice, though, the Church assisted KOR in its attempts

---

6. In Hungary, MDF had its first meeting in 1987, but it did not establish itself legally until the following year. Ramet (1991: 113) reports that George Soros set up a private cultural foundation in 1984, which disbursed around 4 million dollars in 1987 to support research projects, private education, and cultural organizations (museums, theater groups, etc.). In 1986, the authorities permitted a self-help organization called the Retired Persons' Cultural and Self-Assisting Association. These examples show Hungary was more open than the GDR or the ČSSR, but the two groups in question were too small to have much influence on the development of Hungarian politics.

to stop the persecution of workers following the uprising. Moreover, two days after KOR had submitted a letter to the Sejm calling for an official inquiry into the charges of police brutality, the Episcopate announced it was giving aid to people and families who had been deprived of their income due to job loss or imprisonment in connection with the uprising. Local churches in several communities started collections for these families.

Several authors point out that the election of a Polish Pope further strengthened the Church as a legitimate bastion of values in opposition to the party-state. For the first time, some one outside of party-state control could address large audiences, without any need to dress his thoughts in Marxist-Leninist ideology (cf. Bakuniak & Nowak 1987). Frentzel-Zagorska (1990: 766) sums up: "The election of a Polish Pope provided an enormous boost for the hope and morale of Poles in their opposition to the imposed socio-political system." Bakuniak & Nowak (1987: 412) add that the Papal visit in 1979 "became a practical school of organizational action for society and its major lesson was that the authorities do not have a monopoly on organizing and animating social activities."

Nevertheless, the Church remained rather cautious during the *Solidarność* uprising that it helped inspire. Pelczynski (1988: 373) notes that the Church played a moderating role during the strikes of 1980–81. It tried to convince the union to concentrate on building up civil society rather than on making political demands. Ost (1990: 158–9) describes the role of the Church after martial law as follows:

> The Church certainly never supported martial law, and it continued to serve as a refuge and support center for persecuted Solidarity activists, but it was demonstrably willing to work with the government in this period. The government, meanwhile, was interested in working with the Church because it knew it had to reach out in some way to civil society at large. Even after crushing Solidarity, it was still groping for a new kind of compromise.

The Church's caution alienated many people. For example, after the imposition of martial law, Archbishop Cardinal Glemp blamed *both* sides for the crisis. After violent clashes took place during the first week of May—less than five months after the declaration of martial law— "Glemp seemed to endorse the regime's line that underground Solidarity had planned the clashes in advance" (Ramet 1991: 163). In

November of that year, Glemp also criticized underground *Solidarność's* calls for demonstrations; and went on later to assert that the union had lost its significance for society (Ramet 1991: 164–5). The Church was not unified in its complacency, however, and several bishops openly condemned the regime in their sermons (Ramet 1991: 165).

At the same time that Glemp's moderation disappointed many people, the crushing of *Solidarność* left the majority of Poles without any organized non-state alternative to the Church. Consequently, Lisicka (1992: 162) notes:

> The imposition of martial law also speeded up the process of re-catholicization. People turned to the Church as the only institution which was not discredited. As a result of that the Church itself did not become an opposition force but took the side of those values to which the majority of the population was attached and which were rejected by the communist regime.

Rather than acting in opposition to the state, as in the usual state-civil society dichotomy, the Church tried to follow a third course—that of mediator between the party-state and society. Consequently, it did not play the same role as the East German Evangelical churches in harboring "alternative" groups. There were no eco-libraries hidden in Catholic Churches, although, small autonomous Catholic intellectual groups did cooperate closely with the Church (Hirszowicz 1990: 147). When strikes erupted again in 1988, the Church played an important arbitrating role. As former Prime Minister Rakowski recalls: "Whenever we had something important to convey to Solidarity leaders who were active underground, our messenger hurried usually to Archbishop Bronisław Dąbrowski, Secretary of the Episcopate of Poland, or Father ... Alojzy Orszulik, at that time the head of the Press Office of the Episcopate, and they transmitted our proposals to those concerned, who also availed themselves of that channel" (Lisicka, 1992: 163). The Church continued to mediate between the regime and *Solidarność* during the discussions on preparing the Round Table talks (Tymowski 1993: 182). Moreover, at times when the two sides reached an impasse in the course of the Round Table talks, they met unofficially with the Church in order to reach a solution (Tymowski 1993: 182 and Wesołowski 1990: 440).

While the Church could arbitrate between *Solidarność* and the regime in Poland, its role was insignificant in Hungary. Yet in Hungary, the Communists agreed to the principle of multiparty democracy even earlier than in Poland.[7] So although the Church had some influence in bringing down the system in general, one should not exaggerate its role.

A third possibility is to look at the illegal organizations in society. Obviously, Poland provides a special case, because of *Solidarność*. Nevertheless, after the imposition of martial law, *Solidarność* was no longer a well-organized trade union. Rather, it became a collection of decentralized local cells (Ost 1990: 153). The trade union was no longer able to instigate strikes during its underground years, although it was heavily involved in distributing anti-Communist literature. Ramet (1991: 68) reports that by "early 1983 there were more than 500 underground newspapers in circulation." In August 1985, one of underground *Solidarność* leaders, Bujak, estimated that 50,000–70,000 Poles were involved in writing and publishing the underground press, while another 200,000–300,000 provided logistical support (Ramet 1991: 66). Nevertheless, he is hardly an objective source, since it served the organization's propaganda interests to appear as large and powerful as possible at the time. In that same year, the organization's own poll found that *Solidarność* still had far to go in reaching its goal of replacing the official media. Some 80% of the populace relied on the state media for most of its information (Ramet 1991: 91).

The underground union did try to mobilize the populace on some occasions, such as May Day demonstrations. But it met with only moderate success. For instance, Ramet (1991: 92) reports that, on May 1, 1985, around 10,000 supporters demonstrated in Warsaw and in Gdańsk. Although that is more than in other Communist-led countries during this period, this shows the organization was not nearly as strong as it had been during the 1980–1 uprising.

Moreover, *Solidarność* had organizational problems. According to Ost (1990: 169–70), "By late 1987 Solidarity was on the defensive and in disarray." After 1986, there were few underground cells actually functioning in the factories. Moreover, even after *Solidarność* was legalized in 1989, it won back barely one-fifth of its membership from 1981 (Ost 1990: 220). Thus, its strength lay more in its *potential* as a revolutionary organization more than in its actual activities. Given the worsening economic crisis, moreover, *Solidarność* was useful for the regime as a organization which could possibly be coopted into sharing

---

7. See chapters 1 and 9.

responsibility for measures needed to bring the economy into balance. Especially after the failed referendum in 1987, the Polish leaders began to realize they lacked the legitimacy required for carrying out radical economic reforms that would lower living standards for much of the populace.

In Hungary, as noted above, there were also several underground organizations. Yet, in contrast to *Solidarność*, none of them offered an alternative to the ruling regime—at least, not until the establishment of MDF in the fall of 1987. MDF had only a few hundred members at the time. Thus, it was much weaker than *Solidarność*.

The fourth possibility, is that the Polish and Hungarian regimes took advantage of their reformist pragmatic acceptance and liberalized their societies more than the other Soviet-bloc regimes. Under these relatively tolerant regimes, even the rulers came under the influence of thinkers who wanted to transform the system. Ost (1990: 155) remarks that in "overall, cultural policy [in Poland] continued to be the most open in all of Eastern Europe." By 1986, censorship "seemed almost to disappear" (Ost 1990: 176). Censorship was also minimal in Hungary. Consequently, the rulers did not need to read the underground *samizdats* to find sharp criticisms of regime policy. In was enough to read the professional trade papers.

This constant exposure to critical thought hastened their loss of ideological legitimacy. Their ideological legitimacy was based on the claim to having a monopoly on Truth, and on the expectation that they would fulfill certain economic goals, such as improving living standards more quickly than was being done in the West. How could the leaders of the corporate entity still believe they had a monopoly on Truth when *published* reports constantly showed that their policies were failing to meet their goals? How could they believe the Soviet-type system was the best means for improving living standards, when economists at Party and state institutions showed that living standards were declining? The obvious answer is that many of them could not. Thus, as noted in chapter 5, the leaders lost confidence in their ability to rule.

Although some of the most famous academicians were forced to emigrate in the 1960s and 1970s, the Polish and Hungary universities featured world-renowned social scientists who were publishing critical articles in both national and international journals. This includes such people in Poland as the economist Winiecki and the sociologists Staniszkis, Wnuk-Lipiński, Wesołowski, Sztompka, Krzysztof and

Leszek Nowak in Poland; and in Hungary, the economists Kornai and Bauer, and the sociologists Hankiss and Bruszt. Many of the sources in my study are the work of social scientists who lived and published in these two countries during the 1980s. Such famous Western journals as *Social Research* and *Theory and Society* have carried their articles.

That a researcher, such as Trzeciakowski (1987: 23–4), could publish an article in the West arguing that the Polish Communists must enter into a dialogue with society attests to the relative openness of the Polish regime. Another example may be seen in the existence of the critical (but official) newspaper *Polityka*, which freely admitted in 1985 that most Polish intellectuals opposed the Jaruzelski regime.[8] In fact, public-opinion surveys were published regularly even after the declaration of martial law, and many of them were far from flattering.

These researchers worked at official state institutions, but this does not necessarily imply that they were Party members. Some of them met each other at the Round Table negotiations, where they represented both sides. Winczorek (interviewed 1 February 1995), who represented the Democratic Party on the Round Table's constitutional committee, thus recalls that some of his negotiating partners were members of the same university law faculty. They had published articles together. Others, such as Staniszkis, had also been present at the previous negotiations between the Polish regime and *Solidarność* during 1980–1.[9]

So again, it is difficult to draw the line between State and civil society. What is important is that, under the liberalizing regime in Poland, non-dissident researchers at official institutions influenced the thinking of the reformist leadership. They also made it easier for the regime to establish contacts with opposition leaders. In the next chapter, I argue that these contacts made it easier to negotiate an institutional compromise.

Cooperation between intellectuals and regime reformists was even more common in Hungary than in Poland. As Frentzel-Zagórska (1990: 773) remarks,

> Since the mid-1960s Hungarian critical rather than oppositional intellectuals concentrated their endeavours on pressure on the establishment to implement economic reform from above and—in the 1980s—on bringing to power the more radical part of the party's reformist camp.

---

8. As mentioned in chapter 6, *Polityka* acted as a forum for unorthodox views.
9. Staniskis (1984) discusses some of her experiences.

Furthermore, there were many young reform Communists within the Hungarian leadership who were not as constrained as Kádár. They did not feel bound by Kádár's pragmatic acceptance, that had developed in defence of the 1956 Soviet invasion. The young reformers did not feel obliged to defend Kádár's brutal methods of crushing the 1956 uprising and brutally persecuting the leaders of the revolt. Nor were these reformers bound by the notion that they were in power because the Soviet Union had invaded to prevent Hungary from having an independent foreign policy or democratic, multi-party elections. Still, they could build on the other aspect of Kádár's pragmatic acceptance—the notion that the Party was reformist and willing to test the limits of what the USSR would allow. By the late 1980s, the limit of what the Kremlin would tolerate had expanded, and the younger Communists were willing to utilize this opening. Reform Communists around Nyers and Pozsgay actually encouraged critical researchers to provide an alternative program. As mentioned above, Pozsgay commissioned a report on the economy by critical economists. When the Politburo refused to publish it, Pozsgay made it public via the Popular Front, which he headed. Pozsgay also attended the founding conference of the opposition party MDF. In addition, Grósz, who was then prime minister, conveyed his greetings through Pozsgay (Schöpflin, Tőkés, & Völgyes 1988: 36). As in Poland, leading reform Communists had established contacts with opposition leaders well before the Round Table negotiations began. Under this liberalizing regime, critical thought thrived at official Party-state institutions to an even greater extent than in Poland. Critical reports came from institutions extremely close to the center of power. Tőkés (1996: 169) remarks that radical critiques came from the Party's own Institute for Social Sciences as well as from the universities and research academies.

As in Poland, several of the official researchers eventually met each other as negotiators for each of the sides at the Round Table negotiations. In the words of one of the participants, most of the negotiators at the working groups on socio-economic questions fell into one of two groups among reform economists: "those who [had] left the [Party] in time" and "those who had forgotten to leave it in time" (quoted in Tőkés, 1996: 339). This is another reason why I believe it more fruitful to discuss the degree of liberalization of society rather than the strength of civil society. Under liberalizing regimes, official state researchers working at state institutions and publishing in state journals often had more influence on the regime than did opposition leaders. Many of these official researchers also went on to advise the opposition *after* reform Communists convinced the regime to start negotiations.

As Ivan and Balazs Szelenyi (1994: 226–7) point out, the roots of the collapse of the Hungarian regime lay in a generation gap between the "old elite" and a newly emerging elite "composed of skilled or highly skilled professionals, which did not feel comfortable ruling the old way. This intensive struggle within the elite opened up new political spaces, making it possible for a civil society to emerge. Meanwhile, the "new elite"—which was itself a part of the intellectual milieu—began losing its appetite for repressing intellectuals. As a result, intellectual dissent fermented. The dissidents, in turn, influenced and radicalized the liberalizers, who read the underground *samizdat* publications.

In sum, the degree of openness in society in general was more important than civil society (however one defines the term "civil society"). In the Hungarian case especially—which is the case the Szelenyis (1994) write about—Frentzel-Zagórska is correct in emphasizing that the critical intellectuals were more important than the dissidents. Furthermore, I claim the policies of liberalization made it possible for reformists in the regime to establish contact networks with the opposition, which in turn made it much easier to negotiate an institutional compromise (see chapter 9).

THE ANTI-REFORMIST GDR AND ČSSR

According to all four criteria used above, the GDR and ČSSR were much less open societies than were Poland and Hungary. The first criterion was the existence of some sort of private sector. While Poland had a large private sector for agriculture, and Hungary developed a private sector for small businesses during the 1980s, the private sector was almost non-existent in the GDR and the ČSSR. By 1965 the private sector in the ČSSR was less than 0.1% (Brus 1981: 159). In the GDR, some half-private companies still existed when Honecker came to power in 1971, but the new general secretary succeeded rather quickly in nationalizing them completely.[10]

The second criterion is the existence of legal organizations autonomous from the state. In Poland and Hungary, before 1988 the

---

10. See chapter 3.

Catholic Church is the only organization which fulfilled this qualification. The Catholic and Protestant churches were not nearly as important in the anti-reformist countries as they were in Poland, but they had some influence in the GDR and Slovakia. I referred earlier the role of the Evangelical Church in providing an umbrella for alternative movements in the GDR.[11] I noted as well that the Evangelical Church generally wanted cordial relations with the regime, although some pastors allowed alternative groups to use their facilities. Kühnel & Sallmon-Metzner (1991: 373) report that, in the GDR, even those Lutheran churches that offered an umbrella to the alternative groups often came into conflict with them. The church administrators did not want to provoke the regime. They therefore tried to keep these alternative activities under control. The Evangelical Church was not able to provide an alternative set of values in the GDR to the same extent as the Catholic Church in Poland. In contrast to Poland, where the overwhelming majority of the population considers itself Catholic, East Germany had a population which considered itself, in its overwhelming majority, to be atheist.[12] Pollack (1993: 255) therefore concludes, in his article on the role of the churches, that the East German Evangelical Church was definitely not a motor for change in 1989.

In the ČSSR, the Catholic Church was extremely passive before 1988. However, some individual priests became dissidents. Furthermore, Catholic dissidents in Slovakia organized some field trips for Christian youths, at which social questions were allegedly discussed (interview with Jablonický 5 March 1993).

The third criterion is the existence of illegal organizations. In the GDR during the early 1980s, as mentioned above, there was a proliferation of small alternative groups which used the Church as a refuge. This included peace and environmental groups. The peace question is the one issue on which the Church gave its active support to some extent. In 1981, members of the Evangelical Church proposed social service as an alternative to military conscription for conscientious objectors. In 1983, furthermore, the Catholic bishops

---

11. See above in this chapter.
12. *Tagesspiegel* (31 January 1993) cites a survey taken more than three years after the opening of the wall, which showed that only 27% of the respondents considered themselves "Evangelical" (i.e., Lutheran), while fully 67% said they had no religion.

criticized some aspects of East German peace policy in an official statement (Woods 1986: 37–39). In the mid-1980s, human-rights groups also sprout up in the GDR (Ramet 1991: 48). Still, in contrast to *Solidarność* in Poland, these groups of young intellectuals were largely isolated from society. In 1986, Woods (1986: 42) reported: "There have been just a handful of dissident intellectuals in the Honecker era, and although it has been argued by the peace movement that 5000 in the GDR the equivalent of sixty times that number in West Germany, the fact remains that the movement involves thousands, not hundred of thousands."

Similarly, several anti-Communist groups arose in the ČSSR in the late 1970s and the 1980s, but they too were small and isolated from society. Of course, the most famous one was Charter 77, but other well-known groups included the Committee for the Unjustly Persecuted (VONS) and the Jazz Section.[13] In contrast to the situation in the GDR, however, many *samizdat* journals were circulating in the ČSSR. There were even underground book publishers such as *Edice Petlice* (closed down in 1983) and *Edice Kvart* (which put out 120 books; see Ramet 1991: 111). The underground organizations were so isolated from the populace, however, that even during the first week of the revolution in 1989, Havel was basically unknown to the public.[14]

The fourth criterion is a general openness in society. I have maintained that the Polish and Hungarian regimes, which had a reformist pragmatic acceptance, also created more open societies. The openness of official debate influenced the thinking of the reform Communists and facilitated a more critical view of the system. The East German and Czechoslovak Communists, by contrast, were isolated from critical currents of thought. The East German regime was particularly dogmatic. I remember watching East German newscasts in the mid-1980s while living in West Berlin. Every newscast followed the same basic pattern: there was so much coverage of alleged American military aggression that it was easy to believe World War III was about to begin; there was the obligatory report about enterprises which had over-fulfilled their plans-quotas, the obligatory interview with a con-

---

13. Ramet (1991: 108–9). The Jazz Section began as a legal organization, but soon ran into trouble with the regime.
14. I discuss this in chapter 10.

struction worker who explained how additional homes were being built for more people, and the obligatory report about some activity of the Communist youth organization FDJ (*Freie Deutsche Jugend*). I never heard a news report to the effect that Erich Honecker had met Michael Gorbachev and discussed some trade problems (such as Soviet demands that the GDR deliver higher-quality goods, or East German demands for increased shipments of oil and other fuels). Instead, the anchorperson would refer to the various titles of each leader, after which he/she would say something largely free of content. A typical report went something like this:

> Erich Honecker, General Secretary of the Central Committee of the SED, Politburo member, President of the Council of Ministers, and Commander and Chief of the Armed Forces, met yesterday with Mikhail Gorbachev, General Secretary of the Central Committee of the Communist Party of the USSR, Politburo member, and President of the Union of Soviet Socialist Republics. They gave greetings to each other and promised to continue their good fraternal relationship in the struggle for world peace.

While Polish and Hungarian social scientists published abroad regularly and often spent time as guest researchers at prestigious Western universities, one rarely came across anything published in a Western social-science journal by an East German researcher. Nor did one come across more than a few works in Western social-science journals written by a Czech or Slovak researcher before 1989. Writers were still being prosecuted in the 1980s for having published articles or given interviews in the West without the permission of the authorities (Woods 1986: 24 gives examples from the GDR).

A glance at some of the East German textbooks from this period shows the low level of the propaganda which dominated in that country. In their book about economic planning under socialism, Milke, Möller & Schilling (1983: 6) wrote that real income in the USA had fallen to the level of the 1950s, while in the FRG it had fallen to the level of the early 1970s.

The atmosphere in the ČSSR was less dogmatic, but still far from the openness of Poland and Hungary. For example, although social scientists rarely published in well-known Western journals, and although they could not question the regime's policies openly, they could criticize the implementation of policies. Thus, Czechoslovak journals were filled with reports of the failure of industries to cut costs, and the like. By the mid-1980s, moreover, economists were indicating indirectly that market reforms would be valuable. They did this only indirectly, by claiming that the country had to participate to a greater extent in the "international division of labor." Such a participation was not possible, of course, without a more market-oriented economy. Still, these small criticisms and hints were lame compared to what Polish and Hungarian economists were publishing.

The conservative atmosphere in the GDR and ČSSR isolated the elites from critical thinking and reinforced a false sense that all was well. These leaders' pragmatic acceptance was based on the belief that the Soviet Union had put them in power to block reforms. Since they could not imagine the USSR abandoning them, they did not believe they had to pay much attention to public opinion. Thus, while the Polish regime set up a public-opinion institute in the 1980s which published yearly reports, the East German regime did not even commission secret reports for itself, except for those from the Leipzig Institute for Youth Research. Although its reports were secret, they were limited to surveys of the country's youth rather than of the entire population. Consequently, the leaders of these countries were unaware, in 1989, of the seriousness of the crisis and the extent of their unpopularity (see chapter 10). If there had been as much open discussion in the GDR and the ČSSR as in Poland and Hungary, the elites would undoubtedly have been more prepared to deal with the crisis in 1989.

CONCLUSION

In this chapter, I have largely rejected the civil society-based explanation for the collapse of the Soviet-type regimes. As already noted in chapter 1, theorists claiming that the emergence of civil society brought down the regimes were unable to explain why the process of change was so different in the four countries. Moreover, these authors have defined civil society as a sphere separate from the state and opposed to it. I argue that with the possible exception of the Catholic Church and underground *Solidarność* in Poland, none of the four countries had a large enough sphere of activity outside the Party-state sector to substantiate the civil society-based explanation. Furthermore, one should not exaggerate the role of the Catholic Church in Poland. The Church was important because it provided an alternative set of values to the official Marxist-Leninist doctrine. However, its influence on the opposition was moderating rather than radicalizing. It was bent on compromising with the regime rather than on bringing it down. In addition, although underground *Solidarność* in Poland presented a *potential* threat to the regime, it was still much weaker in the late 1980s than it had been at its height during the 1980–81 uprising. Thus, it is not fruitful to describe the situation in 1988 as one in which a growing and mobilizing civil society was on the verge of bringing down the regime.

It is more meaningful to discuss the degree of liberalization in these societies rather than the emergence of civil society. The regimes with a reformist pragmatic acceptance liberalized their society, which in turn allowed society to influence the policies of the regime. It was not necessarily civil society, understood as something separate from the state, that influenced the policies of the liberalizing regimes. Members of the regime and member of Party-state organizations influenced the thinking of regime leaders more than dissidents did. Criticisms put forward by official intellectuals contributed to the erosion of the ideological legitimacy of the regimes. This might have caused the reform Communists in Poland and Hungary to lose confidence in their ability to rule more quickly than the hardliners in the GDR and ČSSR did. In any case, since the Polish and Hungarian reformers took advantage of the liberal climate to establish relations with opposition leaders, they were in a better position than their East German and Czechoslovak counterparts to negotiate an institutional compromise.

Chapter 8

SOCIAL MOVEMENTS BEFORE 1988

In this chapter, I concentrate on analysis of social movements. Social scientists writing about Eastern Europe have at times noted that different groups in society behave differently during revolts. However, very few have offered plausible explanations for these differences. The aim of this chapter is to develop a partial model that can explain the reasons why some groups participate in social movements at certain times, while other groups participate at other times.

FAILED UPRISINGS: PARTICIPATION IN EAST EUROPEAN SOCIAL MOVEMENTS

The revolutions in the GDR and ČSSR in 1989 were not the first attempts at overthrowing the regimes. As early as in 1953, the Soviet Union considered the workers' uprising in Berlin to be serious enough to warrant a military intervention. In this section, I compare the main uprisings within the former Soviet-bloc before 1989, with an eye to demonstrating a certain pattern. In chapter 10, I show that these patterns continued even during the 1989 revolutions. I have chosen the East German worker uprising in 1953, the Polish worker rebellions in 1970, 1976 and 1980, and the Hungarian uprising in 1956. That is, I cover social movements in all of the countries except that of the ČSSR. Since chapter 10 covers the Czechoslovak and East German revolutions, by the end of this study it is demonstrated that the partial model developed in this chapter applies for all four countries, including the ČSSR. It not only is valid for all four countries, it also holds up also over time—from the East German rebellion in 1953 to the Czechoslovak "velvet revolution" in 1989.

Since the relations between workers and intellectuals has been so important for successful rebellions, I also examine the dissident movements in the four countries briefly. I include the demonstrations of Polish intellectuals in 1968, as well as such famous dissident movements as Charter 77 in the ČSSR and KOR (The Workers Defense Committee) in Poland.

The discussion focuses on a comparison between, on the one hand, the less successful rebellions in 1953 (GDR), 1956 (Hungary), 1970 (Poland) and 1976 (Poland), and, on the other, the more successful *Solidarność* revolt in 1980–1. I have chosen to ignore the uprising in Poland in 1956 and that in Czechoslovakia in 1968, since these were not necessarily against the Soviet-type system. Rather, they were against its most oppressive Stalinist elements and *in favor* of either the present reform leadership (Dubček in the ČSSR) or a former Communist leader (Gomułka in Poland). Thus, these uprisings were nationalistic (favorable to their own national Communist regime, rather than purely anti-Communist (against the domestic regime). Both Dubček and Gomułka were national heroes at the time. Because of this, I would not be comparing the same kind of rebellions if I compared them to the those which were directed against the system itself. Nationalist rebellions have different dynamics than anti-systemic ones. However, even if I were to include these cases, the results would be basically the same: the main actors were workers, or workers encouraged by intellectuals; the revolts broke out during periods of economic downturn coupled with rising expectations of political change; and the rebellions were in response to unpalatable measures which the domestic regimes announced (except in the ČSSR, where it was the Soviet invasion that caused the rebellion). Despite these similarities, it would be superficial to note that the pattern of uprisings repeated itself. For example, the rebelling Czechs and Slovaks were certainly more motivated by the foreign occupation of their country than by the preceding economic downturn or by rising expectations of political reform. It is likely they would have protested against a foreign invasion even if living standards had been increasing and even if they tolerated authoritarian rule.

Although I have excluded the Polish and Czechoslovak uprisings that were in favor of national Communist leaders, I have chosen to include the Hungarian revolt of 1956. This rebellion was also, to a large extent, in support of a national reform Communist leader (Nagy). I have two reasons for including the Hungarian revolt. First, despite the support for a national Communist, this rebellion was directed more openly against the Soviet-type system as a system than were those in Poland and Czechoslovakia. Nagy enjoyed the support of the population, but he gained this support by promising such radical changes that we can speak here of *systemic* change. Not only did he announce that Hungary would leave the Warsaw Pact, he also planned to have free, multiparty elections. Thus, both the Hungarian corporate entity and its Soviet masters would have lost their power monopoly.[1]

Chapter 1, discussed the recent attempts at using theories on social movements to explain the revolutions in the GDR and ČSSR. Rational-choice theorists have concentrated on variations of Granovetter's threshold model. This model does not yield any hypothesis about why different groups have different thresholds; nor can it specify the circumstances under which people's thresholds change. These two questions are the most important ones I seek to answer in this chapter and in chapter 10 (which discusses the actual revolutions in the GDR and ČSSR in 1989).

The rationalist theorists have an important point to make in one area: that of regime tactics. Several theorists have pointed out that, if the opposition is unarmed, the regime can quell any rebellion if it uses enough force (cf. Karlkins & Petersen 1993). At each progressive stage of the rebellion, however, the sufficient level of force increases. Thus, if the regime's stance in the beginning is sufficiently tough, it can maintain power. If it waits, it will need to use much more violence to stop the mass movement. Yet even here an non-rational emotive element appears. If the regime uses some violence but *not enough*, this often has the opposite effect: it angers the citizens and drives them to participate. Opp (1993: 199) refers to this as a solidarity effect.[2]

Furthermore, while many public choice theorists have emphasized the importance of selective incentives for collective action (cf. Hardin 1982, Olson 1979 & 1990 and Taylor 1988), I argue that communication has been the most important collective-action problem faced by revolutionaries in Eastern Europe. Public-choice theorists claim, in

---

1. My argument also becomes stronger if I can show that it holds for all four countries. If I leave out Hungary, the reader might wonder if that country constitutes an exception that could invalidate my reasoning. I already include several Polish uprisings in this chapter, and I include the Czechoslovak revolution in chapter 10. In addition, I look at two East German uprisings in this study: the 1953 worker riots in this chapter, and the 1989 revolution in chapter10. The 1956 uprising, however, provides my only opportunity to include Hungary.
2. Elster (1990) adds that if force is used, it might make the regime seem weaker. The populace reasons that if the regime really were strong and the opposition weak, then the police would not have to resort to such violence.

contrast, that the main collective action problem for "political entre-preneurs" normally is to find a means of rewarding participants and punishing "free riders" who refuse to participate. The revolutionaries in Eastern Europe were more concerned about reaching the public with their message than about devising incentives for people to join them. This is especially true of the quick mass mobilizations which occurred in the ČSSR and GDR in 1989, where none of the political entrepreneurs had any selective incentives at their disposal for reward-ing or punishing participants.[3]

Another approach is the neo-Tocquevillian one, which stresses polit-ical openings. Tarrow (1991) names four possible variables that can cause openings. These are: 1) the opening of access to institutional participation, 2) disarray among political alignments before the forming of new ones, 3) conflicts among political elites which the opposition can exploit, and 4) offers of help from influential allies from within or without the system. Although none of these apply to the revolutions in 1989, one can expand the notion of political open-ings to include additional factors, such as the neutralization of outside enemies.[4] While fruitful, this approach fails to explain why different groups have different preferences for rebelling. In addition, it gives only a partial answer to the question of when thresholds change, because it does not provide any hypothesis as to when political openings occur.

I would claim that, in Soviet-Type regimes, political openings usually occur during an economic downturn. As Haggard & Kaufman (1995) conclude, the emergence of grave economic problems often provokes splits within the leadership of authoritarian regimes. As long as the economy is progressing well, it is relatively easy for the rulers to maintain unity. When the rulers must make tough decisions over the

---

3. Turner & Killian (1972: 61) stress the importance of channels of communication for success-ful collective action: "Since collective behavior develops through a communication process and culminates in people's acting together in relatively large collectivities, conditions that facilitate communication and mobilization are essential to conduciveness." Similarly, Tarrow (1989: 52) reflects: "Collective action does not spread like the ripples in a lake when a rock is thrown in the water, but like the channels of other types of diffusion—through natural and social channels of communication. Diffusion never spreads outward evenly, but follows insti-tutional conduits and natural means of communication: as news of early successes spread from center to periphery...."

4. In chapter 1, I discuss why these variables fail to explain the 1989 revolutions.

direction of the economy, conflicts over policy making are likely to arise.[5]

A third approach to the East European revolutions is the J-curve theory (see Dix 1991). According to this hypothesis, revolutions occur when the economy declines after a prolonged period of economic growth. As pointed out in chapter 3, Czechoslovakia and East Germany had experienced a long period of stagnation or decline prior to the revolutions. While the traditional J-curve hypothesis does not provide a persuasive account of the 1989 revolutions, it may be combined with a neo-Tocquevillian approach to explain the dynamics of unmet rising political expectations (cf. Stone 1966: 172). Normally, neo-Tocquevillians have claimed that revolutions occur when a regime begins to reform itself, or when there is a split within the leadership. This did happen in *some* of the pre-1989 revolts, but the 1989 revolutions took place in the anti-reformist countries. Nevertheless, in 1989 as well as during the most successful previous uprisings, *expectations* of political change were rising. In 1989, for instance, East Germans and Czechoslovaks were more hopeful—but on account of the changes in the USSR, Poland and Hungary, rather than because of any reforms which their own regimes had carried out.

A NEO-MARXIAN SYNTHESIS

My framework incorporates several elements from the theorists referred to above. The concepts of political openings, communication, solidarity effects, and rising expectations are meaningful, but they do not tell us why some groups are more willing to revolt at certain times than others.

Thus, it is useful to divide society into groups in order to understand why these groups behave differently. Groups are categorized according to class or stratum. Workers and professionals each comprise a different class, since they occupy different positions in the productive process. Workers hold the lowest position, while professionals sit in the middle between workers and the ruling corporate entity.

---

5. In the East German and Czechoslovak cases, the political opening often came more indirectly, in the sense that the economic crisis caused squabbling among *Soviet* elites, which in turn encouraged the domestic opposition. Yet even in these countries some openings occurred, such as Honecker's greater tolerance for the Church and the support for *glasnost* given by the Czechoslovak youth organization SSM. I discuss this more fully in chapter 10.

Intellectuals, for their part, comprise a stratum, because they belong to the sphere of ideological rather than material production.[6] Of course, the most important issue is whether this classification is *empirically* fruitful. I intend to show that, indeed, these three groups did behave differently.

If these three classes/strata behave differently, one must explain why. I have relied on the notion of institutional and postulated interests. I claim that, while all three groups have postulated interests in systemic change—in order to gain control over their productive process—they have different institutional interests. The latter strongly influence their behavior during normal times. Thus, my study relies heavily on an institutional perspective.

There have been few institutional analyses of social movements in Eastern Europe. In fact, institutional analyses of social movements are lacking in general (cf. Canel 1992: 277 and Escobar & Alvarez 1992: 321). Therefore, I rely on an interpretation of empirical data in order to ascertain the institutional interests of the classes and strata. I maintain below that a clear pattern emerges:

a) Workers tend to rebel when their material conditions are worsening.

b) Intellectuals consistently dominate the dissident movements and oppose the system regardless of the economic situation.

c) Professionals only join the opposition to any substantial extent when the rebellion has become relatively strong.

The question, then, is what institutional incentives do the members of these classes have for acting more (intellectuals) or less (workers and professionals) in accordance with their postulated interests in revolting against the system?

Below I present, first, a logical partial model that can provide a *plausible* explanation. I base this partial model on the trichotomy of postulated interests, institutional interests, and the subjective interpretation of these interests. I then demonstrate, in the following empirical section, that the partial model fares well for the pre-1989 revolts. Since I develop my analysis of institutional interests in order to explain patterns which emerge in the pre-1989 uprisings, the empirical section

---

6. See chapter 2 for a discussion about the theoretical merits of using this division.

does *not* provide a test of my partial model. Rather, it exemplifies the partial model. After showing in this chapter that my partial model is fruitful for explaining the previous revolts, I then apply it, in chapter 10 to the 1989 revolutions. To this extent, I "test it" on the later events. But only the results are testable, not my description of the mechanisms behind them. Postulated interests are a theoretical construct and are not empirically testable.

It *would* have been possible, however, to undertake empirical studies of institutional interests—before 1989. Social scientists could have conducted field studies to discover which incentives motivated workers, professionals and intellectuals to revolt (or to refrain from revolting). To my knowledge, however, no one except for Nowak (1988) has done this and he limits his study to workers in Poland during the *Solidarność* uprising. His investigation shows that job dismissal and a lack of promotion provided the greatest disincentives for workers to rebel.[7] Since I am only aware of one such study, and since it is limited to one class and one country, I can only present a logically reasonable hypothesis concerning the institutional mechanisms that hinder or encourage rebellion.

Workers
Workers in the post-Stalinist era did not face as much pressure as either professionals or intellectuals to support the system. In contrast to intellectuals, workers were not expected to do their job in any particular ideological fashion (no one demands that an assembly-line worker press buttons in a socialist-realist manner).[8] Nor were workers as dependent on patronage as professionals for receiving their jobs. Those who joined the Party at this level did not even receive the same benefits as professionals or those joining the state bureaucratic apparatus. Thus, the material incentives for joining the Party were lower for this group than for others. Consequently, workers were often reluctant to join the Party. So, ironically, workers were under-represented in the so-called "workers' parties" running these countries in their name.

---

7. The other most important factor was withheld bonuses, but it did not seem as important as the first two.
8. Clark & Wildavsky (1990: 71) define socialist realism as "the demand under coercion that art openly support the Soviet state by depicting not how life under communism really is, but rather how it will be when full communism is achieved."

Virtually all workers went through the ritual of joining the Party-controlled union and marching in the annual First of May parades, but otherwise, in the post-mobilization era,[9] they faced minimal demands for political activity. In contrast to an intellectual, finally, an isolated worker had no reason for believing she would have any influence on the rest of society if she becomes a dissident.

So far, I have discussed why workers had a lower propensity to become dissidents than intellectuals had. If workers had weaker institutional interests in opposing the system, however, the question is: why did they tend to rebel during periods of economic decline? Traditional Marxian theory emphasizes the factor of increased consciousness: when workers become impoverished, prevailing class relations become clear to them, making them realize they "have nothing to lose but their chains." The fact that so many Polish workers were willing to rebel already in 1970 shows that they had already achieved a high level of "class consciousness" one decade before the *Solidarność* uprising.

The "nothing-to-lose-but-your-chains" hypothesis has some validity. For workers had less to lose than professionals, since they could assume that they would still be guaranteed jobs after an unsuccessful rebellion—even if they might not be able to keep the exact same job. As noted, Nowak (1988) shows that job dismissal and lack of promotion provided the greatest disincentives to rebel. This implies that blue-collar workers had the least to lose. For unskilled workers who had lost their jobs had little trouble finding a new one. Professionals, in contrast, have more to lose. First, they are more likely to have hopes of promotion. Second, doctors normally consider it a greater loss to be demoted to the status of a window-washer than assembly-line workers do.[10]

---

9. By "post-mobilization era," I mean the period of relative stability in which institutions have already been built, as opposed to the revolutionary "Stalinist" epoch, which is characterized by campaigns of mass mobilization, purges, etc., with much more emphasis placed on ideological purity than on skill. Generally speaking, the totalitarian slogan that "those who are for us are against us" is *de facto* replaced, in the post-mobilization era, by the unspoken slogan that "those who aren't against us are for us."

10. One could assume that, since workers have less to lose than professionals by revolting, they also have a stronger bargaining position. This is not necessarily true. For the regime is also dependent on professionals—such as engineers—to modernize industry. A good engineer is harder to replace than a good assembly line worker.

Moreover, even if a worker revolt fails to change the power structure, it is more likely to influence the regime's policies than a professional or intellectual rebellion. The leaders, who claim to be ruling on behalf of the workers, would feel themselves forced to make some concessions. Beside the factor of ideological legitimacy based on representing the workers, the old argument of strength in numbers is also important. Since workers comprise the majority of citizens, they are the class most easily able to threaten the regime if they unite. Furthermore, it is easier for factory workers than for lawyers to stop producing vital commodities. In view of these considerations, it is not so surprising that Gomułka resigned after the 1970 worker revolt, or that Gierek lowered food prices after the 1976 strikes. A demonstration held by lawyers would hardly have had the same effect!

In normal times, the workers' institutional interest in not opposing the regime prevents them from rebelling. Thus, their institutional interests constrains them from reaching their postulated interests. During an economic crisis, however, workers—being the poorest group in society and the closest to falling below the subsistence minimum—decide in many cases that they have little to lose by revolting.

Although institutional structures are extremely important, they do not determine the behavior of the actors. Rather, they influence and constrain this behavior. It is necessary, therefore, to examine the workers' subjective perception of their institutional and postulated interests. In looking at how workers perceive their interests, two issues are pertinent: First, why do they tend to give precedence to institutional interests over postulated interests *except* when there is an economic crisis? And second, what are the other political interactions that influence their behavior?

Let us look at the first issue. After showing through a comparative analysis that workers in fact do give precedence to their institutional interests over their postulated interests except during periods of economic crisis, I develop a *plausible explanation* as to how workers perceive their interests during an economic crisis. As I have already noted, workers have no institutional interests pushing them in the direction of opposing the regime, although they may well be aware that they could be better off under another system. During periods of economic crisis, on the other hand, they have a tendency to give higher priority to their postulated interests in actively opposing the regime. The obvious reason for this is that, making up some of the poorest groups in society, they are the most vulnerable during an economic crisis.[11] Second, since the regime bases its ideological legitimacy on its economic success, and since it claims to represent the proletariat's best interests, workers probably sense that the regime is especially weak during periods in which workers' living conditions decline. Third, the attitude of the workers towards the regime might change, as they perceive it is no longer able to fulfill its promises of higher living standards.

The fact of an economic crisis does not automatically cause a rebellion. My argument is that it is a *necessary* condition, not a *sufficient* one. Workers do not automatically rebel when an economic downturn begins. But they do not rebel if there is no such downturn, even if they dislike the regime. The behavior of the regime and of intellectuals strongly influences workers' perception of their interests in such situations. Where the regimes are concerned, the manner in which they deal with an economic crisis affects the behavior of the workers. I would argue that decisions which outrage workers and directly lower their living standards increase their willingness to demonstrate. When such feelings arise, people pay less attention to calculations of their institutional interests. As Turner & Killian (1972: 79) put it: "a sense of urgency, a feeling that something can and must be done *now*" is normally the immediate motivation for taking part in a rebellion. Similarly, Elster asserts: "When emotions are directly involved in action, they tend to overwhelm or subvert rational mental processes, not to supplement them."[12] The events in the ČSSR and GDR show that *once* a new wave of protests has already begun, repression by the regime rather than merely economic decisions can still increase feelings of outrage so much that it provokes workers to participate in demonstrations. Under such circumstances, the economic crisis need not be so severe that living standards fall sharply as occurred in Poland right before the *Solidarność* uprising.

Professionals

Parkin (1982: 579) predicted that, under the Soviet-type system, it will be the professionals (whom he calls the *intelligentsia*) rather than the

---

11. As Maslow noted in his famous hierarchy of needs, purely physiological needs must be met before higher goals—love, belongingness, esteem and finally self-actualization—can be fulfilled (cf. Eskola 1988: 71 and Feist 1985: ch. 12).

12. Jon Elster, "Sadder but Wiser? Rationality and the Emotions," *Social Science Information*, Vol. 24 pp. 375–406, quoted in Etzioni (1992: 99).

workers who will take political power away from the Communist leadership. He notes:

> for Marx, a society becomes ripe for social transformation when the stratification order is in disequilibrium; that is, when the class which is (say) economically dominant through its control of the productive process is not the class which is politically dominant (1982: 575).
>
> In socialist society the key antagonisms occurring at the social level are those between the party and state bureaucracy on the one hand and the intelligentsia on the other... The social power of the latter group inheres in its command of the skills, knowledge and general attributes which are held to be of central importance for the development of productive and scientific forces in modern industrial society (1982: 578).
>
> [Professionals comprise the] ascendant class closely identified with the transformation, and capable of pushing it through.... it is because political authority is concentrated elsewhere—in the hands of the party apparatus—that the stratification order can be characterized as one of disequilibrium... Seen from this angle, equilibrium could be restored by the accession to political power of the intelligentsia and the displacement of the apparatchiki (1982: 579).

In contrast to Parkin, I claim that professionals are usually more passive politically than either workers or intellectuals. Professionals find themselves in an ironic situation: although they generally have the most to gain in material terms from systemic change in a market-oriented direction they also face greater incentives than do workers to support the system passively. For them, career advancement is highly dependent either on Party membership or on connections with patrons within the Party-state. In contrast, for example, to authors (who can work alone), professionals normally have to be at a specific work-place, and a repressive apparatus can keep an eye on them. Further-more, while authors can publish abroad (and thereby earn a relatively good income even if they cannot publish in their own country), profes-sionals are completely dependent on their patrons for their incomes and—even more importantly—for their privileges. In a post-Stalinist era, when executions and Gulags are replaced in most cases by short prison sentences or demotion to manual-labor jobs, professionals have much more to lose than workers in opposing the system. In a system guaranteeing full employment, after all, workers cannot fall much lower on the income/status ladder.

At first it might seem strange that professionals worry to such an extent about their careers, since in so many cases they earn little more than workers. In fact, some critics might claim that the high degree of income equality pits society against the state, thus making it unfruitful to differentiate between social classes. Although these critics are certainly correct that many professionals were dissatisfied with the system (since they did not feel "properly" rewarded), I would still assert that the professionals had an institutional interest in trying to keep their posts.

First, there is the obvious point that since nobody forces professionals to become professionals against their own will, they must *want* to practice their profession, even if they feel underpaid. Second, money loses its normal distributive function in a Soviet-type economy; therefore, one must look at the *privileges* which the professionals enjoy through their patronage relations.[13] Third, studies of status in these countries show repeatedly that, despite the regime's glorification of the proletariat, professionals enjoy higher status.[14]

The patterns for professionals are similar to those for workers. The main difference is that professionals have stronger institutional interests in passively supporting the regime than did workers. Thus, institutional interests constrain professionals even more from their reaching their postulated interests. During a period of an economic crisis, on the other hand, professionals are more likely to join the opposition, but for different reasons than the workers. For workers the connection is *direct*: they revolt *because* of the economic crisis. For

---

13. For example, Andorka (1989: 107, 112) cites statistics showing that, while non-manual employees in Hungary earned little more than workers in 1982 (4,022 forints as compared to 3,217), a much higher percentage of them owned cars and had travelled abroad. Thus, while 29% of the engineers and 78% of the medical doctors had vacationed in a foreign country that year, only 5% of the unskilled non-agricultural laborers and 7% of the miners had done so. Similarly, 68% of the engineers and 94% of the doctors owned a car, as compared to 19% of the unskilled workers and 33% of the miners.

14. Since there are numerous examples, it is difficult to choose just one. Still, one random example may be seen in a comparison of social prestige done in Poland in the 1970s. The four professional groups with the highest status included university professors, doctors, teachers and engineers; while the four professions with the lowest status included agricultural workers, cleaning ladies, construction workers and salespeople (Weslowski 1976: 14–15). One example of international comparisons of status sows that, on a scale of 0.0–1.0, professionals in Poland had a status of .97, while state-factory workers had a status of .14; in Hungary, non-manual subordinates had a status of .62, while factory workers had a status of .05; finally, in Czechoslovakia, non-manual subordinates had a status of 0.64, while factory workers had a status of .06 (Słomcyński 1994: 182). This shows that professionals have a lot to lose if punished for participating in an unsuccessful rebellion. Thus, they tend to be more cautious in opposing the regime during normal times.

the professionals, the reason is more *indirect*: they tend to wait until the revolt has become large enough to have a reasonable chance of succeeding, or at least large enough to enable the participants to escape punishment.

I show below that, according to available information, professionals under Soviet-type regimes pay more heed to their institutional interests than do other groups (until, at any rate, a revolt has already gotten under way). The exception is Poland in the 1980s. The reason for this is probably that *once* the professionals had gotten involved in *Solidarność* (which they did later than the workers and the intellectuals), they were already "marked" by the regime. They no longer had as much reason, therefore, to keep their sympathies secret. A possible hypothesis is that, once a civil society emerges—however weak it may be—professionals will become more active in pressing for change.[15]

Intellectuals

Unfortunately, I am forced to make some simplifications when discussing intellectuals' institutional interests. The demands placed by Soviet-type regimes on intellectuals can vary not only between professions but within them as well. For example, even though symphony conductors might suffer from a conservative policy that prevents them from performing certain modern, avant-garde Western works, they do not face as much pressure as do rock groups. Rock musicians have often had trouble convincing the authorities to accept their music style. Then they have the added problem of having to be careful about their lyrics. Writing protest songs is more provocative than performing Beethoven symphonies. Since I want to explain why intellectuals tend to oppose the system openly more often than do professionals or workers, I concentrate on those groups of intellectuals who have most often become dissidents. Of course, this description is a simplification. Intellectuals do not all have exactly the same institutional incentives. Not all are equally articulate; not all have as much access to international contacts, etc. Nor do all they face the same ideological pressures.

---

15. In this sense, their behavior accords with O'Donnell-Schmitter's model (1986: ch. 5) of the birth of civil society, in which professional organizations press for rights once intellectuals have made the first moves. All of the revolts, however, have taken place in countries whose civil societies have been weak—even by Soviet standards. Consequently, professionals have usually given precedence to their institutional interests, except when revolts have already started.

I have two main explanations for why intellectuals have stronger incentives to become dissidents. First, their voices are more likely to be heard. Intellectuals find themselves in a special situation, since they are involved in the production of ideology rather than of goods. This means they are trained to be articulate. Because of their position, they are also more likely to have connections with people within both the national and international media. As Bauman (1976: 139) observes, "their protest is always the most dramatic and easy to notice."

If a famous actress, for example, suddenly criticizes the regime, she is more likely to gain attention than an assembly-line worker. Moreover, famous actors and actresses, musicians, directors, artists and writers are more likely to have Western contacts. It is much easier for a famous musician to gain permission to perform in the West than it is for a car mechanic to gain permission to travel there. Moreover, famous musicians will likely find journalists who wish to interview them. There will also be plenty of Western musicians who want to talk to them about their conditions. It is much more difficult for the travelling car mechanic to make such contacts. Thus, comments made by intellectuals can reach the Western media more easily, and they may be rebroadcast to Eastern Europe through such programs as Radio Free Europe and the Voice of America. If intellectuals are imprisoned, finally, it is more likely that the Western media will find out about it, and that international campaigns for their release will follow.

In addition, modern telecommunications technologies and the globalization of mass media and culture have strengthened the voice of the intellectuals. They became known more fully and more quickly. Musicians, for instance, record records that are immediately sold throughout the world. They perform on television, which makes their faces known throughout the world. Authors can publish their works abroad. The better-known ones see their works translated into international languages within a short time. Dissident authors can also spread their work nationally by printing copies of their work on mimeographs. Later, some gained access to photocopy machines, which speeds up the process. When the authorities decide to arrest dissidents, their colleagues can immediately phone Western journalists. Within hours, it becomes international news. After the East European regimes stopped jamming Western radio broadcasts in the late 1970s, almost all East Europeans could access Western news by listening to their radios. In many areas, they even had access to Western TV.[16]

Second, because of their role in ideological production, they have more contradictory incentives deriving from different sources:

a. the Party-state apparatus
b. their audience
c. the demands of their profession

On the one hand, intellectuals have an institutional interest in pleasing the Communist elite by towing the Party line. Since they are involved in ideological production, they obviously face more pressure to pursue the regime's ideological goals. At times, this can degenerate into demands to reproduce crude propaganda. And even if artists support the Communists' basic politico-economic policy, they might have trouble producing works in the "correct" socialist realist style. Let us assume, for purposes of illustration, that there are two women. One is a communist author; the other is an assembly-line worker with capitalist sympathies. Even if a writer *wants* to write in a socialist-realist style to please the authorities (in whose infallibility she at first believes), she might be *unable* to express herself in that style. Perhaps she is only able to write well in a more surrealistic or stream-of-consciousness fashion. So despite her communist sympathies, she potentially faces pressure from the authorities.[17] The assembly-line worker, in contrast, does not feel as much pressure to change her anti-Communist attitude, since the authorities might not ever discover it. At her workplace, nobody will be able to determine whether or not she is pressing her buttons in a socialist-realist manner.

On the other hand, intellectuals also have an institutional interest in obtaining some degree of "fame and fortune" by pleasing their general audience. Depending on the cultural climate at the time, the audience

---

16. Most East Germans could watch West German TV. In the western Czech lands and in much of Slovakia, antennas could pick up Austrian TV. I assume most Hungarians could also watch Austrian TV, but I have never discussed that question with anyone there.

17. Molnár (1971: 70) gives a typical example of this dilemma. Tibor Déby, a Communist writer, wrote a novel *Reply*, where his "intention had been to provide the a communist answer to the vast political and social question of pre-war Hungary, choosing as his hero the son of a worker. But Bálint [the hero] had not been considered sufficiently positive to be the representative of a class in the name of which the Party judged the living and the dead. The author had allowed his hero to hesitate, to think too long before adhering to the communist movement."

will be more or less favorably inclined toward the Party's policy. If the audience shares the cultural tastes of Party functionaries, there need not be a problem; however, a divergence of tastes places the intellectual in the dilemma of producing either for a few functionaries or a large enthusiastic audience.

With the globalization of culture, moreover, their audience is not limited to the domestic public. East German authors know that, if the authorities forbid their work, its chances of becoming a best-seller in West Germany are increased. Punk singer Nina Hagen and folk singer Wolf Biermann, both East Germans, did not suffer economically from their expulsion to the FRG. Nor did the Czech director Miloš Foreman suffer economically from his move from Prague to Hollywood. The majority of intellectuals who remain in their country can also gain economically from book, film and record sales in the West. This is not to say dissidents are motivated by financial gain. At the very least, though, having an audience in the West gives them moral encouragement. It also makes it more difficult for the rulers to punish them. The arrest of a famous author quickly becomes an international affair. In addition, hard-currency earnings from Western sales make it easier for many intellectuals to survive economically when the authorities forbid them from working within their field.

Finally, intellectuals also have a institutional interest in following the demands for self-expression entailed by their profession. As Lipset and Dobson claim (cited in Frentzel-Zagórka & Zagórski 1989: 99), independence and self-direction constitute the necessary conditions of effective intellectual work.

The manner in which each intellectual solves these potentially contradictory institutional interests depends on the individual intellectual's subjective-level orientation. The author who has difficulty expressing herself in a socialist-realist style will likely find it difficult both to please the regime and to write quality literature. Thus, she faces the choice of writing first-rate literature and having trouble with the authorities, on the one hand, or being an unimportant second-rate author on the other. Certainly, some authors would choose the second alternative, but others might find it necessary to be "true to themselves" and to write in the style which best expresses their innermost thoughts. One could easily imagine similar cases: communist movie directors who cannot express themselves through socialist-realist films; musicians who prefer playing jazz, rock or punk to playing classical or folk music; and so on. Of course, not all intellectuals become dissidents; in fact most do not. As Sampson observes (1990: 22) "for every dissident author there were a dozen who flattered the regime, remained silent or compromised." But while most intellectuals do not become dissidents, most dissidents are intellectuals.

This situation can be analyzed more closely in terms of levels of interest. During normal times intellectuals are constrained by their institutional interests since they face great pressures to support the system. However, intellectuals also have institutional interests which coincide with their postulated interests in opposing the system. Which of the contradictory institutional interests weigh heaviest depends on each intellectual's *subjective perception* of his or her institutional interests.

When society undergoes an economic crisis, and institutional structures begin to breakg down, the non-dissident intellectuals are no longer as constrained from following their postulated interests. As the economic development undermines the regime's ideological legitimacy, the corporate entity gets weaker. This in turn encourages the more utilitarian intellectuals to believe that change is possible. As a result, they feel less constrained by their institutional interests.

Obviously, the decision to become a dissident reflects more than just shifts in the tastes of audiences or changes in the policies of the regime; it also has a lot to with the attitudes and beliefs of the intellectuals themselves. I have pointed out earlier that the intellectuals became much more critical of the regimes over time.[18] By the late 1970s, most East European intellectuals had embarked on a path of "anti-politics;"[19] the object was to fight for human rights and to enlarge the space for civil society.

This change in attitudes can account for the difference in the goals and strategies of the opposition, but it is not enough to explain the increase in the *number* of dissidents. Obviously, repression played a role, as seen in the purging of hundreds of thousands of Party members in the ČSSR following the Warsaw Pact invasion. In the late 1980s, dissident activity increased in all countries, as did the number of active participants. Political openings and rising expectations of change probably encouraged more intellectuals to become dissidents, while convincing more dissidents to organize activities against the regime. For many intellectuals this was not enough: to take the last step to joining the opposition, they had to feel outraged.

---

18. See chapter 5.
19. The phrase comes from Konrád (1985).

Finally, the conscious decision of intellectuals to cultivate worker support is critical for the success of a revolution in Soviet-type societies. For intellectuals cannot topple the corporate entity without gaining the support of workers, who comprise the majority of the population and who provide the basis of legitimacy for the "dictatorship of the proletariat." Without the help of the intellectuals, however, workers have difficulty articulating their demands, organizing themselves, and gaining access to the national and international mass media. Intellectuals can also play an important role in preparing for negotiations with the authorities.

Summary of the Partial Model So Far
A simplified version of my partial model so far is as follows:

1) Since intellectuals have the strongest institutional interests in rebelling, a group of intellectual dissidents potentially exists.
2) If there is a period of economic hardship, workers will have a greater propensity to rebel, because they feel less constrained by their institutional interests; they therefore become more willing to follow their postulated interests in fighting for change.
3) The rebellion, in turn, is sparked off by a Party-state action that causes feelings of outrage. If the economic situation is grave, it will normally be direct decisions on economic policy that causes a worker rebellion. If the economic crisis has not caused any dramatic falls in living standards, then policies of repression can cause intellectuals to feel outraged. This motivates them to act. Their protests can spread to workers, who are dissatisfied with their stagnating living conditions. Furthermore, policies on the part either of the domestic regime or of "allied" regimes can increase expectations among the populace, which strengthen subjective perceptions that the time has come for action.
4) If intellectuals and workers are able to cooperate, the chances of success will greatly increase, possibly inducing professionals to join in. Although professionals have the strongest institutional interests in avoiding conflict with the regime, they follow their postulated interests in pursuing change once the size of the rebellion is great enough to lower the chances for direct reprisals against them. In convincing these groups to participate, the main collective-action problem faced by political entrepreneurs is ensuring the ability to communicate rather than the existence of selective incentives.

5) Since very few of the revolutionaries believe they have a chance of succeeding against either their domestic armies or that of the Soviet Union, they will give up their rebellion after a certain level of armed force is used against them. Consequently, their only hope for ultimate success lies in the paralysis of the regime.

Some readers might criticize my emphasis on economic developments: that workers are only willing to rebel during periods of economic decline. It is true that workers were not just critical of the system for economic reasons. As early as in the East German uprising in 1953, they were demanding more democracy. Still, the task of this study is not to explain why people were against the system. Indeed, I assume that a majority in all four countries was largely opposed to the Soviet-type system. When the citizens supported leaders such as Gomułka and Nagy in 1956 or Dubček in 1968, it was because they thought these leaders would democratize or at least liberalize the system. My question, however, is this: given that the populace did not like the system, why were people not always willing to rebel? The task is to specify the conditions under which they are willing to do so. Finally, according to my definition of systemic change, it is wrong to see democratization as a mere political question. For if workers are to follow their objective interests and to demand control over their surplus production, they must have influence over economic policy, which is not possible without political democracy. Thus, it is not surprising that workers usually demanded the establishment of worker councils before, or at the same time as, demanding political democracy. Both demands have to do with increasing their influence—over the productive process in particular, and over their lives in general.

Below I present empirical data regarding the failed pre-1989 uprisings. I intend to demonstrate that my partial model provides a plausible explanation for these events. In chapter 10, I show that this partial model is also applicable to the successful revolutions of 1989.

EXEMPLIFYING THE PARTIAL MODEL: THE UNSUCCESSFUL REVOLTS

1 The Existence of Intellectual Dissidents

I have stated already that intellectuals have the strongest institutional interests in becoming dissidents. While far from all intellectuals become dissidents, virtually all dissidents have been intellectuals. I traced the development of intellectual dissent in chapter 5. It began in the 1950s. By the 1960s, all four countries had well-known dissidents. These dissidents became increasingly critical of the system. In all four countries, intellectuals dominated dissident circles. Although they acted at first as individuals or in small groups, by the 1980s they had formed dissident organizations in all four countries. Thus, all of these countries had groups of intellectuals who could serve as a catalyst for mass movements. In most cases, the intellectuals formed anti-Communist organizations in protest against specific repressive measures—a fact which fits in well with my hypothesis about importance of feeling outraged.

Going back to the three sources of incentives facing intellectuals, one can say that, by the late 1970s, the intellectuals' audience had become more critical. Much of the domestic like the intellectuals themselves—had lost their illusions after years of economic decline, to say nothing of the invasions of Hungary and the ČSSR. The imposition of martial law in Poland did little to improve the image of the Soviet-types regimes. By this time, moreover, it had become easier for dissidents to reach their audience through non-official means. They could use mimeographs to spread copies of their forbidden novels. Their music and messages could reach a domestic audience through Western radio and TV After signing the Helsinki accords in 1977, the regimes stopped jamming Western radio and TV broadcasts. By the end of the 1970s, moreover, most households owned these appliances.

The increasingly gloomy reality economic situation also meant that the intellectuals had stronger incentives deriving from their profession to be more critical. It became increasingly difficult for a social scientist to write high-quality tracts praising the "Marxist-Leninist" development of society. Nor could as many authors as before write novels glorifying society, while still expressing their innermost thoughts, when reality clearly diverged from the ideals of "socialist realism."

However, the third source—the incentives deriving from the Party-state apparatus—varied among the four countries. In the ČSSR and especially the GDR, intellectuals faced tougher demands for adhering to orthodoxy. Yet even in relatively liberal Poland, the regime took measures which outraged intellectuals—such as arresting striking workers in 1976—thus inducing them to organize against the system. This combination of tolerance and repression in Poland was particularly risky for the Polish regime. The relative tolerance of the Polish regime made it easier for the intellectuals to organize in Poland than in the GDR and ČSSR. Thus, a reversion to repression outrages intellectuals and induces dissidents to organize against the regime. I briefly review the dissident groups of these countries below.

I have already mentioned the names of some of the most famous dissidents in Poland during the 1950s and 1960s.[20] The first time, however, that intellectuals engaged in collective action against the regime was in 1968. In March of that year, students and other intellectuals took to the streets of Warsaw to protest the city theater's closing of Adam Mickiewicz's *Dziady*. In addition to demonstrations, they also organized petition campaigns and informal discussion groups, such as the Club of Catholic Intelligentsia, the as secret opposition movement Ruch, and the dissident/activist circle known as Band of Vagabonds (Adams 1992: 221). Laba (1991) notes that workers distrusted the intellectuals and therefore gave them no support. With the intellectuals standing alone, the regime could easily rout the rebellion.

Just as the workers had left the intellectuals to fend for themselves in 1968, the intellectuals watched passively as the workers' rebellions were quickly repressed in 1970 and 1976. The events of 1976, however, proved to be a turning point. A group of intellectual dissidents gathered around Michnik and Kuroń launched KOR in response to the reprisals against former strike leaders (Bakuniak & Nowak 1987: 420, cf. Feffer 1992: 58). The organization's goal was to help defend strike leaders in their trials. According to Adams (1992: 221–22), the core of KOR consisted of students and intellectuals who had taken part in the 1968 demonstrations. KOR became extremely influential in the *Solidarność* uprising four years later. Although it is not clear whether these intellectuals felt outrage at the repressive steps, the repression of the strikes at the very least had a solidarity effect that induced dissidents to organize an openly anti-Communist group for the first time. By then some workers had joined the opposition, since they suffered as strikers from persecution by the regime; however, workers were still in the minority.[21]

In Hungary, Party intellectuals and students served as the catalyst for the 1956 revolt. During the summer of 1954, the Writers

---

20. These include Brus, Kuroń, Modzelewski and Kolakowski (see chapter 5). They were many others too, of course.

21. Sanford (1992: 5) writes that, until 1980, the majority of those who contested the regime belonged to the "intelligentsia."

Association and its papers (the *Irodalmi Ujság* and *Literary Gazette*) "really became the mouthpiece of Imre Nagy and the opposition" (Molnár 1971: 63). Furthermore, "It was the intellectual élite of the régime who began to detach themselves from those in power, to take the path which led to the uprising of October 1956" (Molnár 1971: 72). One of the main groups of Party intellectuals which encouraged the uprising was the Petöfi Circle. It was officially part of the Federation of Working Youth, but it had become a "second parliament" due to its open debates (Molnár 1971: 82–4).

This core group of Party intellectuals kept the debates on political change open, and raised demands for Nagy's re-instatement as prime minister. The next step came from the students, who met on October 16 in Szegred in order to revive the Students' Association. Within days, independent student organizations had merged throughout the country. Nagy's friends then decided to organize a sympathy demonstration with the Poles, who had succeeded in bringing Gomułka back to power (Molnár 1971: 107). Hundreds of thousands of people joined the demonstration. Some of the demonstrators converged on the radio building, where they wanted to broadcast their demands on the radio. Eventually the security forces at the radio building fired on the crowd. Some of the demonstrators answered by firing their own weapons, and the armed rebellion was under way.

The rebels succeeded at first in their main demands: Nagy returned to his post as prime minister, General Secretary Gerö resigned (Kádár was his replacement), and Nagy declared he would form a coalition government including the non-Communist parties. And the Red Army, which had interceded, returned to the barracks. A few days later, Nagy announced there would be free elections and that Hungary would leave the Warsaw Pact. His announcement came after the Soviet Union had already launched a full-scale invasion.

After 1956, various groups of intellectuals emerged. Especially well-known was the "Budapest school," where young intellectuals met under Lukács' guidance. During the 1970s, intellectuals concentrated mostly on writing and distributing underground *samizdat* journals. In 1979, however, the first independent group emerged: the Foundation for the Support of the Poor (cf. Schöpflin 1983: 76–7). Two years later, students set up the Peace Group for Dialogue. Around the same time, young scientists and intellectuals established the Blue Danube Circle to protest government plans for building a hydroelectric plant and dam on the Danube river (Ramet 1991: 114–5). A more explicitly political opposition emerged in the mid-1980s. In the summer of 1985, 45 writers, actors, sociologists, historians and economists met in the village of Monor to discuss the nation's problems. They met again two years later, together with another 100 or so oppositionalists, to set up an umbrella oppositional organization, Hungarian Democratic Forum (MDF). Politburo member Pozsgay was at the meeting, and he encouraged the new organization to formulate an alternative program, which the government could then take a look at (Ramet 1991: 117–8; see also Swain 1989: 17 and interview with Laszlo Váss 12 March 1993). One year later, the MDF established itself as a political party.

In contrast to Poland, Hungary and the ČSSR, the GDR did not have a large reservoir of dissidents. The first generation of intellectuals shied away from demanding democratic reforms, since they distrusted or even feared their fellow citizens. After all, many of them had enthusiastically supported National Socialism a few years earlier (Meuschel 1989–1990: 5). Furthermore, the division into two countries made it easy for the regime to deport critical intellectuals to the other side of the wall (Ash 1990b). The few famous dissidents were all former Party members who had never tried to organize oppositional groups. Nor did they have much opportunity to do so. The chemist Havermann remained in the GDR, but spent many years under house arrest. Bahro was expelled from the Party and forced to emigrate to the FRG after publishing his book *Die Alternative*. The singer Biermann lost his citizenship while performing a concert in the FRG. Thus, he could not return to his homeland.

During the early 1980s, however, a new generation of critical intellectuals emerged. They took advantage of Honecker's reconciliation with the Evangelical Church. Although the Church had gained more autonomy from the state, it generally preferred a strategy of accommodation to one of conflict. Some pastors, though, opened their facilities to alternative groups. Thus, alternative movements concerned with peace, civil rights, the environment, and the like emerged to take advantage of this political opening. As Meuschel (1989–1990: 18) remarks, young intellectuals dominated these groups (see also Lemke 1991: 209 and Szabó 1991). A sort of generation gap emerged, because (in contrast to the situation in the other East European countries) the elder intellectuals distrusted the alternative groups.

In the ČSSR, there were no famous dissidents before the Prague Spring. During the thaw directly preceding Dubček's rise to power, though, critical writers gained control of the writers' union in Slovakia and then in the Czech lands (cf. Dubček 1993: 145 and Kleberg 1968b: 66). The Czech union used its own journal *Literární noviny* to demand radical political change (Kleberg 1968b: 71–86).[22]

The dissidents did not organize into an autonomous anti-Communist group until 1977, when they created Charter 77. The did not found the organization to protest against the persecution of political activists. Instead, they formed the organization to support the members of the underground rock group Plastic People of the Universe, who were prosecuted for playing the "wrong" style of music. (cf. Gruntorád 1990: 7).

Intellectuals dominated the Charter, as they did other dissident groups in East European countries. Many of them, such as Havel, had never been Communists.[23] Nevertheless, former reform Communists were the largest group within Charter 77. They had suffered the bulk of the persecution during the "normalization" period (cf. Fristedt 1993: 15). Around half a million Party members were either expelled or left the Party voluntarily during this period (Pelikán 1975: 43, cf. Kusin 1978: 85). Of course, not all of them were intellectuals, but the vast majority of those who became engaged in Charter 77 were.[24]

In all four countries, then, there were groups of dissidents who could serve as a catalyst when the right moment arose. These included KOR in Poland, the alternative movements in the GDR, and Charter 77 in the ČSSR. Intellectuals dominated the organizations, although some workers became active in Poland after 1976. After the regime banned *Solidarność*, its working-class leaders became permanent fixtures in the Polish opposition, although intellectuals still played a dominant role during the underground period (by spreading news-

---

22. Among *Literární noviny's* most famous articles was the "Two Thousand Words" manifesto. Written by the author Ludvík Vaculík, it went so far as to claim that the population would be willing to defend itself with arms against a Soviet invasion (reprinted in Norden 1977: 145–53).

23. Besides Havel, other famous authors who joined Charter 77 include the poets Bohumil Hrabal, Petr Kabes, Jiří Kolár and Nobel Prize winner Jaroslav Seifert, and the novelists Eva Kantůrková and Ivan Klíma (Heneka et al. 1985: 287–293). If journalists and literary critics are included, then Jiří Dienstbier (later Foreign Minister), Jiří Ruml (later Interior Minister) and Saša Vondra (later speaker for Charter 77, aid to President Havel and finally, Vice Foreign Minister) should be added.

24. The most prominent former Communist leaders who co-founded Charter 77 include former Secretary for Ideology Zdeněk Mlynář, who became a professor of political science in Austria, and former Foreign Minister Jiří Hajek (also with a doctorate) who became a professor at the Economic University after the 1989 revolution.

papers and the like). In the other countries, intellectuals dominated the anti-Communist organizations completely.

2 Workers Rebel during Times of Economic Hardship

In this section, I argue that workers have only rebelled during periods of economic downturn. At such times, they have been willing to confront the state—*if* the state does something to outrage them, such as announcing a policy that will lower their standard of living. Furthermore, if a rebellion breaks out during a period of declining or stagnating living standards, workers are also willing to join in— especially if the state does something to outrage them.

The 1970 rebellion in Poland occurred during a time of declining living standards for workers. That year the Polish Central Committee discussed a new wage scheme that would a) limit overtime (and thus reduce wages); b) exclude wage increases, premiums, and bonuses for at least two years; c) raise work norms; and d) sharpen discipline. Then, on December 11, Gomułka completed plans for a large, immediate increase in food prices; these were finally announced one week before Christmas.

Workers along the Baltic coast were among the hardest hit, since they lived in an area without private farms, on which they could otherwise have supplemented their incomes by doing extra work (Laba 1991: 199). Thus, coastal workers began striking as soon the price increases were announced. Laba (1991: 25) reports that Gdańsk workers walked down the street singing revolutionary songs such as the "Internationale." Among their demands were greater democracy and the right to have independent trade unions (1991: 82). This shows that workers were already "conscious" of their exploitation. Yet they were not willing to rebel unless they were suffering economically. This is an example of how, during normal times, institutional interests may prevent workers from rebelling even when they are conscious of their postulated interests in changing the system. In times of economic hardship, however, these interests become less constraining. Hence workers are more willing to try to achieve their postulated interests.

In 1976, the regime again announced price hikes in response to worsening economic conditions, and again the workers went on strike. Although it rescinded the increase the next day, by then over 100 factories had stopped work (Laba 1991: 104, cf. Curry 1988: 90 and Touraine et al. 1982).

Even though the strikes ended, the regime was able to do little to improve the economic situation. By the time of the *Solidarność* uprising, economic conditions had become the worst since the Communists came to power. Curry (1988: 487) cites public-opinion surveys showing that, before the *Solidarność* worker uprising in 1980, only 8% of the population thought that the preceding year had been a good one, as compared to 60% in 1974. Furthermore, the official economic growth rates—which had been positive from 1971–1977— declined to –2.3% in 1979 and –6% the following year (Simatupang 1994: 2). When the regime added fuel to the fire by calling for price hikes, strikes were the predictable consequence. At first, the workers only made economic demands. When Wałęsa negotiated an agreement for wage increases at his shipyard, however, the workers voted down his suggestion. They decided instead to continue their strike in *solidarity* with the other workers, who had not received any wage increases. Within a few months, the independent union had around 10 million members and even more sympathizers. One of its main demands was for the establishment of worker councils, which would choose the directors and run the factories. Thus, the workers followed their postulated interests in trying to gain control over their surplus production.

Not much concrete has been written about economic conditions in Hungary prior to the 1956 uprising. But the available literature on the subject indicates that living standards had decreased or stagnated in the preceding years. Molnár (1971: 76) writes: "On the economic level, the standard of living ceased to rise...." Váli (1961) writes about mounting economic problems in connection with failures to meet plans, but he never discusses changes in living standards. Harman (1983: 119) states that "bread production was about 15 per cent less than was needed to feed the population." So the country clearly had economic problems. Under these conditions, the workers were more receptive to the student demonstrations in October 1956. Workers attended the mass rally which started the rebellion. Once the revolt began, workers set up self-governing councils in the factories. They were even encouraged by the Party and the official union (Molnár 1971: 174). Eventually, the workers took the notion of gaining control over their surplus product seriously: they demanded ownerships of the enterprises (Molnár 1971: 178). As in the *Solidarność* uprising, then, workers acted in accordance with their postulated interests.

Similarly, the East German uprising began with measures which lowered workers' living standards. In May 1953, the East German Communist leadership voted to increase work norms by 10% (Simmons 1989: 86–7). Harman (1983: 64) writes that, at a meeting on June 15 in East Berlin, workers calculated that this would decrease their wages by around one-third. He notes further that living standards had been decreasing even before the increases in norms, because of decisions in the previous two years to divert investment from consumer goods to heavy industry.

The day after the workers' meeting, protests and strikes spread through the city and quickly spilled over to the rest of the country. At many rallies the workers demanded democracy. So again, workers made demands for *political* changes as well as economic ones, but they were only willing to rebel during a period of economic hardship—and when they were outraged at state economic policies.

In the ČSSR, the workers never rebelled before 1989, except to protest the Soviet-led invasion in 1968. Even in this instance, the invasion of foreign armies obviously threatened the material standards of the workers. Moreover, the reform Communists had been able to come to power and to launch their economic reforms in the first place precisely because of the recent economic downturn.[25] So even that rebellion took place after workers' living standards had been declining, although the invasion was obviously a more important reason for protesting. Furthermore, the workers' rebellion consisted mainly of establishing worker councils, which means—according to the terms of this study—that they were pursuing their postulated interests in gaining control over the productive process. However, the economic stagnation of the 1980s was not as extreme in Czechoslovakia as in Poland and Hungary, and living standards had been improving during the 1970s. The normalization purges of the 1970s mostly hit higher-lever Party members and intellectuals, so the regime was doing little that could outrage the workers.

The only times when workers revolted, then, were during periods of economic decline. This does not mean they automatically revolted during such periods; however, since there were no instances of worker revolts during an economic upswing, the obvious conclusion is that

---

25. For discussions of the economic downturn and its political consequences, see Dencik & Kenneth (1968: 28–9), Hejzlar (1976: 75) and James (1969: 3).

economic downturn is a necessary but not sufficient condition for workers to participate in rebellions. In addition, the fact that workers demanded democratic reforms during several of their revolts (the GDR in 1953, Hungary in 1956, and Poland in 1970) shows that they were not simply economic robots who were only interested in the economy. Still, the task of my partial model is not to explain people's attitudes in general, but rather their readiness to revolt.

3 Party-State Action
Neither workers nor intellectuals have been willing to engage in collective action until they have felt outraged at some policy decision, which made them feel they had to act *now*. For workers before 1989, these regime decisions were always in the economic arena. For intellectuals, decisions to organize were normally in connection with political repression (the closing of a Play in Poland in 1968, the trials against strike leaders in Poland in 1976 and the trial against the underground rock group Plastic People of the Universe in the ČSSR in 1977). Rising expectations increase the likelihood that outraged citizens will rebel. For example, Polish intellectuals in 1968 probably had expectations of liberalization, since all countries were experimenting with economic reforms during the 1960s, and intellectual pluralism had begun to bloom in neighboring Czechoslovakia during the Prague Spring.

The Polish workers only revolted when they were angry at government measures which lowered their living standards (i.e., the price hikes in 1970, 1976 and 1980–1, and even in 1956). It is not surprising that Gomułka's arrogance in raising prices right before Christmas in 1970 would outrage the workers. Indeed, they showed their wrath directly by burning down the party headquarters in some cities (1991: 35). Laba (1991: 64) quotes a worker who describes how his feelings of outrage influenced him in 1970:

> Up until then I wasn't interested in politics. I returned home that night tremendously upset. My mates, my friends had already come over. All spoke up, one after another. We knew we had to do something.

In another account which Laba gives (1991: 36), the worker states,

> [at] the sound of powerful motors...such anger filled me that I decided to return to the [Party] committee building. But it turned out I wasn't alone, but merely part of a crowd coming from all parts of the city to face the tanks.

The workers acted more calmly in 1980. This does not mean they were any less indignant. Rather, Laba (1991) asserts that, in 1980, they had learned their lesson from 1970: if they left the factories, they were easy targets for the military. By remaining in the factories and refraining from violence, it would be harder for the military to justify an attack. As long as the workers are peaceful and stay away from the streets or Party buildings, the regime cannot claim it needs to repress the workers violently in order to protect itself. In addition, the military could not attack without damaging much of the nation's productive capabilities. Perhaps just as important was the workers' ability to utilize factory facilities for communicating with other factory strike committees. Laba (1991: 129–30) notes that strikers would seize control of factory public-address systems, factory bulletin boards and telefax machines. The fax machines linked the local union with the entire country. In addition, they are less easily tapped than phone lines.

Why did more workers revolt in 1980 than in 1970 or 1976? I have already mentioned the severity of the economic downturn and the lessons the workers had learned regarding communications. The support of the intellectuals was also a major fact, as discussed below. Another difference was probably rising expectations. In contrast to 1970 and 1976, there was a clear split among the leadership in 1980, with a relatively strong "liberal"-softline faction.[26] As Haggard & Kaufman (1995) predict, the split took place during a period of economic decline. Bakuniak & Nowak (1987: 421) report that, prior to the Party conference half a year before the revolt, there were high hopes that the liberal faction would win. In contrast, there had not been any reason for the workers to expect the Party to be open for reforms during their previous revolt in 1970, since it occurred just two years after the regime had been a driving force behind the invasion of Czechoslovakia. Of course, expectations in Poland in 1980 had not risen as much as in the GDR and the ČSSR in 1989. For during the Brezhnev era, East Europeans knew the USSR would likely invade if the changes were too radical. Thus, Solidarność and KOR leaders spoke in the beginning about a "self-limiting revolution" (see Staniszkis 1984).[27]

---

26. See chapter 6 for a discussion of the three factions which had emerged within the Politburo and Secretariat.
27. As Touraine et al. (1983: 19) found in their field study of Solidarność, the union became "a movement which constantly seeks to stay on the right side of the invisible boundary of what is acceptable to the Soviet leadership."

Many Hungarian intellectuals had already decided to act in 1955, after state repression had outraged them. Molnár (1971: 80) notes that, shortly after Nagy had lost the premiership that year, nearly all the writers and journalists who had supported him were punished. The "last straw" was the firing of Literary Gazette's chief editor Györy Hámos. "The members of the secretariat of the Writers' Association, almost all of them communist, handed in their resignations en masse." Other actions soon followed. For example, 58 famous writers, all of them Party members, sent a memorandum to the Central Committee protesting the repression of journalists and writers. Unfortunately, none of the sources I have read have explained why the students decided to get involved in 1956. So it is not possible to judge whether they were driven by feelings of outrage. Many of the intellectuals were probably incensed by the increase in repression after Nagy was sacked, as the above examples of writers and journalists indicate. The rest of the population apparently, was not willing to revolt until events heightened their expectations of change.

Several authors have pointed out that events in neighboring countries increased expectations of change in Hungary in 1956 (cf. Molnár 1971: 82, 104 and Váli 1961). First, Khrushchev condemned the crimes of Stalinism in his famous speech. Thus, the Hungarians hoped that the Kremlin would push for a change of leadership, since General Secretary Rákosi had been responsible for the Stalinist show trials. (He eventually resigned, but Gerö, his replacement, was also a hardliner.) Second, the worker revolt in Poland brought the reformer Gomułka back to power. This gave the Hungarians hope that they could likewise bring back Nagy.

In addition, the split among the leaders caused a political opening. As usual, this opening occurred during a period of economic hardship. Since Nagy's faction was involved in planning the first demonstrations, feelings of outrage were not as necessary for getting people to attend. The regime at first even allowed the demonstration and announced it on the radio. Thus, the Hungarian uprising had a different character than did the other purely anti-Communist uprisings of this chapter.

Like the Polish uprisings, the East German revolt in 1953 broke out in direct response to a change in regime policy—the raising of work-norms. Harman (1983: 64) claims that, at the strike meetings, the workers expressed "resentment" at the new decree. At the sight of the first demonstration, a worker "indicated that the time to act had come." Although Harman does not write anything about expectations of change, it is likely the East Germans had some hopes, since Stalin had recently died. Moreover, the new Soviet leadership was critical of Ulbricht's hardline policies and asked him to moderate them. At this stage, it was not clear what direction Soviet policy would follow. There was even talk of letting the GDR go (see for example Harman 1983: 78). Meanwhile, there was a clear split in leadership (Harman 1983: 79), which according to Tarrow provides a political opening. Again, this split came during a period of economic decline.

Again, Charter 77 emerged to protest a regime decision to prosecute an underground rock band. It is hard to know exactly how "outraged" Czechoslovaks felt over that decision, but most likely they decided that a certain threshold had finally been reached and it was time to act. Otherwise, they could have simply formed the organization at any point during the 1970s, rather than immediately after a particular policy decision. At the same time, the Helsinki Accords provided a slight political opening, since the regimes had pledged to respect human rights. Thus, Charter 77 could demand that the regime actually uphold what it had undertaken. In Schöpflin's words (1993: 180), the organization's "objectives were to compel the party to undertake a dialogue with society and to insist that it abide by its own formal legality, which would, of course, have undermined the system completely." But the Charter intellectuals failed to gain the support of the workers, so they remained largely isolated from society until the 1989 uprising.

4 Cooperation

One of the main differences between other rebellions which lasted a few days and the relatively successful *Solidarność* uprising[28] lay in the cooperation between workers and intellectuals achieved in the latter. As noted above, intellectuals cannot succeed without the support of workers, while workers have a much easier time organizing if they have the support of intellectuals. For intellectuals are usually better at utilizing the media and other forms of communication. They can also be extremely helpful for organizing and negotiating. I assert below that one of the main differences between the relative success of the *Solidarność* uprising as compared to previous revolts lay precisely in this fruitful cooperation between workers and intellectuals. The

---

28. Which continued for one-and-a-half years and gained the support of 10 million members

intellectuals never had any "selective incentives" with which they could induce workers to participate by rewarding or punishing them. Since the Communists had a monopoly over the mass media, the most important collective-action problem during the rebellions was communication. It was necessary to inform other inhabitants that a rebellion had begun.

In 1968 the intellectuals had stood alone in Poland, and in 1970 and 1976 the workers had stood alone (cf. Laba 1991: 91–2). The regime could quickly crush the revolts. Once intellectuals formed KOR to give outright support to workers, the situation changed. Intellectuals used their skills to encourage workers to organize and oppose the regime.

Bakuniak & Nowak (1987: 420) conducted a survey of the Ursus plant in central Poland which had been one of the major strike centers.[29] They note that dissidents maintained close contacts with many of the workers from the plants involved in the 1976 strikes, giving them

> wide access to uncensored papers, books and leaflets (*samizdat*). Secondly, there emerged a group of opinion leaders [at these plants who were] not tied with the existing institutions, [and who were] more or less ideologically connected with the opposition circles.

For the first time in the history of the Soviet bloc, intellectuals tried actively to gain the backing of workers against an allegedly workers' state. KOR organized the Committee for Free Trade Unions in Gdańsk in 1978. Its leaders became the leaders of the Gdańsk *Solidarność* two years later (Ost 1990 cited in Kubik 1994: 443). Among those taken under their tutelage was a certain dock worker by the name of Lech Wałęsa (cf. Syzmanski 1984: 116–7 and Ost 1990: 12–13).

When, in 1980, strikes spread from these plants to the Baltic coast, leading to the formation of a new and independent union, the KOR intellectuals immediately offered their support. A few days after the strikes began, 62 Warsaw intellectuals—many of them internationally known—came out publicly in support of the free trade union. They formed a committee of experts to assist the regional strike. Commenting on this, Touraine et al. (1983: 31) note that, even though the initiative came from the workers, intellectuals were present as

---

29. They actually surveyed two different plants in 1980, interviewing about 60 people at each.

advisors. I have already mentioned how workers used factory facilities to facilitate communication with other strike committees. The intellectuals also helped the workers in their communication with the mass media. Since many of the intellectuals spoke foreign languages, moreover, they were also important for communicating with the international mass media and for gaining foreign support. In addition, the intellectuals helped the workers organize. Thus they were instrumental in helping the movement spread rapidly throughout the country. Furthermore, intellectuals helped develop tactics for negotiating with Communist officials. Later in 1989, many of these intellectuals became involved in negotiations with the Communists on *Solidarność's* behalf. So even if intellectual dissidents did not start the rebellion, they were instrumental in its relative success. This fruitful cooperation between workers and intellectuals is one of the main reasons why the 1980–1 rebellion gained the support of millions of people, while the regime had quickly quelled the previous ones.[30]

Once the fruitful cooperation between workers and intellectuals led to a nation-wide revolt, professionals—who had been passive during previous uprisings—also became involved (cf. Laba 1991: 168).

In Hungary in 1956, it was the intellectuals who clearly took the initiative for revolt. Once they organized demonstrations in October, other groups in society quickly joined them. I have not been able to find any material on the general make-up of the demonstrators, but almost all sectors of society were likely involved—including the Communist Party. After all, as noted above, the Nagy faction of the Party participated in planning the first demonstrations. This was the clearest case of a political opening in pre-1989 Eastern Europe. Workers were among the most active, since they set up worker councils. These councils played an important role in propagating for change during the revolt. Since the radio had announced the demonstration, and since Party members were involved, it is probable that the professionals were not afraid to join in. Since the revolt spread throughout most of the country, and since all groups in society supported it, this revolt was the most successful in Eastern Europe

---

30. Even Laba (1991: 178)—who claims that the role of intellectuals has been vastly overrated— admits that "there would not have been a Solidarity without the intellectuals." But, he continues, "the Solidarity they joined was built on the framework developed by workers. In other words, the roots of Solidarity were in the Baltic working class, and the intellectuals made a necessary but not causal or creative contribution."

until the *Solidarność* uprising 24 years later. As far as I know, the Hungarian intellectuals did not try actively to recruit worker support, as KOR did later in Poland. Nevertheless, all groups cooperated in the sense that they were working for the same basic values: a democratization of society and true independence from the Soviet Union. As during the *Solidarność* uprising, the main collective action problem was communication. Once people knew about the events, they were willing to join the rebellion even without "selective incentives." Thus, the rebels devoted a major portion of their energy to convincing provincial radio stations to broadcast their demands and information. They largely succeeded in this. Consequently, the populace was well-informed of the events (see Molnár 1971).

Harman (1983: 71) and Meuschel (1989–90: 5) agree that, in 1953, the East German workers stood alone. While Meuschel writes that the intellectuals distanced themselves from the workers, Harman quotes a source claiming that "The middle class, bourgeois and intelligentsia kept almost completely out of the events." Again, one main reason was the mistrust felt by the intellectuals, who feared that the German populace still might harbor fascist sympathies.

Even though the workers did not gain the help of East German intellectuals, they were able to spread word of the strike through the *West* German media. The West Berlin radio RIAS broadcast news about the events. Within a few minutes, workers in industrial centers throughout the country knew about the strike. The same day, workers set up strike committees in factories in most cities. Thus, it was Western radio that solved the collective-action problem of communication (as it did later in 1989; see chapter 10).

In contrast to KOR in Poland, Charter 77 in the ČSSR never tried to organize the workers. As Adams (1992: 231) observes, it concentrated on the legal aspects of human rights. Until 1989, the Charter intellectuals remained isolated from the rest of society, without any strategy for gaining worker support.

5. A Certain Level of Armed Force

The rational-choice theorist Przeworksi (1991:intro) claims that in 1989 the Communist leaders gave up because they realized they could not rely on the military to repress the opposition. Chapters 9 and 10 contend that his claim holds true only for Hungary. The East European cases prior to 1989 show that the regimes could quell rebellions without full military support. As Tiananmen Square demonstrated, if the opposition is unarmed, it is not necessary for the regime to enjoy the support of the military *as a whole*. It is enough—*as long as* no other parts of the oppressive apparatus actively support the opposition—to find a few units that are willing to fire on demonstrators (see Schell 1994 for a description of China). Although many Chinese commanders refused orders to attack, the rulers were able to subdue the demonstrators by bringing in troops from far-off provinces. More than two decades earlier, Johnson (1964) concluded that no rebellion can succeed against a modern military unless the rebels themselves are highly armed and well-trained, or a portion of the military actively supports them. In this sense, a reformulated rational-choice hypothesis is more fruitful: there is a certain level of repression which can defeat a rebellion. The required level increases the longer the state waits (see Karlkins & Petersen 1993).

Disregarding for the moment the 1989 cases in East Europe, it is questionable whether the Communist regimes could really have relied on their military even during the failed revolts. In the GDR in 1953, for example, the regular army refused to fire, so elite troops from the Peoples' Militia and the Soviet army quelled the uprising instead (Harman 1983: 72). In Hungary in 1956 the army remained passive. Many soldiers and officers actually helped the rebels. Some handed out weapons; others even fought actively on their side (Molnár 1971: 115, 135). The secret police remained loyal to the regime, but it was extremely ineffective in battle. Again the Soviet army was decisive. Laba (1991: 43–4, 61, 91–92) documents the refusal of some regular military units to shoot demonstrators during the Gdańsk and Szczecin strikes in Poland in 1970. When the regime finally called in special elite troops, these small units were able to crush the rebellion quickly.

The simple conclusion then, is that it is not necessary for most of the military to support the regimes. As long as the military does not actively oppose the regime (as it did in Romania in 1989) a rebellion can be crushed as long as a few divisions are willing to take orders. In the East European context prior to Gorbachev, it was sufficient to use the Soviet Army to stop any revolt. Thus, the main question for the revolutionaries was not whether or not the Party would collapse, but whether or not the national armed forces or the Soviet Union would be willing intervene to save the old regime. In the *Solidarność* uprising, this translated into the fear that either the Polish army or the Soviet Union would eventually intervene if the revolutionaries went too far in their demands. The expectations of the *Solidarność* leadership were accordingly limited: they believed that some changes were possible, such as the establishment of free trade unions. Hence, the perceived strength of the regime was important. The more it caved in to demands, the more radical the demands became. Yet the presence of the Soviet factor dampened revolutionary expectations. In 1989, by contrast, the Soviet Union's position ignited rather than dampened these expectations. Still, as the 1970 Polish case shows, the domestic regimes were capable of stopping rebellions even without full military support. As long as the leaders were resolved to act, and as long as they could count on the support of some units (without the active resistance of others), the opposition had little chance.[31]

CONCLUSION ON UPRISINGS

In all four countries, a certain pattern emerged: there were critical intellectuals ready to act as catalysts for rebellion. Intellectuals are more likely to become dissidents, because they have greater institutional incentives to oppose the regime. They cannot succeed, however, without the help of workers, who do not have as strong institutional interests in opposing the regime. Workers have only been willing to follow their postulated interests and rebel during times of economic decline. Professionals have the strongest institutional interests to remain loyal. Thus, they have only participated in revolts when these have erupted into mass uprisings, which makes the risks of punishment much lower (Poland in 1980 and Hungary in 1956). The *Solidarność* uprising in 1980 was the most successful one in Eastern Europe before 1989.

Here I review the five preconditions for a successful revolt in a Soviet-type society, to suggest why the *Solidarność* uprising was more successful than the previous ones:

- The intellectuals established an anti-Communist organization (KOR), that was ready to play the role of catalyst.
- The economic decline was harsher than in previous cases, which made the workers more willing to rebel.

---

31. Hungary in 1956 was a special case, both because the army resisted actively to some extent and because the rebels were armed (by the military). In addition, the rebels had the advantage of enjoying support from circles around the prime minister. Such a prospect did not exist in 1989—except again in Hungary, where Nemeth, Pozsgay and other radical reformers actively opposed the conservative General Secretary Grósz.

- The state outraged the workers by trying to raise food prices again. The workers were especially frustrated, because the reformist faction had failed to push through radical changes at the Party congress. Thus, the workers' rising expectations went unmet.
- Via KOR, the intellectuals were immediately prepared to cooperate with the workers. Both intellectuals and workers had learned from the past, and thus were able to utilize communications channels effectively (workers with factory resources such as fax machines, intellectuals via the mass media, etc.).

Yet, the fifth variable (the state's use of force) prevented *Solidarność* from completing a true revolution. In the end, the Polish military was willing to use enough force to repress the rebellion. In contrast to the situation in 1989, moreover, the populace was willing to accept this intervention, since it feared that a Soviet invasion would be even worse. In 1989, the East European citizens no longer believed that the Soviet Union would invade to prevent systemic change. Moreover, after the changes in Poland and Hungary in 1989, the East Germans and Czechoslovaks probably had much greater expectations of change than did the Poles of 1980.

Thus, if one applies this partial model to the East European countries in 1988, it becomes clear that these countries were facing a potentially revolutionary situation.

- The intellectuals were better organized and more critical in all four countries than in any previous years. In Poland the intellectuals led underground *Solidarność*. In Hungary, they had built several oppositional organizations, including the MDF, which later won the first free elections. In the GDR, several alternative movements had emerged, while in the ČSSR, several new anti-Communist organizations had joined Charter 77. In all four countries, moreover, the intellectuals had become more openly critical of the regime.
- The economic situation was deteriorating in all four countries. For the first time, these countries had experienced long periods of decline or stagnation. In addition, every country but the ČSSR was facing a mounting debt crisis. Economists and politicians had begun to agree that the debt crisis could only be solved by means of belt-tightening measures which would lower living standards further. Thus, the risk was rising that workers might rebel.

- The regimes had not yet outraged society, but the belt-tightening economic measures which they were considering might have done so. In addition, Gorbachev's reform policy removed the East German and Czechoslovak regimes' pragmatic legitimacy, since they could no longer claim that the Kremlin would not allow reforms. Thus, expectations for change were rising in these countries. Furthermore, the Poles and Hungarians too had good reason to entertain higher hopes for change. There was now a distinct possibility that Gorbachev would encourage their regimes to go further with their reforms. At the very least, they had reason to believe that the Soviet Union would no longer prevent more radical reforms, as it had done in Hungary in the early 1970s. Gorbachev had already allowed Jaruzelski to hold a referendum in 1987 (which the regime lost). Meanwhile, Hungary had carried out an election with multiple candidates, and several independent candidates had obtained seats in parliament.
- In Poland, workers and intellectuals had already set a precedent for cooperation, which could inspire the use of similar strategies in potential uprisings in neighboring countries. Moreover, the telecommunications revolution made communication potentially easier for the opposition, since fax and photocopy machines were becoming more readily available. As a result of the Helsinki accords, morever, the East European regimes had stopped blocking radio broadcasts from Radio Free Europe. Thus, the opposition would be able to appeal to the populace during a rebellion via Western radio.
- Since Gorbachev had become more accommodating toward the West and begun to talk about reducing Soviet forces in the Warsaw Pact countries, East Europeans were no longer certain that the Red Army would prop up the domestic regimes during a rebellion.

The above analysis shows that, if the Communist leaders had examined the causes of previous uprisings carefully, they would have had good reason to be nervous as the decade came to a close.

Chapter 9

INSTITUTIONAL COMPROMISE

THE DISCOURSE

In his recent book, *Democracy and the Market*, Przeworski (1991) predicts that authoritarian regimes (including the Soviet-type) will only agree to democratic elections if they can obtain some guarantees that their basic interests will be protected. Under capitalist regimes, this includes guarantees of property rights. Under Soviet-type regimes, this only includes the political issue of the regimes having continued political influence. In Poland, for example, the Communists obtained the following concessions from *Solidarność*: 1) 35% of the seats in the *Sejm* were reserved for the Communists and another 30% for their allies; 2) the opposition would not block Jaruzelski's election to the presidency; and 3) the Communists would maintain control over matters of defense and internal order (Przeworski 1991: 78). Yet in Hungary, the Communists did not receive any such guarantees—the elections were completely free without any special advantages reserved for the Communists. Furthermore, even Poland falls short of Przeworski's criteria, because the rulers did not behave as strategically as Przeworski suggests. I argue that, while the Polish rulers acted rationally in demanding certain guarantees, when negotiating with the opposition they were not rational in their choice of majoritarian over proportional elections for the freely contested seats.

By non-rational, I mean that given the information available to the Polish leaders, they could have vastly improved their electoral chances by proposing proportional rather than majoritarian elections. It was even less rational to put up more than one candidate in around half of the districts. In general, however, it is difficult to determine what is rational or not. For example, one might claim that the Polish rulers consciously or subconsciously *wanted* to lose power. With such preferences, their behavior could be interpreted as being rational. If one uses a broad enough definition, it is extremely difficult to determine what is rational or non-rational. Therefore, I prefer the term "strategic." By strategic behavior, I mean action that either improves the rulers' chances of maintaining power and influencing developments or at least allows them to go down in history as peacemakers who brought about a democratic transition. In this chapter and subsequently, I assert that only the Hungarian rulers behaved highly strategically, although their Polish comrades were relatively more strategic than the East German and Czechoslovak leaders. Ironically, although Przeworski devotes nearly his entire book to rationalist explanations, the few pages which he devotes to psychological and sociological explanations provide better hypotheses for the Polish, East German and Czechoslovak cases. Przeworski agrees that psychological explanations are useful when rulers screen out information that does not fit their desired outcome (1991: 65). I will maintain that this psychological explanation holds true for the leaders of all of the countries except Hungary. Przeworski's (1991: 54–5) sociological explanation emphasizes the establishment of personal contacts between the liberalizers in the regime and oppositional leaders, which makes a smooth transition possible. The opposition influences the liberalizers, who in turn change their preferences. It should be clear from chapter 7 that this in fact happened in Poland and Hungary, where society was relatively open. The Polish sociologist Sztompka (1995) stresses the importance of trust for society. I maintain that the negotiations in Poland and Hungary went more smoothly than those in the GDR and ČSSR precisely because the rulers and the opposition trusted each other more in the reformist countries.

Even though none of the regimes behaved the way Przeworski expected, he and other theorists of democratization (especially O'Donnell & Schmitter 1986) are correct in emphasizing the dynamics of reformers maneuvering between hardliners and the opposition. To Przeworski's (1991) credit, he takes his analysis one step further than O'Donnell & Schmitter, by dividing the opposition into radicals and moderates. However, he sees the radicals as a threat to the democratization process. The radicals are unlikely to accept any form of institutional compromise, since they "tend to be wary of democratic institutions..." (1991: 73). Yet, the moderates within the opposition must placate the radicals. Przeworski notes (1991: 69) that the "Moderates must either deliver terms tolerable to Radicals, or if they cannot obtain such terms from the Reformers [within the regime], they must leave enough power in the hands of the apparatus to intimidate Radicals." If the moderates choose to ally themselves with the radicals instead of the regime softliners, the softliners will retrench and cooperate with the regime hardliners.

Przeworski begins from the assumption that radicals usually oppose democracy. *If* the radicals do not oppose democracy; however, a democratic transition is possible. It is difficult to argue against the logic of his reasoning. His assumption is questionable, though. He never explains *why* he makes this assumption. Instead, he assumes that the reader shares his belief that radicals are undemocratic. I maintain in this chapter that the radicals in both Poland and Hungary were clearly democrats from the beginning. The differences between radicals and moderates were not about whether the system should be democratic; it rather concerned the pace of change. The radicals successfully pressured both the regime and opposition into speeding up the transitional process. Consequently, the radicals actually made the transitions quicker.

Bova (1991) wrote the only article of which I am aware that uses the O'Donnell & Schmitter model exclusively for a Soviet-type society. He maintains in his article on democratization in the USSR that the farther that the reforms have come, the less credible are threats to reverse them. When the reformers threaten to take back the reforms, the opposition is likely to call their bluff. This, in turn, reduces the reformers' leverage with the opposition. Eventually, the hardliners feel threatened by the pressure for change from below. So they retrench and increase their power. This causes society to become paralyzed, as the center becomes weaker (1991: 124–5). Hence, to ensure a democratic transition, the reformers must gain the support of the hardliners. They can do so either by allowing the hardliners to maintain some political influence in the new system or by securing them the possibility of exchanging political for economic power (1991: 128–9).

Most authors in this actor-oriented tradition, however, have produced hypotheses which have not been born out by the East European cases. First, the Communist regimes did not always act strategically; nor did they always try to gain special guarantees in elections. Second, in stark contrast to Bova's assertion, the reformers in Hungary and Poland did not need to gain the support of the hardliners to ensure democratic transitions. On the contrary, the reformers simply defeated their hardliner adversaries. Third, none of these theorists has seriously considered the possibility of a revolutionary outcome. They remain basically bound to the democratization/authoritarian rule dichotomy.[1]

---

1. Bova does not mention the possibility of revolution at all in his study. Przeworski (1991) has revolution as a possible outcome in his game matrices and diagrams, but he does not seriously discuss this alternative form of transition to democracy.

Thus, they cannot explain the revolutions in the ČSSR and GDR. Finally, like Tarrow in his discussion of political openings, they do not have any theory as to the conditions under which regimes are willing to begin liberalization processes. Above all, they tend to leave out the important interplay between the economy and politics.

I have already claimed that economic problems pressured the Polish and Hungarian leaders to begin liberalizing and then democratizing their countries. The severity of the economic crisis could be the reason why the regimes failed to achieve democracy with guarantees in the manner predicted by Przeworski. Haggard & Kaufman (1995: ch. 2) provide such an explanation. They find in their study of Latin America and Southeast Asia that those regimes which instigated democratization during periods of increased economic growth were usually able to impose their conditions on the opposition. Hence, they could receive some guarantees. In those countries where economic growth had declined, on the other hand, the rulers were usually unable to obtain any special guarantees. The reason being that when there is an economic crisis, the rulers are weakened. Splits arise over economic policy. It is easier to maintain internal unity when the economy is developing positively than when it is developing negatively. In addition, groups in society start mobilizing against the regime when their living conditions deteriorate. This in turn increases the level of repression necessary, if the regime is to maintain dictatorial rule. Softliners may feel the price is too high, and, therefore, favor a conciliation with society.

I basically agree with Haggard & Kaufman that the economic crisis made it more difficult for the leaders of the corporate entity to obtain guarantees. However, the Polish rulers succeeded in obtaining some guarantees, although they did not behave as strategically as many actor-based models would suggest. Haggard & Kaufman's are also correct in claiming that an economic crisis weakens a liberalizing regime by causing splits over policy. I argue in chapter 10, though, that the *non-liberalizing* regimes did not suffer from major policy disputes.

In Eastern Europe, the dynamics of regime policy making were as follows (see Figure 1): Years of economic decline eroded the ideological legitimacy of all four regimes. In striving to find solutions to these problems, the Polish and Hungarian regimes (with their reformist pragmatic acceptance) had greater incentives to liberalize society than the East German and Czechoslovak counterparts (with their anti-reformist pragmatic acceptance). In the relatively open social climate which prevailed in Poland and Hungary, official researchers published extremely critical accounts of the corporate entity's policies. Radical reformers who read these reports became even more doubtful about the possibility of solving the economic problems without systemic change. Not surprisingly, the views of these radical reformists conflicted with conservative *apparatchiks* who were worried about losing their power.

Gorbachev's ascension to power made it easier for the Polish and Hungarian regimes to continue building on their reformist pragmatic acceptance, which was based on the claim that they were testing the limits of what the USSR would allow. When it appeared that society was reaching a potentially revolutionary situation and that Gorbachev would allow a lot more leeway than previous Soviet leaders had done, the path was opened for reaching an institutional compromise with the opposition before a rebellion erupted.

The liberalization of society hastened the process of reaching an institutional compromise. Radical reformers had already established contacts with the opposition before negotiations had begun. Consequently, there was more trust among the negotiators in Poland and Hungary than in East Germany and Czechoslovakia, where both sides still saw the other as the enemy.

Again, I am not using a determinist argument. Instead, I am merely claiming that those regimes with reformist pragmatic acceptance *could*

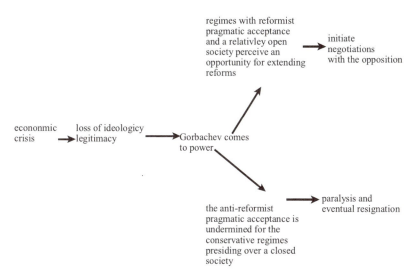

Figure 1: Two Types of Regime Behavior

move more freely than those with anti-reformist pragmatic acceptance. The actual behavior of the rulers depended on their subjective perceptions of their institutional interests. When their ideological legitimacy deteriorates and they stop believing in the system, leaders with reformist pragmatic acceptance are not constrained by their pragmatic acceptance to the same extent as those with anti-reformist ones. Therefore, they *can* follow their institutional interests by taking the first step towards negotiations with the opposition. This gives them the possibility of shaping the transition during a relatively stable period when their bargaining position is still relatively strong. *If* they had waited until a possible mass uprising, they would have negotiated under much less favorable conditions. In order to shape the new institutions to their advantage, it was better to take the initiative to negotiate *before* the opposition had begun fully mobilizing. Even though the reformist regimes had greater opportunities than the anti-reformist ones, this does not mean they made full use of these. For example, the Polish negotiators succeeded in obtaining institutional guarantees, while the radical Hungarian reformers did not strive for such guarantees. Yet, I argue below that the Hungarian rulers behaved more strategically than their Polish comrades.

The regimes with anti-reformist pragmatic acceptance were in a more difficult situation than their neighbors. Since they based their pragmatic acceptance on the concept that the Soviet Union had put them into power to prevent reforms, any steps toward radical reform (such as negotiating with the opposition) would have brought their right to rule directly into question. This is precisely what Gorbachev's rise to power did. They could no longer claim that the Soviet Union wanted to prevent all reforms. Thus, their situation was contradictory. On the one hand, they had institutional interests in continuing to support the USSR, which had put them in power. On the other hand, they had institutional interests in rejecting reforms of the type that the USSR was now trying to implement. In such a contradictory situation, it was difficult for the leaders of the anti-reformist regimes to act. Thus, they tried to wait out Gorbachev and hope that a future Brezhnev would eventually replace him and matters could return to normal.

Put otherwise, when the leaders' institutional interests broke down, they had no mechanism for filtering information and re-orienting in the situation, so they panicked and became paralyzed as their world crumbled around them. At first they could pretend that nothing happened and that the old institutions could continue to exist in their previous form. Therefore they remained comitted to their previous policies. But when the situation went out of control, they gave up rather than seriously seek an institutional compromise, because they mistrusted the opposition and did not have any strategy for dealing with the opposition. This means, I accept Przeworski's (1991) psychological explanation that rulers are in some cases irrational in their filtering of information and responding to the threatening situation. However, I am also specifying the circumstances under which this is likely to occur.

POLAND

I begin this section with an analysis of the Polish rulers' institutional interests, especially their pragmatic acceptance. Then I turn to the subjective level and examine their perceptions of the situation. Afterwards, I look at how the regime and opposition prepared for the negotiations. Here I discuss the goals of both sides for their meetings. Finally, I consider the reasons why the Polish rulers did not behave as strategically as Przeworski expects.

Pragmatic Acceptance and Institutional Interests

Jaruzelski decided to base his pragmatic acceptance on the need to continue reforms, while preventing the Soviet Union from invading. Therefore, he gained considerable maneuvering room once Gorbachev came to power. After the new Soviet leader made it clear that he would not invade, Jaruzelski could instigate more radical reforms without contradicting his pragmatic acceptance. His military background reduced his institutional constraints even more. As a general, he could claim that he had carried out the *coup* to prevent civil war and a Soviet invasion, rather than merely to restore Orthodoxy. Throughout the 1980s he used increasingly non-Communist terms to defend his power. He could portray himself more as a politically neutral officer than as a Communist normalizer. It is no coincidence that he entitled his memoirs "My Life for Poland." He wanted Poles to see him as a nationalist and professional soldier who had maintained Polish independence by preventing a Soviet invasion, rather than as a "proletarian internationalist." Thus, although his Party lost the first elections, he could eventually withdraw from politics and go down in history as the man who brought about the first democratic transition from a Soviet-type system. O'Donnell & Schmitter (1986: 25–6) have observed that a place in history can be as gratifying a reward as continued power. Thus, softliners might be willing to risk losing power for the reward of being remembered as the one who gave their country a "more honorable future."

The Marxist-Leninist dogma of the leading role of the Communist Party was also much less of a constraining factor in Poland than in the neighboring countries. The Polish regime already had the lowest level of ideological legitimacy within the entire Soviet bloc. The *Solidarność* uprising made a mockery of the Party's claim to represent the workers. Meanwhile, the military *coup* dispelled all notions of the Party's declaration that it enjoyed a monopoly of Truth. If the military had to step in to save the Party, the Party could not always claim to be right.

This combination of a non-existent ideological legitimacy and a reformist pragmatic acceptance made it relatively easy for Jaruzelski to begin the transformation process. He was less constrained by the dogma of the "leading role," since the Party had already lost its leading role to the military. Similarly, his pragmatic acceptance did not prevent him from initiating out radical reforms.

The Subjective Level

Even though Jaruzelski had more room to maneuver than most other Soviet-type regimes, his subjective interpretation of the situation was decisive. With the loss of ideological legitimacy, the leaders started doubting their ability to rule. The economic crisis was becoming increasingly serious. Poland's foreign debts were goingg out of control and hyperinflation was a looming threat. Virtually all economists agreed it would not be possible to bring the Polish economy back into balance without measures that would lower living standards in the short run. The previous worker uprisings showed that it was dangerous to implement such policies without obtaining popular support.

Throughout the 1980s, Jaruzelski had tried to coopt the opposition through a consultative democracy. This had little effect. Opinion polls showed waning support for the regime. Former Politburo member Reykowski (1990: 11) cites a survey showing that Jaruzelski's approval rating fell from 71% to 44% between 1985 and 1989. Meanwhile, support for Wałęsa increased from 45% to 85% during the same period. Of course, there are reliability problems with such surveys. It is likely people were more honest in their answers in the more open climate of 1989 than they were in 1985. The point here, however, is that the Communist leaders seem to have *believed* these surveys. The mere fact that a former Politburo member cites them in his article shows that these polls probably influenced the elites. Jaruzelski admits that for him the turning point came when the referendum on economic reforms failed. He came to realize that he needed the support of the opposition in order to stabilize the economy.[2]

As already mentioned, the crisis had gone so far that Poland was facing a potentially revolutionary situation (see chapter 8). Some of the leaders also feared this. Former Politburo member Reykowski (interviewed 23 April 1993) says: "It became clear the longer martial law lasted, the greater the opposition would become and the greater the force that would be needed in the future."

Pressure on the regime to do something increased in 1988. In March and August, new waves of strikes began. To make matters worse for the regime, these strikes broke out independently of *Solidarność*. A younger generation of radicals had emerged which had threatened to draw support away from the more moderate *Solidarność* leaders. In contrast to Przeworski's assertion that the radical faction of the opposition poses a threat to a democratic transition, the Polish radicals became a catalyst. In the relatively open societal climate in the country, softliners had already been able to establish contacts with *Solidarność* leaders. For example, the official magazine *Konfrontace* published an interview with the KOR activist Geremek, in which he suggested guidelines for a dialogue. Thus, some of the high-standing members of the corporate entity had already developed contact networks with the opposition, which gave them opportunities to test out their ideas; it also increased the level of trust between the two groups.

As Przeworski (1991) would predict, the softliners wanted to strike a deal with the moderate opposition. They preferred dealing with the more cautious and experienced *Solidarność* leaders than with the young shopfloor militants. Jaruzelski's decision to start the negotiations was "probably strengthened by the fear that if underground Solidarity also lost its authority over society, there would be no negotiating partner for the régime at all" (Schöpflin's 1993: 213).

On the other hand, I have not found any support for Przeworski's (1991: 6) assertion that the regimes gave up because they could not

---

2. See chapter 3.

rely on the military. First, Jaruzelski himself was a general and commander of the military. His closest and most faithful associates in the regime, such as Interior Minister Kiszczak, were themselves officers. What about the officers who were not in the government? Former Politburo member Reykowski (interviewed 23 April 1993), who led the Round Table talks on political reforms, claims that the problem was not that they could not rely on the military to use force. On the contrary, they had to assure the officers continuously that they were not "betraying socialism." Gebethner, who participated in the Round Table negotiations as an advisor to the communists, adds that the military, police and secret police provided the "most important support of the old regime" (interview published in Kundigraber 1996a:II). Of course, this says little about how the majority of draftees would have behaved. Still, the military repression of the 1970 revolt shows that even if the regular soldiers refused to shoot, it is enough if special units are willing to perform the task.

Preparing for Negotiations: The Regime
There is general agreement that the softliners' main goal was to coopt the opposition. They wanted a trade-off: they would share power with the opposition in return for co-responsibility.[3] According to the political scientist Gebethner, who participated in the Round Tables on the Regime's side, the softliners at first wanted to avoid free elections. Instead, they wanted to allocate the opposition a certain number of seats on a single common list of candidates to the Sejm (1992: 53). Gebethner proposed having one-third of the seats freely contested, but the Party leadership turned him down (1992: 57). Former Politburo member Reykowski (interviewed 23 April 1993), who represented the Party in the Round Table group on political reforms, claims that the final solution of having some seats freely contested and others reserved corresponds to his original intentions. He believed this would be the first step to completely free elections. A transitional period was necessary in the meanwhile, so that pluralistic institutions could emerge—such as new political parties, strong independent newspapers and other civic organizations. He still believes this was a correct strategy.

---

3. Gebethner (1992: 59), a political scientist who participated at the Round Table talks for the Communists, admits this. See also Elster 1993: 202), Tymowski (1993: 182) and Wesołski (1990: 439),

In his eyes, the present unstable, split political system is a consequence of the regime having lost power too early. In other words, in contrast to theorists who claim that the emerging civil society brought down the regime, he maintains that the greatest hindrance to the democratic transition was the lack of a flourishing civil society!

In order for the negotiations to begin at all, the reformers had to defeat the hardliners within the regime. Jaruzelski's dilemma was that he had purged the most reformist members of the leadership to gain support for martial law. This meant the centrists and hardliners out-numbered the softliners. Therefore, Jaruzelski had to purge the hard-liners whom he had bought in during martial law and replace them with "liberals" such as Reykowski (cf. Reykowski 1990). The first step was to gain the Central Committee's approval for negotiations. At first the Central Committee refused to support the proposal. In protest, the military officers Jaruzelski, Defense Minister Siwicki, and Interior Minister Kiszczak threatened to resign, as did Prime Minister Rakowski (Janowski 1992: 166 and Przeworski 1991: 6). Although the hardliners comprised a majority, they had no potential leader or alternative policy to offer in place of the current situation, so the Central Committee gave in. Afterwards, Jaruzelski began to recruit radical reformers to the top leadership. Thus, in contrast to Bova's (1991) claim that a democratic transition is only possible if the soft-liners placate the hardliners, the democratic transformation was made possible in part because softliners *defeated* the hardliners.

Rather than placate the hardliners in the regime, the softliners tried to gain the support of the Party-state apparatus by allowing its members to take over state firms. Frydman, Rapaczynski & Earle (1993: 183) report there were two common forms of corporate-entity privatization. First, state enterprises were transformed into commer-cial companies on the basis of the Law on State Enterprises. Insiders from the Party-state apparatus could gain a large portion of the shares, because these shares were offered to them at unrealistically low prices. Second, members of the corporate entity and their families created private companies, which entered into "sweetheart deals" with state enterprises and siphoned off their resources. They were often involved in exporting goods produced at subsidized prices. They also leased equipment belonging to state enterprises at artificially low prices and exported their products. Although there is no reliable infor-mation on the extent of these types of privatization, Staniszkis (1991: 67–8) estimates that, in 1989, such companies controlled between

10–20% of the fixed capital in the state sector. Ost (1990: 201) cites reports that, in Wałęsa in mid-1987, 25% of those seeking licenses to run private enterprises were members of the corporate entity.

Despite these attempts to coopt portions of the corporate entity, some of the reformists who ran the Round Table negotiations for the regime, claim that eventually, they perceived the conservative members of their own apparatus as the main enemies, rather than the opposition (see the interviews cited in Osiatynski 1996). Zbigniew Bujak, who was one of the main *Solidarność* negotiators at the Round Table agrees: "It was obvious that in the economy there was only one obstacle to agreement, the apparatus. While talking to government experts there were no differences or illusions, everyone wanted to move toward a market economy" (quoted in Osiatynski 1996: 65 fn 27).

In addition to buying off members of the Party-state apparatus, the regime tried to coopt the moderate opposition. The idea was to create a "new center" (Staniszkis 1991: 76). The moderates in the regime would cooperate with the moderates in the opposition. They could, thus, marginalize the dogmatic Communists and the instigators of the recent strikes. In general, as Staniszkis notes, the strategy was to reach an agreement among elites and to demobilize society.

Preparing for Negotiations: The Opposition
The first question is: why would *Solidarność* want to risk entering into negotiations with the regime, when this could easily lead to its cooptation and loss of public support? Some theorists, such as Weigle & Butterfield (1992) allege that the regime really had been brought down by an emerging civil society that had become strong enough to mobilize the population against the regime. If this really were the case, the opposition leaders would perhaps have felt strong enough force their demands on the regime.

Although it might be true that *Solidarność* had recovered somewhat from its repression during the period of martial law, it was still far from enjoying the strength it had at its peak in 1981. Even after its legalization and electoral victory in 1989, it still had only 2.2 million members—about one-fifth of its total in 1981 (Ost 1990: 220). During its years as an underground organization, it had become more decentralized and less unified. Intellectuals and social scientists played an increasingly important role, which pushed the organization away from its original working-class, unionist orientation. As a result, the organization began advocating pro-market policies, including privatization.

Ost (1990: 168) concludes that its economic policy had become "remarkably similar to the program the government had begun to push, and this convergence accelerated Solidarity's crisis as a trade union."

The recent waves of strikes had taken place without *Solidarność* support and its leaders feared that they were losing influence. Holc (1992: 138) remarks:

> The independent and spontaneous strikes took solidarity by surprise. In contrast to the events of 1980, the union's "old guard" leadership headed by Wałęsa emerged almost reluctantly in 1988 to act as negotiator with the state on behalf of the workers. ... Solidarity had become cautious, decentralized, and fractious during the martial law period, and the initiation of the strikes by non-Solidarity workers reflected the changing base of worker activism. Solidarity had to move quickly to salvage its credibility as a representative of the working class against the state and its power to influence the course of events.

Thus, the *Solidarność* leaders had reason to support the softliners' attempt to build a "new center." Otherwise, they risked losing leadership and influence to the younger generation of striking workers. There were not just egoistic reasons for fearing this outcome. If radicals had taken over the opposition movement, this might have forced the softliners in the regime to side with the hardliners. A "Chinese solution" might not have been far away.

Although their fear of losing influence to the radicals gave them an extra impetus to support negotiations, the main opposition leaders had been advocating talks all along. As Geremek (1991) writes, their strategy of building up a civil society was an evolutionary one. They *wanted* to achieve a gradual, evolutionary institutional change, rather than a swift revolutionary one. A revolution might fail and end in bloodshed. Even if the strategy were to succeed, the new regime might also deteriorate into a dictatorship in the absence of a strong civil society.

Now that I have discussed the reasons why the *Solidarność* leaders desired negotiations, the next question concerns their strategy for the negotiations. Their first and most obvious goal was the legalization of *Solidarność* (see Holc 1992: 122). Janowski (1992: 164) recalls that when the Central Committee first approved the Round Table meetings, it was unwilling to recognize *Solidarność*. Instead, it divided the opposition into "constructive" and "destructive" sections. Opposition leaders originally put forward legalization as a prerequisite for holding any talks at all. Later on, they agreed to let recognition be one of the negotiating issues (Elster 1993: 188). In the long run, they also wanted political pluralism and free elections.

Kozłowski (interviewed 22 January 1995), who was a member of the Round Table constitutional committee, admits that the legalization of *Solidarność* was their main goal. He adds that they wanted some sort of "significant breakthrough." Even though they wanted a "free and independent" Poland, they did not believe this was immediately possible. Thus, they would have been satisfied for the moment with establishing the legal foundations for a system based on the due process of law.

The Negotiations
I have claimed that in the countries that reached an institutional compromise, the regimes had a reformist pragmatic acceptance which made it easier for them to initiate negotiations with the opposition. This was made easier by the fact that, in the relatively open atmosphere, members of the corporate entity had already been able to establish contacts with the opposition. This meant there was greater trust between the two sides in these countries than in the revolutionary GDR and ČSSR. Nevertheless, the trust problem was much greater for the Polish negotiations than for the Hungarian.

Many of the Communist leaders at the time of the negotiations had been responsible for breaking the previous agreements which had legalized *Solidarność* before martial law. For instance, Prime Minister Rakowski had been in charge of union negotiations in 1981. If these leaders had broken their promises once, how could the opposition be sure they would keep their promises this time? The new Politburo member in charge of the political negotiations, Reykowski, was well-aware of this problem. He tried to create an atmosphere that would give the opposition leaders confidence that the regime was taking them seriously. He took such precautions as giving the members of the Wałęsa delegation a pompous police escort to the first meeting in order to underscore their importance (interview with Reykowski 23 April 1993). In addition, the first meeting was held privately, without the press. It was very informal. Reykowski (1990: 15) describes the atmosphere as follows:

> During the meeting it was possible to develop the climate of partnership. People talked together (for 12 hours), ate together, drank together, and even

joked together. Toward the end of the meeting the atmosphere was quite free. A group picture was taken and the hosts waved good-by [sic] to the leaving Mercedes bus with [the] "Solidarity" delegation. It should be noted that the meeting resulted not only with the common decision to start the Round Table negotiations immediately, but also it had laid the ground for [the] development of a certain degree of mutual trust. [This] mutual trust is a precondition for replac[ing] a tactic of coercion with cooperation.[4]

When the negotiations started, the regime was careful to grant equal status to the opposition. All working groups were co-chaired by members of the regime and of *Solidarność*; both sides' delegations were equal in size, and so on.

These arrangements contrasted greatly with those in revolutionary Czechoslovakia. Under crisis conditions, negotiations took place directly between Prime Minister Adamec and Havel. Every word was recorded and later given out in book form. In Poland, on the other hand, the real negotiations took place on a much less formal level. To be sure, plenary meetings with ceremonial functions were held, at which both sides could make public declarations. The real negotiations took place, however, within three committees: one on political reform, one on economic reform, and one on trade unions. When problems arose that slowed down the negotiations, a small group met behind closed doors. Jaruzelski and Wałęsa chaired these meetings. Afterwards, the solutions were discussed again at the Round Table committees, in order to assure the legitimacy of the agreement and to assure the public that no secret agreements were being made (Reykowski 1990: 16-7).

The Catholic Church played an extremely important role as well in mediating between both sides and building up a conciliatory atmosphere. The Church had representatives at crisis meetings between Jaruzelski and Wałęsa, where they tried to mediate between the two, rather than to force a solution (interview with *Solidarność* representative Kozłowski (interviewed 22 January 1995). For example, when Kiszczak met with Wałęsa in August 1988 to convince him to call off the strikes, the interior minister was accompanied by Archbishop Dabrowski (Osiatynski 1996: 28). When talks broke down during that

---

4. Note: I quote from his manuscript, in which there are some grammatical errors. When necessary for clarifying the meaning, I add words or parts of words in brackets. Otherwise, I simply add the term "sic" in brackets.

autumn—partially because of the regime's refusal to include the famous dissidents Kuron and Michnik in the negotiations—Bishop Orszulik persuaded the two sides to resume their contacts at a meeting in the parish of Wilanow on November 18, 1988 (Kundigraber 1996: 74 and Osiatynski 1996: 29). Kiszczak recalls that Tadeusz Goclowski, the bishop of Gdansk, "saved" this meeting (Osiatynski 1996: 29). In addition, often when the official negotiations came to a stalemate, the leaders would have an informal meeting at Magdalena, where Church officials were always present (Osiatynski 1996: 32, Kundigraber 1996b: 113). Once when the two sides were not able to even reach an agreement in Magdalena (when negotiating about the number of seats to reserve for the regime in the Sejm), Kiszczak suggested having an even smaller informal meeting with four representatives on each side. Cardinal Orszulik also attended this meeting (Kundigraber 1996a: 78). Former General Secretary Jaruzelski also recalls that the Church played a key role in such moments (interview published in Kundigraber 1996a: XXIX).

Since the main bargaining took place out of the spotlight in the working committees, the issues were less politicized. Experts from both sides could discuss technical details in a factual, non-agitated manner. Gebethner (interviewed 1 February 1995) says the atmosphere was similar to that of a parliamentary committee. As already noted,[5] many of the experts representing both sides at the negotiations were colleagues from the same university faculties. This helped opposition and regime leaders to overcome any initial lack of trust.

Nevertheless, both sides remained under pressure from their radicals. As already mentioned, Reykowski recalls that the military was afraid the rulers were going too far in their concessions to the opposition. Gebethner (1992: 52), who also represented the regime on the political committee, adds that the Communists were afraid the government would split, and that the Sejm might revolt and refuse to pass the laws upon which both sides had agreed. Splits also arose between the Party leadership and the more conservative Communist trade union leaders (1992: 56).

Gebethner adds that meanwhile *Solidarność* was becoming more radical. It was putting pressure on its representatives, not to compromise too much. Former *Solidarność* advisor Staniszkis (1991: 200ff.)

---

5. See chapter 7.

claims that there were four factions within the union: a social democratic one, a neo-conservative one, a liberal one and a populist one. Wałęsa excluded the latter two groups from the negotiations, just because he thought they would be too radical.

It seems that Wałęsa had succeeded rather well in silencing his opponents by the time actual negotiations began. For example, Kozłowski claims that the *Solidarność* Round Table negotiators did not feel any pressure from the grass roots, although some opposition leaders refused to participate in the talks. Although Gebethner (1992) emphasizes the moderate/radical split within the opposition more strongly, he too admits that the regime entered the negotiations more split than *Solidarność*.

One of the most important splits on the regime's side was that between the Communists and the allied parties. Winczorek (interviewed 1 February 1995), who represented the Democratic Party at the negotiations, claims that the Communists still believed that the Democrats would behave as faithful allies. He adds that the allied parties had already sent signals to the Communists that the situation had changed before the negotiations with *Solidarność* began. Before the start of the negotiations, the regime held strategy meetings with the allied parties. At these meetings, the representatives of the allied parties refused to support the regime on most issues. So while *Solidarność* negotiated as a united bloc, the regime was split from within and it was also split from its allies. Winczorek feels that the behavior of the allied parties during the negotiations was important for *Solidarność's* orientation. The *Solidarność* negotiators realized that these parties presented potential allies. He also writes in an article (1992: 285) that the Round Table itself made the allied parties more independent. The talks themselves speeded up the Democratic Party's emancipation from the Communists.

Since the opposition was more unified than the regime, it proved to be a tough bargaining partner. Gebethner recalls (1992: 53) that, at the first meeting, its main demands were for the legalization of *Solidarność*, legal reform, guarantees for freedom of association, an end to the Party monopoly of the mass media, and the instituting of genuine local government. In the end *Solidarność* was able to gain completely free elections to a newly created senate as well as free elections to one-third of the seats in the Sejm. As the talks progressed, it successfully resisted suggestions to have only one national list (which would have led to their cooptation and relegated them to a minor role). *Solidarność* had not originally demanded free elections, so it wound up winning more than it had originally expected.

Not Quite Strategic

So far, the Polish developments appear to follow Przeworski (1991) and O'Donnell & Schmitter's (1986) models quite well. The regime agreed to democratization on the condition that it received guarantees (two-thirds of the seats in the Sejm were reserved for it and its allies). Moreover, to some extent it even succeeded in protecting the property rights of lower level members through corporate entity privatization. The moderates on both sides cooperated with each other and against their respective radicals. Indeed, the Polish regime behaved much more strategically than it counterparts in East Germany and Czechoslovakia, who in the end simply gave up without a fight.

Nevertheless, the Polish regime behaved much less strategically than Przeworski (1991) would have us expect. The most obvious example is the use of majoritarian rather than proportional elections for the Sejm and senate. Reykowski (interviewed 23 April 1993) admits that the Communists only expected to receive 25–30% of the votes in an open election. Under a proportional system, at least, they could have gained a respectable number of elected representatives. Furthermore, they decided to run 186 candidates for the 100 senate seats, while *Solidarność* restricted itself to one candidate per district (see Sanford 1992: 19)! Since the opposition was united around *Solidarność*, the Communists risked losing most of the contested seats.

To make matters worse, the regime insisted on a strange voting system. The voters were to delete the names of all the candidates whom they did not want, rather than to vote for those they preferred. Gebethner (1992: 64) bemoans this, claiming that he "was not alone in attempting vainly to explain that ....[this system] was quite simple a bad one: it created negative protests and aggressive attitudes." It encouraged the voters to strike out the names of candidates for the reserved seats. Therefore, it is not surprising that the Communists did not even win many of the reserved seats. Gebethner believes the leaders failed to behave strategically. They lacked political imagination and refused to consider the possibility that some of their candidates might fail to be elected. They only considered the outcome that they wanted.[6] They refused to think about other possibilities. Gobaua-

---

6. One might claim that they disregarded procedural rationality. As Stein (1985: 52) notes, procedural rationality requires listing the obvious consequences, examining their likely cost and benefit and then comparing policy alternatives.

Klass (interviewed 22 January 1995), a media expert who advised the Communists during the Round Table talks, gives a further example of this. He remembers a Communist senatorial candidate who was convinced three weeks before the election that he would win the election to the senate in his district, although it was clear to any outside observer that *Solidarność* would gain most of the votes.

Similarly, Gebethner (1992: 63) agrees that it was obvious they would not do well in majoritarian elections. When he proposed proportional elections for the senate, one Politburo member told him his proposal was based on academic knowledge, but "political instinct went beyond academic knowledge."

Why did these leaders fail to act strategically? Perhaps age was a factor. Many of the leaders, such as Jaruzelski had belonged to the elite for several decades. They could not believe that the situation was changing so radically. In contrast to the young Hungarian reformers who had joined the elite in the 1980s, these men had built up much of their career around the Party. Gebethner (1992) believes that Jaruzelski simply grew tired in the course of the long, drawn-out negotiations.[7] While a balanced and cautious assessment of the situation would have showed that proportional elections were better than majoritarian ones, the inclination to engage in wishful thinking and to rely on intuition instead of concrete analysis indicates that the Polish leaders were not thinking strategically.[8] As a result of this non-strategic behavior, the regime did not win a single contested seat. Moreover, most of its candidates did even win the seats reserved for them. More than half the voters crossed out the names of most of the Communist candidates, depriving them of the necessary 50%. Consequently, it became necessary to have a second round of voting to fill the vacant seats reserved for the regime.

HUNGARY

I begin this section by examining the institutional factors in the late 1980s which made it possible for the reformists to pursue institutional

---

7. Gebethner goes further and makes the interesting claim that Jaruzelski was tired of ruling and subconsciously *wanted* to give up. This hypothesis is interesting and worth considering, although evidence for this hypothesis is not available.
8. If Gebethner is correct, this behavior might y have reflected a subconscious desire to give up the psychologically demanding task of ruling the country in a crisis situation.

compromise. Second, I discuss the reformists' subjective perceptions of their interests during this period, as well as their strategy for taking power from the conservatives. I prefer the term "conservative" to "hardliner" in the Hungarian context, since the anti-reformist Hungarian Communists also opposed hardline Stalinist repression. Rather, they wanted to *conserve* the Kádárist-type of goulash communism. Third, I discuss the reformers' negotiating strategy. Finally, I bring in the opposition and examine the dynamics of the negotiating process. The interplay between four groups determined the final development of the negotiations and of the first elections. These four groups are the conservatives and the reformers within the regime, and the radicals and the moderates within the opposition.

Pragmatic Acceptance and Institutional Interests
As the economic crisis continued in the 1980s and the country headed toward bankruptcy, the Party completely lost its ideological legitimacy. The regime began losing confidence that it could solve the problems within the framework of the traditional Soviet-type system. Most of the elites believed that more radical market reform was necessary, but they disagreed over whether this could be done under one-party pluralism (Grósz's opinion) or if it required political democracy as well (Pozsgay, Nyers and eventually also Németh). Meanwhile, Gorbachev's rise to power deprived Kádár of part of his pragmatic acceptance. He could no longer claim the Soviet Union was preventing him from going further with reforms. Since the Hungarian Communists had based their pragmatic acceptance on testing the borders of what the Kremlin would allow, the younger Communists were willing to go even further and to democratize society. But Kádár still based his power on the repression of the 1956 uprising. His lesson from these events was that independence from the USSR and multiparty democracy is "counter-revolutionary." So it is not surprising that, as Volgyes (1989: 36) notes, Kádár insisted that they continue to be cautious, since it was not clear yet whether Soviet policy would continue to take a more radical reformist direction.

The younger reformers were no longer as bound by the portion of the regime's pragmatic acceptance that was tied to the repression of the 1956 uprising. Instead, they were more able to exploit the reformist practice of the Party's pragmatic acceptance, based on testing the limits of what the USSR would allow.[9] Since it was clear that these limits had greatly expanded, the younger generation went on the offensive. Among the most famous reformists, Pozsgay and Németh were too young to be implicated in the post-invasion repression of the late 1950s. The older Nyers' reformist credentials were also strong. He had not only introduced the New Economic Mechanism, he had also suffered a demotion from the Secretariat and Politburo in the early 1970s as punishment for being too radical. Furthermore, he had been a Social Democrat before the forced merger of the two workers' parties. Hence, he could claim he had maintained his democratic faith all along. In contrast, the hardliners were mostly older and more directly involved in the post-1956 repression. This includes Berecz, who was the most famous conservative besides Kádár. As chief ideologist, he had also written a book in the 1980s condemning the "counter-revolutionary" uprising of 1956.

Hence, a split broke out between reformers and conservatives. The first showdown came at the Party Congress in May 1988. At that time, the Party was divided into three factions: reformers (Pozsgay, Nyers), conservatives (Berecz, Ivany) and centrists (Grósz, Tatai and Németh).[10]

Grósz had supported far-reaching market reforms as prime minster, and therefore was able to gain the support of the radicals at the Party Congress. As general secretary, though, he became more conservative on political questions and fought for the concept of one-party pluralism (Schöpflin 1991: 62). While Grósz joined the conservatives, Németh joined the reformers. Thus, a clearer split developed between two groups: reformers and conservatives.[11]

By the time the negotiations began in the summer of 1989, the reformers had outmaneuvered Grósz. First, the reformers passed a Central Committee resolution in January 1989 that allowed new parties to register as legal organizations. Then, in June, they replaced

---

9. Volgyes (1989: 31) refers to "the younger (more technocratic) and the older (more ideologically-minded) members of the ruling elite."

10. See for example Volgyes (1989: 33). When he wrote this article, it had not yet become clear how radical the reformists were. Nor was it clear that Németh would become one of the most radical leaders.

11. For example, Körösényi (1992a: 5) follows most authors in dividing the regime into hardliners and reformers. See also Sitzler (1989: 685–6) who describes Grósz and Berecz as representatives of "bureaucratic, enlightened absolutism," and Pozsgay and Nyers as "democratic socialists."

the position of general secretary with a new organ—a four-person presidium. This forced Grósz to share power with three reformers, including Pozsgay and Nyers. Moreover, when Prime Minister Németh switched to the reformers' side, they gained also control over the government.

Initially, the conservatives tried to resist. For example, Berecz launched a counter-attack already in December 1988, when he thought that Ligachev would defeat Gorbachev.[12] When the Ligachev threat receded, the conservatives lost their nerve. They made some futile attempts at sabotaging the negotiations, but they were continuously on the defensive without the support of the Soviet Union. As long as the Kremlin refrained from intervening, the reformers could claim they were continuing the Party's pragmatic acceptance of testing the limits of what Moscow would allow.

Even though the reformist pragmatic acceptance made it possible for the reformists to outmaneuver the conservatives, that does not explain why they chose to negotiate an institutional compromise with the opposition. It only explains why such a choice was possible. To understand the decision to start negotiations, it is necessary to examine how the reformists interpreted their interests at the subjective level.

The Subjective Level
Five main factors influenced the thinking of the reformers.

- The economic crisis convinced the reformers that Kádárism had failed, and that systemic change was necessary in order to save the economy.
- They were also influenced by the debates among critical Hungarian social scientists.[13]
- They believed they were facing a potentially revolutionary situation. I claim in chapter 8 that, in all four countries, a situation was arising in which uprisings could easily ignite. Apparently, the Hungarian reformers reached the same conclusion.
- In the Hungarian case, Przeworski's assertion is correct: the rulers did not think they could rely on the military to put down a potential uprising.

---

12. See chapter 5.
13. See chapter 7.

• Finally, in their battle against conservatives, the reformers decided to try to gain support from the public. This was only possible if they offered something in turn.

Hungary was in a precarious situation. It was experiencing a grave economic crisis. The rulers felt the economy was collapsing. The economic reforms had failed. This further eroded their confidence in the system. According to my knowledge, all experts on Hungarian society who have written on the topic anonymously agree that the economic crisis lay at the heart of the reformers' decision to advocate negotiations with the opposition. Even the conservatives realized—except for Kádár—that the country faced an enormous economic crisis, although they believed they could initiate a transition to a market economy without giving up their power monopoly. Thus, they devised notions of one-party pluralism (see Bruszt 1990, MacDonald 1993 and Schöpflin 1991).[14]

In the open social climate, critical social scientists could publish studies indicating the extent of the crisis. Their criticism influenced the reformers and shook their confidence that reforms within the framework of the system would be sufficient to save the system.[15] In 1988 they went even further, by allowing independent organizations to establish themselves legally. Thus, state-employed social scientists could openly operate and influence the official discourse.[16] In April, FIDESZ was formed as an alternative to the official Communist youth group.[17] Later it became a political party and took part in the Round Table talks. Around this time the Alliance of Free Democrats (SZDSZ)

---

14. See chapter 3 for a discussion of regime fears that the economy was collapsing. See chapter 4 for a discussion of the inability to reform the economy.

15. See chapter 7 for a discussion of the open social climate in Hungary. An example of the co-operation between reformers and critical social scientists is the economic report *Turning Point and Reform*, which Pozsgay, as leader of the Patriotic People's Front, sanctioned in 1986. The economists were allegedly employees from the Hungarian Ministry of Finance and the Institute of Economics at the Academy of Sciences (Schöpflin 1991: 61 fn. 2). When the Central Committee rejected the report, Pozsgay had it published through the Patriotic People's Front. Thus, the above-ground discourse was critical enough to influence the reformists, without them having to dip underground for radical inspiration.

16. The Central Committee did not pass legislation allowing the establishment of independent organizations until the fall of that year, but the government had begun tolerating independent organizations earlier in the year (cf. Bozóki 1993: 277–9).

17. Humphrey (1990) puts the founding date of FIDESZ in April 1988, while Köröséni (1992b) puts it in March.

emerged from dissident circles based on an alliance of base groups called "Network" (Lengyel 1992: 38). In September, the MDF officially announced its intention to register as a political party (Humphrey 1990). Other groups also appeared, which had no aspirations to become a political party but which could directly lobby to influence Party policies[18]

Since I discussed these aspects in more detail in previous chapters, I concentrate here on the remaining three points: the reformers' fear of a possible revolution, their belief that they could not rely on the military, and their need to go outside the Party to gain popular support.

Several former Hungarian Communist functionaries whom I interviewed admitted that the leadership was afraid that, if something were not done soon, the deteriorating economic situation would lead to a revolution.[19] The opposition was becoming increasing active. If these developments had continued, it would only have been possible to stop the opposition by violently repressing it. Nyers (interviewed 8 April 1993) says the system was going through a process of collapse, and the reformers wanted a peaceful transition. The rulers no longer felt they could govern the country, nor could they maintain the one-party system. He links in the process of collapse with the economic situation. Thus, he adds that the reason why they could no longer govern was that the necessary economic measures required sacrifices from the population, which in turn required a legitimate government. They knew the population would not accept these sacrifices as long as the Communists remained in power. Pozsgay's advisor, Váss (interviewed 12 March 1993), adds that Hungarians could accept a compromise if it were tolerable; if provoked, though, they would not accept it. 1956 showed that a rebellion against the Party was possible. Even the Hungarian economist, Urbán (1991: 305), who believes that society

---

18. Peter Szirmai (interviewed 16 March 1993), Co-Chair of the National Association of Entrepreneurs, provides an ironic example of the new lobbying groups. He claims the Communist government in 1988–9 listened more to his organization than the conservative government which came to power in 1990! He adds that he had good relations with the reform Communists and even attended the Party congress in 1989 as an observer. He had especially good contact with Prime Minister Németh, whom he knew from the university. Although he cannot think of any particular issue over which he got the government to change its policy, such contacts probably influenced the thinking of the reform Communists in general.

19. For example, Tibor (interviewed 12 March 1993), the former editor of a secret newspaper for the Party-state elite, asserts that the leaders believed it would be impossible to maintain peace in society if the economy continued to decline.

was far from a revolution in 1989, admits that "in the mind of the Kádárist communist leadership the memory of the 1956 uprising was still very vivid and they were concerned about a repeat scenario of that kind."[20]

The fourth point concerns the possibility of using the military for a "Chinese solution." Váss (interviewed 12 March 1993) claims that Kádár decided in the 1960s to introduce political and social reforms together with economic reforms. Such a liberalization strategy excluded heavy military investments and a reliance on mass repression. During the 1970s and 1980s, he fought Warsaw Pact pressure to increase military spending. Kádár insisted that he needed the money to make investments that would increase living standards. Thus, Váss claims that the Party leaders did not believe the army had the capacity to put down a rebellion. He adds that they never trusted the army. That is why, after the 1956 uprising, they had formed the workers' militia. But the militia was too weak to put down an uprising too. Tibor (interviewed 12 March 1993) confirms there were not enough police for a Chinese solution. The Hungarian economists, Simai (interview published in April 1992 on the Internet) and Magas (1990: 92), agree that military spending was rather low in Hungary.

Finally, in their battle against the conservatives, the reformers felt the need to appeal outside the Party—to the public. Consequently, they promised more radical political and economic reforms. There were probably several reasons why they decided to turn to society. First, Kádár would block their proposals as long as he remained in power. They therefore tried to pressure the leadership by engaging the public. When Grósz replaced Kádár, he too tried to block reforms. In response, the reformers went on the offensive. They realized that, if they obtained the backing of social scientists and of much of the public, they could put the conservatives on the defensive. They would be able to claim they had the best arguments and the strongest social support. The conservatives were opposed to change, but they had difficulty defending the Party power monopoly. After all, hardly anyone believed any longer in the Marxist-Leninist ideology. Moreover, the conservatives could no longer claim that the Kremlin

---

20. He also adds, however, that this fear had existed during the previous three decades. Yet my interviews indicate that, as long as the regime was able to raise living standards, the leaders were not as afraid that society would reject the Kádár compromise of continued authoritarian rule in return for rising living standards and relative cultural freedom.

was preventing change. This left the conservatives with the argument that they have power because they have power.[21]

A second reason why the reformers turned to the public is that they believed a multiparty democracy was necessary in order to solve the nation's problems and they thought that they would have better prospects in free elections if they could gain some popular support.

Third, since they had a reformist pragmatic acceptance, they also had developed reformist identities. This made it easier for them to turn to the wider society than it was for the East German and Czechoslovak leaders.

I have already mentioned some of the ways in which the reformers turned to the public. For example, Pozsgay attended the founding meeting of MDF and commissioned the report of critical economists against Kádár's policies. Furthermore, Nyers requested permission from the leadership to form an alliance with members of the intelligentsia outside the Party and with members of the opposition. At first the rulers dissuaded him from following through with the plan, but Pozsgay quietly established relations with the opposition on his own (Bruszt 1989: 369). Nyers eventually got his wish and founded the New March Front (see for example Bozóki 1993). The New March Front participated in the Round Table talks as a non-governmental organization. Bruszt (1989: 374) reports that Pozsgay brought the issue of the 1956 revolution before the public. This heightened the public pressure for change. This pressure in turn reinforced the reform wing's position within the Central Committee. The reformers also fought to rehabilitate Nagy and to have a funeral for him. This funeral took place on June 16 (Bozóki 1993: 288).

The Negotiations

Why did the Hungarian reformers, in contrast to their Polish comrades, agree to democracy without guarantees contrary to Przeworski's hypothesis? Váss (interviewed 12 March 1993) claims that Pozsgay *did not want* any guarantees. Pure democracy was his first preference. Of course, Váss has an interest in making Pozsgay look democratic, since he was one of Pozsgay's main advisors. Although it is impossible

---

21. As Schöpflin (1991: 63) notes, "Party hard-liners disliked this message, but were stripped of all counterarguments by their fear of popular upheaval à la 1956 and by their lack of an intellectually viable alternative strategy."

to know whether Pozsgay's first preference really was democracy without guarantees, he and his reformist colleagues could expect to do much better in free elections than their Polish comrades. First, they were more popular than the Polish Communists. Second, they faced a much weaker opposition.

The Hungarian reformers were much more popular than the Polish rulers for several reasons. After dumping Kádár, they were no longer connected with the repression of the 1956 rebellion, while Jaruzelski was still responsible for having imposed martial law. Thus, the Hungarian reformers seemed more credible in their claim to have broken with the past. They emphasized this break by changing the Party name at the October congress and expelling the conservatives. So they could enter the first election as a social democratic party, while the Polish Party was still officially Communist. The younger generation of reformers could present themselves as heroes, who had led the revolt against the autocratic Kádár and installed democracy. If they had demanded undemocratic guarantees, they would have appeared as old-fashioned Communists, who had only reluctantly agreed to minimal democratization. Furthermore, Pozsgay was the country's most popular politician according to public-opinion polls; he therefore expected to win the presidential election.[22] Consequently, he pushed for having direct presidential elections rather than having parliament choose the president.

Thus, the Hungarian Communists were more popular than their Polish counterparts. But they also faced a much weaker opposition. In Poland, the opposition was united around *Solidarność*, an organization that had once had 10 million members. Although *Solidarność* had become much weaker during its underground years, it was still potentially strong. Furthermore, it had a popular leader in Lech Wałęsa. No competing leaders emerged from among the more radical young workers who had initiated the wild-cat strikes. Wałęsa remained the uncontested head of the Polish opposition. In contrast, the Hungarian opposition was much smaller, and it was divided into several parties.

---

22. My discussion on Pozsgay's thinking is based on my interview with his former advisor (Váss, interviewed 12 March 1993). Váss also showed me public-opinion surveys (published in Hungarian) confirming that Pozsgay had led in the polls. This is widely acknowledged. For example, Bozóki (1993: 292) writes that "Pozsgay was by far the most popular politician in the country...." Szoboszlai (1991: 203) claims FIDESZ and SZDSZ opposed direct presidential elections because they feared Pozsgay's popularity.

The new parties included the conservative MDF, the liberal SZDSZ, and the Young Democrats (FIDESZ). Meanwhile, some of the "nostalgia parties" which had existed before the Communist takeover came back to life, including the Social Democrats and the Small Holders Party. None of these parties had more than a few hundred members in 1988 or a few thousand by the time negotiations began in the summer of 1989.[23] Nor did they have any leaders as popular or well-known as Wałęsa. In fact, name recognition was a major problem for their leaders in the first few months.

Finally, the Hungarian Communists had less reason than any of their counterparts to fear reprisals if they lost the elections. There was much greater trust between the two sides in Hungary than in the other three countries, and this influenced the negotiations. While Pozsgay and his supporters had not been involved in the repression of the 1956 uprising, Jaruzelski had been responsible for imposing martial law. Jakeš had led the normalization purges of the Czechoslovak Communist Party, while Honecker's replacement Krenz had been secretary of security, and thus connected with the feared Stasi apparatus.[24] Since Hungary had such a low level of political repression, few opposition leaders had spent long periods in prison. Moreover, many of the intellectual advisors to the opposition had thrived under the regime and had published critical studies legally, in general there was less in the way of harsh feelings between the opposition leaders and the Communists. In addition, Pozsgay and his supporters had already taken up contact with opposition leaders several years before the negotiations had begun. I have already noted that Pozsgay attended the founding meeting of MDF, and that Nyers founded the New March Front (which attempted to unite reform Communists with non-Communists).

The Opposition Round Table shows the great roll that the Communist reformers played in supporting the opposition. The Opposition Round Table was formed to unite the opposition in its negotiations with the regime. As Tőkés (1996: 309) notes, five of the

---

23. According to Pekker (1989: 925), for example, the largest Party (MDF) had only 13,000 members in March 1989.

24. It is questionable that he had much influence over the Stasi, since Interior Minister Mielke held it in an iron grip and apparently reported directly to Honecker for the most part. Nevertheless, in the eyes of the populace, Krenz had certainly dirtied his hands by holding a post that officially made him the Party's eye over that organization.

eight organizations[25] participating in the Opposition Round Table had, "in one way or another, been the regime's creations"!

Since the reform Communists had close contacts with the opposition, they had less reason to fear reprisals than any other of the East European rulers. The Hungarian reform Communists were also more popular than their counterparts in Poland, and the opposition they faced was much weaker than the opposition in Poland. Consequently, Pozsgay had a much stronger incentive than Jaruzelski to support democracy without guarantees. He did not expect his party to gain an absolute majority. Yet, public opinion polls showed his party gaining around 35% of the votes (Simai 1991: 54, cf. Swain 1989: 23). Pozsgay assumed this would be enough for the reformed Communists to build a coalition government. After all, he had good relations with MDF and had been at their founding meeting. Together, both parties might be able to gain a majority. He also expected MDF to support his presidential candidacy. As president, Pozsgay would be able to appoint the prime minister and thus to pressure MDF or another opposition party to form a coalition with the reformed Communists.

Since the opposition was divided and Pozsgay was the most popular politician, the regime's optimal negotiating strategy would have been to demand direct elections to the presidency, and single-district, majoritarian parliamentary elections. That was exactly what Pozsgay did. For if only a simple majority is required to win a district, then 30–40% might be enough, as long as the opposition remains divided. In Poland, where the opposition was united, it would have been more rational to follow the opposite strategy and to demand proportional representation (after all, the Communists could not expect to gain a plurality of votes in many districts). Proportional representation would have at least guaranteed them some of the contested seats.

The opposition was rational in its demands as well. Since it knew it would do better under a proportional system, it demanded that as many seats as possible be based on proportionality. In addition, some of the opposition parties preferred to have parliament elect the president. They knew they had a better chance of winning a parliamentary majority than of winning a direct presidential election against Pozsgay. In the end they reached a compromise with the Communists, according to which around half of the seats were based on proportionality

---

25. That is six parties and two intelligentsia groups.

and half on majoritarian elections. The reform Communists got their way on the presidential issue, although FIDESZ and SZDSZ refused to sign the final agreement. They demanded, rather, a referendum on the presidential issue.[26] I look below at the dynamics of the negotiations which brought about this outcome.

The Dynamics of the Negotiations
I have claimed that the Hungarian reform Communists were more popular than their counterparts in Poland, and thus could expect to do better in free elections. In addition, the Hungarian opposition was weaker and more divided than that in Poland. An obvious conclusion might be that the Hungarians were in a stronger bargaining position than their Polish counterparts. Yet, the opposite was true. As O'Donnell & Schmitter (1986) note, reformers are stronger *vis-à-vis* the opposition when they can threaten to revert to authoritarianism. In Poland this was always a real possibility, since Jaruzelski controlled the military and so could threaten to re-impose martial law. In Hungary, by contrast, the reformers had already turned to the public for support against the conservatives. This made them more dependent on the opposition. At the same time, it forced them to fight openly against the conservatives. Therefore, they set up a four-person presidium to curb Grósz's power, and at the October congress they expelled the conservatives from the Party. Having battled the conservatives openly, the reformers could not credibly threaten to revert to authoritarian rule if the opposition did not accept their demands. Since the opposition knew that Pozsgay and his allies would be the first victims of a conservative backlash, it would be disinclined to believe such threats. As O'Donnell & Schmitter (1986: 25–6) conclude, a liberalizing regime reaches a certain point at which threats of a reversion to authoritarianism are no longer credible. Nevertheless, Bova (1991: 128–9) is clearly wrong in claiming that a democratic transition is only possible if the reformers can gain the support of the conservatives. In Hungary, after all, the reformers accomplished the democratic transition by *defeating* the conservatives.

---

26. They also demanded that the Communists dissolve their workplace organizations, and the workers' militia as well. The Communists voluntarily met these two demands before the referendum was held.

Although the reformers did not attempt to satisfy the conservatives within the Central Committee, they did try to placate the economic bureaucracy by allowing its members to take over some state enterprises—through so-called "spontaneous privatization." A 1988 law allowed state enterprises to create subsidiaries with part of their assets. These companies could then sell shares to their managers. In addition, the subsidiaries could turn themselves into joint ventures, of which outside investors could be part-owners. Normally, these investors were foreigners, but domestic investors sometimes took part as well. Although it is difficult to find information on the extent of this spontaneous privatization, an unpublished report by the Ministry of Trade and Industry alleges that 40% of state enterprises in industry, trade and construction had founded private subsidiaries, which accounted for 10% of their total assets.[27]

Another factor making the Hungarian reformers weaker than their Polish counterparts has to with divisions within the opposition. This is paradoxical, since the very split within the opposition that helped them in elections hurt them in bargaining. A split opposition, namely, can make more radical bargaining demands than a united one. The reformers believed it necessary that the population perceive the elections as legitimate. Otherwise it would not accept the belt-tightening economic measures which the new government would surely implement. If any of the opposition parties boycotted the election, the legitimacy of the elections would be in danger. Thus, the most radical group could always exert a pressure at the negotiations disproportionate to its size.

There has been a tendency for theorists to emphasize the split among the political leadership, but to neglect similar splits within the opposition. To Przeworski's credit, he emphasizes—in contrast to Bova and O'Donnell & Schmitter—the role of splits between moderates and radicals in the opposition. Appeasing radicals becomes an important problem for the moderates. He concludes that these radical groups normally make a democratic transition impossible (1991: 71ff.). However, he admits this assumption does not hold if the radical oppo-

---

27. The report is cited in Frydman, Rapaczynski & Earle (1993: 132). I rely on their book for the above account, as well as on Earle, Frydman & Rapaczynski (1993) and Voszka (1993).

sition does not oppose democracy.[28] In the Hungarian case, it was SZDSZ and the Young Democrats (FIDESZ) who played the role of the radical opposition. Yet neither group opposed democracy. They opposed, rather, certain details of the final agreement: in particular, the direct election of the president, so they refused to sign the agreement. They abided by its basic rules, but they exploited its referendum provision to demand a referendum on the method of electing the president.

Finally, I have stressed the existence of contact networks between the regime and the opposition, which facilitated a feeling of trust. Thus, the members of the corporate entity did not fear reprisals, while opposition negotiators were not particularly fearful the regime was merely trying to dupe them. As in Poland, the atmosphere in Hungary was made more cordial by the fact that negotiators from the two sides were often colleagues from the same institution. Tőkés (1996: 341) notes, some of the regime's negotiators got along so well with the opposition that they served as senior officials in the first post-Communist government.

This does not mean the two sides trusted each other completely. First, even if the reformers and the opposition both supported the same basic goal of democracy without guarantees, they still tried to outmaneuver each other in the battle over electoral rules. For example, since the Communists were aware they would do better against a divided opposition, they tried at first to negotiate with each opposition party separately. In response, the various organizations of the opposition formed the Opposition Round Table, so that they could put up a united front in the negotiations. They were successful in their efforts, in the sense that they ensured the opposition parties would all negotiate together rather than separately. Second, the conservatives tried to destroy the opposition's trust for the regime by putting obstacles in the way of negotiations. So when the Central Committee passed a resolution calling for a multiparty system, the conservatives tried to slow down the process, by demanding that a constitutional court first be established which could register all new parties (Bruszt 1990: 374). Also, the conservative Politburo member Fejti tried to prevent FIDESZ from participating in the talks, claiming that, as a youth organization, it could only participate as a part of the National Council of

---

28. I discuss his reasoning in greater detail at the beginning of this chapter.

Hungarian Youth Organizations (Bozóki 1993: 284). Finally, after Pozsgay promised that the Party would abolish its workplace cells, the Central Committee voted him down (Bozóki 1993: 298). There are other examples.[29] Yet, eventually the reformers won each battle against the conservatives, and thus were able to restore their trust with the opposition. These events made it clear to opposition leaders that the *reformers* were trustworthy (although the *Party* could not be trusted completely—at least, not until it purged the conservatives at its congress in October).

According to Pozsgay's advisor Váss (interviewed 13 March 1993), the relations between the two sides were extremely cordial, notwithstanding the conservatives' attempts at sabotage. The atmosphere changed, however, once the negotiations were broadcast on TV. At that point SZDSZ tried to increase its popularity by profiling itself as the most anti-Communist of all the parties. As Ivan and Balazs Szelény (1991: 131–2) note, after SZDSZ refused to sign the final agreement, it accused MDF of being too complacent toward the Communists. When MDF saw its popularity ratings sink, it took an increasingly aggressive stance toward the Communists. It changed its leadership and replaced the pro-Pozsgay leadership with the right-wing, anti-Communist Antall. Then, after MDF took over SZDSZ's anti-Communist strategy, it went pass the liberals by a large margin in the public-opinion surveys. Eventually MDF routed SZDSZ in the elections, so the liberals' anti-Communist strategy backfired.

The biggest losers, though, were the Communists. After their friendly relations with MDF dissipated, they were unable to find a coalition partner. They also suffered when the campaign turned into a referendum on 42 years of Communist rule, rather than a campaign on how best to deal with the current crisis. Thus, in the end, the new social democrats failed to shed their Communist image. Finally, they narrowly lost the referendum on the presidency. Ironically, they probably had the backing of a majority in society for the idea of direct presidential elections, but MDF—which had supported the idea

---

29. For example, when the opposition insisted that the Party rather than the state finance the elections, since the state was already bankrupt, the conservative Fejti sent a letter to the opposition parties claiming that the Party had acquired its assets legally, and thus could use its assets to finance the election unless gaining the approval of its membership Furthermore, although Pozsgay promised that the Party would abolish its workplace units by the end of the year, the Central Committee immediately renounced his promise (Bozóki 1993: 197–8).

also—recommended to its supporters that they boycott the referendum. Thus, the reform Communists also missed a chance to win the presidency.

After all of these unforeseeable events, the reform Communists only received a little more than 8% of the votes in the first election. Yet, while many of the decisions they made might appear sub-optimal in hindsight, they were actually—given the information available to the Communists at the time of the negotiations—extremely rational. In addition, the Communists' democratic behavior during the negotiations turns out to have been a good long-term investment, as their electoral victory in the next elections demonstrates.

CONCLUSION

In this chapter, I have discussed why the communist leaders in Poland and Hungary decided to negotiate with the opposition. Przeworski's hypothesis on the conditions for reaching an institutional compromise fails, at least in part, in the East European cases. In contrast to the predictions of his model, the Hungarian reform Communists—although behaving strategically—did not try to obtain guarantees. Their Polish comrades, furthermore, demanded guarantees, but they did not behave in the strategic manner suggested by Przeworski's rationalist approach. They ignored the advice of their own experts who showed that the Party would do much better under a system of proportional representation than under a system with majority elections. Not only did they demand majority elections to the contested seats, they even ran several competing candidates in most of the senatorial districts. Thus, the united-front *Solidarność* candidates in each of the districts could win even when the two Communists together had received a majority.

Bova's assertion that the reformers will have to placate the hardliners also fails in the East European cases. Rather than gaining the hardliners' support, the softliners *defeated* them in Poland and Hungary.

My conclusion is that the reform Communists in Poland and Hungary took the initiative to negotiate with their opposition because it was easier for them to do so than it was for their East German and Czechoslovak colleagues. All four countries had been suffering from economic problems which had eroded the ideological legitimacy of the regime, and all four countries were facing potentially revolutionary situations. However, in those countries with a reformist pragmatic acceptance, the softliners could take advantage of the opening which Gorbachev gave them. The USSR no longer demanded that the Communist parties maintain their leading roles at all costs. Consequently, the Hungarian and Polish softliners could build upon their reformist identities and take the reforms even farther by meeting opposition leaders. Since the more radical reformers had already established contacts with the opposition during the years of liberalization, the two sides were more trusting of each other in Poland and Hungary than in Czechoslovakia and East Germany.

Even though these factors made it easier to reach an institutional compromise, the outcome was not pre-determined. The Polish and Hungarian reformers, for example, faced similar situations. Yet they utilized the space which had opened up—as a result of Gorbachev's policies and their own reformist pragmatic acceptance—in differing ways. The Hungarians acted strategically in trying to shape electoral institutions to their advantage, though they did not seek any guarantees. For example, they favored majority elections over proportional representation, because—in contrast to the situation in Poland—the opposition was divided into many parties, and these leaders of these parties were relatively unknown to the public. In addition, since public-opinion polls showed they would be the largest party and might gain around 35% of the vote, they expected to be able to win many districts without gaining an absolute majority (with a divided opposition, a mere plurality would suffice to win many districts). In contrast, the Polish reformers did demand guarantees, but they did not act strategically either in their choice of electoral system (they chose majority over proportional elections) or in their manner of campaigning during those elections (they ran several candidates in many districts). Thus, while an analysis of institutional interests gives us a guide to likely behavior, we must go down to the subjective level if we are understand the different outcomes more completely. We must investigate, that is, how the various actors *perceived* their institutional interests.

Chapter 10

NON-VIOLENT REVOLUTIONS

In this chapter, I discuss the non-violent revolutions in the GDR and ČSSR. Again, each section covers a different country. I emphasize both the thinking of the regimes and the oppositional movements in each country, as well as the developments and organization of the revolutionary movements.

I devote more space to the ČSSR than to the GDR, because the East German Round Table talks were not nearly as important as Czechoslovak ones. By the time the East German negotiations began, the regime had already collapsed. Both Honecker and his replacement, Krenz, had already resigned as general secretary, the wall had already been opened for almost one month, and it was clear that Prime Minister Modrow was running a caretaker government until the spring elections. At this point, the unification question began to dominate the political debate. Consequently, international negotiations between the two Germanies and between the four powers (especially the USSR and USA) had already become at least as important as those between the regime and the opposition. Since it was a caretaker government, the Round Table became an organ for the opposition to control the government, rather than an arena where both sides negotiated over the terms of the transition. Therefore, the Round Table discussions in the GDR is only briefly covered. In contrast, the Czechoslovak negotiations have been documented in book form. They were also extremely important for the outcome, since they started at the height of the revolution, and before it had become clear the revolution would succeed.

My basic argument concerning the behavior of the regimes is that they were incapable of rational and strategic action. Instead, they were paralyzed. They had based their pragmatic acceptance on the notion that the USSR had put them into power to prevent all reforms. Gorbachev deprived them of their pragmatic acceptance by making it clear that the Kremlin would no longer prevent the East European regimes from carrying out reforms. The anti-reformist regimes in the GDR and ČSSR had no idea how to behave once their institutional interests in preventing reforms dissipated. Rather than taking steps which could have placated the populace, they stood by idly until mass movements emerged. Moreover, since they had continuously pursued a repressive hardline policy against opposition movements, they had no established the contact networks with the opposition that could have built trust between the two sides.[1] This made it even more difficult for the two sides to engage in constructive negotiations. Since the leaders had already lost their ideological legitimacy, they lost confidence in their ability to rule, when confronted with the new situation, and simply resigned rather than either negotiating seriously with the opposition or attempting a "Chinese solution."

In addition to a consideration of regime behavior, this chapter examines the conditions for revolutions. In chapter 8 it is shown that a pre-existing group of intellectual dissidents acts as a catalyst. Initially, most dissidents are intellectuals, because they have the strongest institutional interests in opposing the system. They increase their oppositional activity if they feel outraged, if their expectations of change increase, and if they find a political opening at home or abroad.

Since intellectuals only compose a small percentage of society, they need to gain the support of the workers if they are to succeed in toppling the system. Workers do not have as strong institutional interests in revolting, but they are more willing to ignore their institutional incentives when there is an economic crisis. If the regime makes decisions that directly affect workers' living standards, they might revolt on their own. Otherwise, during a period of economic stagnation, they are willing to join a protest movement provided the intellectuals have already started one and the regime has committed repressive acts that outrage them. The various Polish worker uprisings and the East German revolt in 1953 are examples of revolts sparked off directly by economic decisions. The 1989 revolutions are instances of revolts being sparked off by acts of repression during a period of economic stagnation. Since the economy stagnated, workers had become more susceptible to revolt once the intellectuals had already organized demonstrations. In both cases, feelings of outrage at state repression also influenced the workers.

In both countries, the revolts also broke out during periods in which expectations of change were rising. Ironically, expectations of change

---

1. The slight exception is the ČSSR, where the advisor to Prime Minister Adamec had met with leader of the group *MOST* (Bridge) on two occasions. But these contacts were much lesser developed than those in Poland or Hungary, and they were not great enough to overcome the trust problem.

in these countries rose more because of events in neighboring countries (especially the USSR) than because of any hopes that their domestic leaders were capable of a regeneration. When the intellectuals tried to gain worker support for revolution, the main problem was communication, rather than providing selective incentives. They had to spread the news of what was happening. They did not have any possibility of rewarding or punishing participants, but this was not necessary. Although public-choice theories about "free-rider" problems were not relevant for the political entrepreneurs, rational-choice threshold theories fare better. The number of participants continuously increased *for a while*. The threshold theory cannot explain, however, why participation decreased after reaching a peak in both countries.

Finally, I claim that the regimes might have been able to repress the revolutions Chinese style. As Opp (1993: 199) notes, some amount of repression ignites a solidarity effect. More people are willing to demonstrate if they feel outraged by the regime's policy. Johnson (1964) observes, however, that the regime can crush any uprising if it uses enough violence, as long as the opposition is not armed and prepared to use weapons. In contrast to Przeworski (1991), I maintain that the reliability of the armed forces was not their main problem. The police used force in both countries. The regime's main problem was that the leaders themselves were too paralyzed to develop a strategy for utilizing their repressive capabilities.

I examine the East German "exit revolution" below, before considering the Czechoslovak "velvet revolution."

THE GDR

According to my partial model, there is a group of intellectual dissidents who oppose the system, but they cannot succeed in overthrowing the system without the support of the workers. They are unlikely to gain worker support, however, unless the economy is stagnating or declining. I have already discussed the existence of small groups of intellectual activists in the GDR. They gathered around "alternative" issues, such as peace and the environment. Many of them worked under the protective umbrella of local parishes. I have also discussed the looming economic crisis in the GDR.[2] An economic

---

2. See chapters 3 and 8.

downturn is not enough to entice the workers to revolt. They are not likely to take action, until some state action outrages them and frustrates their rising expectations of change. By the spring of 1989, expectations were rising and intellectuals were becoming increasingly radicalized and daring in their actions. The regime did not outrage workers enough to cause a rebellion until the fall, but it did outrage the intellectuals enough to make them believe they must try to reach out beyond their small circles and gain societal support.

I discuss the stages which finally led to the revolution below. This includes the rising expectations of intellectuals and society in general, regime actions that outraged these groups, the unusual way in which the intellectuals solved the communication problem in obtaining the support of workers and professionals, and the continuous paralysis of the regime which prevented it from putting down the uprising.

Rising Expectations and Radicalized Intellectuals (Spring and Summer 1989)

By 1989, the East German population had become frustrated. Surveys show that the youth had become increasingly critical of the system (see chapters 3 and 5). Honecker insisted that the GDR did not need any reform. This killed any hopes that the leadership would embark upon reforms. Yet, Gorbachev gave the East Germans reason to believe change was possible. Suddenly, during the last few years, Soviet publications became extremely popular. The journalist Michael Simmons (1989: 122), writing in early 1989 summed up the atmosphere:

> The arrival of Gorbachev in the Kremlin and his spreading of the gospel of perestroika and glasnost (which has not been taken up with any enthusiasm at all by the East German leadership) have led to a new irreverence from the grassroots towards the elderly policy-makers. The pressing need to know more of Gorbachev's thinking is evident from the demand for the Soviet Communist party newspaper, *Pravda*, often unobtainable in East Berlin, and the demand for his book on perestroika. I saw no sign of the book at the Soviet stall at the 1988 Leipzig Book Fair, but there were long queues (of all ages) to find out how it could be obtained.

On the following page, Simmons adds that East Germans had demonstrated in front of the Soviet embassy shouting Gorbachev's name. When the regime banned the Soviet journal *Sputnik* in November 1988, over 200,000 citizens wrote letters protesting the move (Wielgohs & Schultz 1990: 16 fn. 7). These examples do not *prove* the populace had higher expectations that Gorbachev would succeed in changing East German policy, but it would not have been logical for them to behave this way if they did not pin some hopes on the new Soviet leader.

Rising expectations of political change during periods of economic stagnation are not enough to spark off a revolt. Normally, people become more involved in oppositional activity if they feel outraged. The turning point for many intellectual activists was the municipal elections in May. Several independent groups decided to monitor the elections, to make sure that the regime would count the no votes fairly (one could only vote for or against the list of candidates).[3] Despite their presence, the regime clearly falsified the results and claimed nearly 100% support. Wielgohs & Schultz (1990: 18), Meuschel (1991: 24) and Schönsee & Lederer (1991: 313) claim that a wider opposition movement began to form in response to the arrogant manner in which the officials reacted to protests against the elections.

The following month a group of dissident founded the organization *Initiative für den Demokratischen Aufbruch* ("Initiative for a Democratic Awakening" or DA) in response to the elections. In July, the Initiative for a Social Democratic Party in the GDR emerged. Both organizations established themselves officially in October. Thus, the opposition stepped up its activities even before the emigration wave began. Thus, Meuschel (1993: 108) concludes, the intellectual dissidents made the jump from social marginality during the local elections in May 1989 and the ensuing protests against the election falsifications. She adds the factor of rising expectations, since the USSR held secret elections to the Peoples' Congress at the same time, while the Polish and Hungarian regimes had started negotiations with the opposition.

Exodus and Rising Expectations among Non-Intelectuals

As Wielepp (1990: 72) observes, the worsening economic situation had become clear at all workplaces. Meanwhile, the rising living standards in the FRG, together with Honecker's refusal to contemplate reforms, increased East Germans' willingness to leave the country. A

---

3. These groups included among others, the Initiative for Peace and Human Rights, the Church from Below and the internal-Church working group "Rejection of the Practice and Principle of Marginalization" (Wielgohs & Schultz 1990: 18).

few days before the local elections on May 2, the Hungarian government decided to take down its barbed wire fence along its Austrian border. Thousands of East Germans took advantage of this political opening abroad to flee from their country. That month, the number of migrants to the FRG almost doubled from 5,887 to 10,642.[4] During June and July the number of emigrants increased only slightly. In August, the total again doubled—to 20,955. In September, the Hungarian foreign minister announced that he would allow all East German refugees to travel to the West without conferring first with the GDR. This caused a greater pilgrimage to Hungary. 57,024 East Germans emigrated in October. I assume that as word spread of the exodus, more people began thinking about this possibility. In addition, the obvious falsification of the election results, as well as Honecker's clear endorsement of the Chinese massacre, frustrated hopes that the East German regime would be capable of reform.[5]

Although the exodus was partly a result of frustrated expectations of change, it also increased the expectations among the remaining population that change was possible. In Hirschman's words (1993: 187): "Precisely because the East German regime had made the repression of exit into the touchstone of its authority, its sudden incapacity to enforce its writ in this area meant a huge loss of face that emboldened people to other kinds of transgression."

Anti-Reformist Pragmatic Acceptance Leads to Paralysis
The East German regime was not able to recover from this loss of authority. Instead, like an ostrich, it hid its head in the sand and hoped that the problem would disappear. During the hot month of August, when the emigration totals nearly doubled, the ageing Honecker went to the hospital for an operation on his intestine and gall bladder. Since he apparently no longer trusted his "crown prince" Krenz, he sent his heir on a "forced vacation." Honecker gave his more faithful economic secretary, Mittag, the task of running the Politburo

---

4. The statistics come from Harmut Wendt (1991) "Die deutsch-deutschen Wanderungen," *Deutschalnd-Archiv* 24: 390, cited in Hirschman (1993: 188).
5. Hirschman (1993: 189) notes that the endorsement of the massacre led to a loss of authority for the GDR. The populace began to claim that the DDR (the German initials for the GDR) stood for the *Der Dumme Rest* (the dumb remainder).

meetings.[6] This helped guarantee that the Politburo would not make any important decisions during this important period.

Nonetheless, Krenz could have refused to go on vacation, and the other Politburo members could have made important decisions in Honecker's absence. In fact, this would have been a perfect opportunity to carry out a *coup* against the sick leader. Such action, however, requires critical elites, who understand that change is necessary. Even the most radical Politburo member, Schabowski (1992: 224), admits that he did not begin thinking about a leadership change until after Hungary opened its borders on September 10. Finally, at a meeting in September, Schabowski said that they had to talk about some of the important problems such as the emigration situation and the economic shortages. Some other district secretaries gave him cautious support. Hager abruptly ended the debate by stating that the discussion had a fundamental nature. Therefore, they had to wait until Honecker's return before discussing these issues further (Schabowski 1990: 64–6). Schabowski admits that he felt guilty about deviating from Party unity, even though it was obvious that the Politburo should have discussed these problems during the rapidly worsening crisis, (cited in Pond 1993: 93).

If Schabowski was so cautious, one can imagine how the others felt. For example, Stasi chief Mielke complained that the Party and governmental leaders had ignored his information about the unrest in the country (Pond 1993: 9). However, he was unable to understand the depth of the problems. Thus, he thought that the economic problems were purely the fault of incompetent local officials rather than the system. Since his reports showed the economy was drastically worsening, the logical conclusion was either that there were systemic problems or at least that the problems came from the top, where the main economic policy lines were drawn. At the very least, he should have blamed the top leaders for allowing the sudden sharp increase in "incompetent" local officials.

Similarly, Economic Secretary Mittag, who had full knowledge of the collapsing economy, claimed at the Politburo meeting in September that the shortage of consumption goods was a question for the local Party representatives (Schabowski 1990: 64–5). This was a time when he

---

6. Honecker admits that he brought Krenz in the Politburo 10 years earlier, to groom him as a candidate to the general secretary post after Honecker's retirement (interviewed in Andert & Herzberg 1990: 55). Krenz (1990: 42) claims that Honecker forced him against his own will to go on vacation during this period. Schabowski (1990: 63) basically agrees. He writes that Krenz offered to postpone his vacation.

already knew that the debts were so high that the economy faced bankruptcy.

Since ample information was available about the increasing discontent in the population, the rise in oppositional activity, the mass emigration and the near bankruptcy of the economy, it is surprising that the Politburo members were so unwilling to discuss the situation and to attempt to find a solution. Economic stagnation had destroyed their ideological legitimacy, but until recently, they could still base their pragmatic acceptance on the notion that the USSR wanted them to prevent change at all costs. They were so tied to their anti-reformist pragmatic acceptence that they had no idea of how to deal with the new situation. Gorbachev no longer demanded that they continue being guardians of orthodoxy. Thus, the East German rulers no longer had merely to follow orders, but, they were not accustomed to making decisions and taking responsibility for them. Once Gorbachev's reform program removed the pillars of their institutional interests, their house of orthodoxy caved in. Lacking the Soviet-built roof to protect them from their adversaries, they waited hoping the storm would blow over.

Honecker himself provides the most obvious example of the corporate entity's inability to cope with the new situation. During the celebrations of the 40th anniversary of the GDR, Honecker made a speech in which he had only praise for the fantastic accomplishments of his country. His speech was devoid of any criticism or even hints that the country might be having problems. At a closed Politburo meeting in front of Gorbachev, he repeated this speech (Pond 1993: 106). Dresden Party Secretary Modrow writes: "This speech was so decisively removed from reality that it actually increased tensions even more" (1991: 12). Schabowski (1990: 70) comments that he felt embarrassed as he read the draft of the speech, because it was so far removed from reality. He tried to get Honecker to change it, but the general secretary did not make any changes. Modrow concludes that, at this point, "Honecker still believed that [the societal crisis] was a short episode."[7]

---

7. Even one year after the collapse, Honecker was incapable of seeing any problems. For example, when the interviewers Andert & Herzberg (1990: 58) ask about the emigration problem, Honecker protrays himself as a great humanist, who tried to make it easier for East Germans to visit the West! He does not admit, despite the mass exodus, that the populace was discontent with the situation. Instead, he notes that the "simple people" could not understand why the "intellectuals" wanted to travel. He says so, despite the fact, that, as Kühnel & Sallmon-Metzner (1991: 375) observed, the intellectuals were the main group which decided to stay in the country and protest against the system. The workers and professionals were the main groups which left the country.

Fall: Workers and Professionals Join in, the Communication Problem is Solved

As word spread of the mass exodus, tensions were high. The scars of the emigration wave had become noticeable at almost every workplace as the number of employees returning each Monday decreased. The fact that the regime could no longer cage in its people also showed its weakness.

As just noted, by October mass demonstrations had broken out. They started in Leipzig, where the Nikolai Church had been holding its Monday "Prayers for Peace" since 1982. 1,200 people attended when the prayers resumed on September 4 after the summer vacation. By October 30, the number rose to several hundred thousand.[8] Opp & Gern (1993) claim that the Karl Marx Square outside of the church became the perfect place for "spontaneous coordination" of the rallies. The Party-state repressive apparatus was too repressive for dissident groups to organize demonstrations. The police would have immediately arrested the instigators. Most residents knew of the prayers, since the prayers had being going on for such a long time. After the prayers, most participants crossed the square in the center of the city. This made it a natural meeting place. Those who did not attend the prayers knew that people would congregate at the square at a certain time. At first they could act as observers and then cautiously join in if they saw that many others were also there. The greater the number of people congregating there, the lower the risk of a particular person being beaten by the police.

Thus, the communication problem was solved partly by the spreading knowledge that tens of thousands of citizens were leaving the country each month, and partly by spontaneous coordination of demonstrations. Information about the emigration showed the citizens that the regime was becoming weaker, while information about the existence of demonstrations made it easier to "organize" them. During the demonstrations, the police forces did not have any oppositional leaders, whom they could arrest.[9]

---

8. Reich (1990: 81) puts the figure at 300,000. Opp (1993: 195) notes that estimates have ranged from 200,000–500,000. He also puts the September 5 totals somewhat higher than Reich.

9. They could not blame the Church leaders, since the prayers were perfectly legal and had been going on for the last seven years.

Although the demonstrations started spontaneously, a group of intellectuals (i.e. the Church Pastor and his associates) acted as the catalyst. In addition, polls of the participants show that intellectuals were highly overrepresented, although there were many more workers than professionals. Mühler & Wilsdorf's (1991: 40) survey from November 13 shows that intellectuals, university students and other academically trained professionals (i.e. the *intelligentsia*) comprised 38% of the participants, while workers and apprentices comprised 28% and salaried white collar workers (i.e. non-academically trained professionals) amounted to 17% of the demonstrators. Even though more extensive survey data is necessary for making any firm conclusions, this little data that is available basically confirms my assertion that workers are more likely than professionals to join a revolt. However, it is difficult to know if the workers really were more involved than professionals in the early stages of the uprising, since the survey was taken after the revolution had already succeeded in disposing of Honecker and the Wall. Nevertheless, the fact that professionals comprised such a small portion of the demonstrators even at this later stage indicates that they were less willing to revolt than workers.

Although workers did not openly act as a "class for themselves" and demonstrate as a group on the streets as in Poland previously or in the ČSSR a few months later, many did engage in other forms of protest action as a group. For example, in late September, union members from the enterprise VEB Bergmann-Borsig-Berlin wrote a letter to the head of the central union, Tisch, complaining about the economic conditions and lack of personal freedoms (*Taz* 29 September 1989, reprinted in Süß 1990: 16).

Even though the biggest demonstrations in September and early October took place in Leipzig, most of the open organizing occurred in the capital. During the summer, DA was established and the Social Democratic Party was reconstructed. In September, intellectual activists in the alternative movement formed *Neues Forum* (NF or "New Forum"). It quickly emerged as the main opposition group. By November, its membership had reached 200,000, compared to at most 15,000 for its main competitors (Wielgohs & Schultz 1990: 19). Even though it did not organize the first demonstrations, it became the mouthpiece of the opposition. It articulated society's demands in its confrontations with the ruling SED. After the first few weeks it also began openly organizing demonstrations. So again pre-existing intellectual activists took on a catalyst role.

Repression Causes Outrage, Gorbachev Increases Expectations
As Opp & Gern (1993: 676) remark, the Party-state was repressive enough to prevent political activists from openly organizing demonstrations during the first weeks in Berlin as well as in Leipzig. Again, the communication problem was solved by spontaneous coordination. When Gorbachev came to Berlin for the celebration of the country's 40th anniversary, citizens expected crowds to gather around the center where Gorbachev would be.

Opp & Gern leave out, however, one further aspect, namely the connection between Gorbachev and rising expectations. During an official rally to commemorate the anniversary on October 8, crowds embarrassed Honecker by shouting "Gorby! Gorby!" (*Der Spiegel* 17/1990: 90). This indicates that their hopes in the Soviet leader were greater than their hopes in their own leaders.

Gorbachev's visit turned out to be the turning point of the revolution. Protesters took to the streets in Leipzig, Dresden, Plauen, Karl-Marx-Stadt, Magdeburg, Potsdam, Suhl, Erfurt, Halle, and Arnstadt, as well as in Berlin. The police brutally attacked the demonstrators in all of these cities (*Der Spiegel* 17/1990: 92). In Berlin alone, hundreds of people were arrested and beaten. Word of the violence spread quickly through the Western media.[10]

Apparently, even the SED leaders relied on the Western media for their information. Krenz, who was the Central Committee Secretary for Security, (1990: 95) admits that he found out about the October 8 police action from the Western media and from letters he received from artists and relatives of injured demonstrators. The police action outraged the populace and caused a solidarity effect. Thus, the number of demonstrators rose dramatically during the next days. In Leipzig alone, 70,000 people demonstrated the following day. Pond (1993: 113) notes that this was seven times the previous Monday's total.

---

10. A survey of the country's youth from 1988 showed that 57% of the apprentices and 55% of the young workers watched West German TV daily, while almost 80% watched it several times a week. Furthermore, only 4% felt that the East German news reports corresponded to their own experience (Friedrich 1990: 31–2). This indicates that East Germans not only received much of their information from West German TV, but also that they relied on it more for news than their own news reports. Lemke cites a study from 1988 of East Germans who had emigrated to the FRG province Hesse. 82% of the interviewed claimed to have watched West German TV every day. See Kurt Hesse, *Westmedien in der DDR*, (Köln), cited in Lemke (1991: 189–90).

Pond (1993: 115) gives an example of how even people with some sympathy for the regime were outraged into action. She cites an interview with Gudrun Rischer on her participation in the October 9 demonstration:

> I was indignant, because I had never thought that a workers' and peasants' state would go after workers the way it happened on October 7 and 8. The high alert status of the police made such a strong impact on me that I was afraid, afraid for the future of my child, afraid for my husband.[11]

The October 9 demonstration in Leipzig was not only historic for its size, it will also go down in history for its lack of violence. Even though newspapers and SED functionaries threatened that blood might flow, the size of the Monday Leipzig demonstrations grew from thousands to 70,000. Furthermore, the police refrained from attacking for the first time (see Wielepp 1990: 75). According to legend, Egon Krenz personally intervened to prevent a Chinese solution. The evidence indicates something more heroic—but taking place at the bottom rather than at top levels. Kurt Masur, director of the Gewandhaus Orchestra, had become involved in the social movement because he was ashamed of the police harassment against demonstrators. He met together with Pastor Zimmermann and the cabaret performer Bernd-Lutz Lange to issue an appeal against violence. They met three second-rank Party secretaries, who without any authorization from above agreed to make it a joint appeal. The appeal was broadcast on radio and TV that day. Meanwhile, that afternoon, "Leipzig party secretary, Helmut Hackenburg, telephoned Krenz in Berlin to try to get firm instructions—but Krenz would not commit himself either to a crackdown or to disengagement."[12]

Once the Party-state refrained from using violence, the populace lost its fear of demonstrating. From that day the number of demonstrators swelled, until on November 4, a group of artists organized a demonstration in Berlin with over half a million participants (Reißig 1991:

---

11. I assume she must have had some sympathy with the regime. For nobody who considered the regime to be a semi-totalitarian dictatorship is likely to claim that the regime was in any way a "workers' and peasants' state."

12. Pond (1993: 117). Pond's version is supported by *Der Spiegel* (17/1990: 93), which states that Krenz was too busy preparing the *coup* against Honecker to get involved in the Leipzig events. He did not call the Leipzig leadership until 7: 20 P.M.—several hours after the demonstration had already ended.

28). The regime had used the worse possible combination of repression and restraint. It used enough violence to enrage the populace and induce citizens to rebel. Yet, it was not willing to use enough violence to scare the populace into giving up.

This example also shows some of the limits of purely rationalist approaches. For although participation did increase after costs went down, the first major increase came about when the costs went up— that is, after the police attacks on October 8 had enraged the populace and induced a solidarity effect. In addition, although the threshold approach might give a clue to the rapidly rising number of participants in the rebellion, as Opp (1993: 210) notes, it cannot explain why the number of demonstrators suddenly decreased after reaching its peak in early November. An obvious rationalist response would be that, after the wall was opened, they had less reason to demonstrate. But they could just as well have become even more encouraged and willing to demonstrate, since they could see the results of their efforts more clearly. Moreover, until the regime agreed to free elections, they still had good reason to continue demonstrating.[13]

The Regime Is Too Paralyzed to Use Force
Unless the opposition is well armed, the regime can ultimately crush any uprising if it is willing to use sufficient force. However, leaders must be willing to lead if they want to undertake a Chinese solution. The guardians of orthodoxy were too paralyzed to take such measures. When the police mobilized to use mass force in Leipzig on October 9, nobody wanted to take responsibility for a massacre or for preventing one. The local officials had to make decisions in a power vacuum. This is equally true of other cities. Pond (1993: 305 fn.26) interviews the Dresden police officer Horst Zimmermann, who was struck by the total muteness at all levels of command beginning in mid-1989. Since the police actually did use violence throughout the country during previous demonstrations including those in Leipzig, there is little support for Przeworski's (1991) thesis that the rulers

---

13. Information from my interviews in Czechoslovakia leads me to conclude that for most people the utility of participating in a non-violent revolution increases during a short time span, but then decreases after reaching a certain peak. The majority of the population appears to have thought it was fun to demonstrate for a few weeks because they could finally say what they really felt and they enjoyed the carnival-like atmosphere. Most people grew tired of demonstration after a while, except for the student leaders who enjoyed being the center of attraction.

could not rely on its armed forces. Rather, these events indicate that the rulers themselves were too paralyzed to give the necessary orders. The leaders had spent so many years building up their anti-reformist identities that when their pragmatic acceptance collapsed, they simply could not comprehend, and act in the new world around them.

Former Politburo member Schabowski (1992: 180) gives a prime example of their totalitarian mind-set, which prevented them from understanding that they lost all popular support. He recalls that after the crowds shouted Gorbachev's name during the anniversary celebrations, Economic Secretary Mittag mumbled to him, "That was a scandal. We should have organized this differently." Mittag refused to understand that they were in the midst of a revolution, and that they needed more than a few organizational tricks to regain control.

The Fall of the Wall: Continued Paralysis
On October 18, Krenz and Schabowski succeeded in gaining Politburo support for dumping Honecker. The vote was unanimous. Even Honecker's closest allies Mittag and Mielke let him fall. Although the *puchtists* had informed the Kremlin of their plans, Moscow remained passive and simply wished them good luck. Honecker's crown prince Krenz became the new king. But he was a king who could not find any new clothes. He took over during a period in which he was under a great deal of pressure and had to make quick decisions. In October and November, record numbers of people left the country, and record number of people also joined demonstrations. As Hirschman (1993) remarks, "exit" strengthened "voice." The more citizens that left the country, the weaker the regime became and the more citizens dared to voice their discontent in the streets. Krenz, Schabowski and company were simply incapable of shedding their anti-reformist identities and suddenly developing alternative policies. Krenz (1990: 147) sums it up: "We not only acted too late, we also pondered the situation too late. We were quite simply unprepared." Schabowski (1990: 110) agrees with Krenz that the leadership did not have any concept for dealing with the crisis.

Their behavior was marked more by procrastination than by action. In a revolutionary situation, timing becomes a crucial question. It is important to be a step ahead of the populace, rather than a step behind. A radical act that can appease the populace one week seems bleak and defensive if done one week later. As Elster (1990) notes, "Krenz's move—opening the borders to West Berlin, in order to stop the hemorrhage of the country's population—would have been a stroke of genius if made three months earlier." With hindsight, Schabowski (1990: 110) agrees. He concludes that after the Central Committee had elected Krenz, they should immediately have made it clear that they supported real change. They could have proclaimed freedom of association and allowed the media to operate freely. They could have declared their intention to allow free elections and the like. Schabowski also realizes today that they should have initiated the first Round Table meeting on October 18—the day of Krenz' election. By the time they considered that idea, the system had already collapsed (1990: 19).

Instead of working out a strategy, they waited. They thought they had several months to work out a plan (Schabowski 1990: 110ff.). They were so cautious that they elected Krenz both general secretary and head of state. At the time they believed it would add to stability and thus make reforms easier. They did not realize they were sending a signal that nothing would change except the faces. Schabowski concludes (1990: 109), in his first speech on TV, that Krenz should have put forth a vision, even if it had only been a few sentences. He only needed one statement about what they basically wanted to change in the GDR.

> Such a speech would have eliminated the suspicion that we could behave as at Tiananman Square. ...After this TV speech, the mistrust against Krenz crystallized. It would have been better, if he had simply stood before the people without any manuscript and then spoken and answered questions. One needs that much civil courage in such a situation. But at the time the atmosphere was: now we've done it, the door is open, now we must get on.

Since they were unable to recognize the seriousness of the situation, they remained on the defensive and gave in to public pressure, rather than working out an offensive strategy that could have placated the populace. Thus, Schabowski (1990: 127) remarks, Krenz had a tendency to make "the smallest possible number of sacrifices." However, in November a record 133,429 persons emigrated to the FRG (Hirschman 1993: 188). Meanwhile, hundreds of thousands of citizens demonstrated in Berlin and Leipzig. As the pressure increased, less time was available for making decisions. Modrow (1991: 24) recalls that Krenz had originally believed they could work out a law on traveling that would be ready by Christmas.

As Schabowski (1990: 135) admits, the populace was not at all happy with the first proposals, which were bureaucratic and complicated. It would have only allowed 30 days of travel per year, and citizens would need to apply for permission. Not only did the opposition threaten with strikes, the SED leadership also faced threats from the ČSSR, that it would close its borders to prevent further refugees from invading. Modrow (1991: 24–5) claims it was the Czechoslovak threat more than anything else that forced them to rethink the travel restrictions! As is well known, the Politburo approved Krenz' new proposal to allow completely free travel. Schabowski read the decision at a press conference. When a reporter asked him when the law was to take effect, he replied: "now." That evening there was a rush to the West Berlin border. Although not everyone realized it at the time, the spontaneous festival near the Brandenburg Tor marked the end of East Germany's existence. Not even the USSR was informed of this historic decision until the day after (see chapter 6).

Even after opening the Wall, Krenz continued to move far too slowly even for Party members. Pond (1991: 7) reports on the events the following day:

> Four full or candidate members of his new Politburo had to give up their posts immediately because they were voted down in an unprecedented revolt by their local party organizations. Some 150,000 Communist party members again gathered outside the Central Committee building to protest the SED's slow evolution and to demand a full party congress in December with powers to dismiss the old Central Committee.

After a few more weeks of procrastination, Krenz and Schabowski resigned from the Politburo. The new prime minister Modrow announced his intention to have Round Table talks. As Pond (1993: 6) notes, power had already shifted by then from the Party to the prime minister. The Round Table eventually became the policy-making body for the care-taker government until the March elections. Ironically, although the East German revolution helped spark off the Czechoslovak revolution one month later, the incapacitated East German regime did not begin talks with the opposition until several weeks *after* the Czechoslovak regime did.

THE ČSSR

After the fall of the wall, the situation in the ČSSR became more tense. After more than a decade of declining economic performance, the rise of Gorbachev and the democratization of neighboring Hungary, Poland and GDR encouraged the increasingly radical dissidents and other intellectuals. Students became more active and tried to establish an independent student organization. Also workers and professionals could be expected to increase their hopes that reforms would be introduced. Since the rulers claimed to be Marxists, it would not have been strange for them to see a possible connection between declining living standards and a potential willingness on the part of workers to revolt. How did they prepare for this emerging revolutoinary situation?

First, I analyze the behavior of the various factions of the regime, before moving on to the actual revolution. After showing that my partial model for revolutions holds for the Czechoslovak case, I go on to discuss the dynamics of the negotations between the regime and the opposition.

Regime Thinking before November 1989: Anti-Reformist Pragmatic Acceptance Still Guides the Hardline Regime

The Czechoslovak regime's pragmatic acceptance became weaker in the late 1980s, because of Gorbachev's reform policy. Since the regime after 1968 based itself more directly on Soviet intervention than did its East German neighbor, it had more difficulty pursuing Honecker's nationalist line. Instead, it decided publicly to advocate reform, while privately delaying the implementation of any radically new policies. Paradoxically, while the Jakeš team publicly proclaimed the necessity of reform, the regime had become even more conservative internally than the Husák one. After the elimination of the Štrougal faction, the regime was more unified in its conservative sympathies than before 1988. The leaders generally followed a hardline policy toward the opposition, as discussed below. In addition, they often filtered out uncomfortable information especially after the summer of 1989.

An example of the regime's hard line and its tendency to filter out information, can be seen in its attitude toward the 20th anniversary of the invasion on August 21, 1988. Around 10,000 people took part in the first demonstration. Another 5,000 participated in the second. The police broke up the demonstrations violently, using tear gas, water cannons and trained dogs. The 70th anniversary of the founding of the Czechoslovak Republic was marked by similar patterns. On the one hand, the regime was obviously not serious about bringing about any *glasnost*. It chose to continue its confrontationalist attitude toward the opposition. On the other hand, the fact that so many people dared to demonstrate against the regime *despite* the police's harsh methods indicates that the populace was losing patience. To put it into perspective, recall that, in 1987, *Solidarność* was not able to muster more than 10,000 protesters on May Day. The Czechoslovak opposition could muster as many protesters, even though Prague has less inhabitants than Warsaw and Charter 77 had never been nearly as large or well-known as *Solidarność*.[14]

Yet, the regime showed no special concern about these events. It decided to make one exception and to allow an independent demonstration in December celebrating the UN's human rights' day. The rulers gave some impression that they had begun to rethink their strategy by allowing this demonstration. However, they reverted to their hardline strategy the following month. Hence they forbad demonstrations in memory of the student Jan Palach who had burnt himself to death 20 years earlier to protest the invasion. The police arrested Havel and 90 others.[15]

My interviews with former Politburo members show how conservative the leadership was even in its decision to allow the human rights demonstration in December. Former Politburo member and Prague Party Secretary Štěpán (interviewed on 3 June 1992) says it was his idea to allow the demonstration. He claims that the new Party leadership wanted to see how the opposition would react to an opening. Since the opposition comprised more than Charterists, this would give the groups a chance to unite, so that a dialogue could eventually start *within the framework of the constitution.* He never revealed explicitly what he meant by the "framework of the constitution," but one can presume that he meant that the Party had to maintain its leading role and its control over the means of production and coersion. This implies that at most, he was willing to contemplate some sort of consultative authoritarianism, similar to Jaruzelski's failed attempts in the mid-1980s in Poland. Unfortunately for Štěpán, the opposition was not ready to settle for such a minimalist solution. Štěpán believes, instead, its aim was not to have a dialogue, but to change the system. Since demonstrators did not demand a return to capitalism, one must assume that Štěpán was worried about demands for political democracy and respect for human rights rather than a return to capitalism.

---

14. See chapter 1 for more details and a list of sources.
15. See the newspaper reports in *DN, FT, IHT, SvD,* and *UNT,* 16 Jan. 1989.

This shows he was not willing to contemplate any type of serious democratization even within a "socialist framework."

Jakeš (interviewed 9 April 1992), makes similar claims. The leadership allowed the demonstration in order to see how the opposition would behave. In Jakeš' opinion, the opposition failed the test, because it wanted to overthrow the regime rather than reach an accommodation. In contrast to Štěpán, however, Jakeš admits the leaders never wanted a dialogue with the opposition. They preferred toleration to dialogue. Jakeš and Štěpán's interpretations of the events show that they still were incapable of thinking in other terms than their ideological legitimacy, with the Party's leading role in the center. Yet, it does not show they were irrational in filtering information. However, Jakeš' attitude toward the next confrontation—the Jan Palach week—does provide a prime example. He made the incredible assertion that they forbade the demonstration *because the public had complained about the previous demonstration!* So two-and-a-half years after millions of Czechs and Slovaks had taken to the streets to protest against the regime, and nearly two years after the Czechoslovak Communist Party had received just 13% of the votes in free elections, the former general secretary still could express the belief that the Communist Party represented society's interests.

This example shows Jakeš' lack of imagination in adjusting his perspective and in filtering information. Since his pragmatic acceptance was based on preventing reforms and supporting the repression of the Prague Spring, he could not comprehend the changing situation. He was still thinking in terms of "support the Soviet Union" *and* "prevent radical reforms." Moreover, even if he no longer believed completely in the Marxist-Leninist ideology—he, was willing, for example, to accept more marketization of the economy—he was incapable of imagining a system in which the Party no longer had its leading role.

After the Jan Palach week, there were further signs that conditions were worsening for the guardians of orthodoxy. Havel's arrest sparked off a petition campaign for his release. Within weeks around 700 culturally important persons had signed a petition demanding his release (*SvD*, 31 Jan. 1989). According to one dissident, these people were so highly placed, that punishing the petitioners would have meant stopping television broadcasts, closing most of the theaters and interrupting 90% of the film production. After Havel received a nine-month prison sentence (*UNT*, 18 May 1989), the number of signatures on the petition grew to 2,500 (*FT*, 17 March 1989). In May, Havel was suddenly freed for "good behavior" (*UNT*, 18 May 1989). During the summer, another petition circulated which demanded more openness and democratization. According to OF, 40,000 citizens signed it during the summer (unpublished document "Občanské fórum a volby 1990"). In general, society was becoming more active in its opposition to the regime. The state Office for Press and Information reported that, before 1987, there were only 5 dissident groups in the ČSSR. By 1988 the number had increased to 23, and by August 1989 there were 39 groups.

In addition, the regime's own secret public opinion polls showed the Party loosing support. For example, one survey revealed that the number of workers approving of the way the Party was implementing its leading role fell from 57% in 1986 to 26% in June 1989. For other employees (i.e. mostly white-collar professionals) the number fell from 62% to 35% Baburková 1989: 30).[16] So if the leaders had read their own secret reports, they should have understood that the situation was becoming more critical.

To make matters worse, a non-Communist government had come to power in Poland in the summer of 1989 and the Hungarian Communists had reached an agreement with the opposition over the holding of free elections. My interviews indicate that the majority of the Politburo still thought everything could basically continue as before. Prime Minister Adamec's advisor, Krejčí explains:

> the members of the Politburo didn't understand the situation. Nor did they understand modern forms of political analysis and communication, because previously this hadn't been needed in order to maintain power. They thought that Czechoslovakia was different than other Soviet-bloc countries and that they would win. They didn't understand that something new had arisen. Gorbachev was their only problem, because his policies resembled Dubček.[17]

---

16. n = 1,850 for 1986 and 2,041 for 1989. Other polls pointed in the same direction. Over a longer period a survey of the Slovak population, which generally was less critical of the system than the Czechs, the percentage of the population who saw the economic development as "predominantly positive" decreased from 76% in 1975 to only 17% in 1989, while the attitudes towards the political development were not much better: a decline from 79% seeing the development as positive in 1975 to 28% in 1989 (Baburková 1989: 14). Another survey taken in 1988 showed that 59% of the population believed that reconstruction of the economy was "very necessary" and 30% believed it was "necessary;" while 55% also felt that democratization of public life was "very necessary" and 34% that it was "necessary" (Mišovič 1988: 38, n = 3,364).

17. I interviewed him on 13 April 1992. Since I did not record the interview, not everything is an exact quote, but I have not changed the contents.

He adds, though, that they were "shocked and paralyzed" by the events in the GDR. After Honecker's fall, the Czechoslovak Party leadership became more an observer than a participant. From this time on, Adamec went on the offensive and became the most active member of the Politburo. For example, he began to propose economic and political reforms. When the mass demonstrations broke out, he was the only Politburo member who was prepared to start negotiations with the opposition.

Plevza (interviewed 6 March 1993), who was President Husák's official bibliographer, gives a similar account of Husák's mind-set. At first, Husák thought that the negotiations in Poland and Hungary were within the "socialist framework." Furthermore, he was convinced that the Communists would win the elections in Poland and Hungary, so that he had little to worry about. Moreover, he did not feel that such actions were necessary in the ČSSR. He was certain that the USSR wanted the ČSSR to remain "socialist." Therefore, he was not afraid even after the Polish elections. In contrast, the influx of East German refugees to the West German embassy in the fall of 1989 scared him. Yet, even after the collapse of the East German regime, he believed that Czechoslovakia could retain its system. Husák told Plevza that Moscow has always had an influence over Czechoslovakia and will continue to do so.

Štěpán (interviewed 3 June 1992) adds that the Politburo members opposed the actions of their Polish and Hungarian comrades. They felt that this approach was dangerous, and they were afraid. The Communist Parties in these countries had offered the opposition everything without discussing the future. This made the Czechoslovak leadership more conservative.

In contrast to Štěpán, Jakeš (interviewed 9 April 1992) admits he was against a dialogue with the opposition. In a published interview (*Reportér* no. 17, 1991), though, he claims that the regime tried to resume a dialogue with representatives of the reform Communist group *Obroda* ("rebirth") and with Dubček. This development, though, did not succeed. He never says why they could not start a dialogue. Krejčí (1991: 15) points out that the leaders were so concerned about their former Party comrades that a paper which the secret police presented to the Politburo meeting on November 17 [!] considered *Obroda*—and not Charter 77—their main adversary.

The unwillingness to dialogue by itself does not prove that the leaders were paralyzed or not rational in their filtering of information. After the fall of the Honecker regime, it would have been perfectly rational to conclude that they could only keep power by maintaining a hard line. This would have required a plan, though, and willingness to resort to mass repression in the face of a future uprising. Krejčí's description of a paralyzed Politburo is accurate. Plevza's and Krejčí's accounts do indicate that the rulers were incapable of comprehending the radically changed situation.

Adamec Before November 1989: Cautious Reformism
Adamec is another story. His former chief advisor, Oskar Krejčí (interviewed 13 April 1992) claims that Adamec was the only one who advocated serious negotiations with the opposition. His advisor Krejčí has a vested interest, however, in making him appear reformist. Hence, it is hard to know if Adamec seriously considered negotiations before the actual revolution broke out. For example, he had announced in Vienna one month earlier that Havel was a "political zero" (Draper 1993: 16).[18]

Nevertheless, the prime minister was clearly the most reform-minded Politburo member. His behavior deserves closer attention, since he eventually led the negotiations with the opposition during the revolution. In addition, I look more closely below at the other organ which provided an opening for the opposition—the SSM.

Krejčí claims Adamec had suggested negotiations with the opposition as early as January 1989 (interview on 13 April). He did not gain any support for his proposal, however, so he let the issue drop. Nevertheless, when the journalist Michal Horáček and the musician Michal Kocáb formed the organization MOST ("bridge"), to try to start a dialogue between Adamec and Charter 77, Krejčí agreed to meet them several times before the revolution broke out.[19] Although no concrete steps were taken, they had at least established contacts which made it easier to bring about negotiations between Adamec and Havel,

---

18. Pavel (interviewed 29 April 1993) claims Adamec had to say so to placate the conservative Politburo. Of course, Pavel is hardly a unbiased observer. Furthermore, although Krejčí claims that SSM leader Mohorita was the only high-level official to support negotiations, Mohorita himself (interviewed 4 March 1992) denies Adamec's radical credentials. He alleges that Adamec came from the same generation as the rest of the normalizers (he had entered the Central Committee already in 1965) and thus, was tied to the old regime. According to Mohorita, Adamec only supported moderate changes and without understanding the deepth of the crisis. In addition, as mentioned earlier, Adamec's economic advisor Neveřil insists that Adamec only grudgingly accepted the need for economic reforms.

19. I am basing my account on interviews with Horáček (1 June 1992), Kocáb (4 July 1993) and Krejčí (13 April 1992 and 7 June 1993) as well as on their accounts from their memoirs: Horáček's *Jak Pukaly ledy* (1990) and Krejčí's *Proč to prasklo, aneb hovory o demokracii a "sametové revoluci"* (1991).

once the revolution began. For in MOST Adamec and Krejčí found people whom they could trust more than the villainized Charterists.

Meanwhile, Adamec was also allegedly working on economic and political reforms. Matejka (interviewed 5 June 1992) says that Adamec asked three groups of economists to prepare suggestions for reforms during the summer of 1989. The results of their work were kept secret. The StB (secret police) labeled the reports "anti-socialist" and tried to stop the group. So Adamec took no action on the reports.

On the political front, Krejčí (interviewed 13 April 1992) claims that, in August 1989, Adamec asked him to prepare a proposal for changes to the constitution. In addition, he was to prepare materials condemning the invasion.[20] Krejčí says Adamec wanted togive up the leading role of the Party, but does not specify exactly what Adamec wanted instead. It is questionable whether Adamec ever gave such radical directions to Krejčí. For example, even after the revolution had already broken out on November 19, Adamec told MOST initiators Horáček and Kocáb: "Look, I've been in politics for 40 years, I'm a Communist. I've already told you that the Party will never forsake its leading role in society, the Party will never surrender. Perhaps it will need to restructure itself..." (Horáček 1990: 37).[21]

The SSM: An Opening for the Opposition

Since the SSM was a youth organization, it's leaders were by definition too young to be associated with the repression of the Prague Spring. Thus, they were less bound by the regime's anti-reformist pragmatic acceptance. Their leader, Vlasil Mohorita, advocated some kind of Czechoslovakian *perestroika* and *glasnost*. This does not mean he advocated democratization.[22] Nevertheless, Mohorita's *glasnost* created

---

20. Since Krejčí refused to give me a copy of his proposals, so it is not possible for me to judge their content.

21. Krejčí (interviewed 7 June 1993) claims that Adamec knew change had to come, and that his statement was only a political ploy. However, Horáček (interviewed 1 June 1992) casts doubt on Krejčí's democratic ideals. He recalls that, before meeting the advisor, he decided to listen to him speak at a summer camp for young Communists. Krejčí strongly defended the leading role of the Party. Since it was a meeting of young Communists, he expected a positive response, but even the Communist youth turned out to be anti-Communist. Horáček concludes that although Krejčí was a "staunch Communist, who wanted to keep the Party monopoly," he was one of the first to realize that the empire was falling.

22. For example, Karel Švec, a former SSM activist and later diplomat, recalls a conversation which he had with Mohorita in the winter of 1989. Since they were in Africa far away from the ČSSR, Mohorita could be more open over a few drinks. He was very critical over the situation and admitted that changes were necessary. Yet he never spoke of pluralism or democracy.

a political opening, by giving more autonomy to the local SSM organizations. Students did not hesitate to take advantage of this. At several faculties of the Charles University, independent students published newspapers under the auspices of the SSM as early as 1987.[23] One example is the paper *Situace* at the Philosophical Faculty. Since the faculty SSM agreed to print the newspaper, the authorities did not prevent its distribution. To gain SSM support, the students allowed SSM to appoint one of the members of the publishing committee and to exercise some influence on the content of the newspaper. The SSM had to consult with the faculty Party organization on the content. If the students had not accepted these terms, the authorities would have forbidden the paper. The dean and the Party authorities made some attempts to prevent the paper from being distributed, but the students won.

SSM's behavior was very inconsistent, however. While the organization supported independent initiatives at some faculties, students at other faculties claim that the SSM opposed them. For instance, Michael Semín and Ondřej Štindl (interviewed 2 March 1993 and 14 May 1992) claim the organization took a hard line at the pedagogical faculty.

Mohorita and his assistant Lubomír Ledl (interviewed 4 March 1992) both claim that the SSM took initiatives at the top level to support independent groups. For example, it jointly sponsored a musical event in 1987 with the John Lennon Fan Club. The previous year, the club had had a confrontation with the police, but this time with SSM support, there were no disturbances. In June 1989 they co-sponsored a weekend ecological meeting which included international and independent groups such as Green Peace. The SSM leadership also met with some independent peace groups and presented some of their proposals to the ministry of defense and the Party leadership. In an article, Mohorita (1991) claims that the SSM's newspaper *Mladá fronta* invited MOST to publish articles. However, as late as November 20—three days after the revolution had broken out—Mohorita was only willing to publish a censored version of MOST's program (Horáček 1990: 59–60).

Although the extent of SSM's support for various initiatives is debatable, it will go down in history for its support of the student

---

23. Interviews with Pajerová 2 June 1992 and Doubek, Purnama and Ježek on 5 May 1992, Litvák on 26 March 1993, Vidim on 25 June 1993, Marek Benda on 12 June 1993 and Martin Benda on 20 May 1993.

demonstration on November 17. Cooperation between the official and unofficial student organizations started at the local level. The members of the newly created independent student organization knew the students active in the independent student press center. Many of them were SSM members as well, including Martin Mejstřik, the head of the Prague SSM university council. Mejstřik negotiated with the independent students about the possibility of having the SSM jointly sponsor the demonstration in memory of the student whom the Nazis had murdered 40 years earlier. After the murder, the German occupation forces closed down the universities. The independent students were extremely divided on whether or not to cooperate with the SSM in planning the demonstration. After a hot debate the independent students voted in favor of cooperation. They reasoned that if the SSM co-sponsored the demonstration, then it would be legal. If it were legal, more people would come and the risk would be lower that the police would attack them.[24] Mohorita attended the rally and of course claims that he supported the idea of having a joint demonstration.[25] Thus, the SSM can claim to have been a participant in the event which sparked off the revolution.

Intellectual Opposition Radicalizes, Sparked off by Outrage and Rising Expectations

I have already mentioned the growing oppositional activity. The number of opposition groups increased. Between 5–10,000 people attended several demonstrations. There was a petition drive demanding Havel's release from prison. Then came the "Several Sentences" petition which had 40,000 signatures. Again, intellectuals and artists dominated these groups. As mentioned above, the country's cultural elite was the initiator of the petition to gain Havel's release from prison.

---

24. I am basing this account on interviews with Marek Benda (21 June 1993), Martin Benda (20 May 1993), Petr Löwenhöfer (16 June 1993), Semín (2 March 1993), Štindl (14 May 1992) and Honzu Vidim (25 June 1993).

25. Many students whom I spoke to claim that the SSM probably supported it, because it was afraid of losing support to the independent organizations. Katka Švecová, who attended the SSM meeting one week before November 17, claims, however, that Mohorita was rather neutral to the idea of co-sponsoring the demonstration. He did not oppose it, but neither did he openly support it. In general, the SSM leadership was caught off guard by the openness of the radical students who attended the meeting (we discussed this on 21 February 1992).

According to the portion of my model dealing with rebellions, intellectuals usually dominate the opposition until a mass movement emerges, since they have the greatest institutional incentives to revolt. This part is verified by the dominance of intellectuals in the main oppositional groups such as Charter 77. Furthermore, I claim that dissidents increase their oppositional activity when they have rising expectations of political change, and in addition, when they feel outraged. The petition drive to gain Havel's release is an example of reactions based on outrage. It is unlikely that the petition signers were dissidents, who were acting simply because they were continuing previous anti-communist behavior. If they had been active dissidents, they would very likely have been able to reach the upper echelons of the cultural and scientific community. If these people had never engaged in oppositional activities before, then, it is reasonable to assume that they signed the petition because they were outraged at Havel's arrest.

The other aspect of my partial model on rebellions at the subjective level is the emergence of rising expectations. Here I have direct confirmation from my interviews. Virtually every dissident whom I spoke to claimed to have had increasing hopes for change. Among the events which encouraged them were Gorbachev's reform policy, the changes in Poland and Hungary, and finally the collapse of the East German regime. Other factors included the economic crisis and their perception of regime weakness.

For example, former Charter 77 speaker Sašq Vondra (interviewed 1 July 1993) recalls that he felt the regime was becoming "weaker and weaker." Its leaders were older and more "stupid" than in previous years. They no longer enjoyed support from the USSR. To top it all off, the economy was worsening. He adds that the opening of the Berlin Wall was one of the main instigators for him. Even the fact that he had only been imprisoned for two months rather than two years for having signed the Several Sentences petition indicated that the regime was weakening. He concludes that "the question was not *if* but *when* real change would come."

Petr Pithart, who became the first non-Communist prime minister of the Czech lands (interviewed 2 March 1993), recalls that, for him too, East Germany was a turning point. When they saw the thousands of East German refugees in the streets of Prague, the Czech and Slovak dissidents realized the time had come for them to go to the streets as well. The time of petition signing and letter writing was over. OF's campaign manager, Ivan Gabal (interviewed 15 April 1993) also names the collapse of the Berlin Wall as a signal that change would come. Another OF activist, Vladimír Valouch (interviewed 12 December 1993) agrees that the dissidents were greatly encouraged by the East German refugees in Prague.

These interviewees did not mention Gorbachev very often, but that reflected their time horizon. They concentrated in their recollections on the last few months, during which the events in the GDR were particularly important. Those who discussed a longer historical period mentioned the Gorbachev factor as well. For instance, OF activist Žák (interviewed 11 May 1993), remembers that the first sign of change was in 1986. That year, 10 dissidents published an article in the *Moscow News* in which they criticized such policies as the Afghanistan war. "Then it became clear that Gorbachev was not a phoney." Afterwards, there were signs that the domestic regime was weakening. For example, the decision to allow the demonstration for human rights in December 1988 showed that the USSR was pressuring the regime to change.

Interestingly, Václar Žák and others felt that the Czechoslovak regime was so conservative that they interpreted all moves towards liberalization (such as allowing the demonstration) in terms of Soviet pressure. They did not have any confidence in their own leaders, but they thought that change could come from Moscow. Thus, Gabal believes the Czechoslovak rulers were among the most dogmatic in the entire Soviet bloc. Similarly, the long-time dissident Petr Uhl (interviewed 9 May 1995) claims that, before the revolution began, he did not think that there were any Politburo members with whom he could try to start a dialogue. All of them were too conservative to even consider such an endeavor. However, the events in neighboring Poland, Hungary and the GDR encouraged him.

Thus, even though the dissidents had rising expectations that Soviet pressure would bring about some changes, except for Vondra, nobody expected the system to collapse—at least not before the Berlin Wall opened in the GDR. They thought that the USSR would force reforming liberalizers into the leadership, which would had improved the situation, but caused systemic change. As Pithart notes, since nobody expected systemic change they were unprepared for it when it came. Urban recalls (in an (interview 29 April 1995 and unpublished manuscript 1992) that when the group, Independent Intellectuals, employed at the academy of sciences proposed to the Charterists that they copy the Polish example and start preparing negotiating teams, they did not gain any support. The other dissidents replied that it was better to wait.

Horáček (interviewed 1 June 1992), the co-founder of MOST, sums up the irony in the fact that rising expectations were not linked to a belief that the rulers were capable of change. He recalls he and Kocáb founded MOST because, in the summer of 1989, they felt the situation was becoming tense and dangerous. An "us-versus-them" attitude had developed on both sides. The opposition had higher expectations and was becoming more active. Meanwhile, the regime was becoming more repressive. For example, some singers were forbidden from giving TV interviews. He feared the regime might violently repress the outrage of the opposition. This would lead to bloodshed. So he and Kocáb sought a safety-valve by starting discussions between the two sides.

The other half of MOST, Kocáb (interviewed 4 July 1993), does not recall having felt such tension during this period. Yet, he too had higher expectations because of Gorbachev. When Gorbachev appeared, he thought there was a chance to change the system. He also admits to having been encouraged by the increase in oppositional activity in every East European country. As in all the other cases, then he based his expectations for change on activities *outside* of the country, rather than on any political openings provided by the Czechoslovak regime.

The Student Movement: The Most Radical of the Intellectuals
Although the known dissidents had become more daring and radical during the past year, their children at the universities outdid them in boldness. These young adults eventually became the catalysts of the revolution. As noted earlier, students at some faculties of the Charles University began printing independent journals under the protection of the SSM. During 1989 student activity increased in other areas as well. At the pedagogical faculty in early 1989, over 400 students signed a petition to prevent the expulsion of 7 students for participation in the Palach demonstration (document: "Vážený soudruhu děkane"). Around this time, activists created a group called "Student Forum" to organize discussions among the students. And when the faculty committee interrogated the student activist Semín on November 13, over 100 students came to the meeting to support him by singing and blowing bubbles.[26] In the spring of 1989, 32 students at the Prague

---

26. Interview with Semín 2 March 1993. His statements are confirmed by my interviews with Martin Benda on 20 May 1993, Štindl on 14 May 1992, and the document, "Vážený soudruhu vedoucí tajemník," which is a letter from the dean of the pedagogical faculty to the Prague Party secretary and other officials.

Economic University signed a petition which was sent to the Ministry of Education, demanding the abolishment of mandatory courses in the indoctrination subjects such as "scientific Marxism" and "the history of the Czechoslovak workers' movement" (document: "Vážená paní ministryne!"). In the summer of 1989, student activists throughout Prague started an independent student organization, STUHA, with the goal of establishing a self-governing organ for the students.[27] This organization planned the November 17 demonstration which sparked off the "velvet revolution." In short, intellectuals were the catalyst for the social movement.

Organizing in defense of students under threat of expulsion shows that many were motivated by feelings of outrage. Another example of the solidarity effect of repression may be seen in the rise in student activities following the police actions during Jan Palach week. Marek Benda (interviewed 21 June 1993 and in Benda et al. 1990: 15) remembers that the core of STUHA evolved as a loose circle of friends began to meet in the aftermath of the Jan Palach week. As mentioned above, students at the pedagogical faculty organized against the expulsion of students for their participation in the Palach events. Martin Benda (interviewed 20 May 1993) concludes that this particular week, probably was decisvie for many students.

Semín told me that he had expected the opposition movement to increase in size. Moreover, he thought the Party would eventually replace its hardliners with reform Communists, but he never imagined that the regime would give up its power monopoly altogether.

Feelings of Outrage Spark the Revolution; Intellectuals Organize
The newly created independent student organization, STUHA, planned a demonstration on November 17 in memory of the Nazis' murder of a student 50 years earlier. The leaders had no idea that it would have far-reaching consequences. They merely thought that this demonstration would be the first among many other student anti-regime activities. Semín (interviewed 2 March 1993) expected student activity to reach its peak during the next Jan Palach week—in January, 1990.

---

27. Interviews with Martin & Marek Benda on 20 May 1993 and 21 June 1993, Semín on 2 March 1993, and Monika Pajerová on 2 June 1992.

The manifestation took place legally under SSM's protection. Yet, the police attacked the demonstrators as they approached the main square, Václavské náměstí. One student reportedly died. When Uhl found out about this rumor, he called Radio Free Europe and told them the story. By evening, the story had spread throughout the city. The following day, students from the drama academy (DAMU) organized a meeting in their theater. There they launched the idea of a national student strike. A strike coordination committee was set up. During the next few days, students organized strike committees at their faculties. The students also decided to call for a nation-wide general strike on Monday, November 27.[28]

On the same day, Havel returned to Prague and held a meeting at his apartment with some friends from Charter 77. They decided to establish the Citizens' Forum (*Občanské fórum* or OF), which would be a coalition of citizens and groups working for a dialogue with the regime. On Sunday, November 19, OF held its first meeting at the *Činoherní klub*. Havel came prepared with a declaration supporting the students' call for a national strike.[29] Another demand was for the immediate resignation of Štěpán, whom they blamed for the police intervention. They also demanded the resignations of all Central Committee members who had collaborated with the Soviet invaders in 1968. Furthermore, they demanded the release of all political prisoners. Finally, they demanded that the federal assembly set up an independent commission to investigate police beatings. The committee had to include a member of OF. Meanwhile, a group of about 50 Slovak dissidents met in Bratislavia and founded OF's sister organization, VPN (*Verejnos proti násiliu* or "Public Against Violence"). According to former Chair Fedor Gál (interviewed 31 March 1993), the majority of the members were scientists, journalists and other intellectuals.

---

28. General descriptions can be found in English in Draper (1993) and Wheaton & Kavan (1992). For descriptions in Czech see Fleyberk (1990) and Holubec (1990). The students' demands from November 18 are reprinted in Otál & Sládek (1990: 43–5). Uhl's version comes from an interview with him on 9 May 1995.

29. See the previous footnote for general sources. I am also basing my information on interviews with Gabal 15 April 1993, Urban (25 June 1993) and Žák (11 May 1993). OF's declaration is reprinted in Otál & Sládek (1990: 47–8). Havel (interviewed in *Profil* 23 July 1990) also says he held a meeting at his apartment on November 18, where the participants decided to found OF. He claims he had left Prague on Friday, so that he would not give the impression that either he or Charter 77 controlled the demonstration.

The following day (November 20) the student strike committee echoed OF's demands. They went one step further, however, and demanded the removal of the article in the constitution guaranteeing the leading role of the Party (their demands are reprinted in Otál & Sládek 1990: 74–5).

Already a pattern emerges in conformity with my partial model on participation in rebellions. Intellectuals acted as the catalyst for the revolution. First, they organized the rally on November 17. Then they organized strikes and planned further actions. In addition, the core of these new organizations consisted of people who had previously belonged to oppositional groups. Havel utilized his network of Charter intellectuals to launch OF,[30] while students from STUHA and STIS (the independent press center) became the basis for the strike coordinating committee (interview with Pajerová on 2 June 1992). At most faculties, students who had already been active in planning the rally set up strike committees and then simply announced the strike as a *fait accompli* to the students on Monday.[31]

Furthermore, these actions occurred spontaneously in reaction to the police provocation. None of the students to whom I had talked claimed they had discussed the possibility of striking before November 17, except for Semín (interviewed on 2 March 1993). Even he admits it was only a thought, not a plan. Thus, it is reasonable to conclude that the violent intervention had a solidarity effect by outraging the participants so much that they felt they needed to take action. An example is the student Jan Bubeník (interviewed in *Prague Post* 23–29

---

30. Wheaton & Kavan (1992: 56) write: "the forum was based in a relatively narrow social group of Prague intellectuals."

31. Of course, some people first became active during the revolution. For example, the DAMU students, who turned out to be the most radical, had not been involved in planning the November 17 manifestation. But DAMU student Martin Mejstřik had been involved in preparing for the November 17 demonstration. He had been active both within STIS and as the head of the city SSM university committee. Thus, he was the one responsible for getting the SSM to back the action. At some faculties the SSM tried to get a representative to the strike committees, but it failed (interviews with Ježek on 15 May 1992 and Vidim on 25 June 1993). Löwenhöfer (interviewed 16 June 1993) says that some SSM leaders at the economic university tried to convince them not to strike, but they had little influence. Martin Benda (interviewed 20 May 1993) also says, that at the Electro-Techno Faculty, the SSM tried to lead the strike and make it more moderate, but it failed. Two or three active SSM members did manage, however, to get elected to the 15 person faculty strike committee. At the Educational and Sports Faculty of the Charles University, however, the strike leader, Magdalena Staňková (interviewed 30 March 1993) was the SSM chair for her class. She claims there were no confrontations between the SSM and other students at her faculty.

June 1993), who became active in the student movement after the police attack on November 17 sent his roommate to the hospital.

Solving the Communication Problem to Gain Worker Support
Once the intellectuals organized, they sought to gain worker support. After the *Solidarność* uprising, they understood the necessity of gaining worker support for a revolution. Thus, OF and the students organized trips to factories, in order to explain to the workers what had happened at the demonstration. It was often difficult at first to gain admittance to the factories. The opposition came upon a unique solution: they arranged to have famous actors and actresses to accompany the students. Once this was done, it became much easier to enter the premises. The workers might have been distrustful of young intellectual students, but they respected their heroes from film and TV. During the first week, both OF and the students concentrated on building up worker support for the general strike.

The collective-action problem for the intellectuals was not then finding selective incentives to encourage workers to participate, as public-choice theory would lead us to believe.[32] Prague students had no way of rewarding or punishing workers at provincial factories. Rather, the collective-action concern was communication. Not only did the workers use famous celebrities to gain access to the factories, they quickly utilized other forms of communication to spread their message. There are countless examples. Already on the first evening, Uhl used a phone to contact Western radio, which in turn broadcast the event across the country. At most faculties the students seized the communication SSM's facilities—with or without its consent. This

---

32. This does not necessarily mean the participants were not rational. The mere fact that OF and the students were able to gain access to communications equipment and to gain the support of famous actors and actresses was added information for the workers. Yet, the stress on communication goes against the more rigid public-choice theories, which see the free-rider problem as the main concern of revolutionaries. Although most public-choice theorists stress the need for political entrepreneurs who can give selective incentives to participants, Taylor (1988) claims that if a community is small enough, the threat of social exclusion is so strong that a political entrepreneur is not needed. Thus, one would expect participation rates to be highest in the smallest faculties. My interviews with student activists, however, indicate no correlation at all between participation rates and the size of the student body. For example at the Economic University, Löwenhöfer (interviewed 16 June 1993) estimates between 200–300 of the approximately 5000 students were active in the strike. But at the philosophical faculty of the Charles University (with half as many students), Ježek and Purnama (both interviewed 15 May 1992) claim, twice as many actively participated.

included everything from SSM's student radio to its photocopy and fax machines. At the Economic University, the dean allowed the students to use the university's facilities, although at the same time he tried to prevent Charterists from appearing at the campus. At some faculties, teachers helped students translate their declarations into various languages for the Western media. When the students visited the factories, they came equipped with video films of police violence.[33]

In no other East European uprising did the revolutionaries utilize communication channels as effectively as in the Czechoslovak "velvet revolution." In the GDR, for example, the protesters got most of their information from West German radio and TV during the first weeks of the uprising. Due to the spontaneous nature of the revolt, however, the opposition groups did not play a key role in spreading information.

Further help in communication came from the National Front parties, who quickly abandoned the sinking regime. Once the old institutional structures began to loosen, the allied parties no longer limited themselves to being loyal puppets of the regime.[34] On Sunday, November 19, the Socialist Party Central Committee met and condemned the police intervention. They demanded political democracy and guarantees against such further attacks (Fleyberk 1990: 21, the declaration is reprinted in Otál & Sládek 1990: 43–4). The following day, the party newspaper *Svobodné slovo* began writing freely. On Tuesday, the Socialist Party allowed OF's representatives to speak from the balcony of its publishing house at the main square, Václavské náměstí.[35]

Another theoretically interesting development was the emerging split between radicals and moderates, with the students playing the role of the radicals. Already on Monday, the students demanded the removal of the clause from the constitution concerning the leading role

---

33. Based on interviews with Chalupa (December 1990) Purnama (15 May 1992), Rovná (4 June 1992), Staňková (30 March 1993), Urban (25 June 1993), Zbořil (December 1990) and Zbořilová (December 1990). The use of videos is also discussed in Horáček (1990: 54).

34. In contrast to the GDR and Poland, where non-communist allied parties participated in government, the non-communist Czechoslovak parties did not even have any ministerial posts. But as former Chair of the Socialist Party Kučera (interviewed 19 May 1993) told me, "it was better for the Party to exist than to not exist."

35. Václav Malý, a Catholic Priest and Charter 77 signatory, credits Petr Kučera for convincing the Socialist Party leadership to let OF use the balcony of the party newspaper, *Svobodné slovo*. Kučera was a journalist for the newspaper at the time, but quickly joined OF and became one of its leaders. Malý is interviewed in *Profil* 23 July 1990.

of the Communist Party. OF still did not officially demand such measures during this first week. By the end of the week, however, OF had followed the students and declared the general strike a referendum on the leading role of the party.[36]

Attempts at organizing the workers quickly paid off. By Wednesday workers from the TOS enterprise marched together under a banner at Václavské náměstí. The next day, workers at the ČKD plant in Prague booed when Štěpán criticized the students, saying that children cannot run the country. The workers shouted back "we are not children!" (Fleyberk 1990: 59–60 and Holubec 1990: 13). To make matters worse for the regime, TV news reports started becoming more independent of the regime. That evening the news broadcast a film of the roaring crowd of anti-Communist workers jeering the Prague secretary. It is probable that the workers, like the intellectuals, felt outraged at the regime's treatment of the students. One survey shows that 88% of Prague's inhabitants disapproved of the police actions, 8% felt that it was necessary but that it should not have been so harsh none approved of the police behavior.[37]

Finally, although there was a rapid increase in participants during the first week of the demonstrations, this does not necessarily verify the threshold theory of revolutions. As in the GDR, the number of participants decreased after reaching a peak. In the ČSSR, the decrease began already after the first week or two. The students and OF activists whom I interviewed also claim that the number of active participants in their various activities began declining after the first two weeks. Thus, the threshold theory again has difficulty dealing with the time factor. Even though more people are willing to demonstrate when they believe the risks of repression are lower, the utility of demonstrating also decreases with time for a large portion of the public.

The Regime on the First Week of the Revolution: Paralyzed and Afraid of Using Force

Again, if the hardline regime had been willing to use the military, it might have been able to crush the revolt. An anarmed opposition has

---

36. Horáček claims it was his idea (Horáček 1990).
37. Slejška & Herzmann (1990: 42). Their survey was taken between 22 and 24 of November and included 260 inhabitants of Prague.

little chance of defeating a well-armed regime. As long as none of the military organizations fight on the side of the revolutionaries, events will likely develop as in China rather than as in Romania. So the question remains: why did a regime, which was probably more hardline than that in China, refrain from using more force?

There has been no shortage of conspiracy theories concerning the police attacks against the demonstrators on November 17. The alleged death of a student ignited the revolution. Such rumors are not surprising, since the student who supposedly died turned out to be a StB agent who was alive and well. Hardliners claim that reformers planned the police attack in order to force Jakeš to step down, while reformers claim the hardliners planned the attack in part to acquire an excuse to crack down on the opposition and to prevent any future Gorbachev from emerging in Prague. After examining all the available evidence, however, the official parliamentary commission concluded there was no conspiracy (*Prague Post* 4–10 February 1992). Until more material emerges, it is reasonable to accept the commission's conclusions.

Material from my personal interviews and from published interviews indicates that the police probably planned in advance to attack the students.[38] But this is probably the only thing that was planned. Otherwise, the behavior of the police, of the hardliners, and of the Adamec reform-camp indicates chaos and panic, rather than any conspiratorial plans. The police were extremely inconsistent. Sometimes they arrested oppositionalists (such as the student activist Marek Benda); sometimes they merely observed them.[39] They guarded some

---

38. For example, the student activist Ondřej Štindl (interviewed 14 May 1992) recollects that the main doors of the buildings on the street *Národní třida* were locked, but the landlords denied having locked them. Thus, he concludes that the police must have locked the doors in preparation for their attack. In addition, he adds that if they had wanted to prevent the students from approaching the center, they could have attacked them when they were on smaller streets farther away from town.

39. Martin Benda (interviewed 25 May 1993) recalls that, on Sunday, November 19, StB agents stood in front of his building and prevented students from entering. When his brother Marek tried to leave the premises, they arrested him. Marek Benda (interviewed 21 June 1993) says the police seemed extremely nervous when they interrogated him. They threatened that another massacre could occur on Václavské náměstí, but they also showed some understanding for the students' position. The police's behavior in this case says a lot about their behavior toward opposition leaders. If the police had wanted to repress the rebellion, they would have arrested the Benda family, since it was one of the most important families for the revolution. The father Václav was a famous dissident and collaborator with Havel, while the two sons (Marek and Martin) were extremely active in the independent student movement.

apartments and arrested those leaving them. Nevertheless, they never entered the apartments in question to arrest the main instigators.[40] For instance, they arrested Marek Benda when he left his apartment building, but they did not go into the apartment and arrest his more famous father, who had been one of the co-founders of Charter 77. At some faculties the security forces acted tougher than at others. However, at no faculty did they seem to have a set plan of action.[41] In general, the behavior of the security forces is puzzling. Why did they decide to break up some private student meetings while allowing the more important meetings of the central student striking committee at the Disk Theater to take place?[42] Why did the police prevent the Benda family from leaving their building, while letting Havel and other famous dissidents move freely? And why did they allow OF to hold its meeting undisturbed on Sunday evening, while still stopping demonstrations during the first weekend?[43] All these examples indicate that the police was confused. Their behavior was too inconsistent to be part of a detailed conspiracy.

---

40. Again, the Benda family provides an example. The police only arrested family members when they left the apartment. Another Havel colleague, Jan Urban, also had trouble with the police at his apartment. On Saturday, November 18, he held a meeting in his apartment at which Charter 77 members translated the students' texts and phoned the contents to foreign journalists. Eight of his friends were arrested leaving the building, but the police never entered the apartment and arrested Urban himself Horáček 1990: 125). Why the police arrested Marek Benda but not his more famous father, and why they arrested Urban's friends, but not Urban, remains a mystery.

41. Doležal (interviewed 15 May 1992) says that on Monday, the riot police came by the philosophy faculty building four times within one hour. The students met with the dean and demanded a promise that force would not be used. The dean refused to make such a promise. Early Tuesday morning, he hear trucks going around the city collecting rubble stones and putting them in piles. The students considered this a provocation by the police. If one civil police cast a stone against the police, he could have started a civil war. So the students avoided the piles. Ježek (interviewed 15 May 1992) goes further and claims that the dean threatened them, claiming that the police *would* storm the building.

Staňková (interviewed 30 March 1993) gives a more confused picture of the militia at the educational faculty. She remembers that when they arrived, the students went to their trucks and tried to convince them to support them. The militiamen did not really listen to them, but neither did they make any threats. Some officers came to the faculty building and wanted to enter it, but the dean told them they were not necessary. So they left the area after a few hours and never returned. However, several days afterwards, the regular police still blocked the bridges and forced them to show ID cards in order to pass.

42. Semín (interviewed 2 March 1993) remembers that after the police meetings on November 17, people from his faculty met at his apartment to discuss further action. The police came, so they had to break up the meeting.

43. For example, Horáček (1990: 30) writes that the police was less violent on November 18 than 17, but they were "violent enough" in dispersing the crowd.

Below I examine the behavior of the hardline regime and the Adamec camp. I claim that their behavior was not any more strategic or well-planned than that of the police.

The Hardliners during the First Week

Gorbachev's emergence as a reformer destroyed the pragmatic legitimacy of the Czechoslovak leaders, who had based their pragmatic acceptance on the notion that the USSR had put them into power to prevent all reforms. Gorbachev did not demand a Czechoslovak *glasnost* and he did not even support the attempts of the reformist Štrougal camp to defeat Jakeš in the battle over Husák's throne. Neither did he help Adamec in his attempts to replace the conservative Jakeš during the spring and summer of 1989. Nevertheless, the Czechoslovak hardliners had tied their pragmatic legitimacy so strongly to the need to prevent reforms that Gorbachev's domestic reform program, in combination with his passive foreign policy, was enough to destroy the belief that the Kremlin would not allow any change. When the Czechoslovak rulers' institutional interests in avoiding reform evaporated, the hardliners had no clue as to how to deal with the new situation.

Events show that the hardliners were even more confused than the police. They were totally disorganized and without any strategy to deal with the situation. Former General Secretary Jakeš blames the StB for not giving the leaders enough information during that first weekend. He had no idea there was any violence, since the interior minister had clear instructions not to intervene at the demonstration. When Lorenc called him on November 17, he did not give Jakeš any reason to react. Jakeš claims that he had no idea during the weekend about the real situation or about the course of intervention by the StB. He did not call the Politburo together until November 19—two days after the alleged death of a student and one day after the student, musician and actor strikes had already started. During that meeting, the leaders felt "helpless" upon hearing the new information. Lorenc's report "did not correspond to the real course of events." In view of the increasing tension, they agreed to meet again the next day. However, the available information still did not give them a clear picture of what had happened on November 17.[44] Thus, during the

---

44. I am basing Jakeš' account on interviews which he gave to *Haló noviny* on 11 November 1992 and *Reportér* no. 17 1991.

first important weekend, the leaders had no special instructions for the police, and no strategy to deal with the situation except to try and obtain more information.

On Monday, the leaders were concerned about rumors that the radio and TV staff would start supporting the opposition. Therefore, they decided to prepare reserve technical experts from the army who would be able to take over broadcasting. Nothing came of their plans, however, and the media began broadcasting more independently.

As the demonstrations spread on Tuesday, the Politburo had another important meeting. They decided on two measures: 1) they would call in the People's Militia, and 2) they would hold an extra Central Committee meeting on Friday. The opposition was growing exponentially by the day. As rational-choice theorists have pointed out, the level of repression required in such a situation to defeat the opposition increased by the hour. By delaying having a Central Committee meeting until Friday, however, the rulers ensured they would spend the rest of the week preparing for the meeting, rather than working out tactics for combatting the opposition.

The mobilization of the People's Militia provided an occasion for concrete action, but the result was a fiasco, since the Politburo did not give the militiamen any instructions for action. Meanwhile, the top leaders tried to shift responsibility on to each other for the possible measures which the militia might undertake. For example, Štěpán (interviewed 3 June 1992) claims he was not at the Politburo meeting where the militia decision was made. When he found out about it that evening, he immediately called Jakeš. The general secretary was not in. Therefore, Štěpán told the chief of the militia to call Jakeš and to say that he (Štěpán) would take no responsibility for the militia's actions. Of course, as head of the Prague defense council, Štěpán would be blamed for any militia attacks. He was not against the idea of using the militia, but the Politburo had not worked out any plan, so he did not think they should resort to violence. Such an action could only have worked if "political steps" also had been taken. Since the militia was to guard certain important buildings (like the radio and TV buildings and the castle), such an act would have been the equivalent of introducing martial law, but without actually declaring it. Obviously, martial law cannot be effective unless opposition leaders are interned. As far as I know, the Politburo never even discussed this idea during these first days.

At 1:30 a.m., Jakeš called Štěpán back and assured him the militia would not attack. Štěpán believes the decision to call in the militia had the support of everyone except for himself and Adamec (who was absent from the meeting too). If this is true, then we can assume that the Politburo could easily have gone ahead with its intentions. In Štěpán's words, the other Politburo member accepted his decision not to attack, because "they were panicking and under great pressure."

On Wednesday, Jakeš met with the leaders of the allied Parties in the National Front to discuss the recent developments. Former Socialist Party Chair Bohuslav Kučera (interviewed 19 May 1993) recalls that some people like the director of the Socialist Academy Matoš advocated using force. Jakeš said the Party would not use force. All of the National Front parties were also against using force. Later in the afternoon the Politburos of both the Communist and Socialist Parties met. Kučera says he realized at the meeting that the Communist Politburo was completely paralyzed. Two hardliners Kempený and Indra criticized the Socialist Party's new independent stance. Indra was angry and accused them of wanting a "counterrevolution." Yet, they offered no plans of action. Jakeš listened to the Socialist Party leaders, but did not way more than "yes" or "no" to their suggestions. He was not capable of critically analyzing the situation. Jan Škoda (interviewed on 14 May 1993) gives a similar picture of that meeting. He realized for the first time during this meeting how weak the Communist Party had become.[45]

When I asked Jakeš whether he had any strategy during the first week of the revolution, he replied that his strategy was to call the Central Committee together for a meeting (interview on 9 April 1992). So the next questions are, whether he had any strategy during this meeting, and whether the Party leadership in general developed any strategy at that time. The answer to the first question would appear to be negative. As Mohorita (1991) notes, Jakeš' opening speech completely lacked any analysis of the causes of the societal crisis. Nor did he suggest any concrete proposals for solving the crisis. Rather than making strategic decisions himself, he handed over responsibility for the tough decisions to the entire Central Committee. In sum, the Party leaders were paralyzed and without any strategy during the first week.

---

45. He adds that Jakeš was concerned over the journalists who had become less loyal—especially those from TV and the Party newspaper *Rudé pravo*. Then he requested that the journalists at the Social Party newspaper *Svobodné slovo* support the regime. This attests to Jakeš' helplessness. Previously, Communist general secretaries never made requests to the Socialist Party—they gave it orders!

The Party itself was not capable of developing a strategy either. Although the entire Politburo resigned at the first evening, its new composition showed the Party was unable to rejuvenate itself. It included such old-timers as Lenárt, who had been in the Central Committee since the 1950s and the hardline union leader Zavadil. Even more odious for OF was the inclusion of Štěpán—the man whom they blamed for the police attack on November 17. His name topped the list of persons whose resignation OF was demanding. Not a single reformer joined the new Politburo. Not even Adamec was a member.

Of course, the new leadership did not have to be reformist in order to behave strategically. It might have been just as effective to take a tough stance and to attempt a Chinese solution. Rather than electing a strong leader, however, they settled on a listless compromise candidate, Urbánek. Štěpán admits Urbánek was a weak candidate. He reasons that the Central Committee elected Urbánek because he was the only leader who was not in Prague during the week of November 17–24. The following day, Štěpán gave in to pressure and resigned (Mohorita 1991 and Horáček 1990: 141). His replacement, however, was not a known reformer. The Communist Party ceased to be a major actor after this Central Committee meeting. Urbánek basically stood by the sidelines and let Adamec do whatever he wanted (interviews with Krejčí 13 April 1992 and Horáček 1 June 1992).

The paralyzed members of the Politburo filtered out new information and pretended that nothing new had happened and that they would soon be able to continue as before. Yet, already on November 17, important new information arrived which showed that the situation was changing. Even the fact that the StB chief Lorenc had not informed them adequately of what had happened was significant. Even before the November 17 demonstration, major events occurred which radically changed the situation, such as the collapse of the Communist regimes in Poland, Hungary and finally the GDR. During these few months, they were incapable of analyzing this new situation and working out any strategy to deal with future developments. After November 17, they were flooded *every day* with new information that shattered their picture of the world. Within a single day there were several shocks from which to recover. First, the Politburo was surprised by the official youth organization's decision the week before the rally to co-sponsor a demonstration with independent students. Second, there was the shock of the large turnout. Some claim as many as 50,000 persons attended the rally. Then there was the shock of the alleged death of a student.

Then there came a cascade of changes. The Politburo became overwhelmed with the new information. During the weekend the students formed strike committees, the Charterists established OF, Slovak dissidents formed VPN, and the National Front parties joined the opposition. By the fourth day, the demonstrations had grown to around 200,000, and both the Socialist Party and People' Party newspapers began publishing the students demands and writing critically about the regime.[46] Furthermore, virtually all of the nation's universities had closed. By Tuesday, the crowds had exploded into hundreds of thousands, including large groups of workers from the largest factories. By Wednesday, the Party could no longer rely on its own newspaper and Štěpán had been booed out by workers in Kladno, which was normally a Communist stronghold. By Thursday, Dubček was making public appearances at mass demonstrations, and Adamec had broken Party unity by meeting an OF delegation.

This rapidly developing revolution overloaded the cognitive capacity of the aging hardliners. This prevented them from behaving as strategically, as Przeworski would expect. Instead, they became paralyzed. They were no longer willing to take responsibility for their decisions and resigned rather than work out a strategy. This explains more than Przeworski's claim that the regimes gave up, because they could no longer rely on the military. For while it may be the case that the militia was not willing to use violence, we will never know if this is true, since the rulers never gave it instructions to do so. This becomes even clearer when one considers the behavior of the military leaders. On Friday, November 24, they actually offered to repress the opposition, but the Central Committee turned down their offer.[47] So again, the issue is the Communist rulers unwillingness to use violence, not their lack of confidence in the state's repressive capacity.

---

46. For estimates of the size of the demonstrations, see Wheaton & Kavan (1992: 88), Fleyberk (1990) and Konůpek (1990: 18–19).

47. See Barany (1992: 13), *Český Deník* (1 March 1993), cf. Wheaton & Kavan (1992: 72). Schöpflin (1993: 231) also mentions this event. He adds that the Central Committee refused the military's offer to use force, because the interior ministry had claimed that it only had forces at its disposal to deal with up to 30,000 demonstrators—well under the hundreds of thousands that had taken to the streets. It is hard to believe, however, that the well equipped military could not have dealt with much larger crowds if ordered to commit a Chinese-style massacre.

Except for Adamec, the leadership showed itself completely incapable of acting. The rulers were not willing to use violence, but neither were they willing to negotiate with the opposition. As we shall see, even Adamec was cautious and panic-stricken. In addition, once negotiations began with Havel, he became extremely inflexible. He continued to follow his original strategy even when it had clearly failed. Eventually, when it became obvious to him that his original strategy was not working, he simply gave up. Before discussing the negotiations with Havel, I will briefly examine Adamec's behavior during the first week of the revolution, with an eye to showing how weak and isolated he would later become.

Adamec during the First Week: The Cautious Reformer Meets the Opposition
The prime minister does not appear to have been any better informed about the police action on November 17 than Jakeš was. Horáček (1990: 35–7) writes that, when he and his MOST colleague Kocáb met Adamec on Sunday, November 19, the prime minister admitted he had found out what happened from two students from the journalist faculty who had visited him on Saturday. He claimed he still did not have accurate information. Horáček told me (interview 1 June 1992) that Adamec had been "stunned" by the police action.

Krejčí claims that Adamec realized he had to negotiate with the opposition. The Prime Minister's position was extremely weak, however, and he could not be certain he would survive. Krejčí (interviewed 7 June 1993) claims that after Adamec's meeting with MOST on Sunday, November 19, friends called Krejčí and said that the StB wanted to arrest the prime minister. Another advisor to the prime minister, Pavel (interviewed 29 April 1993), agrees that Adamec was afraid of being arrested. The next day, Adamec failed to obtain government approval of his proclamation condemning the police intervention. He then left the meeting, and the government negotiated on the resolution without him. Instead, the government made a declaration supporting the police Krejčí 1991: 72–3 and interview with Pavel on 29 April 1993).Thus, the prime minister's isolation continued.

On Wednesday, November 22, Adamec met with MOST again. Horáček (1990: 71) gives a startling example of how poorly the government understood the swiftness with which change was taking place. Krejčí, who was also present at the meeting, grinned several times and emphasized that the government knew what had been decided at the OF meeting: "we have our information," Adamec's advisor repeated several times. Horáček then pulled out a copy of the Peoples' Party newspaper *Lidoová demokracie* and showed the astonished prime minister that everything that had been decided at OF's meeting was already known to most of the population.

The following day, Adamec agreed to a short meeting with OF, but under the condition that Havel not join the delegation. OF repeated its demands for the resignation ofcertain Politburo members and the release of political prisoners. Adamec replied that he did not have the right to demand the resignation of these persons, but he agreed that freedom of conscience needed to be guaranteed. He also assured the OF representatives that no violence would be used. The prime minister ended the meeting by encouraging the theaters to perform again and the students to go back to their studies. Adamec could continue to have a dialogue with OF, but he did not promise any further meetings (Horáček 1990: 79–80).

According to Krejčí (1991: 75), at the time of this meeting Adamec was still afraid that he would not survive the Central Committee meeting on Friday. He believed the Party would never forgive him if he met with Havel. Apparently, there was good reason for these fears. Adamec received sharp criticism at the Central Committee meeting. In response, he offered his resignation for the third time that year.[48] Later on the next day, when it had become apparent that the Communist Party was finished as a major political player, Adamec agreed at last to start negotiations with Havel.

The "Strategy" of the Negotiators

First, the opposition is discussed. Then the attitude of the regime during the negotiations between Adamec and Havel is analyzed.

Przeworski's division of the opposition into moderates and radicals is once again fruitful here. But again, the impact of the radicals was the opposite of that expected by Przeworski. Rather than hindering

---

48. Horáček (1990: 131) reports Krejčí told him on Saturday morning that nobody at the Central Committee meeting the previous night had supported Adamec. In response, Adamec offered his resignation. Many sources claim the prime minister had offered his resignation earlier that year. Hoření (interviewed in *Mosty* no. 32–3, 1991) puts the total number of resignations at three. Štěpán (interviewed 3 June 1992) mentions that Adamec offered his resignation in June 1989 because he was dissatisfied with the pace of reforms. Čmejrek (interviewed 23 March 1992) says Adamec offered his resignation "several times during that year."

the democratization process, the radicals sped it up. By putting OF's leaders under constant pressure, they induced them to make more radical demands at the negotiations. In addition, the mere existence of the radicals provided an alibi for OF to increase its demands on Adamec. In this case, the main radical group was the students. However, the unorganized masses on the streets and the workers in the factories who threatened to strike, also took on the role of radicals. In contrast, OF's leaders were much more cautious, and they were willing to accommodate Adamec. They wanted to ensure continuity and to avoid a constitutional crisis. As Žák (interviewed 11 May 1993) points out, there would have been no legal president empowered to appoint a new prime minister if Prime Minister Adamec had resigned at the same time as President Husák. OF's leaders wanted Husák to resign; accordingly, they hoped to convince Adamec to stay on as prime minister. This way, they reasoned, a crisis could be avoided and continuity assured on the road to the first free elections. Finally, OF was more cautious than the radicals because it felt a responsibility to prevent a violent reaction from the Party-state.[49]

Since the changes came so quickly, the OF leaders were not able to develop any long term strategy. When I asked former members of OF's leadership what their strategy was, the common reply was "what strategy?" As Pithart (interviewed 2 March 1993) recalls they did not have any strategy at all. They worked out their tactics day by day, hour by hour. Similarly, Vondra (interviewed 1 July 1993) remembers that they had meetings on the night before each negotiation or sometimes in the morning right before negotiations began. But even if they had no well-thought out strategy, they certainly had the long-term *goal* of a transition to a multi-party democracy.

In the short term, they usually united around certain concrete demands. To begin with, it was a concern to avoid violence and the establishment of martial law. In addition, they sought the resignation of certain compromised people, as well as the establishment of an independent commission to investigate the police attacks on November 17. The main organizing goal during the first week, however, was to gain support for the two-hour national strike (inter-

---

49. Pithart (interviewed 2 March 1993) admits they were overly cautious, but says they could not exclude the possibility of a military uprising. There were rumors every day that something was being prepared.

views with Žák on 11 May 1993 and Vondra on July 1993). Subsequently, the main goal became the resignation of President Husák; they also sought influence over the composition of the new government. They did not feel, however, that they were ready to take over ministerial posts themselves. They merely wanted some important posts to go to well-respected non-Communists. In addition, they felt they had no legitimate claim to ministerial posts until they had participated in free elections. In Slovakia, in fact, the OF's sister organization VPN "succeeded" in remaining out of government until the first free elections (interview with former VPN chair Gál on 31 March 1993). I argue below, however, that the reasons why the federal Communist Party forced OF and VPN to take over the majority of ministerial posts, was that it had collapsed so rapidly that it was no longer even capable of running the country for an interim period. At each stage the opposition leaders took a more radical bargaining stance, as the regime showed itself to be weaker and as the "radicals" increased their pressure on OF.

I turn now to Adamec's general thinking before discussing more of the details of the actual negotiations. According to his advisor Pavel (interviewed 29 April 1993), Adamec had no fundamental strategy. Instead, he reacted to the OF's demands. Nevertheless, Pavel maintains that Adamec wanted to avoid violence, and that he wanted the system to remain "socialist." In Krejčí's words, Adamec wanted a democratic socialist system (interview on 7 June 1993). Although one can with good reason question the extent of Adamec's democratic values, it is probable that, by the time serious negotiations had begun, he had already accepted a democratic political system as inevitable. The economic system, therefore, became the main issue for him. Given these long-term goals, it would have been most rational for him to have continued as prime minister and to have tried to influence the transitionary process, rather than resigning as he eventually did. If he had continued as prime minister, he could have greatly increased the chance that the economic reforms would have gone more in the direction he preferred.

At the very least, he would have had the possibility of going down in history as the man who brought about a peaceful transition to democracy in Czechoslovakia. As O'Donnell & Schmitter (1986: 25–6) note, softliners who lose power because they support a democratic transformation can enjoy the privilege of being rewarded by history for having given their country a "more honorable future."

Adamec chose neither of the strategic options. He tried neither to maintain power and shape the process of transformation nor to ensure that he went down favorably in history. Instead, he was so bound by his anti-reformist pragmatic acceptance that he too panicked when his institutional interests collapsed. The pace of change overwhelmed him. He found it easier to give up than to try to salvage anything out of the situation.

Another interesting theoretical development is Adamec's relationship with the hardliners—i.e. the rest of the Politburo. Theorists of democratization have seen hardliners as the greatest enemies of democratization (and to the softliners themselves, since they always threaten to rebound and to punish the liberalizers). According to Bova (1991), the hardliners become so strong during a period of democratization that the softliners must placate them somehow, in order to insure a successful democratic transition. In Poland and Hungary the reformers defeated the hardliners rather than appeasing them. In the ČSSR the opposite happened. According to Krejčí (1991: 102–3), Adamec *wanted* the hardliners to remain players in the transition game, so that he could position himself as a moderate between the hardliners and the opposition. This was not possible, however, because the hardliners collapsed. As Pavel (interviewed 29 April 1993) remarks, Adamec informed the Politburo of what was happening, but the latter was incapable of taking any action. It was extremely passive, and it gave no directions to the prime minister. Thus, Adamec's position *vis-à-vis* the opposition became much weaker. Adamec tried continuously to find groups of people whom he could use as an excuse for slowing down the democratization process. In this sense he did have a tactic of sorts. However, he was extremely inflexible in using this tactic. He continued to use it long after the hardliners collapsed. By the end of the negotiations, his claims that he needed to consult some small, unimportant organizations sounded more pathetic than convincing, and they could have hardly scared the opposition into dampening its demands.

Finally, the willingness of the two sides to trust each other greatly influences their ability to reach an accommodation. In contrast to Hungary and Poland, in Czechoslovakia critical intellectuals were excluded from the universities and public life. Those who conducted research had to hide their true beliefs. Thus, the Party elites did not have the same opportunity to establish contacts with them before the revolution. Nor were they as influenced by their thinking.

Consequently, the opposition had become demonized to a much greater extent than in, for example, Hungary. As Adamec's advisor Pavel (interviewed 29 April 1993) notes, Adamec had told him that he could not work with people such as Havel and Dienstbier. The prime minister's other advisor at the negotiations, Krejčí (interviewed 13 April 1992), admits that neither he nor Adamec trusted (or trusts even today) OF.

Similarly, Pithart (interviewed 14 April 1993) recalls the opposition's fear that the regime might try to trick them. He recalls that during the negotiations with Pitra, the prime minister of the Czech national government, the Communists left the room during a break. Meanwhile, some men entered the room who looked like plain-clothed police. The OF negotiators were afraid that these men would suddenly arrest them. Such thoughts certainly never entered the minds of the Hungarian or Polish opposition leaders during their negotiations.

Nevertheless, the negotiations might never have taken place unless *some* trust had developed. However, Krejčí (1991: 61) never mentions his and Adamec' increased trust for the *opposition* in his book on the events. Rather, he claims that their trust for MOST leaders Horáček and Kocáb increased by the day. This trust for the mediators made it easier to start negotiations than it would have been if the government had had to deal with the opposition directly from the beginning. Although MOST was able to gain Adamec's confidence, the only thing the opposition was able to gain *from* Adamec was his resignation.

The Negotiations

The Politburo resigned on Friday, November 24. Adamec announced the day after that he was willing to meet OF for negotiations and the first meeting took place on Sunday. Fortunately, Havel's assistant Vladimír Hanzel recorded all the negotiations and published their contents in his book *Zrychlený tep dějin* ("The Quick Pulse of History"). We know rather precisely, therefore, what the two sides said. Adamec took up two basic themes at the first meeting. First, the planned national two-hour strike was a threat for the economy, as were the ongoing student and theater strikes. Consequently, all these strikes should be called off. Second, he claimed he needed more time to carry out OF's demands. The actor Petr Čepek countered that OF was under pressure from the public to put these demands on the agenda. Thus, a pattern emerged in which Adamec tried to slow down the process of change, while OF representatives stressed the pressure under which "the public" put them to achieve results. Finally, as a confidence-building measure, Havel invited Adamec to speak at the large rally at Letná park that afternoon.[50]

This demonstration was one of the turning points for Adamec. At this time, he was a popular politician. He had stood up to the hardline Politburo. He was the only Communist leader willing to talk to the opposition. He had been the only Politburo member to advocate reforms. He had assured the populace that the government would not resort to force or declare martial law. Polls showed he was one of the country's most popular politicians.[51] And now he was speaking in front of an enthusiastic crowd of perhaps one million (or 1/12 of the entire population). But rather than play the hero's role which OF had prepared for him, Adamec blew it (Ash 1990c: 46). He spoke using the old jargon and talked about the need for discipline. He encouraged them not to strike and stressed the need for economic rather than political change. Not surprisingly, the cheers quickly turned into boos.

This is a typical example of Adamec's inability to adapt to the new situation. He was still unable to free himself from the chains of Marxist-Leninist dogma, even when he had clearly stopped believing in much of it. Horáček (interviewed 1 June 1992) recalls that after the speech, Adamec turned to him and said "you understand, I had to say what I said." Horáček interprets this as an admission that he was not willing to give up his Communist ideology, even when it hurt him politically. Similarly, Adamec's advisor, Pavel (interviewed 29 April 1993), asserts that as a Communist, the prime minister could not change his ways.

One could defend Adamec by claiming that he was continuing his tactics by placing himself between the regime hardliners and the opposition. However, the Politburo had already showed itself during the weekend to be incapable of dealing with the situation. The entire leadership had resigned, some of the hardliners had won back their positions, and no new strategy had emerged from the Central Committee meeting. Adamec's main advisor, Krejčí (interviewed 13 April 1992), admits that the Party was no longer a major actor in

---

50. For Adamec's statements, see Hanzel (1991: 14–5, 26, 32). Čepek's comment is on page 25. Havel's invitation is on page 16.
51. Slejška & Herzmann & collective (1990: 63) did a survey showing that Adamec was the second most popular politician after Dubček on November 24 (n = 447) and the most popular politician on December 1 (n = 456). His popularity quickly fell afterwards.

the events after that weekend. Thus, the opposition had little reason to believe the Party hardliners were holding Adamec back. Perhaps this is only clear in hindsight. However, after the general strike succeeded and the Party had become even weaker, Adamec continued his tactic, which was based on seeking a middle position between the hardline Party and the opposition. Since he could no longer credibly play the Party against the opposition, Adamec tried to avoid making concessions to OF by claiming that he could not reach any agreement with OF without first negotiating with a variety of small, insignificant opposition groups and some official organizations that were linked to the Party.

The next meeting took place on Tuesday, November 28. OF felt much stronger after the previous day's successful general strike. It began pressuring Adamec on concrete deadlines for the resignation of the president and the appointment of a new government. OF demanded that Adamec propose his new government on Sunday, December 3. Furthermore, they wanted parliament to quickly remove the law on the leading role of the Communist Party. Again, OF used the pressure from radicals as an excuse for laying down such deadlines. Havel also emphasized that the *public* expected these deadlines to be met. Otherwise, he concluded, OF would lose its credibility, and the public would come to believe it was willing to conserve the old system. If their remaining demands were not met, he added, "it could lead to an explosion." The ČKD factor worker, Petr Miller, played on Adamec's socialist ideology and stressed that at the factories, people were ready to strike.[52]

Adamec countered by trying to stall on the dates, although he did not criticize any of the basic contents of the demands. He claimed it would take time for parliament to make the necessary changes in the laws (such as the one on the Party's leading role). Since he was not a member of the federal assembly, he could not force it to pass laws. Moreover, he emphasized that OF was not alone. He had considered the wishes of other groups and the remaining political parties. As many as 18 different groups wanted to meet him, including the parties of the National Front. However, he did agree to reconstitute the government during the week (Hanzel 1991: 53–7).

---

52. Havel's statements are on pages 52 and 44 of Hanzel (1991), while Miller's is on page 55.

So Adamec's next chance to be a hero had come: he had the oppor-tunity to present a broad coalition government that would lead the country to democratic elections. OF did not demand that anyone from its ranks be a member of the new government, although it did "suggest" that the defense minister be someone who was not compro-mised. It also emphasized that it did not want the interior minister to be a compromised person or a Party member.

When Adamec presented his new government on December 3, he again disappointed the populace. His "15 + 5" solution meant that 15 of 20 ministers were to be Communists. If the prime minister himself was included, this meant that 16 of 21 were to be Communists. Čmejrek, a former researcher at the Central Committee (interviewed 23 March 1992), reflects that Adamec was not willing to adapt to the new situation in forming his government. Instead, he merely took up his old proposal to include some of the allied parties in the govern-ment—a proposal which the Politburo had rejected earlier that year. Adamec's inflexibility, though, was not due to a miscalculation. Both Krejčí and Pavel (interviewed 7 June 1993 and 29 April 1993) insist that Adamec knew that OF would reject his proposal. So why did he make it? It hardly made sense if Adamec wanted either to maintain power or to go down in history as the man who had democratized Czechoslovakia. Pavel insists Adamec no longer wanted to remain in politics, so gave up.[53]

By the next meeting, which took place two days later on December 5, the opposition had become still more radical. After Adamec had failed to present even a remotely acceptable proposal for a new cabinet, demonstrators and student activists increased their pressure on OF to make sure *real* change would come about. In an atmosphere filled with distrust, many people feared that Adamec was trying to trick them. Dienstbier (interviewed in Klusáková 1993: 8), the foreign minister in the first post-Communist government, recollects:

---

53. Krejčí (1991: 74) claims that Adamec originally intended this to be a temporary government, but his Deputy Prime Minister, Urban, forgot to say at the press conference that this was only the first step in the reconstruction of the government. Adamec himself, however, emphasized at the next negotiations the necessity of having a stable government until the elections (Hanzel 1991: 189). He adds that it would not be good for the country if he has to present a third government. Such statements do not fare well with Krejčí's claim that Adamec wanted to announce a temporary government which he would change several times before the elections take place.

"When the federal Prime Minister Adamec announced his 'reform' government, in which he didn't reform the basic framework at all, the people were outraged and demanded basic change." Žák (interviewed 11 May 1993) goes so far as to say that many of the opposition leaders were willing to accept Adamec's proposal during the first half-hour, since they were afraid of a constitutional crisis if both Husák and Adamec resigned. They changed their mind, however, after the overwhelmingly negative reaction from the population.

In the course of the previous week, the OF leaders had not demanded any posts in the government—in fact, they did not *want* any. Now they came prepared with a list of people who would make, in their estimation, appropriate ministers. This list was actually drawn up at the regime's own initiative. Adamec had told them the day before, via Pitra (the Czech prime minister), to present such a list (Hanzel 1991: 179). So they had to settle quickly on their proposals. So quickly did they do this, in fact, at times they forgot during the negotiations whom it was that they wanted for each post! (Hanzel 1991: 160–1.)

Thus, OF was forced by the regime as well as the populace to increase its demands. As Pithart (interviewed 2 March 1993) remembers, none of its leaders was prepared for a position in the government. Consequently, they had to improvise a list of ministers in a matter of minutes. The OF leaders felt they needed at least six months to prepare themselves for the responsibility of ruling (Draper 1993: 16–17).[54] Pithart says they had no concrete notion of how the new government should be composed, but they "instinctively understood that the [15: 5] ratio didn't correspond to the situation." He admits their demands had increased as the situation deteriorated. As OF campaign manager Gabal (interviewed 15 April 1993) puts it, they were pushed into taking government responsibility much earlier than they wanted to, because the Communist Party was simply collapsing.

Although OF had merely followed Adamec's instructions when they drew up their list of suggested ministers, the prime minister reacted extremely negatively from the start. His immediate response was to

---

54. Horáček (interviewed 1 June 1992), Pithart (interviewed 2 March 1993) and Gabal (interviewed 15 April 1993) all recall that OF was caught off guard by the sudden collapse of the Communist Party, and that they were unprepared for the sudden need to take government responsibility.

announce his resignation (Hanzel 1991: 165). The strange situation arose in which the opposition appeared more interested in having Adamec continue to rule than was Adamec himself. Pithart pleaded for Adamec to stay on by stating, "eventually the prime minister will reverse his decision" (Hanzel 1991: 172). Later, Pithart reminds him that they had not made any demands; they had only come with suggestions, just as Adamec had told them to do (Hanzel 1991: 177) The following dialogue between Adamec and OF delegates Pithart and Hanzel is worth quoting in full (Hanzel 1991: 175–6):

> Pithart: "I asked you whether there are certain names or numbers of ministers who are not acceptable].
> Adamec: No, I can't get around it—the conditions which you gave me aren't acceptable.
> Hanzel: Mr. Prime Minister, what isn't acceptable?
> Adamec: Everything.
> Havel: Everything?
> Adamec: The people as well as the system. The prime minister must have the right to put the government together in accordance with his own views. I can't appoint a government under pressure...
> Hanzel: What *is* your view?
> Adamec: Please, I can't say in detail today. I just got back from Moscow last night; I've only been here since the morning.

Here we have everything in a nutshell: OF wanted Adamec to continue as prime minister, while Adamec insisted on resigning. OF pleaded with him to tell them what he disapproved of, so that they could reach a compromise. Adamec was determined to resign, however, so he did not want to make any compromise. He could not tell them what he did not like about their suggestion. He could not even tell them what his own recommendation for the government was, since he apparently did not have one. He knew the system must change, but he had no idea of *how*. So he became incapable of action. He preferred giving up all responsibility, therefore, to remaining in office and influencing the transition.

To sum up the argument so far: Adamec's anti-reformist pragmatic acceptance had collapsed, so he had little idea what his institutional interests were in this new situation where the old institutions had collapsed. He had already understood that the old ideological legitimacy had not worked—the economic crisis has falsified the Marxist-Leninist doctrine. Yet he did not know what to replace it with, and he did not really *want* to replace it. Hence, he started losing confidence in his party's and his own ability to rule. He therefore wanted to leave politics rather than to maintain power. Despite this dilemma, however, he continued as prime minister and negotiated with the opposition. But he did not really know what it is he wanted, and he had too little time to prepare a properly thought-through strategy. Meanwhile, the opposition's pressure on the government increased apace with its rising self-confidence. The Politburo had resigned, and the Party was no longer a major actor. The general strike had been a success, proving that the intellectuals had gained the support of the workers. The students continued to strike and to pressure OF's leaders into pushing for faster change. The opposition understood, furthermore, that it had become stronger. So it increased its demands. At first Adamec continued his old tactic of placing himself between the hardliners and the opposition, even though the hardliners had already collapsed. When this tactics failed, he gives up.

Before giving up, however, Adamec made one last desperate attempt to save face. During the December 5 meeting, his advisor Pavel suddenly proposed that Adamec be made president—this after Adamec has behaved extremely aggressively toward his negotiating partners, saying that he would rather resign than consider their demands! Under normal circumstances, this would perhaps indicate Adamec was indeed thinking strategically. As president, after all, he would still have had some influence over the course of events, and perhaps he would still have gone down in history as a statesman who presided over his country's transition to democracy. However, these were not normal circumstances. To be sure, his maneuver showed his behavior to be more strategic than that of the hardline Politburo members who had become completely paralyzed during this period. However, the manner in which he tried to become president almost assured that he would lose face rather than save it.

First, if he had really wanted the opposition to do him a favor and to support his presidential candidacy, it would not have made sense to start the meeting by criticizing the opposition and saying he cannot work with the people they propose as ministers. Moreover, even after Pavel suggested that Adamec be made president and Havel had agreed to consider the possibility, Adamec continued to criticize the opposition. He claimed that his negotiating partners "want some kind of system about which I have reservations." Then he added snidely that "government is not a club for amateurs" (p. 187).

Second, by presenting the presidential plan first at an official nego-tiating meeting, he guaranteed he would lose face if the opposition turns down the proposal. This is especially true in view of the fact that Pavel announced the proposal *after* Adamec had already made it clear that he wants to resign. If the Adamec camp had wanted to leave open the possibility of retreat, it could have sent feelers to OF before the meeting took place. Krejčí, Adamec's advisor, met with MOST members Horáček and Kocáb before each negotiating round. He could have asked them to discuss the possibility with OF. If OF had been definitely opposed to the idea, the Adamec camp could have avoided mentioning it at the official negotiations, and Adamec can continue as prime minister.

Rather than being a well-thought out tactical move, Adamec's behavior came across more as a last desperate attempt to survive a deteriorating situation. Even when he discussed the presidential alter-native with the opposition seriously, he did not hide the fact that he really would have prefered to leave politics. He stresses: "Look—I'm telling you sincerely—it would be best for me if I hand in my resigna-tion tomorow, and then it's goodbye..." (Hanzel 1991: 184).

Later that day, OF and VPN held a meeting and agreed that they could not support Adamec for the presidency.[55] Under these circum-stances, Adamec had little alternative but to resign. The manner in which he sought the office left no room for him to retreat and to remain prime minister.

I conclude now on the question of trust. In previous chapters, I noted the importance of building contacts with opposition leaders well before negotiations begin. For example, as the regime in which they took part was liberalizing society, Polish and Hungarian reformers took advantage of the openings thereby created to establish contacts with the opposition. As the two sides came to know each other, each felt encouraged to trust the other. In the GDR, by contrast, no high-ranking members of the corporate entity had had any contacts at all with the opposition. This is one reason why no serious negotiations were undertaken until the entire old guard had resigned. In the ČSSR, Adamec's advisor, Krejčí, had met twice with some members of

---

55. Their joint letter to Adamec rejecting his presidential bid is reprinted in Hanzel (1991: 197–8) and Krejčí (1991: appendix).

MOST. The MOST connection made it much easier to start negotiations. The organization's leaders, Kocab and Horáček, met with Adamec when the revolution broke out, to make sure that the prime minister would commit himself to a non-violent solution. They acted as a go-between between OF and Adamec and organized the first official negotiations. But although MOST played an important role in establishing negotiations, it was not very successful in arranging meetings *before* the mass demonstrations broke out. It was only able to meet with Adamec's advisor Krejčí twice in the period before Novemember 17. It never met with Adamec (although its leaders did greet him at a theater performance). Two meetings with a prime minister's advisor is hardly enough to establish the kind of trust between regime and opposition that emerged in Hungary. There, the opposition had very strong and frequent contacts with reform communists. For example, the Hungarian Politburo member Pozsgay had become personal friends with opposition leaders and even encouraged them to organize political parties and organizations. Thus, the difference on the matter of trust between the Hungarian and Czechoslovak cases is quite substantial. Whereas Pozsgay *wanted* negotiations with opposition leaders, Adamec clearly undertook them reluctantly. He did not hide his lack of trust for people who were "political zeros."

During the historic meeting on December 5, Adamec was quick to take up the trust issue in connection with his resignation. He insisted that Havel had promised him that the students would end their strike. Havel immediately denied having made such a promise. Already, then, the lack of mutual trust led to squabbles over what OF had promised. Nevertheless, several OF negotiators claimed they had tried to convince the students to break off their strike. This suggests that they wanted to encourage Adamec to trust them. Pithart noted, for example, that he had spent six hours urging the students to end their strike. At first they yielded, but then they revoked their decision and continued their strike. Havel added that he had talked to the student strike coordinating committee, and that they had agreed to stop the strike. But then "there was a storm at the faculties" (Hanzel 1991: 166–7). The students kept up their pressure on OF to demand more radical change. This, in turn, made it more difficult for Adamec to trust the opposition. Nevertheless, Pithart tried to convince Adamec to stay on by claiming that the prime minister "has their trust for the moment. Otherwise he should resign" (Hanzel 1991: 173). And resign he did.

CONCLUSION

The Behavior of the Regimes

The East German and Czechoslovak regimes had built their pragmatic acceptance on the need to support the USSR and to avoid reforms. Thus, they developed institutional interests in maintaining orthodoxy. When Gorbachev started advocating reforms, their pragmatic legitimacy collapsed, as did their institutional interests. The Honecker regime in the GDR decided that it did not need to base its pragmatic acceptance on the Soviet Union. It embarked, accordingly, on a hardline strategy of re-ideologization. The Jakeš regime, in contrast, chose to support the Soviet slogans of *perestroika* and *glasnost* verbally, but without taking much concrete action. Both strategies failed to satisfy the rising expectations of the populace which Gorbachev's policies had inspired. For citizens no longer had any reason to accept their leaders pragmatically as the least evil leaders which the Kremlin would allow. The aging leaders filtered out information pointing to growing unrest. When confronted with a mass movement, they had no notion as to how to respond. A political void arose, as the leaders stood by helplessly. If they had developed a strategy, they might have escaped such mass pressures—either by using sufficient force at an earlier stage or by carrying out enough reforms to placate the populace. Even after a mass movement had emerged, they could at least have tried to shape the transitional set-up more to their advantage. They were under so much pressure, however, that they lost confidence in their ability to rule. After that, they preferred simply to give up.

Yet despite the great pressure they faced, and despite their patent lack of a strategy, they might still have achieved a more favorable result if they had been able to negotiate with the opposition more flexibly. But in contrast to the Polish and Hungarian reformers, who had established contact networks with the opposition, the East German and Czechoslovak Communist leaders did not trust the demonized opposition enough to seriously negotiate with them. The East German leaders did not even agree to Round Table talks until the regime had already basically collapsed. The Wall had already fallen (as had two general secretaries), and reunification was already on the political agenda. In the ČSSR, Adamec was willing to negotiate with OF, but even he mistrusted his negotiating partners, accusing them of putting a knife to his throat. Adamec's lack of trust added to his inflexibility. He decided, apparently, that he would not be able to run any government in which any of the demonized opposition leaders served. Consequently, he preferred to resign.

These two cases contrast sharply with the Hungarian and Polish cases, in which the leaders were able to shape the transition somewhat. The leaders in the countries with a reformist pragmatic acceptance were much more flexible than their conservative colleagues in the ČSSR and GDR. Since their institutional interests did not collapse when Gorbachev came to power, they could continue to build upon their reformist identities, and thus to shape the institutions before they collapsed. Since they took the initiative for negotiations with the opposition before a large-scale mass movement emerged, they had more time and were under less pressure than the leaders in the revolutionary countries. This made it easier for them to work out strategies for influencing the institutional compromise to their advantage.

It was also easier for them to reach an agreement with the opposition, because they had developed greater mutual trust. Regimes with a reformist pragmatic acceptance were able to liberalize their societies gradually. In such a relatively open climate, reformers were able to establish contact networks with dissidents some time before the negotiations began. This gave both sides a chance the feel each other out and to get to know each other. Moreover, universities and research institutions in the liberalized climate became relatively open, pluralist places, where Communists and non-Communists could exchange opinions. University colleagues met each other on opposing sides of the Round Table. In the Polish case, the Communists also took conscious steps to increase *Solidarność's* trust in them.

The Rise of Mass Movements
The other major aim of this book is to explain how mass movements could emerge so easily and bring down the regimes. According to my partial model of participation in rebellions, intellectuals are more likely than others to become dissidents, because they have the greatest institutional incentives to do so. In both the GDR and ČSSR, this indeed happened. In the GDR, the dissidents mostly belonged to a younger generation and centered around the alternative movements. In the ČSSR, their most influential organization was Charter 77. In Prague during the late 1980s, independent student groups also emerged. These student groups planned the November 17 demonstration which sparked off the revolution. In both countries, intellectuals were encouraged by the changes in neighboring countries and in the

USSR, but they had little faith in their own leaders. In both countries, they became more active upon becoming outraged at repressive events. In the ČSSR they reacted immediately after the police arrested Havel and brutally repressed the demonstrators during the Palach week. In the GDR, it was the falsified local elections in May that outraged many intellectuals. In both countries, dissident groups icked up their activities during the summer in response to these events.

Of course, intellectuals can never succeed without gaining support from other groups. The previous Polish, Hungarian and East German uprisings showed that revolts are most successful when intellectuals and workers can unite. Workers, however, are not normally willing to revolt unless they are suffering economically. During an economic downturn, however, they become willing to participate in a revolt if they feel outraged. In previous cases, they had revolted immediately in response to policies which lowered their standards of living. During the two revolutions in 1989, however, they revolted more in response to regime policies that outraged them. My analysis indicates, however, that they would have been much less likely to revolt had the regimes not lost their ideological legitimacy, which had been partly based on promising improved living standards.

In both countries, acts of police repression induced large numbers of workers to revolt. In the GDR, this took place when the police attacked demonstrators during Gorbachev's speech (and not only in Berlin but in other cities as well). In the ČSSR, the solidarity effect came immediately after the police had attacked students on November 17.

One major difference between the two countries lay in the type of cooperation between intellectuals and workers. In the ČSSR, the intellectuals (both students and OF) tried to mobilize workers directly through a general strike. In the GDR, most of the strikes began spontaneously, making it more difficult to organize them. At the time, the repressive apparatus was so threatening that nobody dared openly organize demonstrations. Instead, they broke out at places where everyone knew people would gather—such as the main square in Leipzig on Mondays, after the prayer for peace. Nevertheless, workers and intellectuals cooperated indirectly even in the GDR. Workers gathered at the square after the church officials had held the prayers. NF leaders Voiced the demands of the populace for change. They and other intellectuals also organized demonstrations and threatened strikes after Honecker had resigned and the risk of being attacked had subsided.

In both cases, the collective-action problem was spreading information rather than ensuring the ability to reward or punish participants. In the GDR this was solved in part through spontaneous co-ordination. In the ČSSR, students were able to gain access to the factories by having famous actors and actresses accompany them. In both cases the mass media was also important. East Germans could easily watch West German TV, while Czechs and Slovaks could listen to Western radio broadcasts, such as voice of America. In addition, students often had access to fax machines, photo-copy machines and telephones from the universities and the SSM. Film students also made videos of the police brutality which they were able to show workers in the factories.

According to my partial modelof rebellions, professionals are not likely to revolt unless the uprising has a good chance of succeeding, because they have the strongest institutional incentives to refrain from such activities. They never participated in any uprisings on a large scale until 1980–1 in Poland. A survey of the Leipzig demonstrations also indicates that intellectuals and workers were more willing to demonstrate than are white-collar workers. Unfortunately, there is little data available to say anything conclusive about the behavior of professionals during these revolutions. What is important is that, in the ČSSR as in Poland, the intellectuals realized they needed worker support in order to succeed. I do not know of any special efforts to recruit professionals to the movement. By the time hundreds of thousands had joined the demonstrations, many professionals were certainly taking part too. But, except for Leipzig, no information is available about the point at which their numbers grew in both countries, nor is there much information about the degree of their involvement. The survey taken in Leipzig survey showed that professionals were underrepresented.

Finally, it is possible that the regimes in both countries would have been able to stop the revolution had they been willing to use violence. In contrast to Przeworski's claims (1991: 6), it appears that it was the regimes themselves—rather than the armed forces—that were the main obstacle to a Chinese solution. They were too paralyzed to give the armed forces orders. In the ČSSR, the military even offered to carry out a Polish-type of *coup*, but the Central Committee turned down the offer. In the GDR, the police had showed that they were capable of using violence during previous demonstrations—especially the one on the day of Gorbachev's speech. In Leipzig on the following day, three intellectuals and three lower-rank Party officials were able to prevent a repeat of these police actions, because the central Party leaders failed to give the local police any instructions.

Chapter 11

SUMMARY OF THE MODEL

In the previous chapters, I have developed several partial models capable of explaining different aspects of the collapse. In this concluding chapter, I put the various pieces of this complex puzzle together into a comprehensive model.

1. CRISIS AT THE ECONOMIC BASE

Under the Soviet-type system, the ruling class consisted of the members of the state administration down to the factory managers, and of the members of the Party apparatus down to the heads of the factory Party organizations. The material basis of the power of this class lay in its collective control over 1) the means of production and the productive process, 2) the social surplus product, and 3) the channels of distribution and thus of consumption. At the superstructural level, the ruling class maintained its power through its dictatorial control over the state apparatus, which it used to try to gain monopoly control over all social decisions and all debate. Even if it rarely succeeded in achieving complete totalitarian rule, that was the ultimate goal of the system. In order to legitimize this enormous concentration of power, the members of the corporate entity claimed to have a monopoly on Truth. Consequently, no mechanisms for an open debate or for democratic decision-making were necessary. The second pillar of the ruling class' ideological legitimacy was its claim that, thanks to its possession of the Truth, it would by able to improve living standards markedly. The economy, it promised, would outperform that of the capitalist countries of the West.

The ruling corporate entity maintained its monopoly control over the means of production through a command economy. Such a mode of production may be able to perform relatively well for an economy based on heavy industry. But the social relations of production involved were too inflexible to adapt to modern telecommunications and other advanced technologies. As the forces of production developed more rapidly in a direction requiring greater flexibility, the social relations of production hindered the application of these new technologies.

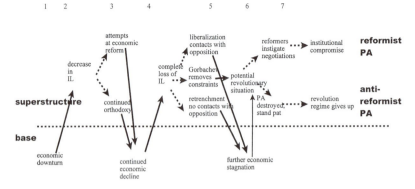

Note: IL = Ideological Legitimacy, PA = Pragmatic Acceptance

This problem in dealing with the new technologies manifested itself in several ways. Capital productivity declined, notwithstanding the fact that the regimes invested more heavily in research and development than Western countries did. Trading patterns began to liken the center-periphery relationship characteristic of trade between so-called Third World countries and the West." That is, exports of finished goods declined while imports of high-tech goods increased. To pay for these imports, the countries of Eastern Europe increased their dependency on the export of raw materials and of half-finished goods. However, their domestic economies were inflexible to such an extent as to be incapable of utilizing the technologies imported from the West efficiently.

As a result, by the late 1970s, the East European economies had entered into a period of economic stagnation and decline. I note in chapter 3 that there is widespread agreement that the economies of Eastern Europe fell further behind those of the West during the 1980s. Some critics claim it is not "fair" to compare the countries of Europe's periphery with those of its center, but even they agree that both rulers and ruled in Eastern Europe did in fact make this comparison. This is not surprising, since much of the regimes' ideological legitimacy was based on their claim to superior economic performance. Furthermore, official statistics show that growth rates were declining. If the calculation of growth rates is amended to take account of realistic rates of inflation, then growth rates may even have been negative for this period, and living standards may have been falling. By 1989, moreover, Poland and Hungary had very high rates of inflation (bordering on hyperinflation). They also had a foreign debt that was rising alarmingly, threatening the solvency of the two countries. Experts often considered the GDR to be in a much better position, but its debts were becoming so high that servicing them became the main focus of economic policy in the late 1980s. Even the ČSSR went through an entire decade of negative growth if realistic inflation rates are taken into account.

The economic crisis would not have had any political consequences had it not influenced the perceptions of both the rulers and the ruled. I cited the memoirs of former Communist leaders, as well as published and unpublished interviews with them, to show that they believed their countries were suffering from economic crisis. Then I turned to the general public. Available public-opinion surveys from Poland and the ČSSR show that an overwhelming majority of the population believed that their country faced an economic crisis. For example, a survey in the Czech Republic showed that no respondents thought there was little or no economic problem. One Hungarian survey from 1986 showed that 61% of the population described its economic situation as hopeless or continually worsening. Later surveys in Hungary and the GDR did not pose these questions directly. Nevertheless, one survey in 1989 showed that 80% of Hungarians believed that their living standards were lower than those in neighboring Austria. Meanwhile, surveys of East German youth showed a dramatic drop in the percentage believing that the world would become socialist. This indicates that at least young people were becoming disillusioned with their country's economic and political development. It is difficult to know how much of their dissatisfaction was caused by political and how much by economic factors. One can assume, however, that the economic situation had some influence on their thinking.

2. THE DECLINE OF IDEOLOGICAL LEGITIMACY

The economic crisis presented major problems for the members of the corporate entity. As already noted, they based their ideological legitimacy on two claims: 1) that they possessed a monopoly on Truth, and 2) that they were able to vastly improve living standards. This type of legitimacy made the regimes particularly vulnerable in a period of economic decline.

To be sure, these regimes never enjoyed much popular legitimacy. The majority of the population never accepted them as their rightful rulers. Nevertheless, the majority of the corporate entity did at one time see itself as the rightful ruler. Since this ideological legitimacy was tied to economic performance, the members of the ruling class were forced to confront their failures when their goals were not met. This undermined their confidence in their ability to rule.

At the same time, poor economic performance offered society the chance to question the regimes' monopoly on Truth. As the decades went on, members of society became more critical of the system, and intellectuals became more radical in their critiques. Although many of the latter had started out as reform Communists, most of them lost faith in the regimes' reformability by the 1980s.

If the regimes had succeeded in reforming their economies and in restoring prosperity, the members of the corporate entity would probably have regained confidence in their ability to rule, and society would have likely been less questioning of the regimes' claims to a monopoly on Truth. For the reasons discussed below, however, none of the reform attempts were able to meet their goals. The regimes sank deeper into crisis.

3. THE FAILURE OF ECONOMIC REFORMS

Despite the mounting economic problems, the regimes might have survived and propped up their sagging ideological legitimacy if they had succeeded in reforming the economy. Not all the regimes reacted similarly to the economic crisis; however, neither those regimes which attempted reforms nor those which avoided them were able to improve economic performance noticeably. The reforms failed because they met too much resistance from different groups within the ruling corporate entity. The only way to break this resistance would have been to liberalize the political and economic system so that the hard-liners lost their influence. Thus, the rulers had to chose between liberalization and reverting to repression. Liberalization is dangerous, because it threatens the Party-state's monopoly on power. Consequently, cycles of reform and repression emerged.

Various groups within and without the corporate entity opposed certain aspects of the reforms, due to their conflicting institutional interests. Among the conflicts between outside and inside groups, I emphasize the conflicting interests between the corporate entity and workers. There were also conflicting interests between professionals and workers; however, since professionals generally have stronger incentives than workers to support market reforms, I do not analyze this conflict. Within the corporate entity, there were conflicts of interests between the Soviet Union and the national Communist rulers. At the national level, there were conflicts between the various levels of the corporate entity.

The most stubborn resistance came from the middle levels of the Party apparatus and state bureaucracy. These were the groups that would suffer the most from market-oriented reforms. If enterprises became more autonomous from state planners, mid-level economic bureaucrats would lose their influence over the enterprises. Many could even expect to lose their job. Meanwhile, mid-level Party bureaucrats would have also become obsolete if the Party were no longer involved in monitoring the activities of individual firms.

There were conflicts between the Party and the state as well, and even among state ministries. Unlike their counterparts in Western democracies, moreover, the elites failed to establish a legitimate system of mediating between these conflicting institutional interests. The leaders also worried that, even if market-oriented reforms were to succeed, increased autonomy for the enterprises and democratization of the workplaces would eventually threaten their power. Often, therefore, they moderated or even drew back their own reform proposals. In the most radical case of economic reforms, i.e. those in Hungary, I come to the rather surprising conclusion that, in fact, members of the Party apparatus worked so strongly against increased state autonomy that the Hungarian government actually enjoyed less autonomy from the Party once market reforms were carried out.

The manner in which the leaders interpreted their institutional interests varied over time and between countries. Some of the decisions made by the Polish, East German and Hungarian leaders worsened the economic crisis. A prime example is the decision in the early 1970s by the General Secretary of the Polish Central Committee, Giereck, to finance capital investment by borrowing heavily from the West. This policy backfired during the oil crisis of the late 1970s, when Western demand for Polish goods dropped. A mounting debt crisis was the result.

4. FURTHER ECONOMIC DECLINE AND THE COMPLETE LOSS OF IDEOLOGICAL LEGITIMACY

Regardless of whether a country chose reform (Hungary and Poland) or retrenchment (the ČSSR and GDR), the economy continued to stagnate. When Gorbachev started talking about reforms and admitting that the economy was not functioning well, the last remains of ideological legitimacy disappeared. How could the East European leaders claim to have a monopoly on Truth when their economic policies had consistently failed over the course of the last two decades? How could the old system be the only correct one, when even the Soviet Union began to move away from it?

Gorbachev's rise to power can itself be described in dialectical terms, in which the economic base and political superstructure constantly influence each other. The Politburo elected this reformer to the post of general secretary in the first place because of the economic downturn. Consequently, the economic crisis was the underlying cause of Gorbachev's rise to power.[1] At first Gorbachev tried carrying out economic reforms. When these met resistance from the state bureaucracy and the Party apparatus, he tried to liberalize the system. He hoped that, by allowing the press to write critical articles, he could put pressure on the conservative hardliners. He also introduced multi-candidate elections, so that the populace could remove hardliners from their positions. All of these measures, along with the worsening economic crisis, called the Kremlin's ideological legitimacy into question still more. This in turn brought into question the ideological legitimacy of the East European satellites.

5. FURTHER DECLINE: GORBACHEV AND THE CHOICE OF LIBERALIZATION OR RETRENCHMENT

The Gorbachev Factor

Despite the economic crisis and their inability to reform the economy, the East European leaders might have remained in power if the Soviet Union had been willing to prop them up with the Red Army's tanks. Consequently, one cannot ignore Gorbachev's role. Gorbachev's policies removed the last vestiges of the system's ideological legitimacy. His political reforms—easing censorship, allowing multi-candidate elections, etc.—encouraged the citizens of Eastern Europe to believe that change could come to their countries as well. This put more pressure on the East European regimes to liberalize their system.

---

1. Even if some readers might dispute this claim that the economic crisis was the cause of Gorbachev's raise to power, Gorbachev's room for carrying out reforms clearly increased as the economy worsened. If he had come to power during a period of increasing growth, then even if he personally had wanted to liberalize the political system, he could have hardly gained the support of the Politburo for such measures.

I maintain, though, that this pressure was indirect. Gorbachev did little to intervene in the East European countries directly. Nevertheless, Gorbachev's passivity toward Poland and Hungary created an opening which the reformists could utilize to initiate negotiations with the opposition. While Gorbachev's policies made life easier for the Polish and Hungarian reformists, it had the opposite effect on the East German and Czechoslovak hardliners. The available evidence indicates that Gorbachev did not try to force the conservative East German and Czechoslovak regimes to alter their policies. Once the USSR embarked on the path of reform, however, the orthodox regimes could no longer compel their citizens to accept their power pragmatically—i.e., on the grounds that the Kremlin had put these regimes in power in order to prevent reforms, while the Red Army would see to it that they would not propose any meaningful reforms. Thus, these regimes' institutional interests (which I term "pragmatic acceptance") collapsed, giving the former Soviet puppets little clue as to how to behave in the new situation. Gorbachev's mere decision to stay neutral rather than to support repression also made it more difficult for the orthodox regimes to defeat the rebellions with violent means.

The Reformist Regimes Liberalize Society

In chapter 6, I introduced the notion of pragmatic acceptance. All of the countries except for Poland had suffered Soviet invasions. Even Poland faced threatened invasions twice (in 1956 and 1981). Each of these events was marked by a change of leadership in the satellite regime.[2] These new leaders tried to induce the populace to accept their rule for pragmatic reasons. In Poland and Hungary, the leaders gained the people's pragmatic acceptance on a relatively reformist basis. Moscow would not let these leaders do whatever they wanted, but said leaders could still try to expand the boundaries of what the Kremlin would allow. For example, the Red Army marched into Budapest in 1956 in order to prevent the country from leaving the Warsaw Pact and from carrying out free elections. Thus, the new regime knew it had to remain a faithful ally of the Soviet Union, and it had to maintain its political monopoly. But this still left a relatively

---

2. Technically, Jaruzelski had become general secretary in Poland a few months before declaring martial law. Still, he became general secretary during a period of threatened invasion, inasmuch as the indirect threats began well before his rise to power. Moreover, he did not consolidate his power until after he had carried out the military *coup*.

large space to maneuver in the fields of economic reform and cultural openness. Although the populace might have preferred to leave the Warsaw Pact and to introduce political democracy, it realized this was unrealistic, given the Soviet Union's dominance. Thus, the citizens were willing to accept the regime on *pragmatic* grounds.

Both the Polish and Hungarian regimes established reformist identities, which gave them institutional interests in continuing to appear as reformists. Steps back toward orthodoxy would have endangered their pragmatic acceptance and turned the populace against them. Even after martial law came to Poland, the new leadership insisted it would continue to experiment with reforms.

Although reform usually began with economic reforms, the Polish and Hungarian regimes also started liberalizing society. They could liberalize even further when Gorbachev became general secretary. In the relatively open atmosphere that arose, official researchers at the universities and academies could publish critical reports on social and economic developments. These reports further eroded the regimes' ideological legitimacy and caused the reformers to lose even more confidence in the system. As the reformers lost confidence, they took advantage of the liberal atmosphere in society to establish contacts with opposition leaders. Thus, leaders from the corporate entity and from the opposition got to know each other, with increased trust between the two sides. This made it easier to negotiate an institutional compromise when the time was opportune.

The Orthodox Regimes Oppose Reforms

In contrast to their Polish and Hungarian comrades, the Czechoslovak and East German leaders developed a pragmatic acceptance based on the need to prevent reforms. The Czechoslovak leadership had come to power after the Warsaw Pact invasion in 1968. The new Czechoslovak leadership claimed that its allies had offered "fraternal help" in order to prevent a reversion to capitalism. Thus, all economic reforms were by definition "capitalist." Since the new leaders had come to power to prevent capitalism, they would not engage in any reformist experiments.

Similarly, the East German regime based its pragmatic acceptance on the need to prevent all deviations from orthodoxy. The orthodox East German leadership had only survived because the Red Army had saved it from the irate workers during the 1953 rebellion. Afterwards the USSR made it clear that it was not about to accept any destabilizing reforms in the country against which it had fought two world wars.

Thus, both the East German and Czechoslovak regimes tried to avoid reforms even after Gorbachev came to power. However, the new Soviet leader eroded their pragmatic acceptance more and more with each passing year. When the USSR started carrying out radical reforms, it became progressively difficult for the orthodox regimes to claim they were in power because the USSR wanted them to prevent reforms. Their institutional interests in supporting orthodoxy and Soviet policy simultaneously became contradictory. When their institutional interests broke down, the members of the orthodox regimes lost their bearings: they no longer knew how to act.

Most members of the Czechoslovak elite believed that Gorbachev would eventually lose power, so they tried to wait him out. In the meanwhile, they publicly advocated some cautious reforms, which fell far short of those proposed by Gorbachev and far short of those seen during the Prague Spring. Basically, these leaders tried to pretend that nothing new had happened. Moreover, despite their decision to allow one independent demonstration in 1988, they basically continued their hardline policy against the opposition. The police broke up several demonstrations violently, for example, and they continued to jail dissidents. Thus, in contrast to the situation in Hungary and Poland, no contacts emerged between the regime and the opposition until the fall of 1989, when an advisor to the prime minister met twice with two members of the organization *MOST*.

Similarly, the East German rulers tried to act as if nothing had changed. In fact, they became even more hardline (undertaking, for example, a re-ideologization campaign). At the same time, they suddenly claimed that the GDR faced different conditions than the USSR, and so did not have to follow the same policies. This turnaround was hardly convincing for a population which had only recently been accustomed to hearing slogans about how they had to "learn from the USSR." As in the ČSSR, then, the regime did not establish any contacts with the opposition which might have facilitated feelings of trust and eventually negotiations between the two sides.

6. A POTENTIALLY REVOLUTIONARY SITUATION EMERGES

In chapter 8, I constructed a partial model to explain the pattern of revolts that emerged in the East European countries. I examined the revolts in the GDR in 1953; in Hungary in 1956; and in Poland in 1968, 1970, 1976 and 1980. In addition, I took a look at the dissident movements in all four countries. Then, in Chapter 10, I showed that this partial model can explain the mass uprisings in the GDR and the ČSSR in 1989.

I began with an analysis of interests. I claimed that the members of the corporate entity comprised a ruling class which exploited the workers, the professionals and the intellectuals. Consequently, the members of these classes or strata had interests in changing these relations of exploitation. I called these interests "postulated interests," because they are not directly empirically observable. They are, rather, a theoretical construction based on an analysis of the relations of production.

The next step was to analyze why most members of the different classes and strata only follow their postulated interests under certain circumstances. For example, workers usually only rebel during periods of economic decline, while many intellectuals oppose the system even when the economy is doing relatively well. Meanwhile, professionals have a tendency to wait until a rebellion has already began before actively participating.

I devised a partial model according to which members of these groups experience structures of institutional incentives for following their postulated interests in fighting for change.

Institutional Interests

Intellectuals, for several reasons, are more likely to become dissidents than are members of other groups. First, their voice is more likely to be heard. In general, they are more articulate and better known than members of the other classes. They are also more likely to have Western contacts. These contact-persons can spread their message (via Radio Free Europe, for instance). Moreover, when intellectual dissidents wind up in prison, their Western colleagues can start international campaigns demanding their release.

Second, intellectuals often face contradictory institutional incentives deriving from a variety of sources. Their superiors from the Party-state apparatus may demand they adhere to a "socialist-realist style," while their audience may favor something very different. Their profession, meanwhile, may demand something else again. For example, an author who truly supports the Communist Party, may face an audience which does not want to buy books written in a socialist-realist style. Thus, if the author wants to become popular, he or she faces contradictory incentives. While genuinely supporting the Party, moreover, this author might find it difficult to express his- or herself in a socialist-realist style. He/she faces the choice, accordingly, of being a second-rate official author or an internationally acclaimed dissident author. In sum, an author who actually supports the Communist Party politically may still face some pressures to become a dissident.

In contrast, workers face no such pressures. Even if workers oppose the system, they can keep their opinion to themselves. Nobody demands that an assembly-line worker press buttons in a socialist-realist manner. In contrast to professionals, moreover, they are not so dependent on patronage. A doctor can only get a good position at a hospital with the approval of certain Party functionaries. This is not the case for a cleaning lady or an assembly-line worker. Patronage relations become more important the higher one climbs up a career ladder. Thus, unskilled workers face less pressure to conform to the party than do ambitious professionals. In brief, workers face less pressure than intellectuals do to oppose the system, and less pressure than do intellectuals and professionals to support it.

The question is: why are workers more willing to rebel during economic downturns? First, they are the hardest hit by economic problems. Their income in terms of money may not be much lower than that earned by professionals, but their access to privileged goods is much more limited. In the Soviet-type economy, the ability to buy many goods is a function not of money but of connections.

Second, since workers are at the bottom of the social hierarchy, they have the least to lose by rebelling. As long as they are not sent to prison, they have the right to a job. While a doctor may consider it a punishment to be forced to work as a window-washer, a window-washer will hardly consider it a punishment. This does not mean workers face no risks at all, but their risks are lower than those face by other groups.

Third, being the worst-off economically, they are also likely to be the most angry when the regime does not keep its promises of higher living standards. After all, these regimes staked much of their ideological legitimacy on the promise of surpassing the West economically.

Fourth, workers also know their protests will be more effective than those of other groups. Since the regimes claim to represent the working class, they are more susceptible to a working-class uprising than to a demonstration of lawyers. The workers also know that they have strength in numbers. In these countries considered in this book, they comprised the majority of society.

The last group is the professionals. They have usually been the most passive group, even though they would probably gain the most in material terms from a transition to a more market-oriented system. Because of their position, however, they have the strongest institutional incentives to remain loyal to the system irrespective of their personal opinions. In contrast to workers, they are highly dependent on the patronage system for advancing in their careers. And in contrast to intellectuals, they normally lack international contacts and domestic fame. They tend as a result to be cautious, becoming active in the opposition only *after* a revolt has begun. At this point, their chances of being punished have declined, which frees them to pursue their postulated interests in socioeconomic change.

Subjective Level

At the subjective level, feelings of outrage and rising expectations are important factors in decisions to rebel. Intellectuals often take the step to becoming active dissidents when the Party-state commits a repressive act that outrages them. Similarly, workers are more likely to join a rebellion if the regime announces policies that will directly lower their living standards. In addition, if a crisis prevails economically, and if— under such conditions—the security forces attack demonstrators, this is likely to enrage workers enough to persuade them to join the emerging rebellion. An uprising is more likely to succeed if intellectuals and workers cooperate with each other. There are some telling differences in this regard between certain events in Poland: between, on the one hand, the failed intellectual protests in 1968 and the failed worker rebellion in 1970; and, on the other, the more successful *Solidarność* revolt in 1980. By 1980, intellectuals had learned the importance of cooperating directly with workers. Once workers and intellectuals cooperate in a mass uprising, professionals are more likely to risk getting involved.

Two further factors are also important for the success of a rebellion in the Soviet-type system. One is the ability to build up communication networks. The other is the behavior of the regime toward demonstrators. Since the Party-state has a monopoly on the legal mass media, instigators of rebellion must find some means of spreading their message to the rest of the populace. Moreover, although mildly repressive acts will likely induce others to join in, the regime can crush the uprising if it is willing to use sufficient force. As long as the opposition is not armed, a regime does not need the support of the entire armed forces to put down an uprising. It is enough that *some* units are willing to attack demonstrators and that—at the same time—there are no other units which are willing to fight against the regime.

Summary of the Partial Model
By combining the institutional and subjective levels, I developed a partial model of the collapse of the Soviet-type system. This partial model does not explain the entire collapse, but it explains when people are willing to rebel in the Soviet-type system. I built this partial model in chapter 7 on the basis of an analysis of the failed rebellions in Hungary, Poland and the GDR before 1988, as well as on the basis of a look at the dissident movements in all four countries (including the ČSSR). This partial model has the advantage, therefore, of being applicable to all four countries, and for all periods of Communist rule. Then, in chapter 9, I applied this partial model to the East German and Czechoslovak revolutions. In a simplified form, my partial model is as follows:

1) A group of intellectual dissidents already exists, since intellectuals have the strongest institutional interests in rebelling. If they feel outraged at certain acts of repression, they are likely to rebel. They have no chance of success unless they gain working-class support. During a period of rising expectations, the number of intellectuals who are willing to engage in oppositional activities increases, as does the level of activities among previous dissidents.

2) If there is a period of economic hardship, workers will have a greater propensity to rebel, because—being the worst off economically—they feel less constrained by their institutional interests. Consequently, they become more willing to follow their postulated interests in fighting for change. They know, moreover, that a regime which bases its ideological legitimacy on the notion that it represents the true interests of the workers will have a harder time repressing them than in repressing other groups.

3) The rebellion, in turn, will also be sparked off by a Party-state action that causes feelings of outrage. If the economic crisis is grave, it will normally be decisions bearing directly on economic policy that cause a worker rebellion. If, on the other hand, the economic crisis has not caused a dramatic fall in living standards, a rebellion may still be sparked off if the regime applies repressive methods which outrage the

intellectuals and inspire them to acts of resistance—act of resistance which may then spread to workers.

4) If intellectuals and workers are able to cooperate, the chances of a successful uprising greatly increase; this induces professionals to join in (notwithstanding their stronger institutional interests in avoiding conflict with the regime). Professionals have such strong postulated interests in change, that they are likely to join in once the rebellion is large enough to lower the chances of direct reprisals against them. The ability to communicate is the main collective-action problem for political entrepreneurs seeking to persuade these groups to participate.

5) Since very few of the revolutionaries believe they have a chance of succeeding against either their domestic army or the Soviet army, they give up if the regime uses enough force. Consequently, their only hope for success lies ultimately in the paralysis of the regime.

Revolutionary Situation

Chapter 8 concluded with the claim that the regimes in all four countries were facing a potentially revolutionary situation in 1988. The intellectuals had become more critical and were better organized; they were potential political entrepreneurs for a revolt.

There was also an increasing risk of a workers' rebellion, since the economic situation was deteriorating in all four countries. A growing consensus had emerged among official economists that the economy in these countries were going out of balance. Belt-tightening measures would be necessary to re-establish this balance. The regimes had not yet outraged society, but the economic measures they were contemplating would likely have led to this result. Furthermore, Gorbachev's liberalization policies and passive foreign-policy stance increased expectations among the populace that change might come to their countries. The Round Table discussions in Poland and Hungary raised expectations further among East Germans and Czechoslovaks. The *Solidarność* uprising set a precedent for cooperation between intellectuals and workers. It had also become easier for potential revolutionaries to communicate their messages. Since signing the Helsinki accords, the regimes could no longer block Western radio broadcasts. Thus, dissidents could spread their message via radio. In addition, the advent of video, fax and photocopy machines facilitated the quick spread of information. Finally, since Gorbachev gave high priority to improving relations with the West, the East European regimes could no longer be certain of receiving Soviet military help during a rebellion.

All these factors indicate that the East European countries were faced with a possibly revolutionary situation. At this point, the regimes had three basic options. They could take the initiative for negotiations with the opposition, they could clamp down on the opposition, or they could continue behaving as before. a) The advantage of starting talks with the opposition lies in the fact that the negotiating position of the regime in question will be stronger *before* the outbreak of a revolt than after. b) If the regime clamps down hard enough, it might be able to prevent a revolt from breaking out. (If a revolution breaks anyway, however, the risk that society will demand vengeance against the former rulers will be much greater.) c) Finally, there are at least two possible advantages with the cautious approach of continuing as before. First, if no mass movement emerges (e.g., because intellectuals and workers refuse to cooperate), then the leaders will be able to maintain power without making any concessions. Second, if the leaders do end up losing power to a revolutionary movement, the demands for vengeance will be weaker than they would have been if the regime had increased its repression immediately preceding the revolution.

7.A. REFORMERS START NEGOTIATIONS IN POLAND AND HUNGARY

As a revolutionary situation developed, the reformist regimes in Poland and Hungary behaved much differently than their orthodox counterparts in the GDR and ČSSR. Since the Polish and Hungarian Communists based their pragmatic acceptance on a reformist identity, it was not difficult for them to take their reforms a few steps further and to negotiate with the opposition. They had claimed to be testing the limits of what the Soviet Union would allow. Then, suddenly, this dominant country indicated that there were not many reforms it would not allow. The reformist regimes were able to take advantage of this political opening. As the economic crisis worsened, moreover, they grew fearful that a revolt might break out when they introduced the belt-tightening measures, which they believed were necessary for averting economic collapse. They believed it better, then, to meet the opposition at the negotiating table rather than to wait and meet it on the streets.

The existence of contact-networks between reform Communists and the opposition also facilitated the negotiations. These contacts increased trust between the two sides, making it easier for them to cooperate. Both regimes had established contacts with the opposition, but the Polish regime had a more difficult time getting the opposition to trust it. The Polish rulers had already reneged once on an agreement to allow free trade unions. (It had allowed *Solidarność* to operate freely but suddenly banned the organization upon proclaiming martial law.) The

Hungarian regime, by contrast, consisted of newly elected reform Communists without any connection to the repression that had followed the 1956 rebellion.

Nevertheless, the Polish regime enjoyed more trust than the East German and Czechoslovak regimes did. Like their counterparts in Hungary, representatives of the Polish regime had already come into contact with opposition leaders several years before the negotiations began. In addition, the relatively open cultural atmosphere in Poland and Hungary meant that colleagues from the same university department often ended up sitting across the table from each other at the round table negotiations. Moreover, the Polish regime consciously tried to create an atmosphere of trust at the negotiations. To signal that it took the opposition seriously, for example, the regime closed down the motorway and gave the *Solidarność* delegation a police escort to the first meeting. Other measures included having representatives from each side co-chair the various subcommittees, and ensuring that the delegations from the two sides were of an equal size. So the trust factor favored the Polish regime over its East German and Czechoslovak counterparts, but left it in a weaker position than the Hungarian regime.

The Reformist Regimes: Subjective Perceptions

Although the leaders in Poland and Hungary *were able* to take advantage of Gorbachev's opening, this does not mean that they *had* to do so, or that they had to do so in the same manner. They had a similar reformist pragmatic acceptance, but the result was different: the Hungarians reached a different sort of institutional compromise than the Poles did.

The Polish leaders did obtain certain guarantees. For example, in return for the instituting of completely free elections to the senate, 65% of the seats in the *Sejm* were reserved for the Communists and their allies. Nevertheless, the rulers proposed an electoral system that made it difficult for them to win the freely contested seats in the *Sejm* and the senate. Their own advisors warned them they would have trouble gaining a majority in the single member-districts, since they faced a united opposition behind *Solidarność*. These advisors calculated that the Party would most likely win a great many more seats under a system with proportional representation. Yet, they turned down this professional advice. The results were telling: the Communists did not win a single contested seat.

In contrast, the Hungarian rulers behaved much more strategically, notwithstanding the fact that they did not demand any special institutional guarantees. They supported completely democratic elections instead. But they tried to shape the democratic institutions to their advantage. First, they advocated majority elections. Proportional representation may have made more sense for the Polish Communists, but majority elections would have been better for the Hungarian party, because the Hungarian opposition was split into a number of small parties. In contrast to the situation in Poland, moreover, none of the opposition leaders were well-known. So while the Polish Communists needed more than 50% of the vote to win an average single-member district, it might have sufficed for the Hungarian Communists to gain 30%. Moreover, while the Hungarian party did not expect to win an absolute majority, it expected to post a strong enough showing to be able to build a coalition government. Second, the Hungarian leaders favored direct presidential elections. Polls showed that their candidate was the most popular politician in the country. They expected, therefore, that they would be able to win such an election.

The results were not as they expected, however. When negotiating with the opposition, they had agreed to a compromise solution in which only about half of the parliamentary seats would be elected from single-member districts, while the other half would be elected on the basis of proportional representation. Furthermore, the electoral results were much worse than previous polls had indicated. Finally, they did not foresee the petition drive to hold a referendum on the manner in which the president would be elected. The radical opposition proposed to have parliament elect the president. It won the referendum by a very slim margin. Consequently, parliament would now elect the president, rather than the electorate as in the original agreement. This meant the popular leader of the reform Communists no longer had a chance to become the first freely elected president.

7.B. THE ORTHODOX REGIMES REMAIN PARALYZED IN THE FACE OF REVOLUTION

For both the East German and Czechoslovak regimes, the events in Poland, Hungary and the USSR came as a shock. Reforms were no longer taboo once Gorbachev had started calling for them. When he furthermore allowed the Polish and Hungarian Communists to undertake negotiations with their opposition, the Czechoslovak and East German leaders could no longer claim that Moscow opposed all liberalizing reforms. Their pragmatic acceptance therefore evaporated. The populace no longer believed that the Kremlin wanted the ageing orthodox leaders to remain in power. As the rulers' institutional interests broke down, they became disoriented. Advocating reforms would have undermined their power position. At the very least, it would have brought demands for their replacement by reform Communists. Consequently, they tried to oppose change as long as possible.

The Orthodox Regimes: Subjective Perceptions
Some of the leaders in the GDR and ČSSR realized that their countries were sinking deeper into crisis. Yet none of them developed a strategy for dealing with the situation. Most of the leaders instead became paralyzed, preferring to give up rather than to negotiate a compromise with the opposition. Their Hungarian and Polish comrades could follow their institutional interests in the preservation of their reform legacies. So it was not difficult for them to take the reforms further and to initiate negotiations with the opposition. The East German and Czechoslovak leaders, in contrast, did not have the luxury of being able to build upon their reformist policy. For they had based their pragmatic acceptance on the notion that the USSR had put them in power to prevent reforms and to guarantee stability. When Moscow pulled the rug out from under them, they wandered around aimlessly, without any clear conception of how to act strategically.

When at last they were confronted with a mass movement, the East German and Czechoslovak leaders were under much greater pressure than their Hungarian and Polish counterparts, and they had far less time to work out a strategy. While the Polish rulers had six months to prepare for their negotiating strategy, and the Hungarians had five months, the East German and Czechoslovak leaders had just a few days.[3] Furthermore, the Polish and Hungarian rulers could reach a compromise with opposition leaders at the elite level while a relativley demobilized society waited and watched. In the GDR and ČSSR, by

---

3. In Poland, the regime had announced in August 1988 that it was willing to meet with the opposition. The actual negotiations started in February. In Hungary, the Central Committee passed a resolution in February calling for multiparty elections. The negotiations began in June. In the ČSSR, by contrast, the prime minister met for the first time with opposition leaders six days after the police had attacked student demonstrators. This was also four days after the main opposition organization OF had been established. In the GDR, finally, the leaders refused to negotiate directly with the opposition in the beginning. The round table was set up after the entire leadership had already resigned. Nevertheless, after the mass demonstrations broke out in October, the original leadership only had a few days to work out a strategy—both for forcing General Secretary Honecker to resign and for dealing with the demonstrators.

contrast, the regimes faced an enormous pressure from mass movements demanding rapid and radical change.

The negotiating climate, furthermore, was less congenial in East Germany and Czechoslovakia than in Poland and Hungary, where greater political liberalization had allowed regime members to come into contact with dissidents and loyal opponents. In the course of this process, members of the regime and of the opposition had began to trust one another. The heavier repression in the GDR and ČSSR, on the other hand, had prevented any trust from developing between regime and opposition. Opposition leaders could not imagine their neo-Stalinist rulers suddenly becoming democrats. Similarly, the conservative Communist leaders had difficulty believing that subversive "criminal elements" could suddenly take responsibility for running the country. This lack of trust undermined the prospects for institutional compromise further. Instead, in the end, the paralyzed regimes simply capitulated.

The Behavior of the Exploited Classes as the Revolution Breaks Out
In the GDR and ČSSR the regimes were basically passive once the rebellions broke out. Their previous repressive actions, however, helped spark off the rebellion. These events took place against the background of radical changes in Poland, Hungary and the USSR, which naturally increased hopes among the populace that some changes would come to their own countries too. In the USSR, Gorbachev was advocating radical reforms; in Poland, a *Solidarność*-led government had come to power; in Hungary, the Party had renamed itself a "Social Democratic" party and had agreed to hold free elections. In the GDR itself, moreover, hundreds of thousands of citizens had left the country via Hungary.

In what follows, I place these revolutionary developments within my partial model on rebellions:

1) In both countries, groups of intellectual dissidents had already existed before the revolution broke out. The East German opposition was centered on the alternative movements which had found shelter in several of the Evangelical churches. In the ČSSR, it was Charter 77 and later the independent student organizations that supplied the main opposition. The intellectuals of Charter 77 became the core of OF, the movement which led the revolution and won the first elections. There were rising expectations of change in both countries, once Gorbachev had embarked on his reformist course. These hopes increased when the

Polish and Hungarian rulers decided to start negotiations with the opposition. However, the East German and Czechoslovak regimes were so tied to their anti-reformist pragmatic acceptance that they did not dare contemplate meaningful reforms. Instead, they continued their hardline policies against the opposition, which eventually outraged intellectuals and induced them to radicalize their activities. The East German intellectuals became outraged when the regime falsified the results of the local elections in May 1989. In response, they established new political organizations during the summer, such as *Demokratischer Aufbruch*. Many of the Czechoslovak intellectuals had become outraged earlier that same year. When the regime arrested Havel during the Jan Palach week, thousands of cultural figures signed a petition demanding his release. Meanwhile, the repressive actions taken this week prompted dozens of students to become involved in independent student groups.

2) While intellectuals had gotten angry at the regime's repressiveness, workers were now becoming more receptive to intellectuals' calls for opposition. Living standards had been stagnating or even declining in both countries for most of the decade.

3) In both countries, police repression sparked off mass rebellion. In the GDR, it was the police attacks during the 40-year anniversary celebrations. In the ČSSR, it was the brutal repression of the November 17 student demonstration.

4) In both countries, intellectuals and workers were able to cooperate to bring down the regime. In the GDR, this cooperation occurred at first through "spontaneous coordination." People gathered at places where they knew there would be crowds. These crowds often assembled in connection with activities organized by religious and other intellectuals.[4] Once the demonstrations started, the intellectual leaders of NF became the voice of the revolution. They also organized some of the later demonstrations. In the ČSSR, the cooperation between intellectuals and workers was more direct. The students organized the strike and immediately received support from OF. It is difficult to ascertain the involvement of professionals in these revolutions. Nevertheless, surveys of the Leipzig demonstrations in the GDR show that professionals were much less active than intellectuals and workers. East German intellectuals solved the communication problem initially through spontaneous coordination and later through West German media, while the Czechoslovaks used modern communications technology to spread their message (faxes, videos, Western radio broadcasts, xeroxed leaflets, etc.). The Czechoslovak revolutionaries also obtained help from popular

---

4. For example, crowds emerged after the weekly "Prayer for Peace" in a Leipzig church next to the main square.

actors and actress, who could gain access to factories more easily than the students could.

5) In both countries, the military and police were probably willing to attack the demonstrators. In the ČSSR, the military even offered to carry out a Polish-style *coup*. We will never know, however, whether the soldiers of these countries would actually have been willing to suppress the rebellions, because the rulers were unwilling to give the order to shoot. Instead of working out a strategy to keep power, they became paralyzed and gave up without a fight.

THEORETICAL IMPLICATIONS

My adaptation of several elements of Marxist theory has four major theoretical implications: 1) a rejection of historicism; 2) a rejection of purely structuralist adaptations of Marx, and a consequent emphasis on the dialectical interplay between actors and structures; 3) a rejection of rational-choice Marxism, and a related support for a more cognitive approach to the actor level; and 4) an emphasis on the need to complement class analysis with institutional analysis.

1) Anti-Historicism

Obviously, it is not possible to reconcile Marx's historical determinism with the view that the Soviet-type system comprised a special mode of production. The orthodox Marxian view of history does not leave open the possibility that a mode of production can emerge which is neither socialist nor capitalist. Nor does it allow for the possibility that a new mode of production can exist for a relatively short period of time and then die out, without ever becoming a world-dominant production mode. The non-capitalist Soviet-type system is a bothersome type that does not fit into Marx's historical categories.

The mere fact that I consider the corporate entity to be a ruling class excludes the possibility of the Soviet-type system being "socialist" in the Marxian sense of the term. A basic tenet for Marx was that a socialist society must be *classless*. It would be a logical impossibility for a classless society to have a ruling class. Since, moreover, the Soviet-type society was a historically unique type of class society—one based on collective ownership for members of the corporate entity—my approach excludes the possibility of labelling these societies "state capitalist."

Although I personally reject all forms of historical determinism, one possibility remains. One might claim that a socialist society will *definitely* arrive at some future point in history. The Soviet-type societies could not succeed because they tried to install a socialist system before the time was ripe. The forces of production still had not developed fully enough to allow for a classless society, in which machines take over all manual labor and the "necessary labor time" approaches zero. According to this approach, the October Revolution came centuries too early, just as one might argue that the Cromwellian revolution in England came too early and so eventually failed. It is impossible to "falsify" this claim, since however far we might be from this stage of technological development, it might still come in the future. This "wait-and-see" attitude would have been embarrassing for Marx himself, since he was convinced over 100 years ago that the forces of production had already developed enough to make a world socialist revolution possible.

2) Actor-Structure Dialectics

Even if the forces of production did reach such astounding levels that it were possible for machines to take over most production—thus laying the foundations that would make full communism possible—it still is not clear that we would organize society in a socialist manner. My adaptation of Marx is anti-structuralist. Structures influence actors; they place them in a situational context. This *does not* mean, though, that they determine all behavior. Two people in very similar structural situations might behave differently. An example is the fact that the Hungarian reform Communists wanted completely free elections, while the Polish reformers sought guarantees at least for the first elections.

Moreover, not only do structures influence us, we also influence them. For example, when the Soviet Union invaded Hungary in 1956 and the ČSSR in 1968, it was not clear what kind of pragmatic acceptance the new leaders would develop. The Soviet and Hungarian leaders could have emphasized the danger that the domestic changes under Nagy were leading the country toward a "capitalist" road of development. Similarly, the Soviet and Czechoslovak leaders could have stressed the original claims that the ČSSR was falling into the hands of West German "revanchists." There was no compelling structural reason to refrain from emphasizing the foreign-policy aspects of Czechoslovak "revisionism". Nor was there any compelling reason not to claim that the danger posed by Nagy's policies—to the continued application of a Soviet economic model within the country—

was a great as the corresponding danger posed by the reforms of the Prague Spring. There was no compelling structural reason, finally, why Jaruzelski had to continue the regime's reformist pragmatic acceptance after having declared martial law, while the Husák regime, by contrast, had abandoned a similar pragmatic acceptance under similar conditions. However, once these regimes had established a pragmatic acceptance, this institutional structure influenced their future behavior.

3) A Cognitive Approach

I have emphasized the role of actors, but this does not necessarily imply a rational-choice approach toward Marxism. During normal times, the majority of society often behaves in the manner predicted by rational-choice theory. In my analysis of institutions, therefore, I have essentially followed the rationalist tradition of examining the institutional incentives of actors. However, my analysis of Eastern Europe also shows that during times of crisis actors often behave differently than what most rational-choice theories would predict. Individual actors may behave unstrategically even during normal times. During periods of crisis and change, moreover, both political leaders and large social groups are unlikely to behave in accordance with the expectations generated by most rational-choice models.

The Czechoslovak and East German leaders became paralyzed and then gave up, rather than behaving in any kind of strategic fashion which might have ensured them influence over the future direction of their societies. The Polish leaders, moreover, may have acted in accordance with Przeworski's predictions when they sought certain guarantees, but their choice of electoral system and their behavior during the actual elections runs contrary to rationalist models.

In my analysis of East European social movements, moreover, I found shortcomings in rationalist approaches. First, contrary to the predictions of public-choice theory, the main collective-action problem was not devising selective incentives but establishing communication links. This does not mean the workers were "irrational" to evince a greater concern with establishing communications than with devising future rewards or punishments for the revolutionary leaders. On the contrary, it was perfectly rational for them to be encouraged by the messages sent by the students and dissidents that the revolution was spreading. In this case, then, my finding merely requires some revision in rationalist theory, rather than a rejection of it.

A second criticism of rationalist approaches, however, is more serious. My investigations indicate that psychological factors were more important for inducing people to participate in revolution than were rational calculations of the chance of success and the costs of failure. Such factors as rising expectations of political change and feelings of outrage after acts of repression radicalized the intellectuals. The same held true for workers during periods of deprivation caused by economic decline. (I leave open the question of whether this deprivation was absolute or relative, although I note that living standards were probably falling in absolute as well as relative terms.)

4) Institutions

In this study, I have shown it is possible to analyze the Soviet-type system with the use of class analysis. I have also essentially retained the traditional dichotomy between objective and subjective interests, although I have renamed them "postulated interests" and "the subjective interpretation of interests." However, these two levels—the systemic and the individual—are not enough. It is necessary as well to examine the institutional arrangements and institutional interests which the members of different classes and strata derive from these institutional arrangements. Without taking into account institutions, one cannot fully understand the mechanisms which allow a ruling class to keep its power over other classes and strata. As I made clear in my analysis of social movements in Eastern Europe, it was not enough for the revolutionaries to make the workers "conscious" of their exploitation. Many workers were "class-conscious" and opposed to the system already. Certain institutional and psychological barriers had to be overcome, however, before these class-conscious workers were willing to participate in collective action. Finally, since actors in my model have both postulated and institutional interests, I stress that it does not make sense to talk about subjective *interests*. What is important, rather, is how actors *perceive* their possibly contradictory postulated and institutional interests.

THE LINZ & STEPAN MODEL

Since I wrote my manuscript, a seminal work on transitions to democracy has come out by Juan J. Linz & Alfred Stepan (1996), entitled *Problems of Democratic Transition and Consolidation: Southern*

Europe, South America, and Post-Communist Europe. In contrast to many of the earlier works on democratic transition, they discuss the possibility of non-violent revolutions in which the regimes give up rather than repress the rebellion or negotiate guarantees. They claim that the ageing, inflexible regimes in the GDR and ČSSR remained frozen in a post-totalitarian stage and suffered from decades of decay. Since these regimes did not give any space for reformers, no split arose between reformers and hardliners. The ageing conservatives were unable to respond to the rapidly changing circumstances, so when confronted by mass uprisings they suffered rapid defections and quickly collapsed (1996:316ff).

In Hungary, by contrast, the regime had developed into a "mature post-totalitarian" system with a large private sector for small scale private enterprises and a relatively reliable legal framework. These economic and legal reforms created new economic opportunities for both members of the "second economy" and members of the party-state apparatus. Although economic society had developed, Hungary still did not have a civil society that was any where nearly as strong as in Poland. As the economic crisis deepened, reformers within the regime encouraged critical groups to organize so that the reformers could increase their influence within the regime. The reform Communists began to accept competitive politics because of the dynamics of reformers looking to the opposition for support. Linz & Stepan note that in Hungary the civil society did not grow through its opposition to the state. Rather, civil society could grow because of a momentary alliance between parts of the party-state with the civil society (1996: 304).

According to Linz & Stepan, Poland never was a truly totalitarian society, but rather "authoritarian Communist" because the state was never able to wipe out societal pluralism. The Church was always strong and independent, private farming dominated agricultural holdings, and because of the regime's relatively low level of cultural repression a relatively strong civil society could develop. Finally, in contrast to dogmatic totalitarian countries, policies often changed directions with the relatively often changes in party leadership (1996: 255-258). In 1988, the regime agreed to start negotiations, because it did not want *Solidarność* to boycott the upcoming 1989 parliamentary elections and it hoped to gain support for economic reforms. *Solidarność's* main goal was to gain legal recognition. The result was a "pact" that likens Przeworski's democracy with guarantees, in which

Solidarność agreed to participate in the elections in turn for legal recognition and a completely democratically elected senate.

The Linz & Stepan approach has the advantage over Przeworski and O'Donnell & Schmitter in that it places actors in an institutional setting. Nevertheless, there are several advantages to the approach used in this book compared to Linz & Stepan. First, they do not explain the reasons *why* the countries had different regime types, which has been a central theme in this book's discussion of "pragmatic acceptance." Second, it is not clear how fruitful Linz & Stepan's division is between authoritarian-Communist Poland and mature, post-totalitarian Hungary, since both countries according to their own account basically achieved the same result: negotiated transition to democracy. One could claim that there were important differences between the transition in Poland and in Hungary, since the Polish rulers obtained guarantees, while the Hungarian rulers did not. Another difference was that the Hungarian reformers acted more strategically than their Polish counterparts, because they supported the electoral system that would most likely improve their chances of winning elections. Since the Hungarian rulers faced a divided opposition, with little name recognition, they could expect to do best in a system of majoritarian rule, and thus they advocated such a system and eventually reached a compromise in which half the seats were based on single-member districts. Meanwhile, the Polish rulers could have expected to do best under a system of proportional representation, since they faced a united opposition (behind *Solidarność*) which had a popular, well-known leader Wałęsa). Yet, they insisted on majoritarian elections. However, since Linz & Stepan do not try to explain these differences, their division into three regime types does not add any explanatory value to the dichotomy used in this book of regimes having either a reformist or an anti-reformist pragmatic acceptance.

Epilogue

THE RIGHTWING SHIFT AFTER 1989

A key notion in the theoretical framework presented in this book is that workers had a postulated interest in wrestling greater control of the surplus product from the party-state. It is not clear what form a democratic alternative of worker control would take; it could include such possibilities as worker ownership of enterprises or continued state ownership, with indirect control over the enterprises exercised through free and democratic elections of the national governments. Since workers have an interest in ending their exploitation, *under certain circumstances*, they can be mobilized against the system. Thus, the analysis of postulated interests indicates the *potential* for various groups to revolt against a system, but their actual revolt is not predetermined. Throughout this book the conditions for worker participation in revolts have been analyzed. It was shown that worker participation was essential for the Czechoslovak and East German revolutions, which adds credence to the fruitfulness of using the concept of postulated interests as an analytical tool. Critics, though, will be certainly quick to point out the problem that in all four countries, the first post-communist governments carried out rightwing, pro-market policies. Why did workers not follow their postulated interests and demand control over the surplus product? Why were they willing to accept a new economic system in which a different class would replace the party-state and take control over the surplus product, and therefore, become a new group with power over the workers?

I will argue below that in all four countries, workers did, in fact, support policies in line with their postulated interests. Since they had not mobilized around their interests, however, they were not able to pressure the new governments into enacting such policies. The key to the rightwing swing was the change in attitudes of the intellectuals professionals, who dominated the new governments. They did so, to a large extent, without an electoral mandate from the populace. Briefly, I will examine the rightwing shift of each country.

CZECHOSLOVAKIA

In Czechoslovakia it is clear that the overwhelming majority of the population wanted change. Public opinion polls taken shortly after the events of November 17, 1989 show that the populace was extremely dissatisfied with the political and economic situation (see table 2, chapter 3). On the other hand, surveys taken after the Politburo resigned and then after President Husák resigned both show that there was hardly any support at all for a return to capitalism (only 3%!) The vast majority either wanted a socialist system or some sort of "middle-way." Furthermore, popularity polls show that one week after the initial demonstration, Dubček (who was seen as a symbol for both democratic socialism and a "third way,") was by far the most popular politician, with Prime Minister Adamec in second place. Havel was far behind. Already on December 1, Dubček's popularity collapsed and never recovered, but this need not be interpreted as a drift rightward, because Adamec replaced him and the economist Vatr Komárek—who also was considered a supporter of a third way—came in second. In the next survey on December 12, Komárek took over the top spot, with Havel moving into a close second and Adamec losing a great deal of ground. First 10 days later Havel's backing exploded, leaving the others far behind in the aftermath (Slejška & Herzmann 1990: 63).[1]

Havel was no representative of Thatcherite conservatism. On the contrary, he often emphasized the need to maintain a welfare state and protect the environment. He was previously even considered a "critical sympathizer" with the West German Greens (Morley 1990: 374). At this point, the free-market economist Václav Klaus, who eventually became chair of OF, was hardly known at all.

---

1. A skeptic might wonder how reliable surveys can be that were taken by an official state institution. While also admitting a small dose of skepticism might be justified, it is hard to imagine that a survey which is biased in favor of the Communist regime could show that 98% of the population considers the environment a great problem or that 92% consider to economy and 88% the political system to be one (see the results of this survey in Chapter 3, table 2). In addition, these findings on preferences for economic system are surprisingly consistent with earlier studies done. In 1968, during the Prague spring, for example, one poll taken in June, 1968 shoed that only 5% preferred a capitalist road of development as opposed to 89% favoring continued socialist development (Piekaliewicz (1972: 4). Later, Radio Free Europe, which can hardly be suspected of having a pro-Communist bias in its polling, showed that in 1971–2 in free elections the Communist Party would win 7%, a Democratic Socialist Party 41% and a Christian Democratic or Peasant Party would only gain 31%. In 1979–80 the figures were 3% Communist, 44% Democratic Socialist and 36% Christian Democratic/Peasant. In other words, those favoring either a democratic or authoritarian form of socialism had a clear majority in both surveys (cited in Lewis (1984: 53). The only investigation that I have which goes somewhat against this trend is a doctor's dissertation from 1968, which concludes that a large number of students were doubtful about the future of socialism (Kubríčková 1968: 317).

Table 1: Support for Socialism and Capitalism in Czechoslovakia

"Our society should develop along…"	November 23–24	December 9–12
A socialist path	45%	41%
A middle-way	47%	52%
A capitalist path	3%	3%
Doesn't matter/don't know	5%	4%

Source   Slejška & Herzmann (1990: 51)

When millions of people entered the streets to protest against the former regime, they demanded the resignations of the former rulers and called for democratic reforms. There was no discussion, however, over what type of economic system should replace the Soviet-type economy. In other words, citizens were unified more *against* a previous system, rather than *for* a new one. When the dissident-led organizations OF and VPN entered into the federal government, nobody knew what kinds of social and economic policies they would pursue. In fact, the "third-way" socialist, Komárek, as Vice-Prime Minister in charge of economics, originally had responsibility for working out the economic reform.

It was not even apparent which direction the economic reform would take after the first free elections half a year later. Those voting for OF did not know that they were voting for a market-liberal reform team centered around Klaus. On the contrary, OF's election platform emphasized the need for social justice and environmental protection. Its main author, Miloš Zeman, later became leader for the Social Democratic Party, where he advocated privatization via worker ownership of the enterprises—a solution that would be perfectly in line with the workers' postulated interests in getting control over their surplus product. When OF and VPN together received a majority, President Havel had substantial influence over the choice of ministers. However, by then Komárek had alienated the other politicians by his lack of engagement in working out the economic reforms and Klaus had established himself as an extremely capable economist and hard worker. Consequently, Klaus built up support even among social democratically inclined leaders, who were afraid that only Klaus could guarantee the continuation of reform. Therefore, although Havel reportedly tried to avoid re-appointing Klaus to the post of finance minister, in the end the president relented. Thus, Klaus' rise into prominence was not based on his being a supporter of market-liberalism, but rather on his ability to convince the former dissidents that he was a genuine reformer.[2]

Being an extremely charismatic leader, Klaus was able to sway the populace to the right by playing on the populace's fears that without him, the country would revert back to the former Stalinist system. Although the majority of the populace had been favorable to a non-"capitalist" transformation, it was nevertheless extremely critical of the previous regime. In other words, a strong, charismatic leader could have potentially gained popular support for both relatively market liberal and relatively "democratic-socialistic" reforms. Thus, the outcome hinged much on the behavior of the elites: both in the sense that Klaus gained the support of the former dissidents in wrestling control of the economic reforms from Komárek and that he could persuade the populace that—in contrast to the wishy-washy intellectuals—he was a man of action, who knew what the country needed. A self-confident, determined, Left-leaning politician, with similar characteristics, could have just as well succeeded.

In fact, part of the failure of Klaus was the fact that despite his charisma, he was unable to convert the populace to market-liberalism. As Orenstein (1998) shows, Klaus' popularity as finance minister was based on the fact that social democratically inclined people still had control over social policy. Once Klaus became prime minister after the breakup of Czechoslovakia in 1992 and began streamlining social benefits, his popularity plunged. Meanwhile, the Social Democrats under Zeman's leadership continuously gained in strength, until they eventually formed their own government in 1998.

Slovakia also fell prey to a charismatic leader. This time, it was a Leftwing, populist, Vladimír Mečiar. Mečiar built his career more around Slovak nationalism then any clear economic ideology, but his ability to win several elections with a "Leftist" profile also shows that the Slovaks could have potentially been mobilized to support a democratic socialistic alternative. In both the Czech Republics and Slovakia, the problem was that workers participated in the 1989 revolution on a

---

2. Much has been written about this topic. See, for example, Saxonberg (1999) for details.

mass scale, but since they were not organized around their own interests, they quickly lost influence once the populace demobilized and a
group of intellectuals and professional experts took control of the
"technicalities" of socio-economic transformation.

EAST GERMANY

In spite of the temptation to join West Germany, the direction of the
East German revolution was also far from certain several months
after Honecker's resignation. A poll published in *Der Spiegel* (18 Dec
1989) showed that while almost half the voters were undecided, the
Communist SED was by far the greatest vote getter, with the
Social Democrats in second place and the "alternative-New Left"
oriented *Neues Forum* tied with the liberals for third place. Another
poll published in that magazine which measured the East Germans'
degree of sympathy for West German parties on a scale of −5 to +5,
showed that the Social Democrats and Greens were the most popular,
while the right-wing parties (Christian Democratic Union/Christian
Social Union and the Republicans) all received negative values.
Moreover, 71% wanted East Germany to remain a separate
state.

There were several reasons for this quick turnabout in opinion.
First, the intellectuals from *Neues Forum* alienated themselves from
the populace. They were so fearful of a possible German unification,
that at times they seemed to align themselves more with the old regime
than the participants in their own revolution. They gave the impression of being afraid of the populace. Consequently, they failed to take
over the leadership role over the revolution as their Czech and Slovak
colleagues had done. They did not organize more than a few demonstrations themselves; nor did they demand that the communist government resign and schedule free elections. They did not even enter into
Round Table negotiations with the regime until December 7, 1989—
nearly two months after Honecker's resignation!

Second, public opinion swung after the revelation of several scan-
dals, such as the existence of separate living quarters for the political
elite, with their own special stores. Another big scandal was the existence of secret party funds, whose income came from the illegal sale of
weapons to such politically incorrect countries as South Africa. Until
then, the populace perceived the SED regime as being authoritarian,
but principled. Now all illusions of the regime evaporated.

Finally, one cannot ignore the role of West German Chancellor Helmut Kohl. He toured the GDR and promised the populace that if they voted for the Christian Democrats, they would soon enjoy the same living standards as in West Germany. The Left (SED, *Neues Forum* and Social Democrats) was rather disorganized and failed to present an appealing alternative scenario. Eventually, nationalist sentiments took over and the urge to rejoin the West became greater than any socio-economic ideologies. The East German Christian Democrats also benefitted greatly from both the economic aid and the political counseling from their ruling sister party in the West, an advantage which *Neues Forum* and the SED did not enjoy.

HUNGARY

As in Czechoslovakia and East Germany, public opinion was extremely critical of the communist-led regime, but at the same time favorable to "socialist" reforms. A Gallup poll taken in June, 1989 showed that a majority of citizens either believed that state companies should remain in state hands (33%) or given to the workers and employees under a system of self-management (26%). Only 38% thought the property should either be given back to the original private owners (9%) or sold to the highest bidders (29%) (Hankiss 1989: 55). That poll also showed that the communists were still by far the most popular party, with the Social Democratic Party coming in third place, after MDF (Hungarian Democratic Forum) (Hankiss 1989: 53). Despite this, the conservative MDF went on to win the elections, the reformed communists barely received 10%, and the social democrats failed to enter parliament.

Again, the election results to not necessarily indicate that the Hungarians wanted "rightwing" policies, rather it shows that they wanted to rid the government of communist control. The MDF had originally advocated a "third way" and stood close to the reform communists around Pozsgay. During the Round Table negotiations, however, the Free Democrats began attacking MDF for being quasi-communists. The Free Democrats' anti-communist campaign attracted media attention and put the MDF on the defensive. The MDF responded to its sinking popularity by sacking its Leftleaning leadership and electing a conservative leader, who successfully pointed out that the prominent Free Democrats were mostly former Marxists. Hence, the MDF gave the Free Democrats a taste of their own medicine. This competition between the two leading opposition parties over who was the most anti-communist stirred up anti-communist feelings in the country, which in turn hurt the chances of the reformed communists, who had now changed their party into an official social democratic party.

The original Social Democratic Party, which had once been nearly as popular as the MDF fell prey to vicious infighting between several different factions. A group of old social democrats from the interwar period gained control and prevented youthful leaders from attaining meaningful influence. As a result, the party split into several small competing parties. None of these small parties had the infrastructure and finances to be able to compete with the enormous apparatus which the reformed communists controlled. However, the reformed communists failed to convince the populace of their democratic credentials. During the first free elections since the communist take-over, the citizens resisted electing an old wolf in new clothing. As Szelényi & Szelényi (1991) show, with a lack of a viable social democratic alternative, a large portion of Left-leaning workers stayed at home rather than vote for a rightist party. Nevertheless, those who did vote, chose the least market liberal of the two main opposition parties. MDF won the elections handily on its promise of piecemeal reform, while the Free Democrats' failed to gain support for their calls for rapid transition and shock therapy.

Later political developments also show that the Hungarian populace largely has refused market liberalism. After four years in opposition, the reformed communists gained enough trust to be able to defeat the conservative MDF and return to power. Although they had an absolute majority, the socialists decided to form a coalition with the liberal SZDSZ. Despite their "socialist" name, they actually pursued much more radical market reforms than their conservative predecessors. Among others, they made many social programs means tested. Since the population still rejected market liberalism, voters retaliated by electing the FIDESZ, who despite their official liberal label, criticized the socialists from the Left and promised more generous social benefits. The pro-business weekly, *Business Central Europe* (July/August 1998, p. 11) sums up the last two elections: "the Hungarians have essentially been voting for a form of social democracy."

POLAND

Poland provides another example of how the elites moved to the right against the wishes of the population. When *Solidarność* was a mass union, which organized millions of workers, it made Leftist demands for worker self-management and supported relatively generous social policies. Rather than supporting market liberalism, one of its main demands was continued price control. Once it went underground, the organization lost much of its union character and became more of a general opposition movement, dominated by intellectuals. Nevertheless, the *Solidarność* grouping which Wałęsa invited to the Round Table negotiations still officially supported worker self-management of industry and gave absolutely no indication of supporting any kind of "shock therapy" or market liberalism. On the contrary, experts at the time claimed either that Wałęsa specifically excluded market-liberals from his team and surrounded himself with social democrats and Christian democrats (Staniszkis 1991) or Wałęsa's cohorts were all "Leftists" (Ziemer 1989b).

As is well known, the 1989 elections led to a resounding victory for *Solidarność*, which won all of the freely contested seats in the Sejm and 99 of 100 seats in the senate (with one seat going to an independent). Since *Solidarność* never expected to form a government, it did not present a program of economic reforms, although, as already mentioned, it still officially supported worker self-management. Thus, the electorate had no idea that a *Solidarność*-led government would eventually carry out "shock therapy" policies. In fact, there was still large support for socialistic economic policies. Grosfeld (1990: 146–7) cites a survey taken in the summer of 1989 among Polish workers showing that 64.6% of the industrial workers thought that the transformation of state companies into worker owned ones would have a positive impact on the economy, while 71.1% felt so about their own company. In contrast, only 17% supported selling shares to non-employees. A general survey of the entire population showed that in 1990, 61.8% of Poles favored worker self-management "decidedly" or "rather," while only 10.7% were "rather" or "decidedly" against it and 26.4% were undecided (Kolarska-Bobińska 1994: 26). A majority of the population also supported limitations of earnings on the most wealth (54.8%), full employment policy (66.9%), and state control of prices (65.9%). On the other hand, there was also support for the dismissal of inefficient employees, increased possibilities for private enterprises and the adoption of laws of the market and competition. A majority opposed central management of the economy or the abandonment of privatization of industry. In other words, the populace harbored a combination of socialistic and market-oriented beliefs. This meant the voters could potentially be mobilized by both the democratic Left and the right, although a program of market-socialism, based on worker self-management of the large enterprises and pluralistic ownership forms would probably have come closest to the voters' wishes.

Once the *Solidarność* government moved in a market-liberal direction, it immediately lost popularity. By 1993, when the reformed communists had gained more trust for their claims to be social democratic, they were able to return to power in a coalition with the Peasant Party. Again, we have a situation where voters, who potentially were willing to vote for Leftist economic policies, voted for a party because of its anti-communism, without knowing what the economic consequences would be. As in the other countries of this study, the shift to the Right occurred among the ruling intellectual elite in government, rather than among the voters. Of course, the ensuing political climate in all of these countries also influenced the voters, who eventually became less socialistic in their opinions. The point, however, is that workers were probably willing to support viable parties that would have pursued policies in accordance with their postulated interests in obtaining greater control over the surplus product. The new political elite, who had themselves moved in a more market-liberal direction, did not have to address these issues in order to win the first elections. Anti-communism, combined with vague promises of reform were enough. If the workers had been able to form their own organizations and rally around leaders, who promoted their interests, then the outcome would have probably been much different.

Appendix

NOTES ON THE INTERVIEWS AND DOCUMENTATION

INTERVIEWS

Here the following will be discussed: 1) the criteria for choosing people to interview, 2) the types of interviews conducted and 3) the manner in which the results were used.

1) The Criteria

Even though I did have a set of priorities of which types of people I wanted to interview, I never turned down anybody who was willing to be interviewed. Furthermore, the actual group of people whom I interviewed did not always correspond to my order of priorities. It also depended to a large extent on who was willing to meet me for an interview, which in turn depended to some extent on what kind of contacts I was able to make in each country.

The main categories of people whom I wanted to interview included high ranking members of the Party and state apparatus as well as student and opposition leaders. Within the Party and state organs, I was interested in interviewing people who could discuss either the regimes' strategies toward the opposition or the relationship between the various Party and state organizations and their roles in supporting or blocking attempts at implementing economic reforms. I gave highest priority to those with the greatest power (i.e. former members of the Politburo or Party Secretariat and former prime ministers and economic ministers). I also tried to interview their advisors, since these people were often more open and less worried about their reputations. In order to understand the Party-state relations better, I also wanted to interview mid-level people (people working at economic ministries or Central Committee organs) as well as former managers of state enterprises. I succeeded best at obtaining interviews with those at the top level positions and their advisors. My greatest failure was the inability to conduct any interviews with former managers, since this would have allowed me to gain some insight to Party-state relations and the reform process from their point of view.

Among the opposition, my highest priorities were anybody who participated in negotiations with the old regimes and in Czecho-slovakia, anyone who was a member of the strike committees. I also tried to interview people in Czechoslovakia who were involved in either organizing the strikes and information campaigns and those who were involved in the organizational work of the Czech and Slovak oppositional organizations OF and VPN. In Czechoslovakia, where a revolution broke out, I considered it equally important to interview opposition leaders as the former Communist rulers. In Hungary and Poland, however, where I had much more limited time, I gave higher priority to interviewing former Communist leaders. My main question in these countries was to know *why* these rulers took the initiative to start negotiations. The issue of why the opposition accepted these proposals was less interesting.

The reader might have noticed that the majority of the interviews came from Czechoslovakia. I decided to concentrate on this country, because it was the only country to have an organized revolution. East Germany had a revolution, but it happened more spontaneously. Moreover, in contrast to East Germany, the negotiations between the regime and opposition took place at the height of the revolution. The East German Round Table talks took place after two general secretaries had resigned and it was already clear that democratic elections would be held. Moreover, in contrast to East Germany, there were some reform attempts. Thus, the Czechoslovak revolution had all the elements that I was interested in: I could look at why reform attempts had failed; I could examine the regime's strategy (or lack of it) toward the opposition; I could do the same for the opposition leaders and I could investigate how the revolution was organized.

I spent several months in Poland and Hungary, which enabled me to conduct some interviews there as well. I gave these countries priority over East Germany, because a great deal of information has been published internationally on the East German case than the other two. This is hardly surprising, since many West German researchers followed the events on the other side of the wall very closely. Besides the richly available reports from East and West German researchers, most of the most important former Communist leaders have either published memoirs or allowed journalists to publish interviews with them. In addition, many documents have also appeared in various books. Since more published information was available on East Germany than on Poland and Hungary, I decided that I should compensate for this gap by doing interviews in the latter two countries. Furthermore, in the original manuscript, I placed greater emphasis on the question of economic reform, which meant that I wanted to interview members of the Party and state apparatuses on this question. Since East Germany had only made slight reforms in the 1960s and had not attempted any more afterwards, it was natural for me to seek out interviews from the two relatively reformist countries.

2) Types of Interviews

My interviews were opened ended. I came to each interview with a list a questions. I tried to ask basically the same questions to the same categories of people. As time went on, new questions would emerge and I often wanted new interviewees to confirm or deny statements made by other interviewees or even other published sources that I had read after conducting the first interviews. Otherwise, the lists of questions were basically the same.

Unfortunately, the interviews were not always as systematic as I would have liked them to be. I could never know ahead of time how long the interviewee would be willing to talk. Even when they said they only had an hour, the interviews could still continue over three hours. Other interviews could be much shorter than planed. One interview, for example, which I had expected to last at least an hour, was cut short after some15 minutes due to unforeseeable events.

Another problem that I had was that some of the interviewees did not only want to stick to my questions about the events in 1989; they also wanted to talk about current politics. This was especially a problem with some of the former Communist leaders, who wanted to point out that they were not so bad and that the current regimes are not so good. This forced me to do a balancing act. On the one hand, I did not want to offend them and appear rude by cutting them off and telling them that I am not interested in what they are saying. For some of them, the interviews also served a psychological function of allowing them to tell "their side of the story." If I had deprived them of too much of this, they might not be as relaxed and open in answering the questions that I needed answered. On the other hand, I also wanted to use the time as efficiently as possible, so that I could be sure to discuss my main questions. This balancing act was especially difficult since I could never know how much time I would have for the interviews. It was even more difficult in the cases where the interviewees used an interpreter, since it was hard to interrupt the interviewee to speak to the interpreter.

Even though some interviewees used interpreters, the language barrier did not present a problem. Most of the time, the interviewees brought with their own interpreters, whom they trusted. Whether an interpreter was present or the interviewees spoke a language other than their native tongue (i.e. English or German), I was careful about the possibility of misunderstandings. If somehow the answers to my questions seemed illogical or indicated a possible misunderstanding of my question, then I repeated my question with different wording. Thus, I did not experience any important language problem during any of my interviews. Generally, the interviews in Hungary were conducted in German without interpreters, the interviews in Poland were conducted in English without interpreters, and the interviews in former Czechoslovakia were conducted in English or German. In former Czechoslovakia interpreters were used several times for interviews especially in the early stages of the project before my Czech skills had reached high enough levels to conduct interviews fully in Czech. Only one of the interviews in Poland and two in Hungary were conducted with the help of interpreters.

3) Using the Results of the Interviews

All types of sources have their advantages and disadvantages. Interviews have the advantage of allowing the researcher to inquire about events that have not been thoroughly documented. They also give the researcher some insight about what the participants were thinking when these events took place. Moreover, a personal interview allows the researcher to ask questions which the participants themselves have not answered in their published memoirs, interviews or articles which they have written. Furthermore, when the interviewer detects an apparent contradiction in a person's story, the interviewer has the possibility of directly confronting the person with contradictions.

The disadvantage, obviously, is the reliability problem. There is always a risk that the interviewee will be less than completely honest in order to present a more favorable picture of him- or herself. Of course, this problem also arises in any memoirs, published interviews or articles written by the participants. Such reliability problems even exist to a lesser extent in all other available materials. For example, journalists reporting on the events also have preconceived values which affect their interpretations of what they have seen and what they report. They also have their own sources which they rely on to a large extent to the exclusion of other sources. Any observer—whether participant or observer—is going to view the events through subjective glasses. A reliability problem which only pertains to the case of interviews is the question of how much the interviewees might have forgotten by the time I interviewed them.

In both cases, I dealt with the interviews the way I would with any other materials. I checked and cross-checked *all* types of sources with each other. For example, in the case of interviews dealing with the negotiations in Czechoslovakia, I tried to interview as many participants as possible from both the Communist and opposition side. I also interviewed some of the participants from the Socialist Party. I compared their responses to each other and to the published sources. The published sources included transcripts of all the negotiations which Havel participated in. In addition, I also compared the published documents and my interviews to the secondary literature on all subjects. Finally, in the Czechoslovak case, I was in the country long enough that I was able to contact some of the participants for a second interview to clarify misunderstandings or contradictions between what they said the first time around and what others said later. In one case, I interviewed the assistant of one of my previous interviewees. I considered this partially a continuation of the previous interview, since this assistant had been present at the first interview as a translator.

If ever an important discrepancy occurred among the interviewees, I noted this in my book. Fortunately, such occasions were rare. Most of the differences in answers were of the sort that are more interesting for historians than for social scientists. For example, in Czechoslovakia, all students present at the meeting of independent students agree that the decision to collaborate with the official youth organization, SSM, was only reached after a long and heated debate. Although they all agreed that the final vote was close, they disagreed on the exact voting totals and they also disagreed over which students supported and opposed collaboration. However, these types of details were not important for my main findings.

There were several cases, though, in former Czechoslovakia, in which former Communist leaders made claims that were completely refuted by other interviewees. The most important discrepancy in the Czechoslovak case, was Krejčí's claim that OF had offered Adamec the presidency during one of the negotiations. Krejčí claims that this offer was not recorded, because he asked Hanzel to turn off the microphone. (Hanzel was Havel's assistant, who recorded the negotiations, which he later published in the book *Zrychlený tep dějin*). Not only did all of OF's negotiators deny that such an offer was made, even Adamec's other main advisor, Pavel, also denied this. When I met Krejčí again, I told him what Pavel and the OF negotiators had said. In response, he merely smiled and shrugged his shoulders, as if to say "so you caught me on this one." Rather than discuss Krejčí's claim in the text, I left it out, on the grounds that it was clearly a false claim and not worth pursuing, given the limits of space for this book. This example shows that I was actually much more critical of my interviewee's responses than might appear in the book, because for reasons of space I chose to leave out questionable statements rather than refute them.

In Hungary, there were never any discrepancies among the interviewees. In Poland, it only arose on one occasion, in which a former *Solidarność* leader denied that there were any divisions between the organization's negotiators and its more radical grassroots. This particular person was still an active politician and generally gave more "official" answers than open, detailed responses.

DOCUMENTATION

Two kinds of sources were used in this book: theoretical and empirical. For the theoretical works, most of the material used in this book was based on theoretical explanations of the collapse of the Soviet-type regimes in 1989. The exception is the theoretical works that I used for building my model. As noted in the introductory chapter, so many theoretical schools of thought are touched upon in this book, that the book would have become many thousands of pages long if each theoretical discourse were discussed in its entirety. Instead, it was assumed that since so many scientific works have been devoted to the collapse of the Soviet-type regimes, if members of a theoretical school had something important to say about this event, they probably would have already said it. Of course, the possibility has been left open that important new theoretical works will be written in the future on this topic and that these works might come from traditions not represented in this book.

Both secondary and primary sources are richly represented among the empirical works referred to in this book. Secondary sources are especially important for this type of comparative study, because one author cannot be expected to have mastered the six languages of English, German, Czech, Slovak, Polish and Hungarian. However, primary sources were used as much as possible. In addition, an effort was made to read secondary sources by East European social scientists, so that the book would not rely too much on the Western interpretation of the East.

The primary sources include published interviews, memoirs, statistical yearbooks, published and published documents. Because of language limitations, the documents cited are mainly German and Czech. The published documents include documents from the German Politburo, statements made by the East German regime during the fall of 1989, documents about the East German opposition movements, the minutes of the Czechoslovak negotiations between the government and opposition, a collection of the official statements, brochures and press releases made by both the Czechoslovak government and opposition during the November revolution, and the findings of the official parliamentary commission investigating the "velvet revolution." The unpublished documents all come from the Czech Republic and are clearly shown in a separate section of the reference list.

The question arises of what status the "subjective" sources, such as interviews, published interviews and memoirs should be given. It is common to look at interviews or memoirs with some suspicion. If a Western news reporter claims, for example, that there were rising expectations of change in 1989, some critics consider this more believable than if a former dissident says that the dissents had higher expectations of change. Why a news reporter, without any statistical evidence is always more credible than a participant is hard for me to understand.

Of course, the accuracy of one interview may be inferior to the accuracy of one document, although even documents can be fabrications. Interviews and memoirs, however, have the advantage of giving greater insight to the subjective level, in order to understand how the actors thought and experienced certain events. The statements of actors are always more believable if they describe mistakes that they made, rather than merely defend themselves. Their statements are also more believable if they are confirmed by other people. Especially if they are confirmed by both members of the old the opposition and the old regime and by different groups within the opposition and regime. For this reason, I tried to get as many interviews as possible. I also tried to make sure as much as possible that the answers given corresponded to the available documents. This was especially easy concerning the interviews on the Czechoslovak negotiations, since the minutes of these meetings have been published.

At times I used interviews to assess theoretical hypotheses. For example, there is not much literature about which groups opposed economic reforms in the Soviet-type economy, but hardly any empirical work done on this issue. Thus, it was interesting to see that these hypotheses were basically confirmed by members of the former regimes in Poland, Hungary and Czechoslovakia. It is unlikely that all the theorists and all the interviewees of three countries would all be completely wrong.

Nevertheless, the absence of hard data at times is a regrettable problem in doing this type of study. One must make the best of the available material and try to gain more material by conducting interviews and asking people to make copies of any documents that they might have. Imperfect data is still better than no data at all.

REFERENCES

Published Books and Articles, and Manuscripts

Adam, Jan (1987) "The Hungarian Economic Reform of the 1980s," *Soviet Studies*, 4:610–627.

Adams, Tenley (1992) "Charter 77 and the Workers' Defense Committee (KOR [sic] the Struggle for Human Rights in Czechoslovakia and Poland," *East European Quarterly*, 2:219–239.

Adamski, Władysław W. (1982) "Structural and Generational Aspects of a Social Conflict," pp. 49–57 in *Sisyphus Sociological studies Vol. III: Crises and Conflicts. The Case of Poland 1980–81.* Warsaw: Polish Scientific Publishers.

Ágh, Attila, (1991) "Emergence of the 'Science of Democracy' and its Impact on the Democratic Transition in Hungary," *AULU Society and Economy*, 2:96–111.

Albæk, Erik (1988) *Fra sandhed til information: Evalueringsforskning i USA—før og nu*, Denmark: Akademisk Forlag.

Allardt, Erik (1971) "Culture, Structure, and Revolutionary Ideologies," *International Journal of Comparative Sociology*, 1:24–40.

Altman, Franz-Lothar (1980) "Tschechoslowakei," pp. 181–229 in Klaus Bolz ed., *Die wirtschaftliche Entwicklung in ausgewählten Ländern Osteuropas zur Jahreswende 1979/80*, Hamburg: Verlag Weltarchiv.

Altman, Franz-Lothar (1981) "Tschechoslowakei," pp. 269–314 in Klaus Bolz ed., *Die wirtschaftliche Entwicklung in ausgewählten Ländern Osteuropas zur Jahreswende 1980/81*, Hamburg: Verlag Weltarchiv.

Andert, Reinhold & Herzberg, Wolfgan (1990/1991) *Der Sturz: Erich Honecker im Kreuzverhör*, 3rd ed., Berlin & Weimar: Aufbau-Verlag.

Andorka, Rudolf (1989) "The Development of the Sociological Views on the Structure and Stratification of the Hungarian Society" pp. 85–119 in Rudolf Andorka & Miklós Hadas eds., *Social Structure, Stratification and Mobility in Central and Eastern Europre*, Papers presented at the Conference in the Inter-Unversity Centre of Postgraduate Studies, Dubrovnik, April 14–17, 1989, Budapest: BUES.

Anonymous (Member of the Czechoslovak Communist Party's Central Committee Organ For Culture) (1991) *Aparát: Soumrak polobohů*, Prague: Fajma.

Aragon, Louis (1985) "The Biafra of Spirit," p. 15, in Heneka A., et al. eds., *A Besieged Culture*, Stockholm & Vienna: The Charta 77 Foundation and International Helsinki Federation for Human Rights.

Arato, Andrew (1991) "Social Theory, Civil Society, and the Transformatoin of Authoritarian Socialism," pp. 1–26 in Ferenc Fehér & Andrew Arato eds., *Crisis and Reform in Eastern Europe*, New Brunswick & London: Transaction Publishers.

Arrighi, Giovanni (1991) "World Income Inequalities and the Future of Socialism," *New Left Review*, 189:39–65.

Ash, Timothy Garton (1990a) "Eastern Europe: The Year of Truth," *The New York Review*, Feb. 15:17–22.

Ash, Timothy Garton (1990b) "Mitteleuropa?" *Dædalus*, 1:1–22.

Ash, Timothy Garton (1990c) "The Revolution of the Magic Lantern," *The New York Review*, January 18:42–51.

Ash, Timothy Garton (1990d) *We The People: The Revolution of '89 Witnessed in Warsaw, Budapest, Berlin & Prague*, London, Granta Books.

Askanas, Benedykt (1985) "Niveau und Entwicklung der Reallöhne in den RGW-Ländern im Vergleich mit Österreich," *WIIW Forschungsberichte nr. 103*, The Vienna Institute for Comparative Econoimic Studies.

Åslund, Anders (1989a) *Gorbachev's Struggle for Economic Reform*, London: Printer Publishers.

Åslund, Anders (1989b) "The Soviet Union Seeks a New Role for the CMEA (COMECON)," pp. 53–70 in *Europe and the Soviet Union, Proceedings of the CEPS Fifth Annual Conference*, volume 2, CEPS Paper No. 41, Brussels: Centre for European Policy Studies.

Åslund, Anders (1990) "Systemskifte i Sovjetunionen," *Svensk tidskrift*, 6:343–349.

Babúrková, Jolana (1989) *Závěrečna správa: "Nazory občanů ČSSR na vedoucí úlohu KSČ,"* Prague: Institut pro výzkum veřejného mínění.

Balla, Bálint (1972) *Kaderverwaltung: Versuch zur Idealtypisierung der Bürokratie sowjetisch-volks-demokratischen Typs*, Stuttgart: Ferdinand Enke Verlag.

Bakuniak, Grzegorz & Nowak, Krzysztof (1987) "The Creation of a Collective Identity in a Social Movement: The Case of 'Solidarność'" in Poland," *Theory and Society*, 16:401–429.

Barany, Zoltan D. (1992) "East European Armed Forces in Transitions and Beyond," *East European Quarterly*, 1:1–31.

Barker, Colin & Weber, Kara (1982) *Solidarność: From Gdansk to Military Repression*, London: International socialism 15.

Bartha, Ference (1989) "The External Financial Situation and the Macro-Level Flow of Sources between 1986 and 1988," *The Hungarian Economy*, 1:3.

Bates, Robert H. (1991) "The Economics of Transitions to Democracy," *Political Science & Politics*, 3:369–390.

Batt, Judy (1991a) *East Central Europe from Reform to Transformation*, London: Pinter.

Batt, Judy (1991b) "The End of Communist Rule in East-Central Europe: A Four-Country Comparison," *Government and Opposition*, 3:369–390.

Bauer, Tamas (1988) "Reforming or Perfecting the Economic Mechanism," *Social Research*, 4:715–746.

Baumann, Manfred-Jürgen (1989) "Verschuldung und Verschuldungsfähigkeit sozialististischer Staaten," pp. 23–36 in Rüdiger Zellentin ed., *Ostpanorama Sonderausgabe 1989*, 22nd international seminar on East-West Trade, Linz: Gesellschaft für Ost- und Südostkunde.

Bauman, Zygmunt (1976) "Social Dissent in the East European Political System," pp. 115–142 in Bernard Lewis Faber ed., *The Social Structure of Eastern Europe: Transition and Process in Czechoslovakia, Hungary, Poland, Romania, and Yugoslavia*, New York et al.: Praeger Publishers.

Bauman, Zygmunt (1987) "Intellectuals in East-Central Europe: Continuity and Change," *Eastern European Politics and Societies*, 2:162–186.

Beck, Carl (1961) "Party Control and Bureaucratization in Czechoslovakia," *The Journal of Politics*, 2:279–294.

Benda, Marek et al. (1990) *Studenti psali revoluci*, Prague: Univerzum.

Benditt, Theodore, M. (1975) "The Concept of Interest in Political Theory," *Political Theory*, 3:245–287.

Benn, S.I. (1960) "'Interests' in Politics," Meeting of the Aristotelian Society at Bedfor Square, London.

Berend, Ivan T. (1990) *The Hungarian Economic Reforms 1953–1988*, Cambridge: Cambridge et al., University Press.

Beschloss, Michael R. & Talbott, Strobe (1993) *At the Highest Levels: The Insinde Story of the End of the Cold War*, London: Warner Books.

Beyme, Klaus von (1990) "Die vergleichende Politikwissenschaft und der Paradigmenwechsel in der politischen Theorie," *Politische Vierteljahresschrift*, 3:457–474.

Bialer, Seweryn (1986) *The Soviet Paradox: External Expansion, Internal Decline*, London: I.B. Tauris & Co. LTD.

Blaha, Jaroslav (1985) "1984: La Tchéchoslovaquie face au défi de lá modernisation," *Le courrier des pays de l'Est*, 295:37–43.

Blaha, Jaroslav (1986) "Les résultats du plan 1985 en Tchéchoslovaque: à la recherche de la qualité," *Le courrier des pays de l'Est*, 304:54–60.

Blanchard, Olivier and Richard, Layard (1990), "Economic Change in Poland" pp. 63–83 in Beksisak, Janusz et al., *The Polish Transformation: Programme and Progress*, London, Centre for Research into Communist Economies.

Block, Fred (1977) "The Ruling Class Does Not Rule: Notes on the Marxist Theory of the State," *Socialist Revolution*, 33:6–28

Böhm, Arnost (1985) "Hospodářská spolupráce s nesocialistickými zeměmi," *Plánované Hospodářství*, 1:56–63.

Böll, Heinrich (1985) "Cultural Cemetery," p. 15, in Heneka A., et al. eds. *A Besieged Culture*, Stockholm-Vienna: The Charta 77 Foundation and International Helsinki Federation for Human Rights.

Botsas, Eleftherios (1992) "Trade and the Collapse of Central Planning in Europe," *East European Quarterly*, 2:239–259.

Bottomore, Tom ed. (1983) *A Dictionary of Marxist Thought*, Oxford: Basil Blackwell Ltd.

Bova, Russell (1991) "Political Dynamics of the Post-Communist Transition: A Comparative Perspective," *World Politics*, 12:113–38.

Bozóki, András (1993) "Hungary's Road to Systemic Change: The Opposition Roundtable," *East European Politics and Societies*, 2:276–308.

Bradley (1992) *Czechoslovakia's Velvet Revolution: A Political Analysis*, Boulder: East European Monographs (distributed by Columbia University Press in New York).

Brand, H. (1992) "Why the Soviet Economy Failed," *Dissent*, 2:232–244.

Breslauer, Goerge W. (1990) "Soviet Economic Reforms Since Stalin: Ideology, Politics and Learning," *Soviet Economy*, 3:252–280.

Brunner, Georg (1982) "Legitimacy Doctrines and Legitimation Procedures in East European Systems," pp. 27–44 in T.H. Rigby & Ference Fehér eds., *Political Legitimation in Communist States*, London & Basingstoke: The Macmillian Press LTD.

Brus, Włodzimierz (1971) *Funktionsprobleme der sozialistischen Wirtschaft*, Edda Werfel trs. Frankfurt: Suhrkamp.

Brus, Włodzimierz (1981) *Österuropas ekonomiska historia efter 1945*, trs. by Gunnar Sandin Lund: Liber förlag.

Brus, Włodzimierz (1988) "The Political Economy of Reforms," pp. 65–79 in Marer, Paul and Siwinski, Włodzimierz eds., *Creditworthiness and Reform in Poland, Western and Polish Perspectives*, Blommington: Indiana University Press.

Brus, Włodzimierz (1989) "Evolution of the Communist Economic System: Scope and Limits," pp. 255–277 in Victor Nee & David Stark eds., *Remaking the Economic Institutions of Socialism: China and Eastern Europe*, Stanford: Stanford University Press.

Bruszt, László (1990) "1989: The Negotiated Revolution in Hungary," *Social Research*, 2:365–389.

Bryson, Phillip J. & Melzer, Manfred (1991) *The End of the East German Economy: From Honecker to Reunifiaction*, Hampshire & London: MacMillan.

Brzezinski, Zbigniew (1990) *The Grand Failure: The Birth and Death of Communism in the Twentieth Century*, New York: Collier Books.

Bukač, Vladimír (1985) "Aplikace Souboru opatření v ekonomice ČSSR," *Plánovaní hospodárství*, 1:23–31.

Bunce, Valerie & Csanádi, Mária (1993) "Uncertainty in the Transition: Post-Communism in Hungary," *East European Politics and Societies*, 2:240–275.

Canel, Eduardo (1992) "Democratization and the Decline of Urban Social Movements in Uruguay: A Political-Institutional Account," pp. 276–290, in Arturo Escobar & Sonia E. Alvarez eds., *The Making of Social Movements in Latin America*, Boulder et al.: Westview Press.

Čap, V. & Rybnikář, K. (1985) "K vývoji národního hospodařství v roce 1984," *Plánovaní hospodárství*, 2.

Cerny, Philip G. (1990) *The Changing Architecture of Politics: Structure, Agency, and the Future of the State*, London et al.: Sage Publications.

Český Statistický úřad (1993) *Statistická ročenka české republiky '93* Prague: Český statistický úřad.

Chirot, Daniel (1991) "What Happened in Eastern Europe in 1989?" pp. 3–32 in Daniel Chirot ed., *The Crisis of Leninism and the Decline of the Left: The Revolutoins of 1989*, Seattle & London: University of Washington State.

Cipkowski, Peter (1991) *Revolution in Eastern Europe: Understanding the Collapse of Comunism in Poland, Hungary, East Germany, Czechoslovakia, Romania, and the Soviet Union*, New York et al.: John Wiley & Sons.

Clapham, Christopher (1985) *Third World Politics: An Introduction*, London: Routledge.

Clark, John & Wildavsky, Aaron (1990) *The Moral Collapse of Communism: Poland as a Cautionary Tale*, San Francisco: ICS Press.

Cohen, Mitchell (1990) "Creating a New-Old Europe," *Dissent*, 2:161–170.

Cohn, Stanley H. (1987) "Economic Burden of Soviet Defense Expenditures: Constraints on Productivity," *Studies in Comparative Communism*, 2:145–161.

Collins, Randall & Waller, David (1993) "Der Zusammenbruch von Staaten und die Revolutionen im sowjetischen Block: Welche Theorien machten zutreffende Voraussagen?" pp. 302–325 in Hans Joas & Martin Kohli eds., *Der Zusammenbruch der DDR*, Frankfurt am Main: Suhrkamp.

Cornelsen, Doris (1986) "Bilanz der DDR-Wirtschaft," *FS Analysen: Teil I*, Forschungsstelle für gesamtdeutsche wirtschaftliche und soziale Fragen, 4:25–48.

Crusius, R., Kuehl, H., Skála, J., Wilke, M., eds. (1973) *ČSSR Fünf Jahre "Normalisierung" 21.8/21.8.1973 Dokumentation*, Hamburg: Verlag Association Gmb.

Csaba, László (1989) "Some Lessons from Two Decades of Economic Reform in Hungary," *Communist Economies*, 1:17–29.

Csanádi, Maria (1990) "Beyond the Image: The Case of Hungary," *Social Research*, 2:321–346.

Csanádi, Maria (1991) "The Diary of Decline: a Case-study of the Disintegration of the Party in One District In Hungary," *Soviet Studies*, 6:1085–1099.

Curry, Jane L. (1988) "The Psychological Barriers to Reform in Poland," *East European Politics and Societies*, 3:484–123.

Czege, Andreas Wass von (1987) "Hungary's 'New Economic Mechanism': Upheaval or Continuity?" pp. 121–144 in Peter Gey, Jiří Kosta & Wolfgang Quaisser, eds., *Crisis and Reform in Socialist Economies*, Boulder & London: Westview press.

Czesaný, Slavoj (1989) "Structural Development of the Czechoslovak Economy," *Czechoslovak Economic Papers*, 28:81–95.

Dahlkvist, Mats (1978) *Staten, socialdemokratin och socialismen*, Lund, Prisma.

Davidheiser, Evenly B. (1992) "Strong States, Weak States: The Role of the State in Revolution," *Comparative Politics*, July:463–475.

Davies, Jamces C. (1962) "Toward a Theory of Revolution," *American Sociological Review*, 1:5–19.

Dencik, Peter & Kvist, Kenneth (1968) "Ekonomisk utveckling i Tjeckoslovakien," *Zenith*, 5:27–30.

Denitch, Bogdan (1990) "Reform and Conflict in Yugoslavia," *Dissent*, 2:151–3.

Di Palma, Guiseppe (1991) "Legitimation from the Top to Civil Society," *World Politics*, 1:49–79.

Dix, Robert (1991) "Eastern Europe's Implications for Revolutionary Theory," *Polity*, 2:227–242.

Djilas, Milovan (1957/63) *Die Neue Klasse: Eine Analyse des kommunistischen Systems*, trs. by Reinhard Federmann, München: Kindler Verlag.

Doktór, Kazimierz (1982) "Industrial Conflicts and the Ultrastability of the System," pp. 69–80 in *Sisyphus Sociological Studies, Volume III: Crisis and Conflicts. The Case of Poland 1980–1981*, Warsaw: Polish Scientific Publishers.

Draper, Theodore (1993) "A New History of the Velvet Revolution," *The New York Review*, 42:16–18.

Dubček, Alexander (1973) "Speech to the Central Committee of the Communist Party, 29 May" pp. 146–148 in *Czechoslovakia. The Party and the People*, Oxley *et. al*.eds., London: Penguin Press.

Dubček, Alexander (1993) *En självbiografi*, Jiri Hochman ed., Lars Olov Skeppholm trs., Sweden. Wahlström & Widstrand.

Dubček, Jiří (1986) "Bez kompromisů," *Hospodářské noviny*, 34:1&4.

Dvořáková, Vladimíra (1993) "Transition to Democracy in the Czech Republic," unpublished manuscript, Prague Economic University.

East, Roger, *Revolutions in Eastern Europe*, London: Pinter Publishers.

Earle, John S. & Frydman, Roman & Andrzej Rapaczynski eds.(1993), *Privatization in the Transition to a Market Economy: Studies of Preconditions and Policies in Eastern Europe.* London: Pinter Publishers.

Ebel, Horst (1990) *Abrechnung: Das Scheitern der ökonomischen Theorie und Politik des "realen Sozialismus,"* Berlin: Verlag Die Wirtschaft Berlin GmbH.

Eckstein, Harry (1988) "A Culturalist Theory of Political change," *American Political Science Review,* 3:789–804.

Ekiert, Grzegorz (1991) "Democratization Processes in East Central Europe: A Theoretical Reconsideratin," *British Journal of Political Science,* 21:285–313.

Eklund, Klas & Reichard, Per (1976) *Är Sovjet kapitalistisk?,* Stockholm: Röda rummet.

Elster, Jon (1989a) *The Cement of Society: A Study of Social Order,* Cambridge et al.: Cambridge University Press.

Elster, Jon (1989b) *Nuts and Bolts,* Cambridge, New York & Melbourne: Cambridge University Press.

Elster, Jon (1990) "When Communism Dissolves," *London Review of Books,* 28 January.

Elster, Jon (1993) "Constitution-Making In Eastern Europe: Rebuilding the Boat in the Open Sea," *Public Administration,* 71:169–217.

Engman, Ingemar, (1969) "Invasion och motstånd i tjeckoslovakien," *Fock och försvars skriftseries nr 5,* Stockholm.

Escobar, Arturo & Alvarez, Sonia E.(1992) "Conclusion: Theoretical and Political Horizons of Change in Contemporary Latin American Social Movements," pp. 317–331 in Arturo Escobar & Sonia E. Alvarez eds., *The Making of Social Movements in Latin America,* Boulder et al.: Westview Press.

Eskola, Antti (1988) *Socialpsykologi,* 9th ed., trs. by Synnöve Ståhle, Stockholm: Awe/Gebers.

Etzioni, Amitai (1992) "Toward a New Decision-Making Model," pp. 89–111, in Marty Zey ed., *Decision Making: Alternatives to Rational Choice Models,* Newbury Park et al.: Sage.

Falus, Katalin Szikra (1991) "Expertise and Loyalty—the Top-level Managers of the Economics," *AULA. Society and Economy,* 2:81–95.

Federální statistický úrad (1990a) *Statistická ročenka české a slovenské federativní republiky 1990,* Prague: SNTL.

Federální statistický úrad (1990b) *Statistické údaje, které jsme nesméli znát,* Prague: SNTL.

Feffer, John (1992) *Eastern Europe after the Revolutions,* Boston: South End Press.

Fehér, Ference (1992) "Marxism as Politics: An Obituary," *Problems of Communism,* **January-April:**11–17.

Fehér, Ference & Heller, Agnes & Márkus, György (1983) *Dictatorship over Needs,* Oxford: Basil Blackwell.

Feist, Jess (1975) *Theories of Personality,* New York et al.: Holt, Rinehart & Winston.

Fellegi, Tamas L. (1992) "Regime Transformation and the Mid-Level Bureaucratic Forces in Hungary," pp. 119–150 in Peter M.E. Volten ed., *Bound to Change,* Colorado: Institute for East-West Studies, Westview Press.

Filip, Václav & Valach, Josef (1986) "Globální hodnotový ukazatel," *Hospodářské noviny,* 33:4.

Flathman, Richard E. (1975) "Some Familiar but False Dichotomies Concerning 'Interests,'" *Political Theory,* 3:277–287.

Fleyberk, Jiří (1990) *Československé probuzení,* Prague: Orbis.

Freeman, Michael (1972) "Review Article: Theories of Revolution" *British Journal of Political Science,* 2:339–359.

Fremera, Miloslav et al. (1984) *Základy politické ekonomie,* Prague: Nakladatelství svoboda.

Frentzel-Zagórska, Janina (1990) "Civil Society in Poland and Hungary," *Soviet Studies,* 4:759–777.

Frentzel-Zagórska, Janina & Zagórski, Krzysztof (1989) "East European Intellectuals on the Road of Dissent: The old Prophecy of a New Class Re-examined," *Politics & Society,* 1:89–113.

Friedrich, Walter (1990) "Mentalitätswandlungen der Jugend in der DDR," *Aus Politik und Zeitgeschite,* B 16–17:25–37.

Fristedt, Karin (1993) *Charta 77—ett moraliskt alternativ?* Graduating paper presented at the Department of Government, Uppsala University.

Frydman, Roman & Rapaczynski, Andrzej & Earle, John S. et al. (1993) *The Privatization Process in Central Europe*, Budapest, London & New York: CEU Press.

Fukuyama, Francis (1993) "The Modernizing Imperative: The USSR as an Ordinary Country," *The National Interest*, **31**:10–18.

Gál, Peter (1987) "Der Strukturwandel in der Weltwirtschaft und der ungarische Westhandel," pp. 53–71 in Rüdiger Zellentin ed., *Ostpanorama Sonderausgabe 1989*, 22nd international seminar on East-West Trade, Linz: Gesellschaft für Ost- und Südostkunde.

Gati, Charles (1990) *The Bloc that Failed: Soviet-East European Relations in Transition*, Bloomington & Indianapolis: Indiana University Press.

Gazsó, Ference (1992) "Cadre Bureaucracy and the Intelligentsia," *The Journal of Communist Studies*, **3**:76–90.

Gebethner, Stanislaw (1992) "Political Reform in the Process of Round Table Negotiations," pp. 50–68 in Sanford ed., *Democratization in Poland, 1988–90: Polish Voices*, New York: St. Martin's Press.

Gella, Aleksander (1989) *Development of Class Structure in Eastern Europe: Poland & Her Southern Neighbors*. Albany: State University of New York Press.

George, Alexander L. (1991) "The Transition in U.S.-Soviet Relations, 1985–90: An Interpretation from the Perspective of International Relations Theory and Political Psychology," *Political Psychology*, **3**:469–486.

Geremek, Bronislaw (1991) "Die *Civil Society* gegen den Kommunismus: Polens Botschaft," trs. by Holger Fliessbach, pp. 264–273 in Klett Cotta ed., *Europa und die Civil Society*, Stuttgart: Ernst Klett Verlag.

Gerrits, André (1990) *The Failure of Authoritarian Change: Reform, Opposition and Geo-Politics in Poland in the 1980s*, Aldershot et al.: Dartmouth.

Gill, Graeme (1982) "Personal Dominance and the Collective Principle: Individual Legitimacy in Marxist-Leninist Systems," pp. 94–110 in T.H. Rigby & Ference Fehér eds., *Political Legitimation in Communist States*, London & Basingstoke: The Macmillian Press LTD.

Gill, Graeme (1991) "Sources of Political Reform in the Soviet Union," *Studies in Comparative Communism*, **3**:235–257.

Glaeßner, Ger-Joachim (1993) "Am Ende des Staatssozialismus—Zu den Ursachen des Umbruchs in der DDR," pp. 70–92 in Hans Joas & Martin Kohli eds., *Der Zusammenbruch der DDR*, Frankfurt am Main: Suhrkamp.

Główny urzad statyzstyczny (1986) *Rocznik statystyczny 1986* Warsaw: Główny Urzad Statystyczny.

Główny urzad statyzstyczny (1990) *Rocznik statystyczny 1990* Warsaw: Główny Urzad Statystyczny.

Golan, Galia (1973) *Reform Rule in Czechoslovakia: The Dubček Era 1968–1969*, Cambridge, Cambridge University Press.

Gołębiowski, Janusz W. et al. (1994) *Transforming the Polish Economy*, Volume I, Warsaw: Warsaw School of Economics.

Gomulka, Stanislaw (1985) "The Incompatibility of Socialism and Rapid Innovation," pp. 12–31 in Mark E. Schaffer ed., *Technology Transfer and East-West Relations*, London & Sydney: Croom Helm.

Goodwin, Jeff & Skocpol, Theda (1989) "Explaining Revolutions in the Contemporary Third World," *Politics & Society*, **4**:489–509.

Gramatzki, Hans (1977) "Die polnische Arbeiterselbstverwaltung" pp. 117–140 in Gudrun Lemân and Hans Gramatzki, *Arbeiterselbstverwaltung und Mitbestimmung in den Staaten Osteuropas*, Hanover: Fackelträger Verlag.

Granovetter, Mark (1978) "Threshold Models of Collective Behavior," *American Journal of Sociology*, **6**:1420–1443.

Gregory, Paul R. (1990) *Restructuring the Soviet Economic Bureaucracy*, Cambridge et al.: Cambridge University Press.

Griffith, William E. (1989a) "Central and Estern Europe: The Global Context," pp. 1–11 in Griffith ed., *Central and Eastern Europe: The Opening Curtain?* Boulder et al.: Westview Press.

Griffith, William E. (1989b) "The German Democratic Republic," pp. 314–337 in Griffith ed., *Central and Eastern Europe: The Opening Curtain?* Boulder et al.: Westview Press.

Gruntorád, Jiří (1990) "Oberoende medborgarinitiativ i Tjeckoslovakien," pp. 7–38 in Michal Konůpek & Miroslava Slavíčková eds., *Den "leende revolutionens" rötter*, trs. Lenka Elvingson & Karin Mossdal, Stockholm, Charta 77-stiftelsen.

Guess, Raymond (1981) *The Idea of a Critical Theory: Habermas and the Frankfurt School*, Cambridge et al.: Cambridge University Press.

Gulcyński, Mariusz (1992) "Systemic Change in Poland: a Historical-Philosphical Approach" pp. 35–50 in George Sanford ed., *Democratization in Poland, 1988–90: Polish Voices*, New York: St. Martin's Press.

Gurr, Ted Robert (1970) *Why Men Rebel*, New Jersey, Princeton University Press.

Habermas, Jürgen (1977) *Legitimationsprobleme im Spätkapitalismus*, 4th edition, Frankfurt am Main: Suhrkamp Verlag.

Habermas, Jürgen (1988) *Theorie des kommunikativen Handelns*, two volumes, 4th edition, Frankfurt am Main: Suhrkamp Verlag.

Habermas, Jürgen (1990) "What Does Socialism Mean Today? The Rectifying Revolution and the Need for New Thinking on the Left," *New Left Review*, 183:3–21.

Haendck-Hoppe (1986) "Startschwierigkeiten in der Außenwirtschaft," *FS Analysen: Teil I*, Forschungsstelle für gesamtdeutsche wirtschaftliche und soziale Fragen, 4:46–74.

Haffner, Friedrich (undated) *Grundbegriffe der marxistischen Politischen Ökonomie des Kapitalismus*, Berlin: Colloquium Verlag.

Hage, Jerald & Meeker, Barbara Foley (1988) *Social Causality*, Boston: Unwin Hyman.

Haggard, Stephan & Kaufman, Robert R. (1995) *The Political Economy of Democratic Transitions*, Princeton: Princeton University Press.

Halik, Jan (1986) "Ceny nepodporují efektivnost," *Hospodářské noviny*, 23:4.

Hankiss, Elemér (1989a) "Between Two Worlds," *Research Review*, 2:39–58.

Hankiss, Elemér (1989b) "Demobilization, Self-Mobilization and Quasi-Mobilization in Hungary, 1948–1987," *East European Politics and Societies*, 1:105–151.

Hankiss, Elemér (1990a) "In Search of a Paradigm," *Dædalus*, 1:183–213.

Hankiss, Elemér (1990b) "What the Hungarians Saw First," pp. 13–38 in Gwyn Prins ed., *Spring in Winter: The 1989 Revolutions*, Manchester & New York: Manchester University Press.

Hanzel, Vladimír ed. (1991) *Zrychlenýtep dějin: Reálně drama o desiti jednáních*, Prague: OK centrum.

Hardin, Russell (1982) *Collective Action*, Baltimore & London: John Hopkins University Press.

Harman, Chris (1983) *Class Struggles in Eastern Europe 1945–83*, 2nd ed., London & Sydney: Pluto Press.

Hatschikjan, Magarditsch A. (1987) "Prag, Gorbačov und die Umgestaltung," *Interne Studien, Nr. 8*, Bonn: Konrad-Adenauer-Stiftung.

Havel, Václav (1973) "On the Theme of Opposition" pp. 131–140 in Oxley et al. eds., *Czechoslovakia: The Party and the People*, London: Penguin Press.

Haverman, Rober (1981) *I morgon*, trs. by Frederik Sjögren, Stockholm: Ordfronts förlag.

Havlik, Peter & levcik, Friedrich (1985) "The Gross Domestic Product of Czechoslovakia 1970–1980," *World Bank Staff Working Papers Number 772: A Background Study for Dollar GNPs of the USSR and Eastern Europe*. Washington, D.C.: The World Bank.

Hechter, Michael (1994) "Theoretical Implications of the Demise of State Socialism," *Theory and Society*, 2:155–168.

Hejzlar, Zdenek (1976) *Reformkommunismus: Zur Geschichte der Kommunistischen Partei der Tschechoslowakei*, trs.Peter Aschner, Köln-Frankfurt am Main: EuropäischeVerlagsanstalt.

Hejzlar, Zdenek (1978) *Tjeckoslovakien tio år efteråt*, Stockholm: Utrikesolitiska institutet.

Hela världen i faka '87 (1987) Stockholm: Bonniers.

Heller, Agnes (1982) "Phases of Legitimation in Soviet-Type Societies," pp. 45–63 in T.H. Rigby & Ference Fehér eds., *Political Legitimation in Communist States*, London & Basingstoke: The Macmillian Press LTD.

Heneka A., et al. eds. (1985) *A Besieged Culture*, Stockholm-Vienna, The Charta 77 Foundation and International Helsinki Federation for Human Rights.

Henyś, Otta (1985) "Poválečný vývoj československého zahraničního obchodu," *Československý Zahraniční Obchod*, 5:3–5.

Hermansson, Jörgen (1992) "Democratization of Eastern Europe: A Game Theoretic Perspective," *Scandinavian Political Studies*, 3:217–233.

Herzmann, Jan (1992) "Volby v kontextu vývoje veřejného mínění 1989–1991," *Sociologický časopis*, 2:165–183.

Higley, John & Pakulski, Jan (1992) "Revolution and Elite Transformation in Eastern Europe," *Australian Journal of Political Science*, 27:104–119.

Hill, Ronald J. & Löwenhardt, John (1991) "*Nomenklatura* and *Perestroika*," *Government and Opposition*, 2:229–243.

Hill, Ronal J. & Frank, Peter (1986) *The Soviet Communist Party*, 3rd ed., Boston et al.: Unwin Hyman.

Hirschman, Albert (1993) "Exit, Voice, and the Fate of the German Democratic Republic: An Essay in Conceptual History," *World Politics*, 45:173–202.

Hodný, Martin (1991) *Českoslovenští politici 1918/1991: Stručné životopisy*, Prague: Nakladatelství M. Hodný.

Hoffman J. (1966) *Zentralverwaltungswirtschaft*, Frantfukt am Main et al.: Verlag Moritz Disterweg.

Holc, Janine P. (1992) "Solidarity and the Polish State: Competing Discursive Strategies on the Road to Power," *East European Politics and Societies*, 2:121–140.

Holesovsky, Vaclav (1970) "Planning and the Market in the Czechoslovak Reform," unpublished speech given at the Research Conference on Economic Reform in Eastern Europe, November 16–18, 1970 at the University of Michigan Comparative Economics Program and Center for Russian and East European Studies, Michigan.

Holtmann, Dieter & Strasser, Hermann (1990) "Comparing Class Structures and Class Consciousness in Western Societies," in Max Haller ed., *Class Structure in Europe: New Findings from East-West Comparisons of Social Structure and Mobility*. Amonk, New York: M.E. Sharpe 1990.

Holubec ed., (1990) *Kronika sametové revoluce*, Czechoslovakia: ČTK-Repro.

Horáček, Michal (1990) *Jak Pukaly ledy*, Prague: Ex libris.

Hough, Jerry F. (1989) "The Politics of Successful Economic Reform," *Soviet Economy*, 5:3–46.

Hough, Jerry F. (1993) "The Logic of Collective Action and the Pattern of Revolutoinary Behavior" pp. 347–368 in Frederic J. Fleron, Jr. & Erik P. Hoffmann eds, *Post-Communist Studies & Political Science: Methodology and Empirical Theory in Sovietology*, Boulder et al.: Westview.

Huinink, Johannes & Mayer, Karl Ulrich (1993) "Lebensverläufe im Wandel der DDR-Gesellschaft," in Hans Joas & Martin Kohli eds., *Der Zusammenbruch der DDR*, Frankfurt am Main: Suhrkamp, pp. 151–171.

Humphrey, Sarah (1990) "A Comparative Chronology of Revolution, 1988–1990," pp. 211–240 in Gwyn Prins ed., *Spring in Winter: The 1989 Revolutions*, Manchester & New York: Manchester University Press.

Hungarian Central Statistical Office (1991) *Hungarian Statistical Yearbook 1990*, Budapest: Hungarian Central Statistical Office.

Huntington, Samuel P. (1968) *Political Order in Changing Societies*, New Haven & London: Yale University Press.

Huntington, Samuel P. (1984) "Will More Countries Become Democratic?" *Political Science Quartely*, 2:193–218.

Huntington, Samuel P (1991) *The Third Wave: Democratization in the Late Twentieth Century*, Norman & Longon: University of Oklahoma Press.

Isaac, Jeffrey C. (1987) *Power and Marxist Theory: A Realist View*, Ithaca & London: Cornell University Press.

Israel, Joachim (1982) *Alienation och byråkratisering—industrisamhället i omvandling*: Stockholm: Awe/Gebers.

James, Robert Rhodes (1969) *The Czechoslovak Crisis 1968*, London, Weidenfeld & Nicolson.

Janos, Adrew (1991) "Social Science, Communism, and the Dynamics of Political Change," *World Politics*, 1:81–112.

Janowski, Karol B. (1992) "From Monopoly to Death-Throes: the PZPR in the Process of Political Transformation," pp. 162–176 in Sanford ed., *Democratization in Poland, 1988–90: Polish Voices*, New York: St. Martin's Press.

Janson, Carl-Heinz (1991) *Totengräber der DDR*, Düsseldorf et al.: ECON Verlag.

Jaruzelski, Wojciech (1992/1993) *Erinnerungen: Mein Leben für Polen*. Trs. by Hans Kray, Munich & Zurich: Piper.

Jeffries, Ian (1992) "Industrial Reform in Historical Perspective," pp. 1–43 in Jeffries ed., *Industrial Reform in Socialist Countries: From Restructuring to Revolution*, Hants England: Edward Elgar.

Johnson, Chalmers (1964) *Revolution and the Social System*, Stanford: Hoover Institution Press.

Johnson, Chalmers (1983) *Revolutionary Change*, 2nd ed., London: Longman.

Jowitt, Ken (1992) *New World Disorder: The Leninist Extinction*, Berkeley et al.: University of California Press.

Judt, Tony (1991) "The Dilemmas of Dissidence: The Politics of Opposition in East-Central Europe," pp. 253–302 in Ferenc Fehér & Andrew Arato eds., *Crisis and Reform in Eastern Europe*, New Brunswick & London: Transaction Publishers.

Judt, Tony (1992) "Metamorphosis: The Democratic Revolution in Czechoslovakia," in Ivo Banac ed., *Eastern Europe in Revolution*, Ithaca & London: Cornell University Press.

Kaminski, Antoni Z. (1992) *An Institutional Theory of Communist Regimes: Design, Function, and Breakdown*, San Francisco: ICS.

Kamiński, Barłomiej (1991) *The Collapse of State Socialism: The Case of Poland*, Princeton: Princeton University Press.

Kagarlitskij, Boris (1989) "Perestrojka: förändringens dialektik," *Zenith*, **104/105:51–66**.

Karklins, Rasma & Petersen, Roger (1993) "Decision Calculus of Protesters and Regimes: Eastern Europe 1989," *The Journal of Politics*, **3:588–614**.

Karlsson, Christer (1993) "Hegel och den tredje ståndpunkten," graduating paper presented at Uppsala University, Department of Government.

Kaśpárek, Pavel (1985) "Normativy mezd a jejich vazba na produktivita práce," *Plánované hospodařstvi*, **9:46–49**.

Kende, Jiři (1982) "Tschechoslowakei: Ziele, Problem und Strategien der Wirtschaftspolitik zu Beginn der 80er Jahre," *Berichte des Osteuropa Instituts und der Freien Universität Berlin, Heft 127*, Berlin.

Kirkpatrick, Jeane (1979) "Dictatorships and Double Standards," *Commentary*, **11:34–45**.

Kitschelt, Herbert P. (1986) "Political Opportunity Structures and Political Protest: Anti-Nuclear Movements in Four Democracies," *British Journal of Political Science* **16:57–85**.

Kleberg, Olof (1968a) "En mänsklig socialism: Det tjeckoslovakiska kommunistpartiets aktionsprogram" pp. 109–128 in *Reform. Ockupation: Tjeckoslovakien 1968*, Stockholm: Bokförlaget Aldus/Bonniers.

Kleberg, Olof (1968b) "Författarna och demokratiseringen" pp. 65–108 in *Reform. Ockupation: Tjeckoslovakien 1968*, Stockholm: Bokförlaget Aldus/Bonniers.

Klusáková, Jana (1993) *Jiří Dienstbier rozmlouvají nadoraz: Nejen o tom, jak si stojíme ve světě*, Prague: Primus.

Knight, Amy W. (1988) "The KGB and Soviet Reform," *Problems of Communism*, **September-October:61–70**.

Kolakowski, Leszek (1978/1987) *Main Currents of Marxism: Vol. 1. The Founders*, Oxford & New York: Oxford University Press.

Kolarska-Bobińska (1990) "The Myth of the Market and the Reality of Reform," pp. 160–179 in Stanisław Gomułka & Antony Polonsky eds., *Polish Paradoxes*, London & New York: Routledge.

Kołodko, Grzegorz W. (1990) "Crisis, Adjustment and Growth in Socialist Economy: Political Challenges and the Dilemmas of Economic Sciences," *Polish Institute of Finance Working Papers No 7*, Warsaw.

Konrád, György (1985) *Anti-Politik*, trs. by Maria Ortman & Staffan Holmgren, Stockholm: Alba.

Kontorovich, Vladimir (1993) "The Economic Fallacy," *The National Interest*, **31:35–45**.

Konůpek, Michael (1990) *Dagbok fra Praha*, Oslo: Exlibras forlag.

Korbel, Josef (1959) *The Communist Subversion of Czechoslovakia 1938–1948: The Failure of Coexistence.* New Jersey: Princeton University Press.

Korbonski, Andrzej (1989) "The Politics of Economic Reforms in Eastern Europe: The Last Thirty Years," *Soviet Studies*, **1:1–19**.

Kornai, János (1986) "The Hungarian Reform Process: Visions, Hopes, and Reality," *Journal of Economic Literature*, **24:1687–1737**.

Kornai, János (1990) *The Road to a Free Economy: Shifting from a Socialist System: The Example of Hungary*, New York & London: W.W. Norton & Company.

Körösényi, András (1992a) "The Decay of Communist Rule in Hungary," pp. 1–12 in András Bozóki, András Körösényi & George Schöpflin eds, *Post-Communist Transition, Emerging Pluralism in Hungry*, London & New York: Pinter Publishers & St. Martin's Press.

Körösényi, András (1992b) "The Hungarian Parliamentary Elections, 1990," pp. 72–87 in András Bozóki, András Körösényi & George Schöpflin eds, *Post-Communist Transition, Emerging Pluralism in Hungry*, London & New York: Pinter Publishers & St. Martin's Press.

Kosta, Jiří (1974) *Sozialistische Planwirtschaft: Theorie und Praxis*, Opladen: Westdeutscher Verlag.

Kosta, Jiří (1978) *Abriß der sozialökonomischen Entwicklung der Tschechoslowakei 1945–77*, Frankfurt am Main: Suhrkamp Verlag.

Kosta, Jiří (1984) *Wirtschaftssysteme des realen Sozialismus: Probleme und Alternativen*, Köln: Bund-Verlag.

Kosta, Jiří (1985) *Neue Reformansätze im Wirtschaftssystem der CSSR*, Berichte des Bundesinstituts für ostwissenschaftliche und internationale Studien, nr. 21, Köln.

Kosta, Jiří (1990) "Systemwandel in der Tschechoslowakei: Ökonomische und politische Aspekte," *Osteuropa*, **9:802–818**.

Krejčí, Oskar (1991) *Proč to prasklo, aneb hovory o demokracii a "sametové revoluci"*, Prague: Trio.

Krenz, Egon (1990) *Wenn Mauern fallen: Die friedliche Revolution. Vorgeschichte—Ablauf—Auswirkungen*, Vienna: Paul Neff Verlag.

Krisch, Henry (1982) "Political Legitimation in the German Democratic Republic," pp. 111–125 in T.H. Rigby & Ference Fehér eds., *Political Legitimation in Communist States*, London & Basingstoke: The Macmillian Press LTD.

Kubíčková, Miluše (1968) *Typologie nalnotcých, zvláště politicleých orientaci vysokoškolských studentů*, doctoral dissertation in pedagogy, Charles University, Prague.

Kubik, Jan (1994) "Who Done It: Workers, Intellectuals, or Someone Else? Controversy over Solidarity's Origins and Social Composition," *Theory and Society*, **3:441–466**.

Kuhn, Ekkehard (1939) *Gorbatschow und die deutsche Einheit: Aussagen der wichtigsten russischen und deutschen Beteiligten*, Bonn: Bouvier Verlag.

Kühnel, Wolgang & Sallmon-Metzner, Carola (1991) "Protestkulturen und Protestdiskurse im Wandel der DDR-Gesellschaft," *Berliner Journal für Soziologie*, **3:369–382**.

Kundera, Milan (1985) "I Am Weighing My Words Carefully," p. 128 in A. Heneka et al. eds. *A Besieged Culture*, Stockholm-Vienna: The Charta 77 Foundation and International Helsinki Federation for Human Rights.

Kundigraber, Claudia (1996a) *Polens Weg in die Demokratie: Der Runde Tisch und der unerwartete Machtwechsel* (Göttingen: Cuvillier Verlag).

Kundigraber, Claudia (1996b) "Political Culture of Compromise in Poland," pp. 107–120 in Andrzej W. Jabłoński & Gerd Meyer eds., *The Political Culture of Poland in Transition*, Wrocław: Wydawnictwo Uniwersytetu Wrocławskiego.

Kuran, Timur (1991) "Now out of Never: The Element of Surprise in the East European Revolution of 1989," *World Politics*, **44:7–48**.

Kurz, Robert (1994) *Der Kollaps der Modernisierung: Vom Zusammenbruch des Kasernensozialismus zur Krise der Weltökonomie*, Leipzig: Reclam Verlag.

Kusin, Vladimir V. (1978) *From Dubcek to Charter 77: Czechoslovakia 1968–78*, Edinburgh: Q Press.

Kyn, Oldřich (1972) "Die tschechoslowakische Wirtschaftsreform und ihr Ende," pp. 139–180 in Höhmann, Kaser & Thalheim eds, *Die Wirtschaftsordnungen Osteuropas im Wandel: Band I*, Freiburg.

Kwiatkowski, Stanislaw (1992) "Public Opinion in Poland during the 1980s," pp. 127–135 in Sanford ed., *Democratization in Poland, 1988–90: Polish Voices*, New York: St. Martin's Press.

Laba, Roman (1991) *The Roots of Solidarity: A Politcal Sociology of Poland's Working-Class Democratization*, Princeton: Princeton University Press.

Lebow, Richard Ned (1981) *Between Peace and War: The Nature of International Crisis*, Baltimore & London: John Hopkins University Press.

Lemân, Gudrun (1977) "Die tschechoslowakischen Reformvorstellungen von 1968/1969," pp. 141–153 in Gudrun Lemân & Hans Gramatzki, *Arbeiterselbstverwaltung und Mitbestimmung in den Staaten Osteuropas*, Hanover: Fackelträger Verlag.

Lemke, Christiane (1991) *Die Ursachen des Umbruchs 1989: Politische Sozialisation in der ehemaligen DDR*, Opladen: Westdeutscher Verlag.

Lengyel, László (1992) "The Character of the Political Parties in Hungary (Autumn 1989), pp. 30–44 in András Bozóki, András Körösényi & George Schöpflin eds, *Post-Communist Transition, Emerging Pluralism in Hungry*, London & New York: Pinter Publishers & St. Martin's Press.

Leptin, Gert (1986) "Aktuelle und unaktuelle Probleme der Wirtschaftspolitik in der DDR," *FS Analysen Teil I*, Forschungsstelle für gesamtdeutsche wirtschaftliche und soziale Fragen, 4:9–24.

Levčik, Friedrich (1985) "Wirtschaftsentwicklung und Wirtschaftsmechanismus in der Tschechoslowakei," *Europäische Rundschau: Vierteljahreszeitschrift für Politik, Wirtschaft und Zeitgeschichte*, 2:131–143.

Levčik, Friedrich (1986) "The Czechoslovak Economy in the 1980's" in *East European Economies: Slow Growth in the 1980's: Vol. 3*, Washington: Congress of the United States, March 1986.

Levčik, Friedrich & Skolka, Jiri (1984) *East-West Technology Transfer Study of Czechoslovakia*, Paris: OECD.

Lewin, Moshe (1988) *The Gorbachev Phenomenon: A Historical Interpretation*, London: Hutchinson Radius.

Lewis, Paul G. (1992) "Introduction" pp. 1–15 in Lews ed., *Democracy and Civil Society in Eastern Europe*, Hampshire & London: St. Martin's Press

Lijphart, Arend (1971) "Comparative Politics and the Comparative Method," *The American Political Science Review*, 64:682–693.

Linz, Juan J. & Stepan, Alfred (1996) *Problems of Democratic Transition and Consolidation: Southern Europe, South America, and Post-Communist Europe* Baltimore: John Hopkins University Press.

Lipp, Wolfgang (1978) "Bürokratische, Partizipative und Kaderorganisation als Instrumente sozialer Steuerung," *Die Verwaltung*, 11:1–25.

Lipton, David & Sachs, Jeffrey (1990) "Poland's Economic Reform" in *Foreign Affairs*, Summer 1990, pp. 47–66.

Lomax, Bill (1990) "The Rise and Fall of the Hungarian Working Class," *Journal of Communist Studies*, 2:45–60.

Lowenthal, Richard (1983) "Beyond Totalitarianism?" pp. 209–267 in Irving Howe ed., *1984 Revisited: Totalitarianism in Our Century*, New York et al.: Harper & Row.

Lukes, Steven (1974/87) *Power: A Radical View*, Hampshire & London: Macmillan Education LTD.

McDonald, Jason (1993) "Transition to Utopia: A Reinterpretation of Economics, Ideas, and Politics in Hungary, 1984 to 1990," *East European Politics and Societies*, 2:203–239.

McSweeney, Dean & Tempest, Clive (1993) "The Political Science of Democratic Transition in Eastern Europe,"*Political Studies*, XLI:408–419.

Magas, Istvan (1990) "Reforms Under Pressure: Hungary," *East European Quarterly*, 1:65–100.

Mandel, Ernest (1991) *Beyond Perestroika: The Future of Gorbachev's USSR*, 2nd ed., trs. by Gus Fagan, London & New York: Verso.

Manicas, Peter T. (1987) *A History and Philosophy of the Social Sciences*, Oxford: Basil Blackwell.

Marer, Paul (1989) "Market Mechanism Reforms in Hungary," Peter Van Ness ed., *Market Reforms in Socialist Societies: Comparing China and Hungary*, Boulder & London: Lynee Reinner Publishers.

Marx, Karl (1844/1985) *Ökonomisch-philosophische Manuskripte aus dem Jahre 1844*, MEW 40, Berlin: Dietz Verlag.

Marx, Karl (1859/1985) *Kritik der Politischen Ökonomie*, pp. 3–160 in MEW:13, Berlin: Dietz Verlag.

Marx, Karl (1885/1987) *Der achtzehnte Brumaire des Louis Bonaparte*, pp. 88–170 in *Ausgewählte Werke*, Moscow: Progress.

Marx, Karl & Engels, Friedrich (1848/1987) *Manifest der Kommunistischen Partei*, pp. 27–57 in *Ausgewählte Werke*, Moscow: Progress.

Mason, David S. (1992) *Revolution in East-Central Europe: The Rise and Fall of Communism and the Cold War*, Boulder et al.: Westview Press.

Matějů, Petr (1992) "Beyond Educational Inequality in Czechoslovakia," *Czechoslovak Sociological Review Special Issue*, **August:37–59.**

Meuschel, Sigrid (1989–90) "The End of East German Socialism," *Telos*, **82:3–22.**

Meuschel, Sigrid (1991) "Wandel durch Auflehnung: Thesen zum Verfall bürokratischer Herrschaft in der DDR," *Berliner Journal für Soziologie*, **1:15–27.**

Meuschel, Sigrid (1992) *Legitimation und Parteiherrshaft in der DDR*, Frankfurt am Main: Suhrkamp.

Meuschel, Sigrid (1993) "Revolution in der DDR: Versuch einer sozialwissenschaftlichen Interpretation," pp. 93–115 in Hans Joas & Martin Kohli eds., *Der Zusammenbruch der DDR*, Frankfurt am Main: Suhrkamp.

Meyer, Gerd (1991) *Die DDR-Machtelite in der Ära Honecker*, Tübingen: Francke Verlag.

Migdal, Joel S. (1994) "The State in Society: an Approach to Struggles for Domination," pp. 7–34 in Joel S. Migdal, Atul Kohli & Vivienne Shue eds., *State Power and Social Forces: Domination and Transformation in the Third World*, Cambridge: Cambridge University Press.

Milanovic, Branko (1991) "Poverty in Esatern Europe in the Years of Crisis, 1978 to 1987: Poland, Hungary, and Yugoslavia," *The World Bank Economic Review*, **2:187–205.**

Miliband, Ralph (1969) *The State in Capitalist Society* (New York: Basic books).

Milke, Harry & Möller, Uwe & Schilling, Gerhard (1983) *Die Planmäßigkeit der Entwicklung der sozialistischen Volkswirtschaft*, 3rd edition, Berlin: Dietz Verlag.

Mišovič, Ján (1988) *Záverečná správa z výskumu č. 88–4: Názory našich občanov na vedúcu úlohu strany*, Prague: Ústav pro výzkum veřejného mínění při FSÚ.

Mittag, Günter (1991) *Um jeden Preis: Im Spannungsfeld zweier Systeme*, Berlin & Weimar: Aufbau-Verlag.

Mlynář, Zdeněk (1973) "Towards a Democratic Political Organization of Society" pp. 114–122 in *Czechoslovakia: The Party and the People*, Oxley et. al., eds., London: Penguin Press.

Mlynář, Zdeněk (1980) *Nattfrost*, trs. Gunnar Gällmo, Stockholm: Ordfronts förlag.

Modrow, Hans (1991) *Aufbruch und Ende*, Hamburg: Konkret Literatur Verlag.

Mohorita, Vlasil (1991) "Konec vlády jedné strany," *Edice Mosty*, **30–31.**

Molnár, Miklós (1971) *Budapest 1956: A History of the Hungarian Revolution*, trs. by Jennetta Ford, London: George Allen & Unwin Ltd.

Molnár, Miklós (1987/1990) *From Béla Kun to János Kádár: Seventy Years of Hungarian Communism*, trs. by Arnold J. Pomerans, New York: St. Martin's Press.

Moltz, James Clay (1993) "Divergent Learning and the Failed Politics of Soviet Economic Reform," *World Politics*, **45:301–25.**

Moreau, Jacques (1965) "Ou va l'economie des pays socialistes de l'Est?" *L'Economie*, 29 January.

Mühler, Kurt & Wilsdorf, Stefan H. (1991) "Die Leipziger Montagsdemonstration," *Berliner Journal für Soziologie*, **Sonderheft:37–45.**

Mujzel, Jan (1989) "Social-Economic Reforms in Eastern Europe and Real Socialism," *Communist Economics*, **1:3–16.**

Müller, Aleksander (1987) "Structural Change and Economic Reform in Poland," *Forschungsberichte*, nr. 133, The Vienna Institute for Comparative Economic Studies.

Munck, Gerardo (1994) "Democratic Transitions in Comparative Perspective," *Comparative Politics*, **3:357–372.**

Myant, Martin (1992) "Economic Reform and Political Evolution in Eastern Europe," *The Journal of Communist Studies*, **1**:108–127.

Narayanswamy, Ramnath (1992) "Causes and Consequences of the East European Revolutions of 1989," *Economic and Political Weekly*, 15 February, pp. 365–370.

Neumann, Thomas (1991) *Die Maßnahme: Eine Herrschaftsgeschichte der SED*, Hamburg: Rowohlt.

Norden, Peter (1977) *Prag 21 August: Das Ende des Prager Frühlings*, München: Wihelm Heyne Verlag.

Nove, Alec (1982) "Is There a Ruling Class in the USSR?" in Anthony Giddens & David Held eds., *Classes, Power, and Conflict*, Hampshire: Macmillan Press.

Nove, Alec (1983) "The Class Nature of the Soviet Union Revisited," *Soviet Studies*, **3**:298–312.

Nove, Alec (1984) *The Soviet Economic System*, 2nd ed., London, Goerge Allen & Unwin.

Nove, Alec (1989) *An Economic History of the U.S.S.R.*, 2nd ed., London, Penguin Books.

Nowak, Krzysztof (1988) "Covert Repressiveness and the Stability of a Political System: Poland at the End of the Seventies," *Social Research*, **1–2**:179–208.

Nuti, Domenico Mario (1990) "Internal and International Aspects of Monetary Disequilibrium in Poland" in *European Economy*, No. 43, pp. 169–182.

Nyírő, András (1992) "The Last Days of the Elite of the Communist Bureaucracy in Hungary," unpublished stencil.

O'Donnell, Guillermo & Schmitter, Philippe C. (1986) *Transitions from Authoritarian Rule: Tentative Conclusions about Uncertain Democracies*, Baltimore & London: The John Hopkins University Press.

OECD (1989) *External Debt Statistics*, Paris: OECD.

OECD (1991) *OECD Economic Surveys: Hungary 1991*, Paris: OCED.

OECD (1992) *Short-Term Economic Statistics Central and Eastern Europe*, Paris: OECD.

Offe, Claus (1985) *Disorganized Capitalism: Contemporary Transofrmations of Work and Politics*, John Keane ed., Oxford & NY: Polity Press.

Offe, Claus (1993) "Wohlstand, Nation, Republik: Aspekte des deutschen Sonderweges vom Sozialismus zum Kapitalismus," pp. 282–301 in Hans Joas & Martin Kohli eds., *Der Zusammenbruch der DDR*, Frankfurt am Main: Suhrkamp.

Offe, Claus (1994) *Der Tunnel am Ende des Lichts: Erkundungen der politischen Transformation im Neuen Osten*, Frankfurt: Campus Verlag.

Olson, Mancur (1979) "Die Logik des kollektiven Handelns," in W.W. Pommerrehne & B.S. Frey eds., *Ökonomische Theorie der Politik*, Berlin, Heidelberg, New York: Springer Verlag.

Olson, Mancur (1990) *How Bright are the Northern Lights? Some Questions about Sweden*, Lund: Lund University Press.

Opp, Karl-Dieter (1993) "DDR '89: Zu den Ursachen einer spontanen Revolution," pp. 194–221 in Hans Joas & Martin Kohli eds., *Der Zusammenbruch der DDR*, Frankfurt am Main: Suhrkamp.

Opp, Karl-Dieter & Gern, Christiane (1993) "Dissident Groups, Personal Networks, and Spontaneous Cooperation: The East German Revolution of 1989," *American Sociological Review*, **58**:659–680.

Orenstein, Mitchell (1988), "Václar Klaus: Revolutionary and Parliamentarian," *East European Constitutional Review,*Winter: **46**–55.

Osiatynski, Wiktor (1996) "The Roundtable Talks in Poland," pp. 21–68 in Jon Elster ed., *The Roundtable Talks and the Breakdown of Communism*, Chicago: University of Chicago Press.

Ost, David (1990) *Solidarity and the Politics of Anti-Politics: Opposition and Reform in Poland since 1968*, Philadelphia: Temple University Press.

Ost, David (1993) "The Politics of Interest in Post-Communist East Europe," *Theory and Society*, **22**:453–486.

Otál, M. & Sládek, Z. eds. (1990) *Deset pražských dnů: 17–27. listopad 1989*, Prague: Academia.

Owsiak, Sanisław (1992) "The Collapse of the Reform and the Decomposition of the System of Economic Regulation" pp. 55–66 in Jerzy Hausner & Tadeusz Klementewicz eds., *The Protracted Death-Agony of Real Socialism*, Warsaw: PANISP.

Parkin, Frank (1982) "System Contradiction and Political Transformation," pp. 574–587 in Anthony Giddens & David Held eds., *Classes, Power, and Conflict*, Hampshire: Macmillan Press.

REFERENCES

Pekker, Zsolt (1989) "Politische Veränderungen in Ungarn," *Osteuropa*, **10**:922–928.
Pelcynski, Z.A. (1988) "Solidarity and 'The Rebirth of Civil Society' in Poland, 1976–81," pp. 361–380 in John Keane ed., *Civil Society and the State: New European Perspectives*, London & New York: Verso.
Pelikán, Jiři (1975) *Prag tiger inte*, Stockholm: Tidens förlag.
Piekalkiewicz, Jaroslaw A. (1972) *Pulic Opinion Polling in Czechoslovakia, 1968–69: Results and Analysis of Surveys Conducted during the Dubcek Era*, New York: Prager Publishers.
Pithart, Petr (1992) manuscript of a speech given in Budapest, 23 Oct. 1992.
Plato (1970) *The Republic*, F.M. Cornford trs., New York & Oxford: Oxford University Press.
Plevza, Viliam (1991) *Vzostupy a pády: Gustáv Husák k prehovoril*, Slovakia: Tatrapress
Poland: Stagnation, Collapse or Growth? A Report by an Independent Group of Economists in Poland, (1988) London: Centre for Research into Communist Economies.
Pollack, Detlef (1993) "Religion und gesellschaftlicher Wandel: Zur Rolle der evangelischen Kirche im Prozeß des gesellschaftlichen Umbruchs in der DDR," in Hans Joas & Martin Kohli eds., *Der Zusammenbruch der DDR*, Frankfurt am Main: Suhrkamp, pp. 246–266.
Pond, Elizabeth (1993) *Beyond the Wall: Germany's Road to Unification*, Washington, D.C.: The Brookings Institution.
Poulantzas, Nicos (1978) *Political Power and Social Classes*, trs. by Timothy O'Hagan, London: Verso.
Przeworski, Adam (1986) "Some Problems in the Study of the Transition to Democracy," in Guillermo O'Donell, et al., eds. *Transitions from Authoritarian Rule: Prospects for Democracy*, Baltimore: John Hopkins University Press.
Przeworski, Adam (1988) "Democracy as a Contingent Outcome of Conflicts," pp. 59–80 in Elster & Slagstad eds., *Constitutionalism and Democracy*, Cambridge: Cambridge University Press.
Przeworksi, Adam (1991) *Democracy and the Market: Political and Economic Reforms in Eastern Europe and Latin America*, Cambridge et al.: Cambridge University Press.
Przeworski, Adam & Teune, Henry (1985) *The Logic of Comparative Social Inquiry*, Florida, Robert E. Krieger Publishing Company.
Przybylski, Peter (1991) *Tatort Politbüro: Die Akte Honecker*, Berlin: Rohwolt.
Przybylski, Peter (1992) *Tatort Politbüro: Band 2: Honecker, Mittag und Schalck-Golodkowski*, Berlin: Rohwolt
Ramet, Sabrina P. (1991) *Social Currents in Eastern Europe: The Sources and Meaning of the Great Transformation*, Durham & London: Duke Univeristy Press.
Reeve, Andrew & Ware, Alan (1980) "Interests in Political Theory," *British Journal of Political Science*, **13**:379–400.
Reich, Jens (1990) "Reflections on Becoming an East German Dissident, on Losing the Wall and a Country," pp. 65–98 in Gwyn Prins ed., *Spring in Winter: The 1989 Revolutions*, Manchester & New York: Manchester University Press.
Reißig, Rolf (1991) "Der Umbruch in der DDR und das Scheitern des "realen Sozialismus," in Rolf Reißis & Gert-Joachim Glaeßner eds., *Das Ende eines Experiments: Umbruch in der DDR und deutsche Einheit*, Berlin: Dietz Verlag.
Reißig, Rolf (1993) "Das Scheitern der DDR und des realsozialistischen Systems—Einige Ursachen und Folgen," in Hans Joas & Martin Kohli eds., *Der Zusammenbruch der DDR*, Frankfurt am Main: Suhrkamp, pp. 29–69.
Reykowski, Janusz (1990) "Resolving of the Large Scale Political Conflict: The Case of the Round Table Negotiations in Poland," revised version of paper presented at the 1990 Texas A&M Symposium on Group conflict.
Reykowski, Janusz (1994) "Why Did the Collectivist State Fail?" *Theory and Society*, **2**:233–252.
Roskin, Michael G. (1994) *The Rebirth of East Europe*, 2nd ed., Engelwood Cliffs: Prentice Hall.
Rothstein, Bo (1988) "Aktör-struktur ansatsen: Ett metodiskt dilemma," *Statsvetenskapliga tidskrift*, **1**:27–40.
Rothstein, Bo (1992) *Den korporative staten: Intresseorganisationer och statförvaltning i svensk politik*, Stockholm: Norstedts.
Rüddenklau, Wolfgan (1992) *Störenfried: DDR-Opposition 1986–1989*, Berlin: BasisDruck Verlag.

Rush, Myron (1993) "Fortune and Fate," *The National Interest*, 31:19–25.

Rychard, Andrzej (1992) "Politics and Society after the Breakthrough: the Sources and Threats to Political Legitimacy in Post-Communist Poland," pp. 136–161 in Sanford ed., *Democratization in Poland, 1988–90: Polish Voices*, New York: St. Martin's Press.

Saiedi, Nader (1988) "Agency and Freedom in Neofunctionalist Action Theory: A Critique," *Social Research*, 4:775–806.

Sakwa, Richard (1990) *Gorbachev and His Reforms 1985–1990*, New York et al.: Philip Allan.

Sampson, Steven (1990) "De östeuropeiska 'revolutionerna,'" *Zenith*, 108:19–27.

Sanford, George (1983) *Polish Communism in Crisis*, London & Canberra: Croom Helm (also New York: St. Martin's Press).

Sandford, George (1992) "The Polish Road to Democratisation: from Political Impasse to the 'Controlled Abdication' of Communist Power," pp. 1–34 in Sanford ed., *Democratization in Poland, 1988–90: Polish Voices*, New York: St. Martin's Press.

Sannerstedt, Anders (1991) "Implementering—hur politiska beslut genomförs i praktiken," in Bo Rothstein ed., *Politik som organisation*, Stockholm: SNS Förlag.

Saxonberg, Steven (1999) "Václav Klaus: The Rise and Fall of and Re-Emergence of a Charismatic Leader" *East European Politics and Society*, 2:391–418.

Schabowski, Günter (1990) *Das Politbüro: Ende eines Mythos*, book-long interview conducted by Frank Sieren & Ludwig Koehne, Hamburg: Rowholt.

Schabowski, Günter (1992) *Der Absturz*, Hamburg: Rowholt.

Schell, Orville (1994) *Mandate of Heaven: A New Generation of Entrepreneurs, Dissidents, Bohemians, and Technocrats Lays Claim to China's Future*, New York et al.: Simon & Schuster.

Schönsee, Reinhard & Lederer, Gerda (1991) "The Gentle Revolution," *Political Psychology*, 2:309–330.

Schöpflin, George (1983) "Opposition in Hungary: 1956 and Beyond," pp. 69–81 in Jane Leftwich Curry ed., *Dissent in Eastern Europe*, New York: Praeger.

Schöpflin, George (1991) "Conservatism in Hungary," *Problems of Communism*, January-April:60–68.

Schöpflin, George (1992) "From Communism to Democracy in Hungary," pp. 96–110 in András Bozóki, András Körösényi & George Schöpflin eds, *Post-Communist Transition, Emerging Pluralism in Hungary*, London & New York: Pinter Publishers & St. Martin's Press.

Schöpflin, George (1993/1994) *Politics in Eastern Europe*, Oxford UK & Cambridge USA: Blackwell.

Schöpflin, George & Tőkes, Rudolf & Völgyes, Iván (1988) "Leadership Change and Crisis in Hungary," *Problems of Communism*, 5:23–46.

Schroeder, Gertrude E. (1991) "The Soviet Economy on a Treadmill of Perestroika: Gorbachev's First Five Years," pp. 31–48, in Harley D. Balzer ed., *Five Years that Shook the World: Gorbachev's Unfinished Revolution*, Boulder et al.: Westview Press.

Scott, Alan (1990) *Ideology and the New Social Movements*, London et al.: Unwin Hyman.

Selucký, Radoslav (1969) *Reformmodell ČSSR—Entwurf einer sozialistischen Marktwirtschaft oder Gefahr für die Volksdemokratien?*, Hamburg. Rowholt.

Shen, Raphael (1993) *Economic Reform in Poland and Czechoslovakia: Lessons in Systemic Transformation*, Westport, Connecticut & London: Praeger.

Short, Nancy C. (1990) "*Perestroika* and Industrial Reform: Lessons from Hungary's New Economic Mechanism," *Coexistence*, 27:17–51.

Šik, Ota (1966) *Die tschechoslowakische Wirtschaft auf neuen Wegen*, 2nd edition, Prague: Orbis.

Šik, Ota (1972a) *Czechoslovakia: The Bureaucratic Economy*, White Plains: International Arts and Sciences.

Šik, Ota (1972b) *Sozialismus und Marktwirtschaft*, Trierer Scripte 2, Trier.

Šik, Ota (1981) *The Communist Power System*, trs. by Marianne Grund, Freidberg & New York: Praeger.

Simai, Mihaly (1991) "Hungarian Problems," *Government and Opposition*, 1:52.63.

Simatupang, Batara (1994) *The Polish Economic Crisis: Background, Causes and Aftermath*, London & New York: Routledge.

Simmons, Michael (1989) *The Unloved Country: A Portrait of East Germany Today*, London: Abacus.

Sitzler, Kathrin (1989) "Die Anfänge eines politischen Pluralismus in Ungarn," *Südosteuropa*, 38:678–694.

Skocpol, Theda (1979) *States and Social Revolutions: A Comparative Analysis of France, Russia, and China*, London et al.: Cambridge University Press.

Skocpol, Theda & Somers, Margaret (1980) "The Uses of Comparative History in Macrosocial Theory," *Comparative Studies in Society and History*, 22:174–97.

Skocpol, Theda (1985) "Bringing the State Back In: Strategies of Analysis in Current Research," pp. 333–43, in Evans, Rueschemeyer & Skocpol eds., *Bringing the State Back In*, Cambridge et al., Cambridge University Press.

Slejška, Dragoslav & Herzmann, Jan & collective (1990) *Sondy do veřejného mínění (Jaro 1968, Podzim 1989)*, Prague: Nakladatelství Svoboda.

Słomczyński, Kazimierz M. (1994) "Class and Status in East-European Perspective," pp. 167–190 in Matti Alestalo, Erik Allardt, Andrzej Rychard & Włodzimierz Wesołowski eds., *The Transformation of Europe: Social Conditions and Consequences*, Warsaw: IFiS Publishers.

Smith, Gordon B. (1992) *Soviet Politics: Struggling with Change*, 2nd edition, London et al.: MacMillan.

Šourek, S. (1986) "Modifications in the System of Financial Management of Economic Production Units and Enterprises for the 8th Five-Year Plan," *Czechoslovak Economic Digest*, 2:11–23.

Spittman, Ilse & Helwig, Gisela (1989/90) *Chronik der Ereignisse in der DDR*, 4th edition, Köln: Edition Deutschland Archiv im Verlag Wissenschaft und Politik.

Staar, Richard ed. (1981, 1983, 1986, 1988, 1989) *Yearbook on International Communist Affairs*, Stanford: Hoover Institution.

Staatliche Zentralverwaltung für Statistik (1989) *Statistisches Jahrbuch 1989 der Deutschen Demokratischen Republik*, Berlin: Staatsverlag der Deutschen Demokratischen Republik.

Staatliche Zentralverwaltung für Statistik (1990) *Statistisches Jahrbuch 1990 der Deutschen Demokratischen Republik*, Berlin: Staatsverlag der Deutschen Demokratischen Republik.

Staehle, Dr. Wolfgan H. (1987) *Management*, Munich: Verlag Franz Vahlen.

Staniszkis, Jadwiga (1984) *Poland's Self-Limiting Revolution*, Jan T. Gross ed., Princeton: Princeton University Press.

Staniszkis, Jadwiga (1991) *The Dynamics of the Breakthrough in Eastern Europe: The Polish Experience*, Trs. by Chester A. Kisiel, Berkeley et al.: University of California Press.

Statistisches Amt der DDR (1990) *Statistiches Taschenbuch der Deutschen Demokratischen Republik*, Berlin: Rudolf Haufe Verlag.

Statistisches Bundesamt (1960) *Statistisches Jarhbuch für die Bundesrepublik Deutschland 1960*, Stuttgart & Mainz: W. Kohlhammer GmbH.

Statistisches Bundesamt (1990) *Statistisches Jarhbuch für die Bundesrepublik Deutschland 1990*, Stuttgart: Metzler-Poeschel Verlag.

Stein, Janice Gross (1985/89) "Calculation, Miscalculation, and Conventional Deterrence 1: The View from Cairo" pp. 34–60 in Robert Jarvis, Richard Ned Lebow & Janice Gross Stein eds., *Psychology and Deterrence*, Baltimore & London: John Hopkins University Press.

Steinberg, Dmitri (1990) "Trends in Soviet Military Expenditure," *Soviet Studies*, 4:675:699.

Stokes, Gale (1991) "Lessons of the East European Revolutions of 1989," *Problems of Communism*, Sept-Oct.:21.

Stone, Lawrence (1966) "Theories of Revolution," *World Politics*, 2:159–176.

Štouračová, Judita (1989) *Československá ekonomika a její hospodářské organizace v mezinárodní délbé práce*, Prague: Academia.

Sułek, Antoni (1994) "Systemic Transformation and the Reliability of Survey Research: Evidence from Poland," *Polish Sociological Review*, 2:85–100.

Süß, Walter ed. (1990) *TAZ DDR Journal zur Novemberrevolution August bis Dezember 1989*, 2nd edition, Berlin: TAZ.

Syrop, Konrad (1982) *Poland in Perspective*, London: Robert Hale.

Swain, Nigel (1989) "Hungary's Socialist Project in Crisis," *New Left Review*, 176:3–29.

Swain, Nigel (1992) *Hungary: The Rise and Fall of Feasible Socialism*, London & New York: Verso.

Swanton, Christine (1980) "The Concept of Interests," *Political Theory*, **1**:83–101.

Syzmanski, Albert (1984) *Class Struggle in Socialist Poland*, Now York: Praeger Publishers

Szabo, Mate (1991) "Die Rolle von sozialen Bewegungen im Systemwandel in Osteuropa: Vergleich zwischen Ungarn, Polen und der DDR," *Österreichische Zeitschrift für Politikwissenschaft*, **3**:275–288.

Szajkowski, Bogdan (1983) *Next to God. Poland: Politics and Religion in Contemporary Poland*, New York: St Martin's Press.

Szakolczai, Árpád & Horváth, Ágnes (1992) "The Discourse of Civil Society and the Self-elimination of the Party," pp. 16–31 in Paul Lewis ed., *Democracy and Civil Society in Eastern Europe*, Hampshire & London: St. Martin's Press.

Szelenyi, Ivan (1991) "Foreward," in Jadwiga Staniszkis, *The Dynamics of the Breakthrough in Eastern Europe. The Polish Experience*, Trs. by Chester A. Kisiel, Berkeley et al.: University of California Press.

Szelenyi, Ivan & Szelenyi, Balazs (1994) "Why Socialism Failed; Toward a Theory of System Breakdown—Causes of Disintegration of East European State Socialism," *Theory and Society*, **2**:211–232.

Szoboszlai, György (1991) "Political Transition and Constitutional Changes," pp. 195–212 in Szoboszlai ed., *Democracy and Political Transformation. Theories and East-Central European Realities*, Budapest: Hungarian Political Science Association.

Sztompka, Piotr (1995) "Trust: The Missing Resource of Post-Communist Society," forthcoming in German, in Sonderheft 1995, "Politische Soziologie," *Kölner Zeitschrift für Soziologie und Sozialpsychologie*, edited by Birgitta Nedelmann.

Szulc, Tad (1971) *Czechoslovakia Since World War II*, New York: Viking Press.

Taborsky, Edward (1961) *Communism in Czechoslovakia 1948–1960*, Princeton, Princeton University Press.

Taborsky, Edward (1968) "La réforme économique en Tchécoslovaquie: Bilan de la première année," *Témoignages*, **61**:43–49.

Taras, Ray (1984) *Ideology in a Socialist State. Poland 1956–1983*, Cambridge et al.: Cambridge University Press.

Taras, Ray (1986) *Poland. Socialist State, Rebellious Nation*, Bouldern & London: Westview Press.

Taras, Ray (1990) "The Crises of East European Communism: The Grand Failure of Manipulated Participation," *Journal of Communist Studies*, **3**:1–21.

Taras, Raymond (1992) "Marxist Critiques of Political Crises in Poland," pp. 81–114 in Raymond Taras ed., *The Road to Disillusion: From Critical Marxism to Postcommunism in Eastern Europe*, Armonk, New York; & London: M.E. sharpe, Inc.

Tarrow, Sidney (1989) *Struggle, Politics, and Reform: Collective Action, Social Movements, and Cycles of Protest*, Cornell Studies in International Affairs, Western Societies Papers, Occasional Paper No. 21, Center for International Studies, Cornell University.

Tarrow, Sidney (1991) "'Aiming at a Moving Target': Social Science and the Recent Rebellions in Eastern Europe," *Political Science & Politics*, **3**:12–20.

Taylor, Michael (1988) "Rationality and Revolutionary Collective Action" in Michael Taylor ed., *Rationality and Revolution*, Cambridge: Cambridge University Press.

Therborn, Göran (1971) *Klasser och ekonomiska system*, Sweden: Zenitserien 14.

Therborn, Göran (1980) *Vad gör den härskande klassen när den härskar?* trs. Gunnar Sandin, Sweden: Zenit.

Ticktin, Hillel (1987) "The Political Economy of Class in the Transitional Epoch," *Critique*, **20–21**:7–25.

Ticktin, Hillel (1992) *Origins of the Crisis in the USSR: Essays on the Political Economy of a Disintegrating System*, Armonk New York & London: Sharpe.

Tocqueville, Alexis de (1848/1981) *Democracy in America*, abridged with an introduction by Thomas Bender, trs. by Henry Reeve et al., New York: McGraw-Hill Inc.

Tocqueville, Alexis de (1856/1988) *The Ancien Régime*, trs. by John Bonner, London: Everyman's Library.

Tőkes, Rudolf L. (1990) "Hungary's New Political Elites: Adaptation and Change, 1989–90," *Problems of Communism*, 6:44–65.

Tőkes, Rudolf L. (1996) *Hungary's Negotiated Revolution: Economic Reform, Social Change and Political Sucession,* Cambridge: Cambridge University Press.

Toranski, Teresa (1987) *Oni: Stalin's Polish Puppets,* trs by Agnieszka Kolakowska, London: Collins Harvill

Touraine, Alain et al. (1982) *Solidarity: The Analysis of a Social Movement: Poland 1980–1981,* trs. by David Denby, Cambridge et al.: Cambridge University Press.

Trzeciakowski, Witold (1987) "Can the Polish Debt Problem be Solved?" *WIIW Forschungsberichte nr. 128,* The Vienna Institute for Comparative Econoimic Studies.

Trotsky, Leon (1937/1972) *The Revolution Betrayed: What is the Soviet Union and Where is it Going?,* 5th edition, New York: Pathfinder Press.

Trotsky, Leon (1942/1973) *In Defense of Marxism,* 2nd edition, New York: Pathfinder Press.

Turner, Ralph H. & Killian, Lewis M. (1972) *Collective Behavior,* 2nd ed., New Jersey: Prentice-Hall.

Tymowski, Andrzej W. (1993) "Poland's Unwanted Social Revolution," *East European Politics and Societies,* 2:169–202.

Typolt, Jiří (1966) "Le nouveau systeme des prix en Tchécoslovaquie," *Problèmes economiques,* 25 August.

UN (1989) *Economic Bulletin for Europe,* volume 41, New York: UN.

UN (1990) *Handbook of International Trade and Development Statistics 1989,* New York: UN.

UN (1991) *National Accounts Statistics: Main Aggregates and Detailed Tables, 1989,* parts I & II, New York: UN.

Urban, Jan (1992) "The Powerlessnes of the Powerful," unpublished manuscript.

Urban, László (1991) "Why was the Hungarian Transition Exceptionally Peaceful?" pp. 303–309 in in György Szoboszlai ed., *Democracy and Political Transformation: Theories and East-Central European Realities,* Budapest: Hungarian Political Science Association.

Váli, Ferenc A. (1961) *Rift and Revolt in Hungary: Nationalism versus Communism,* Cambridge Massachusetts: Harvard University Press.

Vanek, Jaroslav (1990) "On the Transition From Centrally Planned to Democratic Socialist Economies," *Economic and Industrial Democracy,* 11:179–203.

Varga, László (1991) "Geschichte in der Gegenwart—Das Ende der kollektiven Verdrängung und der demokratische Umbruch in Ungarn," pp. 167–181 in Rainer Deppe, Halmust Dubiel & Ulrich Rödel eds., *Demokratischer Umbruch in Osteuropa,* Frankfurt am Main: Suhrkamp.

Vintrová, Růžena (1989) "Continuity or Restructuring? (Some Problems of Long-Term Socio-Economic Forecasts)," *Czechoslovak Economic Papers,* 27:7–24.

Vlačil, Jan (1992) "Logika a retorika reformy," *Sociologické aktuality,* 2:14–15.

Volgyes, Ivan (1989) "Leadership Drift in Hungary: Empirical Observations on a Normative Concept," *Studies in Comparative Communism,* 1:23–41.

Voráček, Michael (1987) "Außenwirtschaftsbeziehungen der CSSR nach dem XVII. Parteitag der KPTsch," *Außenhandel der Tschechoslowakei* 2:6–11.

Voskamp, Ulrich & Wittke, Volker (1991) "Industrial Restructuring in the Former German Democratic Republic (GDR): Barriers to Adaptive Reform Become Downward Development Spirals," *Politics and Society,* 3:325–340.

Voslensky, Michael (1980/1984) *Nomenklatura: Anatomy of the Soviet Ruling Class,* trs. by Eric Mosbacher, London et al.: The Bodley Head.

Voszka, Eva (1993) "Spontaneous Privatization in Hungary," pp. 90–107 in Earle, John S. & Frydman, Roman & Andrzej Rapaczynski eds., *Privatization in the Transition to a Market Economy: Studies of Preconditions and Policies in Eastern Europe.* London: Pinter Publishers.

Wacker, Vladimír, (1983) *Internationale wirtschaftliche Zusammenarbeit,* Prague, Orbis.

Walder, Andrew J.G. (1994) "The Decline of Communist Power: Elements of a Theory of Institutional Change," *Theory and Society,* 2:297–324.

Waller, Michael (1994) *The End of the Communist Power Monopoly,* Manchester & New York: Manchester University Press.

Walter, Gregor (1990) "Der Kollaps der zentralen Machtstrukturen der DDR," *Sozialwissenschaftliche Informationen*, 3:158–169.

Wasilewski, Jacek (1990) "The Patterns of Bureaucratic Elitte Recruitment in Poland in the 1970s and 1980s," *Soviet Studies*, 4:743–757.

Weigle, Marcia A & Butterfield, Jim (1992) "Civil Society in Reforming Communist Regimes: The Logic of Emergence," *Comparative Politics*, 1:1–24.

Weir, Margaret & Skocpol, Theda (1985) "State Structures and the Possibilities for 'Keynesian' Responses to the Great Depression in Sweden, Britian, and the United States, in Peter B. Evans, Dietrich Rueschemeyer & Theda Skocpol eds, *Bringing the State Back In*, Cambridge et al.: Cambridge University Press.

Wesołowski, Włodzimierz (1990) "Transition from Authoritarianism to Democracy," *Social Research*, 2:435–461.

Wheaton, Bernard & Kavan, Zdeněk (1992) *The Velvet Revolution: Czechoslovakia, 1988–1991*, Boulder, San Francisco & Oxford: Westview Press.

Wielepp, Christoph (1990) "Montags abends in Leipzig," pp. 71–78 in Thomas Blanke & Rainer Erd eds., *DDR—Ein Staat vergeht*, Frankfurt am Main: Fischer.

Wielgohs, Jan & Schultz, Marianne (1990) "Reformbewegung und Volksbewegung: Politische und soziale Aspekte im Umbruch der DDR-Gesellschaft," *Aus Politik und Zeitgeschicte*, B 16–17:15–25.

Wielgohs, Jan & Schultz, Marianne (1993) "Von der 'friedlichen Revolution' in die politische Normalität: Entwicklungsetappen der ostdeutschen Bürgerbewegung," pp. 222–245 in Hans Joas & Martin Kohli eds., *Der Zusammenbruch der DDR*, Frankfurt am Main: Suhrkamp.

Wienert, Helgard & Slater, John (1986) *East-West Technology Transfer: The Trade and Economic Aspects*, Paris: OECD.

Wightman, Gordon (1989) "Czechoslovakia under Miloš Jakeš," *Journal of Communist Studies*, 3:349–355.

Winczorek, Piotr (1992) "The Internal Evolution and Changig Policies of the Democratic Party," pp. 177–194 in in George Sanford ed., *Democratization in Poland, 1988–90: Polish Voices*, New York: St. Martin's Press.

Winiecki, Jan (1987) *Economic Prospects—East and West: A View from the East*, London: Centre for Research into Communist Economies.

Winiecki, Jan (1989) "Large Industrial Enterprises in Soviet-type Economies: The Ruling Stratum's Main Rent-seeking Area," *Communist Economies*, 4:363–383.

Winiecki, Jan (1990a) "Hur det hela började—orsaker till sovjetekonomiernas sammanbrott," *Ekonomisk Debatt*, 6:535–545.

Winiecki, Jan (1990b) "Why Economic Reforms Fail in the Soviet System—A Property Rights-based Approach," *Economic Inquiry*, 1:195–221.

Winiecki, Jan (1991) *Resistance to Change in the Soviet Economic System: A Property Rights Approach*, London & New York: Routledge.

Wolchik, Sharon L. (1991) *Czechoslovakia in Transition: Politics Economis & Society*, London: Pinter Publishers.

Woods, Roger (1986) *Opposition in the GDR under Honcker, 1971–85: An Introduction and Documentation*, London: Macmillian.

World Bank (1991) *Czechoslovakia: Transition to a Market Economy*, Washington D.C.: The World Bank

Yin, Robert K. (1991) *Case Study Research: Designs and Methods*, revised edition, Newbury Park: Sage Publications.

Žabža, Josef (1984) "Exportní uvědomění—předpoklad úspěchu československé vyvozní ofenzívy," *Československý Zahraniční obchod*, 12:2–4.

Zagorin, Perez (1973) "Theories of Revolution in Contemporary Historiography" in *Political Science Quarterly*, 1:23–52.

Zhang, Baohui (1992) "The State Central Economic Bureaucracies and the Outcome of Systemic Economic Reform: An institutional Explanation for the Soviet and Chinese Experiences," *Governance: An International Journal of Policy and Administration*, 3:312–341.

Ziemer, Klaus (1989a) "Auf dem Weg zum Systemwandel in Polen: 1. Politische Reformen und Reformversuche 1980 bis 1988," *Osteuropa*, 9:791–805.

Ziemer, Klaus (1989b) "Auf dem Weg zum Systemwandel in Polen: II. Vom 'Runden Tisch' zur 'IV. Republik'?" *Osteuropa*, 11–12:957–980

Zubek, Voytek (1991) "The Threshold of Poland's Transition: 1989 Electoral Campaign as the Last Act of a United Solidarity," *Studies In Comparative Communism*, 4:355–376.

Newspapers and Magazines

Aftonbladet (Sweden)

Aftonbladet/Kultur (Sweden)

Außenhandel der Tschechoslowakei (former Czechoslovakia)

Business Central Europe

Český Deník (Czech Republic)

ČTK (Czech Republic Wire Service), available on the internet address: http://www.ios.com/~jirim/czech.html#CTKsum

Czechoslovak SR (from the Radio Free Europe Reports)

DN (Dagens Nyheter—Sweden)

FAZ (Frankfurter Allgemeine Zeitung—Federal Republic of Germany)

FT (Financial Times—Great Britian)

Haló noviny (former Czechoslovakia)

IHT (International Herald Tribune—USA)

L'Express (France)

Mladý svét (former Czechoslovakia)

Mosty (former Czechoslovakia)

NZZ (Neue Zürcher Zeitung—Switzerland)

PlanEcon Report (USA)

Prague Post, The (The Czech Republic)

Profil (Austria)

Reportér (former Czechoslovakia)

Socialistický směr (former Czechoslovakia)

Spiegel, Der (Federal Republic of Germany)

SvD (Svenska Dagbladet—Sweden)

Tagesspiegel (Federal Republic of Germany)

TAZ (Tageszeitung—Federal Republic of Germany)

Time Magazine (USA)

Times, The (Great Britain)

UNT (Uppsala nya tidning—Sweden)

Zeit, Die (Federal Republic of Germany)

Unpublished Documents

Letter from František Nevaříl to the author, 12 April 1993.

"Některá fakta k přípravě a hodnocení návrhu 9. pětiletky," memo from František Nevařil to Prime Minister Adamec, 1 November 1989.

"Občanské forum a volby 1990"—election pampflet from OF (Civic Forum) from 1990.

"Vážená paní ministryne!" petition of students from the Prague School of Economics to the Minister of Education in 1989.

"Vážený soudruhu děkane," protest letter to the dean of the Pedogogical Faculty of the Charles University, dated 20 Feb. 1989.

"Vážený soudruhu vedoucí tajemníku," letter from the dean of the Pedogogical Faculty of the Charles University to responsible Party, State and university functionaries—including to Jan Fojtík, the Secretary of the Central Community for Ideology and Secretary of the Prague Party, dated 15 Nov. 1989.

Personal Interviews
(In Czechoslovakia)*

Benda, Marek: member of STUHA, the Student Strike Coordinating Committee and of the Strike Committe at the Math-Physics Faculty of the Charles University, presently member of parliament for the Christian Democrats. *Interviewed 21 June 1993.*

Benda, Martin: member of STUHA, the Student Strike Coordinating Committee and of the Strike Committe at the Electro-Technical Faculty of the Charles University, presently studying theology. *Interviewed 20 May 1993.*

Chalupa, Pavel: member of Student Strike Committee at DAMU, presently has a radio program. *Interviewed 22 December 1990.*

Čmejrek, Jaroslav: former researcher at the Central Committee's institute for international affairs. Presently a teacher. *Interviewed 23 March 1992.*

Doležal, Jiří: member of the strike committee at the Pyschological Institute of the Philosophical Faculty at the Charles University, presently working as a journalist. *Interviewed 15 May 1992.*

Doubek, Vrátá: member of the strike committee at the Philosophical Faculty of the Charles University. At the time of the interview was doing research on Tomaś Masaryk. *Interviewed 5 May 1992.*

Fiśera, Ivan: advisor to OF (Civic Forum), one of its four organizationl leaders until the first elections, previously taught managers at the Research Institute of Technology and Economy, presently working for the Central Trade Unions. *Interviewed 6 May 1993.*

Gabal, Ivan: at the founding meeting of OF (Civic Forum), later campaign manager for Civic Movement, previously member of the Circle of Independent Intellegentsia. Presently director of a market research company. *Interviewed 15 April 1993.*

Gál, Fedor: Slovak dissident, became chair of VPN, presently professor of sociology at the Charles University. *Interviewed 31 March 1993.*

Gerle, Ladislav: Czechslovak Minister for Metallurgy and Heavy Industry, 1979–81; Vice Prime Minister, 1981–88; and Minister for Metallurgy, Machinery and Electronics, 1988. Presently a private businessman. *Interviewed 17 August 1993.*

Holub, Jiří: activist in the Socialist Party; was candidate to become the Party's leader at the time of the interview. *Interviewed 28 April 1993.*

Horáček, Michal: journalist, co-founder of the group MOST (English: "Bridge") which established the first contacts between the Communist Regime and Czech dissidents. Presently working for a betting agency. *Interviewed 1 June 1992.*

Hoření, Zdeněk: former editor of the Communist Party daily, *Rudé Pravo* with obersver status in the Politburo, presently writing for the pro-Communist weekly *Naśe pravo. Interviewed 30 March 1992.*

Jablonický, Jozef: dissident historian living in Bratislava, presently doing research at the Slovak Academy of Sciences. *Interviewed 5 March 1993.*

Jakeś, Miloś: former General Secretary of the Communist Party (1987–89), presently retired. *Interviewed 9 April 1992.*

Ježek, Vlasta: member of the strike committee at the Philosophical Faculty of the Charles University, was active in the campaign for *Občanské hnutí* at the time of the interview on *5 May 1992.*

Kocáb, Michal: well known Czech musician, co-founder of MOST, presently owner of a radio station and other businesses. *Interviewed 4 July 1993.*

Krejčí, Oskar: former advisor to Prime Ministers Adamec and Čalfa. *Interviewed 13 April 1992* and *7 June 1993.* At the time of the first interview, he was doing research at the Academy of Sciences, which was closing down during the time of the second interview.

Kučera, Bohuslav: Chair of the Socialist Party 1968–1990, Justice Minister 1968, presently retired. *Interviewed 19 May 1993.*

Ledl, Lubomír: former member of the SSM leadership in charge of contacts with independent organizations. At the time of the interview member of parliament for the Czech Communist Party. *Interviewed 4 March 1992.*

Lenárt, Jozef: member of the Politburo from 1962–1968 and 1970–1989, Prime Minister 1963–1968, 1988–1989 Central Committee Economic Secretary, presently retired. *Interviewed 3 June 1993.*

Lér, Leopold: Finance Minister 1973–1985, presently working as an economic consultant. *Interviewed 3 May 1993* and *10 June 1993*.

Litvák, David: member of the Student Strike Coordinating Committee, presently working as a translator. *Interviewed 26 March 1993*.

Löwenhöfer, Petr: member of STUHA and the strike committee at the Prague Economic University, presently private businessman. *Interviewed 16 June 1993*.

Matějka, Milan: member of the Governmental Committee for the Management of the National Economy and advisor to Prime Minister Adamec (1988–1989), presently researcher at the Prague Economic School. *Interviewed 5 June 1992*.

Mohorita, Vasil: former leader of the Socialist Youth Union (SSM), general secretary of the Communist Party (1990–1991), member of parliament for the Communist Party at the time of the interview. *Interviewed 4 March 1992*.

Nevařil, František: economic advisor to Prime Ministers Štrougal, Adamec and Čalfa, presently working as an accountant. *Interviewed 30 March 1993*.

Pajerová, Monika: former editor of a semi-legal student paper at the student press center (STIS), one of the leaders of the Student Strike Coordinating Committee and presently culture attaché in France. She was also a candidate to parliament for *Občanské hutní*,"Civic Movement," in the 1992 elections. *Interviewed 2 June 1992*.

Pavel, Miroslav: former press secretary for Prime Ministers Štrougal and Adamec, 1987–1989. *Interviewed 29 April 1993*; presently working for an economic journal.

Pithart, Petr: signer of Charter 77, participant in the several of the negotiations between OF (Civic Forum) and the regime, elected Czech Prime Minister as OF's candidate in the first post-Communist elections. Professor at the Central European University at the time of the interviews. *Interviewed 2 March 1993* and *14 April 1993*.

Plevza, Viliam: Previusly the "official historian" of the Communist regime during the normalization period and a close associate of former General Secretary Husák. Retired at the time of the interview, *6 March 1993*.

Poledník, Jindřich: former Secretary of the Central Committee for Social Organizations and the National Committees (local governments), candidate to the Politburo. *Interviewed 6 April 1992*.

Potáč, Svatopluk: Planning Minister 1981–1988, earlier head of the National Bank, presently retired. *Interviewed 9 July 1993*.

Purnama, Alan Rezner: member of the strike committee at the Philosophical Faculty of the Charles University. *Interviewed 15 May 1992*.

Rovná, Lenka: teacher at the Prague Economic University (then and now) who helped the students there organize the strike. *Interviewed 4 June 1992*.

Rusmich, Ladislav: economist, former employee of the central planning commission. Presently employed by the Czech National Bank, *interviewed 29 May 1992 and May 1993*.

Sedlák, Jaromír: former advisor to Prime Minister Štrougal, presently active in the Socialist Party and doing research. *Interviewed 11 May 1992, 12 May 1992* and *3 June 1992*.

Semin, Michael: student leader at the Pedagogical Faculty in Prague, member of the committee planning the Nov. 17 demonstration and later member of the Student Strike Coordinating Committee. Presently working for the conservative think-tank "Civic Initiative." *Interviewed 2 March 1993*.

Škoda, Jan: former Secretary of the Socialist Party in Czechoslovakia, is now retired. *Interviewed 14 May 1993*.

Staňková, Magalena: member of the Strike Committee of the Educational and Sport Faculty of the Charles University and of the Coordinating Committee of OF (Civic Forum). Presently runs a news service for members of parliament. *Interviewed 30 March 1993*.

Šťastný, Dr.: Former assistant to Planning Minister Potáč. Interviewed 28 July 1993.

Štěpán, Miroslav: former member of the Politburo (1988–89) and secretary of the Prague Party; the only Communist leader to have served a prison sentence after the "velvet revolution." *Interviewed 3 June 1992*. One year later he tried to make a come-back in the Communist Party of the Czech Lands.

Štindl, Ondřej: member of the strike committee at the Pedegogical Faculty of the Charles University; *interviwed 14 May 1992*; presently working at a radio station.

Sucharda, Bohumil: Finance Minister 1964–1969, researcher at the Prognostic Institute 1985–90, is now retired. *Interviewed 4 June 1993.*

Švec, Karel: Former SSM activist and diplomat. *Private discussion on 21 February 1992.* Worked at a private bank at the time of the discussion.

Švecová, Katka: former SSM activist, now working as a translator; *private discussion on 21 February 1992.*

Uhl, Petr: former member of OF (Civic Forum) and later Civic Movement, he was a famous socialist dissident who had surved a prison sentence in the early 1970s for forming an oppositional socialist group, later was active in the Committee for the Defense of the Unjustly Prosecuted. After the revolution, he became head of the Czechoslovak wire services. Interviewed by Eva Frödin on *9 May 1995.*

Urban, Jan: founding member of OF (Civic Forum), became the organization's general manager and then chair. *Interviewed 25 June 1993* and *29 April 1995*; was working as a free-lance journalist at the time of the first interview and at the time of the second interview was working for the state television company.

Valenčik: former researcher at the Prague Economic School, the Academy of Sciences in Northern Bohemia, at the time of the interview advisor to the leader of the Czech Communist Party, Svoboda. *Interviewwed 18 March 1992.*

Valouch, Vladimír: former researcher at the Institute for Mathematical Mechanics, worked at the office of OF at the time of the interview—*20 December 1990.*

Vidim, Honza: member of the Student Strike Coordinating Committee and strike committee at the Prague Economic University. Assistant to the conservative ODS mayor of Prague at the time of the interview. *Interviewed 25 June 1993.*

Vondra, Saśa: former speaker of Charter 77, the only member of OF (Civic Forum) to have attentended all the negotiations with the Communist government; *interviewed 1 July 1993.* Vice Minister for Foreign Affairs and member of the conservative ODS at the time of the interview.

Žák, Václav: at the founding meeting of OF (Civic Forum), today vice-chair of Civic Movement; *interviewed 11 May 1993.*

Zbořil, Zdeněk: former lecturer at DAMU, was elected student advisor to DAMU's strike committee. He was a professor of political science at the Charles University at the time of the interview. *Interviewed 21December 1990.*

Zbořilová, Zlata: student activist at the Philisophical faculty of the Charles University, *interviewed at the end of December, 1990.* She was still a student at the time of the interview.

(In Hungary)

Faluvégi, Lajos: Hungarian Finance Minister 1970–78, President of the Planning Commission 1978–86. Presently Professor of Public Finance at the Budapest University of Economic Sciences. *Interviewed 11 March 1993.*

Farkas, György: formerly executive at the metal works then at the National Bank; took part int the trade talks for the Ministry of Trade with the EC 1987–89. Presently Vice-General Secretary at the Hungarian Chamber of Commerce. *Interviewed 12 March 1993.*

Hajdu, Tibor: Former employee of the Party archives and employee at the Central Committee Department for Economic Policy as well as Agriprop ("aggitation and propaganda"). Presently head of the section of modern history at the Historical Institute of the Hungarian Academy of Sciences; *interviewed 12 March 1993.*

Hetényi, István: Finance Minister 1980–1986, worked in the Planning Office 1949–1980. Presently Professor of Public Finance at the Budapest University of Economic Sciences. *Interviewed 8 April 1993.*

Nyers, Rezső: member of the Politburo 1962–74, Economic Secretary 1963–74, considered the architect of the New Economic Mechanism. Presently one of the leaders of the reformed Communists (now calling itself "social democratic"). *Interviewed 8 April 1993.*

Sándor, Nyírő: Party Secretary for an industrial enterprise. Presently among the leadership of the Hungarian Socialist Workers' Party—a Communist splinter group from the reform Communists after the latter became declared a social democratic orientation. *Interviewed 9 April 1993.*

Szirmai, Peter: Co-Chair of the National Association of Entrepreneurs. *Interviewed 16 March 1993.*

Tibor, Györffy: Former editor of *Background*, a magazine for the *nomenklatura* given out in 3,500 copies which translated articles from feign magazines (including Wetern ones) and also former editor at the Hungarian news agency MTI. Is presently retired. *Interviewed 12 March 1993.*

Timár, Mátyás: member of the Central Committee 1966–88, Finance Minister 1963–67, Deputy Prime Minister 1973–1975, Chair of the government's economic commission 1967–73, Chair of the National Bank 1975–88. Presently doing research on the Hungarian banking system. *Interviewed 17 March 1993.*

Váss, Laszlo: formerly department chief to Minister of State Pozsgay (who was in charge of political reforms) and vice-director of the ministry. Previously employed at the Ministry of Education (1982–86) before working at the Central Committee Department of Higher Education (1986–88). Presently Professor of Political Science at the Budapest University of Economic Sciences. *Interviewed 12 March 1993.*

(in Poland)

Gebethner, Stanislaw: participant in the Polish round table talks for the Communists in the constitutional committee. Presently Professor of Political Science at the Waraw University and member of parliament for the former Communist party, which now calls itself "social democratic." *Interviewed 1 February 1995.*

Gobau-Klass, Tomasz: took part in the Polish round table discussions as an advisor to the Communists in the expert group on the media. Presently professor at the Jagellonian University; *interviwed 22 January 1995.*

Kozłowski, Krzyszłof: member of the constitutional committee for *Solidarność* at the Polish round table discussions. Later Minister of Interrior in the first *Solidarność* government. Presently member of the senate for the Democratic Union. *Interviewed 22 January 1995.*

Kubiak, Hieronim: Central Committee Secretary for Science and Culture 1981–1982, Politburo member 1981–1983. Presently Professor of Sociology at the Jagellionian University. *Interviewed 25 January 1995.*

Reykowski, Janusz: Professor of Psychology at the Polish Academy of Sciences, joined the Polish politburo in December 1988 and became responsible for designing the Communists' negotiating strategy. At the time of the interview working as a researcher in psychology. *Interviewed 23 April 1993.*

Winczorek, Piotr: Participant in the Polish round table talks in the constitutional working committee for the Democratic Party. Presently a member of parliament for the Democratic Union. *Interviewed 1 February 1995.* Presently professer of law at the Warsaw University.

Published Interviews

Bubeník, Jan (student activist during the Czechoslovak revolution) published in *Prague Post*, 23–29 June, 1993.

Diesntbier, Jiří (former Foreign Minister in Czechoslovakia's first post-Communist government), interview in book form in Klusáková 1993).

Gebethner, Stanislaw (participant in the Round Table talks for the regime), published in the appendix of Kunigraber (1996a).

Haval, Václav (Co-founder of Charter 77, dissident playwrite, founder of OF, elected president December 1989) interviewed in *Profil* 23 July 1990.

Honecker, Erich (former General Secretary in the GDR) interview in book form in Andert & Herzberg (1990).

Hoření, Zdenek (former editor of the Czechoslovak Communist Party daily *Rudé pravo*) published in *Mosty*, nr. 32–33, 1991.

Jakeś, Miloś (former General Secretary of the Czechoslovak Communist Party) interviews published in *Reportér*, nr. 17, 1991 and *Haló noviny* 11 November 1992.

Jaruzelski, Wojciech (former General Secretary of the Polsih Communist Party) interviews published in *Time Magazine*, 31 December 1990 *Aftonbladet/Kultur* nr. 3–95 and *Dagens Nyheter* 19 November 1995 and appendix of Kundigraber (1996a).

Malý, Václav (Catholic Priest, signer of Charter 77, moderator at OF's mass rallies during the revolution), published in *Profil* 23 July 1990.

Simai, Mihaly (Professor of Economics and Business at the Budapest University of Economics), published in April, 1992 in internet: gopher://csf.Colorado.Edu/00/eforum/EconConv/Simai_mihaly.hungary_.

Sindermann, Horst (1973–1976 Prime Minister, 1976–1989 President of the parliament in the GDR) published in *Der Spiegel* 19/1990.

Urbánek, Karel (1988–9 head of the National Front and Secretary of the Central Committee organization for party work, he became General Secretary of the Communist Party on November 25, 1989) published in *Mladý svět*, nr. 37, 1991.

*Note: for the ČSSR I have checked all the dates in which former government ministers held office in Hodný (1991).

Index